A History of

Western Philosophy

Volume IV

A History of

Western Philosophy

PHILOSOPHY FROM THE ROMANTIC AGE
TO THE AGE OF POSITIVISM

by

A. Robert Caponigri

UNIVERSITY OF NOTRE DAME PRESS

Notre Dame   London

Library of Congress Catalog Card Number: 63-20526
Manufactured in the United States of America
by NAPCO Graphic Arts, Inc.

For my father-in-law and mother-in-law,
Franklin A. and Catherine Franco,
in honor of their
fifty years of married life

TABLE OF CONTENTS

Part I

The Restoration

Introduction

Our basic reason for undertaking the authorship of this work is to promote the return of the history of philosophy to its rightful place of honor and usefulness in the academic program. This return is long overdue; it is becoming painfully clear that philosophy cannot be pursued in an historical vacuum. Indeed, in a very real sense philosophy is identical with its history and torn from this context it loses its particular character and force.

Philosophy pursued in an unhistorical or ahistorical manner cannot help but warp the individual and social consciousness at whose heightened refinement it is aimed. To pursue philosophy, one must either enter into the rich heritage of its history or run the risk of falling victim to a kind of speculative barbarism.

The form of these works has been determined by the authors' conviction that the history of philosophy itself can be fully appreciated only when taken as a basic element in the whole cultural complex of the West. Philosophy is not a specialized but a pervasive discipline. It finds its interest everywhere in the life of the spirit and it takes form as a response to all of the needs of the spirit. Philosophy is never a *part* of a culture but a pervading influence and mode of awareness. For this reason, in these volumes the chief architectural principle has been to place philosophy as firmly as possible in the cultural context, seeing it in this living relation to all the interests of culture and the life of the spirit.

It is our belief that the division of the work into five volumes and the articulations of the history of culture within which the history of philosophy has been placed is justified and even demanded by that history itself and has nothing artificial or contrived about it. For this reason, the student and the general reader will, we believe, be able to relate the flow of philosophical speculation directly to what he already knows about the general architecture of the history of Western Culture and will immediately experience the history of philosophy as an enrichment in depth of his cultural consciousnss. It is hoped that the student will come to perceive that it is precisely the quality of its philosophical experience which gives an age its special character and it is precisely its philosophical discontent which, stirring in one age, prepares and induces the vast labors which usher in a new.

While the volumes have been so planned that they may be read profitably by the general reader, they have a special orientation toward the academic world of the classroom. It is the authors' conviction that the basic book used in an academic course ought to be the meeting ground for the minds of both teacher and student. To this end, both will find that these volumes contain something which suits their particular needs and functions.

The particular need of the student is background; he can profit little from any contact with even the best of teachers unless he brings the richest possible preparation to this encounter. Therefore, these volumes are addressed to him in the hope that he will be drawn into them by a natural and spontaneous response. Frankly, we hope that the student will enjoy reading them and not find that reading a chore.

The need of the teacher, by contrast, is for an instrument of focus; something which will enable him, in the limited time at his disposal, to select the points of greatest impact with the student mind and those which will bring about the most significant student discussion and mutual exchange. The flexible construction of these books should meet this need. The teacher may assess and evaluate the whole and/or parts according to his own needs and interests and select for treatment in the classroom those articulations which will give him the greatest direct access to the minds of his students. In this process of selection, the volumes may be used as a guide to serve him by indicating the structure of the history of philosophy. They do *not* undertake *to make that selection for him* or dictate to him, by their structure, what his selection should be. He too, it is hoped, will enjoy teaching with this book (note we carefully avoid saying *teaching this book*) because it ministers to his own irreplaceable activity and does not dictate or constrain it.

In the text, reference to original sources and to the best secondary sources has been constant. In every way the authors have made an effort to place the student in contact with these sources in the context in which they will be most beneficial. In addition, lists of supplementary readings have been appended at important junctures. The quality of these reading lists should be clear from the start. They are not mere bibliographical lists nor are they "outside readings" in the current, vague sense of that term. These readings have a utilitarian purpose; they are closely related to the process of the narrative of the text itself. It is the authors' hope that as specific issues arise in class discussion, corresponding readings may be found which may extend the discussion or give it direction and emphasis. Again, it is hoped that the composition of studies will always be made a part of the student obligation in any course in the history of philosophy. The supplementary readings are so planned that the student will find in them direct help in the researching, planning and composition of such papers.

In closing, the authors would emphasize again one salient point: they hope that from these pages the reader will derive above all a renewed sense of the universal relevance of philosophy to the life of the mind and of the spirit.

Philosophy is above all a humanistic pursuit in the basic sense of that term; namely, philosophy takes for its own all that touches man. Only when seen in this perspective can philosophy be appreciated and enjoyed. Only in this way will it inevitably be recognized by every man as the supreme human discipline, the one activity of mind and spirit from which he cannot isolate himself and still achieve stature and maturity as a human being.

Notre Dame, Indiana   A. ROBERT CAPONIGRI
and
RALPH M. McINERNY

PART I
THE RESTORATION

Introduction

In the philosophical system of Hegel the romantic period reaches its apogée—that is, in a Hegelian sense, the moment in which it is both fulfilled and transcended. It was succeeded by the period of the Restoration. This period falls naturally between the end of the Napoleonic adventure (1815) and the Year of Revolutions (1848).

In retrospect, three important features of this period impose themselves. In the first place, the Enlightenment, with which the romantic spirit had been in constant tension and conflict, was not entirely banished. The Enlightenment was a movement and a period of remarkable inward vigor, and the impetus of romanticism did not overwhelm it. The spirit of the Enlightenment endured even when romanticism was triumphant and persisted into the succeeding period, the Restoration. Especially in England, where the impact of romanticism had been buffered by distance and slow response, the spirit of the Enlightenment informed the vigorous thought of utilitarianism and the narrow but acute and far from uninfluential analyses of the Scottish philosophers.

In the second place, so strong was the impetus of romanticism that even where it did not sweep all before it, it set up eddies and side currents which stirred long quiescent waters parallel to its own wake. These para-romantic movements are an important feature of the Restoration and have one note in common: They illustrate the perturbations which romanticism aroused in places ostensibly remote from and immune to its particular spirit. Within the Catholic ambit, for example, the spirit of romanticism in Italy touched both the speculative thought of Rosmini and the political, cultural reflections of Gioberti; in France many of its basic themes offered support to reconstructive efforts in political and social thought in such figures as de Maistre and Lamennais. In the English-speaking world, this disturbing influence is clearly evidenced in the soaring eloquence and powerful political and historical thought of Burke, in the subtle meditations of Coleridge on poetry and the movements of the human spirit in general, and in America, in the gentle moralism of Emerson.

Finally, it was evident that the social upheaval of the French Revolution, despite whatever countermovements of neo-imperialism

3

or archconservatism might be provoked against it, had worked an irreversible change. This change, in turn, released the social imagination of men at the same time that it aroused their social consciences. The spirit of romanticism touched both this social imagination and conscience in utopian social thought as well as in the soaring constructions of Comte, in whom the spirit of romanticism touched the scientific imagination as well.

Even while it was having such wide-reaching effects, romanticism itself was passing through its own period of crisis, inevitable, it might be supposed, after the eminence reached in the Hegelian synthesis. Schopenhauer, who had, as it were, long lurked in the shadow of Hegel, now became a voice which, if not heeded immediately, grew stronger with the decades. Within the very structure of the Hegelian system itself, moreover, the tremendous cohesiveness which the presence of Hegel had seemed to render unassailable now began to exhibit the flaws which must infect every human creation. The "dissolution of Hegelianism" was an inward process which the inherent vigor of the system indeed resisted but which it could not finally fend off.

The first effects of this process are to be seen in those figures to whom Marx was later to refer, somewhat contemptuously, as the "Holy Family," Bauer and those in his circle. But the full force of the process was to be seen only in the vigorous thought of such authentically powerful thinkers as Feuerbach, Marx, and Kierkegaard. Yet what these latter exhibit, in the last analysis, is not really the dissolution of Hegelianism but its remarkable power of transforming all that it touched and of coloring most precisely those movements, like the thought of Kierkegaard, which ostensibly are most in opposition to it. The result is that the thought of the nineteenth and twentieth centuries becomes, as Whitehead alleged of the whole of western philosophy with respect to Plato, a series of footnotes to Hegel.

CHAPTER I

Persistences of the Enlightenment

A. *Utilitarianism*

The consideration of utilitarianism turns one back from the advances of philosophical romanticism to the intellectualistic atmosphere of the Enlightenment. Utilitarianism is an essential and integral dimension of the Enlightenment mentality, and consequently its course followed a pattern like that of the Enlightenment itself. Its origins can be traced partly in the rise of the Cartesian type of rationalism in France and partly in the rise of British empiricism. That the relationship between these two movements is very close is illustrated by the fact that the notion of the normative character of mathematical concepts, which was essentially the heritage of French rationalism, remained constant in the development of British empiricism in Locke, Hume, and Berkeley. There was a constant exchange of influence across the channel, which reflects the essential cosmopolitanism of the spirit of Europe at the time. Utilitarianism too passed back and forth, manifesting itself in French as well as in English writers and thinkers. At the same time, however, it remained a dominantly British viewpoint and doctrine, the British giving it its most complete and coherent statement and its widest applications.

Utilitarianism is eclectic or syncretic in composition. Its basic concern is ethical and social, and it found telling expression in the social and juridical reform movements which it inspired. Its method is psychological and analytical. Its presuppositions are mechanistic, and its ideal approaches what, in the twentieth century, has been called a behavioral science of man; its modern descendants are the behaviorists, the semanticists, and logical positivists. The utopian and humanitarian element which characterizes the thought of the Enlightenment is quite evident in the composition of utilitarianism. Also in evidence are both

5

the remote image projected by the Cartesian philosophy of the "human machine" and the strong analogical influence of the Newtonian ideal in the philosophy of nature, with its conception of the cosmos as a closed system of forces which are exhaustively calculable. And last, but not least, this eclectic structure contains a logical element, which finds fullest expression in the preoccupation of the later utilitarians with the theory of probability as applicable to human motives.

Utilitarianism assumes a basic analogy between the mechanistic conception of nature and human action. Each is a closed system of forces, within which both constant and variable factors exist, while the whole is governed by universal laws, whose enunciation yields both the explanation and the controlling principles of individual and social human conduct. The task is to discover these constant and variable factors and these universal principles and to erect closely analogous normative principles. As early as Hobbes, the most universal and constant factor had supposedly been discovered in the basic egoism of human appetites; a less harsh view had seen in man but a vehicle of pleasure and pain, while an even milder conception had seen man's personal and social life moved by sentiments of sympathy and repulsion. Correlatively, the chief controlling principle had been identified with a calculus of personal interests and public good; with a calculus of personal pleasure and personal pain; with an appeal to the life of the sentiments and a surrender to them; or, finally, with social legislation and administration. Through all, the basic analogy between man and mechanistic nature persists.

B. *Earlier Utilitarians in England and in France*

The Fable of the Bees, 1705, of Bernard de Mandeville (1670–1733) is one of the earliest, most urbane, and most ironical expressions of the utilitarian point of view. The work presents a paradox which has become a byword in the language: private vices are public benefits. Men appraise conduct in terms of its consequences, not in terms of a transcendent law or norm of action. The consequences most to the fore in de Mandeville's opinion are social. His position can be seen as a response to the alternative which Plato had sought to construct in the *Republic:* whether it is better to be good and run the risk of being thought evil, or to be evil and to be thought good. The second, for de Mandeville, is the only possible attitude for a reasonable man; viz., to have one's way and yet to win public approval. The irony of the situation is that a man pursuing his own interests will more frequently than not reap the reward of public approval and bring benefit to the group. The satirical vein is strong in de Mandeville, however, and it is difficult to say when he writes in earnest and when tongue-in-cheek.

The *Observations on Man*, 1749, by David Hartley (1705–1757) contributed much to the progress of utilitarianism by its development of the associationistic psychology earlier suggested by Hobbes and Locke. Since association is essentially mechanical and calculable, it was inevitable that it would become a tool for the utilitarian analysis of human conduct and motivation.

In France, utilitarianism found its most influential expression in Etienne de Condillac (1715–1780) and Claude Helvétius (1715–1771). Condillac brought associational psychology to its most complete formulation. He traced the origins of reflective thought to language, rather than to any innate power of reflection, and discovered the springs of human conduct and motivation in the associational processes of pleasure and pain. In two works devoted to the problems of man and his conduct, *De l'esprit*, 1758, and *De l'homme*, 1772, Helvétius formulated a single, quantitative standard for all human conduct. This standard of the "greatest happiness of the greatest number" is to linger with slight variations through all utilitarian literature. Helvétius carries to its ultimate implication Locke's insight that the perfection of man is attainable through control of his environment. He transfers the arena of ethics from the individual consciousness to society, for the formula cited above is clearly a social principle. Hope for the improvement and happiness of men rests in laws; these he holds, if they are conformable to the true calculus of human motives, will direct men to the public good by leading them to seek their private advantage. De Mandeville's paradox is here advanced in all seriousness, without any ironic or satirical purpose, for Helvétius is innocent of both.

A less mechanistically determined form of the utilitarian doctrine was expressed by David Hume (1711–1776). His point of departure lay in the critique of the natural law and natural rights theory of the jusnaturalistic tradition. The latter tradition, in line with the general tendency of the dominant rationalism, had tried to establish the concept of a natural law and the existence of natural rights as truths of reason alone, independent of empirical reference. From the empirical point of view, a similar, though more limited, attempt had been made to give evidence for the same concepts. Hume applied to this procedure the same two-edged skepticism which he had previously applied to such rationalistic concepts as "cause" and "substance." He sought to demonstrate that neither natural law nor natural right could be established as truths of fact by either of these means. Moral judgments required for their consummation another factor, the presence of a human preference, the option of "sentiment." His utilitarianism has therefore been called sentimental utilitarianism to distinguish it from the more calculatory forms. Hume also pointed out, against the Hobbesian or egoistical point of view, that utility, in both its empirical and its ideal dimensions, could not be restricted to the individual and his reactions of pleasure and pain but required a consideration of convention and social conditioning. Thus he expanded the psychological horizon of utilitarianism and pointed to the possibility of a sociology of human motivation.

The motive of "sentiment" became the common principle of a utilitarian current which was dependent upon Hume and included many eminent names. This current did not remain isolated and self-contained, but tended to modify the egotistical and calculatory current. By emphasizing sentiment, Hume had placed himself in the tradition of the morality of sentiment expressed, but with other preoccupations, by Joseph Butler (1692–1752), Lord Shaftesbury (1671–1713), and Francis Hutcheson (1694–1746). These thinkers had postulated among the faculties of man a "moral sense" which was the specific organ of the moral judgments. The preference or option of Hume exercised the same function, without enjoying the status of "faculty".

The current of sentimental utilitarianism received its most finished expression from the moralist and economist Adam Smith (1723–1790). Smith gave the notion of sentiment the meaning which it later enjoyed almost universally, that of "sympathy." In his work the *Theory of Moral Sentiments*, 1759, Smith traced the springs of moral behavior precisely to this power of sympathy. It is by our ability to enter sympathetically into the feelings of others that we are able to stand off and judge ourselves impartially. His formulation is famous: "I divide myself into two persons, I, the examiner and judge . . . and I, the person whose conduct is examined into and judged of." We are here for the first time in the presence of the moral attitude, and from its structure the whole theory of morals must be derived.

In France, the doctrine of the moral "sentiments" and their relation to human conduct was carried to an extreme point by Jean-Jacques Rousseau (1712–1778). Rousseau interpreted sentiment to mean the spontaneous movement of the sympathetic self. On this ground he rejected the analytic method in moral philosophy which had been practiced even by other "sentimentalists" such as Hume and Smith. On the same ground he rejected both such analytic structures and the social structures which, in his opinion, they mirrored. He suggested a moral anarchism, in which the only true moral conduct flows spontaneously from the feeling of the acting subject and finds expression in a free mode of conduct corresponding, not to the analytic precepts of reason or to the conventions of society, but only to this pure spontaneity of feeling. This is the morality of the "heart" as contrasted with that of the "head." With Rousseau, it is clear, one passes over the border of utilitarianism into the morality of romanticism and precisely that sentimental romanticism which must be distinguished from its philosophical counterpart.

C. *Classical Utilitarianism*

Classical utilitarianism is almost exclusively an English phenomenon. In England, alone of the countries of Europe, the Enlightenment, in its empirical vein, remained the dominant "forma mentis." This is to say, England remained the country of Hume and of Locke. Even as sensitive a figure as Newman, at heart a romantic and an idealist, is still, in his instincts as an Englishman, a Humean. This was to remain the situation until the romantic revolt of Coleridge and Carlyle was to disturb the intellectual peace of the island. In the area of moral speculation the expression of this continuation of the Enlightenment is utilitarianism.

The dominant figure of classical utilitarianism, who made the doctrine logically articulate and socially effective in the areas of politics and social legislation, was Jeremy Bentham (1748–1832). Unlike similar movements on the Continent, English philosophical movements have rarely formed schools or parties. Utilitarianism is an exception. Under the leadership of Bentham, who was a practicing lawyer and an excellent speaker as well as a writer in the best tradition of the English prose of the Enlightenment, it achieved articulate organization with an eloquent organ in the *Westminster Review,* which was founded by Bentham in 1824, and which from that date until the year of his death played a major part in English political life. The monument of this movement and of the influence of utilitarianism is the Reform Bill of 1832, which, introducing vast changes into the patterns of British legislation, translated into fact the principles of tolerance which form one of the chief merits of the utilitarian mentality. With Bentham in this movement was an alert and capable group of men who collectively offer a remarkable example of high-minded public-spiritedness. Some were undoubtedly touched with speculative genius. Among the group were James Mill, the father of John Stuart Mill; Ricardo, the economist; and Malthus, the statistician and population theorist. Bentham was a man of action even more than a thinker or writer; his published works, as a consequence, follow a somewhat sporadic pattern. These include: a *Panopticon,* 1802, a project for prison reform marked by a rational approach to this difficult social problem; *An Introduction to the Principles of Legislation and of Morals,* 1789, perhaps his most effective work; a treatise on morals in the classical manner, the *Deontology,* which appeared posthumously in 1834; and two smaller tracts which were first published in French and later translated into English, *The Rationale of Punishment,* 1830, and *The Rationale of Reward,* 1825.

Because of his preoccupation with the social dimension of human conduct and with the nature and effect of legislation, the principle of utility appears first in Bentham as a principle opposed, in its actuality, to the fiction of a social contract. Sound legislation needs no such fictitious base; it needs only to discover its own fundamental principle in the actual nature and character of men and to build upon that with common sense and sound reason. The function of the principle of utility in his theory of legislation and morals is to establish a relationship between the *fact* of human nature and the rule of conduct, individual or social. The *fact* which he discovers is the classical insight of utilitarian doctrine: that pleasure and pain provide the rule and motive of human conduct. This is for Bentham a primitive fact and, hence, a *primum verum* for all theory and a *primum practicum* for all action.

What is the good law or the good rule of moral conduct? For Bentham it is that rule which will produce, in the nature of the case or in the long run, the greatest credit of pleasure against the corresponding debit of pain. The work of the legislator is to discover and enact such laws, or to alter the existing laws in conformity with Bentham's reformatory propensities.

The implications of this theory of legislation are tremendous. It must, in the first place, establish that primitive fact; and while this is an empirical principle, in Bentham's view, and consequently needs only to be discovered, it is obviously not a self-evident fact and its discovery entails much effort. In the second place, it must establish the balance of pleasure and pain with respect to the law under consideration and seek the rule for determining that balance in principle. Bentham discovers the latter in the classical formula of the "greatest good of the greatest number." The theory must, further, examine all of the circumstances both of pleasure and of pain—their intensity, their duration, their certitude, their proximity or remoteness, their fecundity, that is, their power to engender further experiences of the same quality, and the purity of pleasure, that is, its freedom from the tendency to engender its opposite, as the ancient stoics had pointed out that pleasure is inclined to do. Finally, it must consider the function of the number of subjects of legislation. To the credit of their fortitude, if not their perspicacity, Bentham and the utilitarians about him did not shrink from these tasks but even hopefully concluded that, by this enormous labor of reason, legislation and morality might be reduced to a science of mathematical exactitude.

In Bentham's view the principle of utility is, above all, a principle of legislative and social reform; that is to say, the utilitarian contemplates his own action within a society that is already established and directs that society toward a conversion of existing law in the direction which the principle of utility indicates. It presupposes that the interests of all in a society will not be identical; if they were, the principle of utility would be useless. Its purpose is to compose natural differences rationally, or artificially as some like to say. For this reason Bentham was readily led by the influence of James Mill to a political radicalism, a kind of Jacobin democracy; only in such a democracy are the natural diversity of interests and the community engendered by law seen in their clear opposition and relation.

Important and interesting variations and applications of the basic utilitarian insight flourished. The social radicalism or nihilism of William Godwin (1756–1836) is perhaps the most arresting, though, by its very extremism, this proved self-defeating as a doctrine and as a program. In the work *Political Justice,* 1793, Godwin concludes, in the name of the principle of utility, that all law and all government is nocuous. The stability of law is in effectual contradiction to the continual variation of utility; thus it must be inimical to the notion of man's perfectibility. In the name of utility, Godwin adds a criticism of the concept of property; it is the product of an artificial institution, that of heredity or inheritance. As the complement of this nihilism Godwin offers a positive "credo" which might be called the doctrine of the natural identity of interests. Godwin holds that laws and institutions not only disrupt this natural identity but also impede the natural perfectibility of man.

Godwin's notion of the natural identity of interests was obviously in contradistinction to Bentham's insight that interests were naturally divergent and had to be brought into conformity by precisely those structures and institutions which were interdicted by Godwin. A consideration which militated against the assumption of the natural identity of interests was advanced by the economist and statistician Thomas Malthus (1766–1834). In *An Essay on the Principle of Population,* 1798, he demonstrates that the natural identity of interests and an indefinite increase of happiness in man is contradicted by an ineluctable law of nature. He formulates this law in his famous "principle of population." This principle affirms, on the one hand, that, unless impeded by some obstacle, natural or artificial, population doubles itself in every twenty-five-year period, and from twenty-five-year period to period increases geometrically and, on the other hand, that for like periods it is impossible to increase the means of subsistence except arithmetically. Malthus concludes that to support and sustain the population it is necessary that there be some artificial barrier to its geometrical increment. Ordinarily these barriers are provided by vice, poverty, famine, war, and emigration. These are, therefore, necessary components of the fabric of society. Their removal would bring about a disequilibrium between the factors of population and sustenance which would be fraught with consequences of utmost gravity. Poverty and its attendant phenomena cannot therefore be obliterated from the human scene. This doctrine has been called the "melancholy theory" because of the unrelieved picture it paints, in sharp contrast to the bright canvasses of other utilitarians. Politically, Malthus derived democratic consequences from the theory. He argued against communism or socialism, because these, imagining that poverty could be checked by a division of lands, would lead only to overpopulation and a greater universal poverty. Likewise, he argued against revolution, because the people, holding governments to account for their poverty, do nothing by revolution but bring down upon themselves the added miseries of oppression and despotism.

Another law which militates against a natural identity of interests and the indefinite increase of happiness and progress was formulated by the economist David Ricardo (1772–1823) in his *Principles of Political Economy and Taxation*, 1817. His is a complex principle based on phenomena of two different economic orders—the agricultural and the industrial—but merging toward one conclusion. The profit of the landed proprietor must increase by the degree to which the needs of people force them to have recourse to the land for sustenance; in the industrial area, a like phenomenon prevails: Wages tend to seek their lowest possible level according to the ratio of available workers, while profits tend to become concentrated in the hands of the smallest possible number. This last part of Ricardo's principle, it may be noted, bears certain resemblances to the point of departure of Marx's famous theory of wages and of surplus value. Although Ricardo shares with utilitarianism the framework of its general assumptions, he does not share its optimistic tone. Poverty, conflict of interests, and the frustration of many are conditions for the existence of wealth and for the happiness of a few. Ricardo's picture is no less melancholy than that of Malthus.

James Mill was the most devoted and the most literal of Bentham's continuators. Mill's importance for philosophy lies chiefly in the fact that he worked out most consistently and completely the associationist psychology which is the theoretical basis of the utilitarian movement. The force of Mill's logical analysis of this psychological theory shows that its point of view is that of a retrospective analysis of experience and that it is not an attempt to seize experience in its unity and wholeness. This view enables Mill to resolve experience into supposedly "simple" elements which are thought to precede, whether logically or temporally, the larger unities of which they form a part. Reduction to these elements is considered to "explain" the complex wholes to which they give rise. This point of view was not new; it had been illustrated in both the rationalistic and the empirical traditions; in addition, as Kant pointed out, it constituted their common fallacy.

The elements to which Mill reduced the complex unity of experience are the units of "sensation." These possess an "atomic dispersity," one from the other—an image borrowed from the physical sciences and applied metaphorically to this new area. These basic elements are then thought to be united into larger and more complex unities by "laws of association." These laws are "mechanical"; they operate in a closed order of cause and effect. Thus eliminated from the structure of experience are the two elements which give it a unity and autonomy of its own: the activity of a self or a subject and the concept of a real relation, which is as much a given as any of the "elements" into which experience is analytically resolved. Utilitarianism draws the conclusion that control of the whole process of experience is secured through knowledge of these laws of association. Mill draws conclusions in the orders of ethics, politics, economics, and education. The clarity of his presentation of this analysis earns him the right to be called the theoretist and methodologist of utilitarianism.

D. *The Scottish School*

Equally redolent of the spirit and the atmosphere of the English Enlightenment is the philosophy of the Scottish school. Established by the work of Thomas Reid, this current received successive elaboration in the thought of J. Beattie, J. Oswald, Dugald Stewart, Thomas Brown, Sir William Hamilton, and others. Its doctrine has been called the "philosophy of common sense," and in some accounts it has shared with the eclectic philosophy of the Frenchman Victor Cousin the title "perceptionism." It was a strong reaction against the extreme consequences of British empiricism, especially the alleged skepticism of Hume, which had denied the objectivity of material and spiritual substance alike. Reid expounded the fundamental idea of the school, namely, that all men have naturally the capacity of knowing external reality, not, indeed, by any recourse to reasoning, but through the agency of an *instinctive credence* tightly connected with the act of perception. This credence thus manifested that "common sense" which is the universal and proper character of all men.

The development of the school passed through a number of stages. The first is that of the "triumvirate," as Priestley called it, of Reid, Beattie, and Oswald. Dugald Stewart initiated its second phase through his teaching of moral philosophy at the University of Edinburgh. In his train followed Thomas Brown, who was somewhat critical, however, of the thought of his master, and Sir James Mackintosh, who accepted the postulates of the school with greater fidelity. Sir William Hamilton developed the epistemological doctrine of the school in the direction of agnosticism. James McCosh, a student of Hamilton, was responsible for carrying the doctrine of this school across the Atlantic to America. The final phase of the school is marked by a progressive separation from its first postulates and a movement in the direction of continental idealism in such men as Fraser, Laurie (the historian of the school), and especially J. F. Ferrier. Without question, the most vigorous exponents of this current under its various aspects were Reid, Stewart, and Hamilton. Consequently, it is to them that the brief notice possible here will be given over.

Thomas Reid (1710–1796) developed his philosophical ideas with the purpose of combatting the extreme skeptical implications of Hume's thought. His *Inquiry into the Human Mind on the Principles of Common Sense*, 1764, is limited to a theory of *sensation* but sets the framework for his later doctrine concerning sensation and *instinctive belief*. Its line of thought is continued in his other substantial work, the *Essays on the Intellectual Powers*, composed in 1785. In 1788 his essays on moral philosophy appeared.

Reid's position can be developed about a number of salient points. The first is his indictment of skepticism and the quest for its origins. He traces the latter not merely to Berkeley but, by way of Locke, to Descartes. Reid counsels a return to the "inductivism" propounded by Francis Bacon; to observation, which he thought possible, of the *facts* of consciousness just as they present themselves. Reid thus became the philosopher of "pure experience" as Kant was later to be the philosopher of "pure reason."

The naive realism present in Reid's criticism of Locke and Descartes becomes clear in his further accusation that these philosophers made ideas the mere *representations* of reality, implying nothing about the existence of the objects represented. Sensation, he claims, does contain such implication. This anti-representationalism involves many difficulties, as Hamilton pointed out in the introduction to his edition of Reid's works. This position is of basic importance in the structure of Reid's thought because it leads to the formulation of a theory of perception.

In formulating this theory Reid arrives at his most important doctrine: the distinction between *sensation* and *perception*. Sensation is strictly *subjective; perception* is not only the apprehension of an external object but the *presence* of an object so apprehended. The perception implies both a *conception* of the object and a *belief* in its actual existence. Thus, perception is both immediate and complex for Reid. While perception explains how we apprehend the external world as actually existing, philosophy is at a loss to explain perception itself, which has no "ground." Reason is but a marvelous and unintelligible instinct in our souls. Perceptions are *facts;* they are immediately identifiable and therefore they exist. We cannot know why we have perceptions, but because we have perceptions, to whose complex structure *belief* in the reality of the external world is integral, we are able to affirm such a world.

This *belief* becomes an object of direct interest. Reid's position is formed against the background of that of Hume. Hume held that we have *belief* concerning the probable, such as the existence of the external world, while we have *knowledge* of what is certain. For Hume, belief depends on the force of a certain idea, by means of which it acquires a validity equal to that of an immediate impression. Reid introduces important modifications into this view. He agrees with Hume that belief must be a sensorial act rather than a cognitive one; but he insists that between an idea which is imagined and one which engenders belief there is more than a difference of intensity; there is a difference in *nature* as well. He gives no definition of belief, however, preferring to assign it to a natural impulse which may be called "instinct." He maintains its primitive, underived character. *Belief, assent, conviction* are terms which do not admit of logical definition because the operations of the mind which they indicate are perfectly simple and of a special character. There is no necessity to define them, for they are common words and well understood by all. (Cf. *Works,* ed. Hamilton, p. 327b.)

The introduction of the notions "common" and "well understood by all" leads immediately to the notion most closely associated with this school and with Reid in particular, that of "common sense." By all indications, common sense for Reid is precisely this instinctive belief which informs all perceptions and of which a prime example is the principle of induction. It is immediately pointed out by the best recent commentators on Reid, such as M. M. Rossi, that there is nothing original about this notion. The term *sense* in this phrase is ambiguous because it is not clear whether Reid considers it immediate, like sensation, or a mediate act of thought, that is, a judgment or an opinion. Sometimes he speaks of it as the common *opinion* of men, to which philosophy may not go counter; again, in reply to certain difficulties advanced by Priestley, he tries to establish a distinction between *sense* and *sensation,* calling the former a judgment while affirming that sensation contains no such element. The notion "common" in the phrase *common sense* is also freighted with ambiguity. Sometimes it is used to imply something which is common to all rational mankind; at other times, it is used to mean the sameness of the character of evidence with which all different fundamental principles present themselves to the mind; at still other times, the term is used to imply a notion of basic *consensus*, as when Reid affirms that there are universal opinions shared by all men because they are reflected in diverse languages, and that the validity of common sense therefore is founded on a universal consent.

Reid's last work, *Essays on the Active Powers,* 1788, takes up themes in moral philosophy but exhibits little originality. These essays continue the line of thought of his great predecessors, Hutcheson and Smith.

Dugald Stewart (1753–1828) began his career as a professor of mathematics but in 1785 succeeded to the chair of moral philosophy at the University of Edinburgh. His chief work is *Elements of the Philosophy of the Human Mind,* published in three volumes between 1792 and 1814. His *Outlines of Moral Philosophy* appeared in 1793; his *Philosophy of the Active and Moral Powers of Man* in 1828.

One cannot speak of an original problematic or an original doctrine in Stewart; he exhibited too close a dependence on Reid and his school. He did, however, make advances on Reid in a number of points. He clarifies the concept of the "Principles of Common Sense" and "Metaphysical Axioms," which Reid asserted somewhat dogmatically, in a manner which suggests affinities to the Kantian criticism. He prefers to call these "Fundamental Laws of Human Belief" and "Constituent Elements of Human Reason." Stewart makes clear that such elements are not "objects of knowledge" but conditions "necessarily and unconsciously [i.e., unreflectively] involved" in the exercise of our powers. They are "necessary conditions on which every step of the deduction tacitly proceeds." He tends to refine these elements in the direction of a constitutent formalism and functionalism and away from any kind of merely psychological status.

He similarly refines Reid's doctrine of perception. Intuition, he holds, accounts only for the existence of an objective quality while we are actually perceiving it; its continued existence, independent of our perception, is due principally to the circumstance that we cannot, as we can in the case of the imagination, recall or set aside the object at will.

In the *Elements* he examines the control which the mind has over the streams or currents of association and then attempts to explain, by the principle of association, processes and relations—such as wit, fancy, invention, dreaming—which Hume and Reid had not included. He discusses the influence of association upon the formation of speculative conclusions, evaluations of taste, and decisions of moral conduct. In the important second volume of the same work, his affinity for the aprioristic point of view in considering the dynamism of mind is clear. While he perhaps contributed nothing absolutely new, Stewart is responsible for keeping the Scottish movement alive; through him younger philosophers, especially Hamilton, were attracted to it and saw its possibilities for development.

Sir William Hamilton (1788–1856) brings to culmination all that was significant in the "Scottish philosophy." Hamilton exercised his considerable influence more through discussion of the opinions of others and in fragmentary writings and lectures than in any carefully worked out statement of his views. Attempts have been made (for example, that of Bowen) to weave his fragmentary writings into some sort of continuity. During his lifetime he published but one volume, which brought together many of his critical essays: *Discussions on Philosophy and Literature, Education and University Reform,* 1852. His writings on logic and metaphysics, his preferred topics, were edited after his death by H. L. Mansel and John Veitch (*Lectures on Metaphysics and Logic,* 4 vols., 1859–60).

Following Reid, he seeks to prove that the human mind *presents* and does not merely *represent* its object. Hamilton goes beyond the original arguments of Reid and the Scottish school, almost to the point of annulling that position. He notes that the quality of immediate presentation belongs only to the sensible perception; it does not characterize recall, in which only an image of memory is presented but not the actually existing object. He takes a step further, invoking a kind of "principle of relativity" which indicates that existence cannot be known directly and absolutely in itself but only under certain special aspects or modes, which can be known only if they stand in certain determinate relations with our faculties, under conditions determined by these faculties.

By this position, Hamilton advances that affinity with Kantianism and that divorcement from the doctrine of Reid which has already been noted in Stewart. An adumbration of the distinction between "things in themselves" and phenomena seems to appear, especially since Hamilton makes it clear that primary as well as secondary qualities are knowable only in a "relative" way. From this point Hamilton advances his principle of the "total conditionality" of all knowledge. He rejects any "philosophy of the unconditioned," that is to say, of the wholly immediate. To think, to know, is to posit conditions and to condition that which is known and which is the object of thought. The unconditioned can be conceived only as the negation of conceivability;

as, the concept of the infinite. A final step toward the displacement of the "naive realism" of the Scottish school is Hamilton's distinction of the function of "belief." The function of belief in Reid was precisely to establish the warrant of presentation; it was the principle of knowledge, i.e., of the actual presence of the object as existing. Hamilton asserts that the range of our belief is far wider than that of our knowledge, that the claims of the two not only are not coextensive but are actually different. The fact that we cannot know the infinite does not at all deny that it can and must become the object of our belief. The reversal seems complete when Hamilton seems to suggest that the exteriority and presence of the object as existing is the object of belief, not in Reid's sense, but in his own. To be sure, belief for Hamilton is a necessary, or unconditioned, imposition of our nature; but it is, nevertheless, not itself a "fact" or a logical illation.

Hamilton's philosophy enjoyed for a time an undisputed dominance in the Scottish universities and even some influence beyond; eventually it was to draw the double attack of positivism and neo-idealistic criticism. The *Examination* by J. S. Mill sounded the death-knell of both Hamilton's influence and of the significance of the Scottish school.

E. *Ideology in France*

The term *ideology* has become current in our day; its associations are such, however, that the current use must be distinguished from the use which characterizes the philosophical movement in France at the end of the eighteenth and the beginning of the nineteenth centuries. The more recent use implies a social and political orientation of thought; the older employment refers to the study of "ideas" in the traditional sense: their origins, their validity, etc. This school resolutely restrains this problem within the limits of psychological analysis, proving in this process that the problem strains to transcend these limits. These concerns form a bond between the chief figures of the movement of ideology—DeStutt de Tracy (1754–1836), Pierre Cabanis (1757–1808) and Maine de Biran (1766–1824)—despite the great diversity of attitudes and doctrines among them.

The immediate antecedents of ideology are to be found in the thought of Condillac of which it is the prolongation. The ideologues themselves, however, make frequent reference to the English sources of their thought, especially Bacon. This is one reason, no doubt, that their most severe critics, the traditionalists, directed such harsh censure against Bacon.

The golden age of the movement opens with the foundation in 1795 of the Institute of France. The "second class" of the Institute was the

Academy of Moral and Political Sciences, and it included in its membership all of the men associated with the ideological movement. Many of its members were partisans of Napoleon, from whom some of them received signal honors; this attachment lessened quickly, when the ideologues experienced the frustration of the liberal expectations they had rested in the First Consul.

Historically, the movement of ideology links the theory of knowledge of the Enlightenment and the scientific positivism of the nineteenth century; hence, its abiding importance. Its view of the problem of knowledge was not narrow. It saw this problem as the cornerstone of the philosophical edifice and hoped, through its solution, to be able to address more effectively the whole range of moral, political and social problems.

This derivation from Condillac resides in its acceptance of his analytic method, which reduces the complex structures of the psychic life to the simple elements of sensation, and in the corresponding notion that through progressive composition the sensorial datum and the act of sensation give rise to all the contents of the psychic life and to the differentiation of the "faculties." From sensible impressions in turn derive the moral and social sentiments, making ethics and politics an *applied ideology*.

Of the three chief figures of the movement, DeStutt de Tracy will engage our attention first. The substance of his thought is contained in the work *Eléments de idéologie,* which comprises three volumes: *Idéologie,* 1801, *Grammaire générale,* 1803, and *Logique,* 1805. In addition, he wrote the *Traité sur la volonté,* 1815, and a *Commentaire de l'esprit des lois,* 1811–19. To de Tracy we owe the classical definition of ideology: "the science which has for its object ideas in all their dimensions." The important term here is "dimensions," for this term embraces for him the whole universe of discourse and the unity of the sciences, with which he is much concerned. The basic function of ideology is to reestablish the unity of the sciences. It is identical with the "first philosophy," which applies itself to the real in general and its conditions, rather than to a particular class of objects. Ideology, in his view, studies the "true" logic, which is not merely the practical art of reasoning but the speculative study of the means of knowledge. The scientific part of this logic is the object of that type of anlaysis for which Condillac has furnished the model. In its pursuit of this unity of the sciences, however, ideology is not metaphysical but "humanistic," since it seeks its basis in man, specifically in the origin of the three operations of the judgment, signs, and the will, which exhaust the activities of the human spirit.

The *Idéologie* constitutes an analysis of the human faculties.

Though relying heavily on Condillac, de Tracy occupies a position by no means identical with his. Condillac had been concerned with the "genealogy" of the faculties; thus, for him, sensation comes before judgment, and judgment influences desire and the will. De Tracy's position is more complex. He distinguishes four basic and irreducible modes of sensibility: will, judgment, sensation, and memory. The inner dialectic of these, rather than any simple genealogical progression, generates the "faculties." A faculty is a concrete condition for the effectuation of all of these primitive elements in a complex pattern. The constitution of consciousness is thus at once firm in its morphology but fluid and functional in its actual forms.

The portions of the *Elements* comprising the *Grammar* and the *Logic* relate to the judgment. De Tracy offers both arresting conceptions of these sciences and arresting notions within them. Grammar, he agrees, is the study of signs and their significations. He at once, however, separates himself from that eighteenth-century tradition which had taken the simple *word* as the sign of the idea. The first is an interjection which contains a judgment. Attribute and subject are distinguished by subsequent analysis. The judgment is not constructed out of these elements; they are, rather, derived from the judgment. The effect of this in logic is striking. It leads de Tracy to deny validity or force to reasoning which rests merely on form, save among purely identical propositions. Effective judgment, consequently, does not involve relations of extension, which are few in number and may be enumerated beforehand; it involves the content of the ideas, and the content can be determined only by direct inspection of the ideas employed. Here a certain affinity can clearly be discerned with "ideology" in the sense that it will have later in history. Since reasoning has its basis in the content of the ideas, the validity of reasoning cannot be determined by recourse to rules but only by a review of the various ideas involved in a chain of reasoning.

The treatise on the will, an integral part of the *Elements,* studies the will and its effects. Morality, for de Tracy, resides, not in rules, but in the study of the origin and character of our desires and passions and the study of their conformity with the actual character of our mode of being.

Pierre Cabanis is the author of twelve reports or "memoirs" which were brought together to comprise his work *Rapports du physique et du moral de l'homme,* 1802. The way in which these reports are conceived and their problem formulated, however, reflects the fact that Cabanis was a physician. Their argument reflects a prevalent concern to which their author subscribed, that of establishing moral sciences which would possess evidence and certitude equal to those of the physical sciences. These would provide a basis for an individual morality independent of religious dogma. Since the welfare of the individual is indissolubly united with the welfare of others, such sciences would become basic in the formation of a just social order.

Cabanis directs a telling criticism at the very fathers of ideology, Condillac and Helvétius. They did not consider the gnoseological and moral operations of the human principle in complete integration with the living body, but in abstraction from the conditions body imposes. They treated as independent of the body, operations whose relation to the body they did not understand. The solution of Cabanis: both theory of knowledge and morals should be reestablished on the sound basis of physiology. He anticipates the objection that such a procedure would involve a return to a kind of metaphysical materialism. This could be avoided, he notes, if the whole question of "first causes" is bracketed and the physiological processes are taken as first and ultimate in the order of their complex resultants.

In the first six memoirs, Cabanis tries to make a start in the direction indicated. He offers studies on the intellectual and moral life based on such factors as age, temperament, sex, disease, and climate. These studies are rich in analysis and detail. Cabanis cannot be considered a mere mechanist. He advances a distinction which places his thought in a direct line with the eventual development in France of the point of view called "spiritualism." He makes this distinction in a typically medical fashion; *irritability* is not to be confused with *sensibility,* and the latter is not to be reduced to the former. The significance of the distinction is far-reaching. Irritability can account for movement, but it cannot account for the *coordination* of movement; hence, it is necessary to recognize a principle of coordination and organization which is not reducible to the simple stimulus-response pattern. This principle must be an internal sensation which is the psychic basis of coordination and organization. Here we are at the most basic and rudimentary level of the self and of the life of spirit, and that precisely in the physiological matrix.

Consciousness is not the distinctive mark of sensibility. For consciousness to arise, that organizing and coordinating sensibility must itself become the object of the apprehension of the self. There arises, consequently, in Cabanis, a dualism between *unconscious sensibility,* which organizes many patterns of response and may have many centers within the life of the organism, and *consciousness* as distinctively consciousness of self, which organizes the entire psychic life.

Although these distinctions point to an eventual spiritualism, Cabanis himself remains an organic monist. It is not necessary to go beyond the resources of the organism, the organized body, to account for any of the distinctions he has established. The economy of the body can account for every level of its operations, including even those which were traditionally referred to some "higher" principle, immanent, but not reducible, to organized matter.

Maine de Biran published nothing during his lifetime; nevertheless, he is generally accounted the most accomplished of the ideologues. His writings were edited by Victor Cousin and published in a complete edition in 1841 and again by Naville in 1859. The latter also edited a volume of his *Pensées* in 1857. A modern edition of his works was published under the editorship of Tisserend in 1920–39.

In his thought ideology reaches its highest point of development, the point at which, inevitably, it transcended itself, to take that direction, already noted in a rudimentary form in Cabanis, toward a recognizable but heavily psychological spiritualism. This spiritualism will eventually come to have an independent career in France, though with constant reference to de Biran.

De Biran's thought is divided into a number of periods. The document of his first period is the *L'influence de l'habitude sur la faculté de penser*. De Biran shows that while he has mastered the technique of ideology, he had already begun to sense its limitations. The central point of this document and of this period of his thought is his analysis of the notion of "habit." The mechanism, he notes, which habit tends to introduce into psychic life does not in any sense extend to all its manifestations. There remains a very considerable area which transcends mechanism and even organicity. For example, *effort* reveals the conscious sense and constitutes the primitive fact of the self. The self resists all mechanistic explanation.

This distinction ushers in the second phase of de Biran's thought, of which the most representative document is the *Essai sur les fondements de la psychologie* [Essay on the foundations of psychology]. Continuing in his analysis of habit and effort, he is led to accept the Cartesian *cogito* as the initial intimation of the basic importance of the self as the first form of direct contact with *being*. De Biran refuses to limit this intimation, as Cartesianism does, to the *cogito*. The self has a wider range of manifestation, and he remains open to all evidences of its presence and its testimony to being. Under another aspect, while not rejecting the value of the Cartesian testimony, he shows himself closer to a position taken by Leibnitz, by his preference of the notion of the self as *agent force* to that of the self as *substance*. This preference releases him from many of the naturalistic complications which the concept of self as substance implies. As agent force, the self is not reducible to any of its forms of expression; it cannot be brought within the range of any categorical schema. It remains pure being in and for itself, and hence *act*. This hyperorganic activity establishes the self as the dynamic and operational principle of the unity of consciousness; it renders *knowledge* possible, for the form of knowledge is precisely the kind of living synthesis which the self, in this dynamic aspect, can engender. The sense of the self extends to the sense of the self as body, as being in the world, and in this way establishes both itself as in the world and the exterior world as an object of knowledge through its relations to the self through its body. De Biran is here sketching an inclusive *fundamental ontology* or theory of the being of the self in the world and of the world as established by that being.

The process of his liberation from ideology is completed in the third stage of his thought, of which the most representative document is the *Nouveaux essais d'anthropologie* [New essays on anthropology]. The agent force undergoes a further transformation. It is identified as liberty, as a pure mode of initiative activity. The self is identified with this liberty, i.e., pure capacity of initiative action or, even better, pure actualty as initiative action. The human subject is recognized as *moral* subject. The conception of the moral subject establishes the context for the notion of person. The person is the ontological region of the interior, the realm of liberty, independent of spatial, temporal and organic relations. Here the concrete man achieves existence, the moral phenomenology of concrete man has its special field of inspection.

The thought of Maine de Biran makes it possible to assess the historical significance of ideology. The movement began as an attempt to continue and reenforce certain views first advanced in the eighteenth century, views closely associated with the thought of Condillac, Helvétius, and d'Holbach and sometimes referred to as materialism. The consequence of ideology was in this aspect, and throughout its career, precisely the opposite of its purpose. It constitutes, not the reenforcement and continuation, but the gradual dissolution of that point of view. From an intended materialism it moves by its own inner logic toward a spiritualism and within the area of its spiritualism toward an *actualism,* culminating in a dynamic conception of the human moral subject as the creator of values in the moral and political order through its capacity of initiative action. Moreover, it achieves a notable movement forward in the area of the metaphysics of the human subject as person, away from the substance concept to the operational conception, which effectively marks the end of certain dualisms (such as the mind-body dualism) which had plagued thought since Descartes.

Readings

I. UTILITARIANISM: GENERAL

Hodgson, D. H. *Consequences of Utilitarianism: A Study in Normative and Legal Theory.* Oxford: Clarendon Press, 1967.

Lyons, David. *Forms and Limits of Utilitarianism.* Oxford: Clarendon Press, 1965.

Narveson, Jan. *Morality and Utility.* Baltimore: Johns Hopkins Press, 1967.

Rescher, Nicholas. *Distributive Justice: A Constructive Critique of the Utilitarian Theory of Distribution.* Indianapolis: Bobbs-Merrill, 1967.

II. UTILITARIANISM: PARTICULAR FIGURES

Francis Hutcheson

Blackstone, William T. *Francis Hutcheson and Contemporary Ethical Theory.* Athens, Ga.: University of Georgia Press, 1965.

Scott, W. R. *Francis Hutcheson: His Life and Position in the History of Philosophy.* Cambridge: Cambridge University Press, 1900.

Adam Smith

Cropsey, Joseph. *Polity and Economy: An Interpretation of the Principles of Adam Smith.* The Hague: M. Nijhoff, 1957.

MacFie, Alec Lawrence. *The Individual in Society: Papers on Adam Smith.* London: Allen & Unwin, 1967.

Marrow, Glenn R. *The Ethical and Economic Theories of Adam Smith.* Reprint of 1923 edition. New York: A. M. Kelley, 1969.

Taylor, William L. *Francis Hutcheson and David Hume as Predecessors of Adam Smith.* Durham, N. C.: Duke University Press, 1965.

Jeremy Bentham

Atkinson, Charles Milner. *Jeremy Bentham: His Life and Work.* Reprint of original 1905 edition. New York: A. M. Kelley, 1969.

Baumgardt, David. *Bentham and the Ethics of Today.* Princeton, N. J.: Princeton University Press, 1952.

Kayses, Elmer Louis. *The Grand Social Enterprise: A Study of Jeremy Bentham in his Relation to Liberal Nationalism.* New York: Columbia University Press, 1932.

Keeton, G. W., ed. *Jeremy Bentham and the Law: A Symposium.* London: Stevens, 1948.

MacCunn, John. *Six Radical Thinkers.* Reissue of a 1910 edition. New York: Russell & Russell, 1964.

Mack, Mary P. *Jeremy Bentham: An Odyssey of Ideas, 1748–1792.* New York: Columbia University Press, 1963.

William Godwin

Fleisher, David. *William Godwin: A Study in Liberalism.* London: Allen & Unwin, 1951.

Grylls, Rosalie G. *William Godwin and His World.* London: Odhams Press, 1953.

Monro, David H. *Godwin's Moral Philosophy.* London: Oxford University Press, 1953.

Thomas Malthus

Ambirajan, S. *Malthus and Classical Economics*. Bombay: Popular Book Depot, 1959.

Glass, D. V., ed. *Introduction to Malthus*. London: Watts, 1953.

McCleary, George F. *The Malthusian Population Theory*. London: Faber & Faber, 1953.

Meek, Ronald L., ed. *Marx and Engels on Malthus*. London: Lawrence & Wishart, 1953.

David Ricardo

Blaug, Mark. *Ricardian Economics: An Historical Study*. New Haven: Yale University Press, 1958.

St. Clair, Oswald. *A Key to Ricardo*. New York: A. M. Kelley, 1965.

James Mill

Bain, A. *James Mill*. Reprint of 1882 edition. New York: A. M. Kelley, 1967.

Hamburger, Joseph. *James Mill and the Art of Revolution*. New Haven: Yale University Press, 1963.

Murray, Robert H. *Studies in English Social and Political Thinkers of the Nineteenth Century*. 2 vols. Cambridge: W. Heffer, 1929.

III. THE SCOTTISH SCHOOL

Bryson, Gladys. *Man and Society: The Scottish Inquiry of the Eighteenth Century*. Princeton, N. J.: Princeton University Press, 1945.

Fraser, A. Campbell. *Thomas Reid*. New York: Scribner, 1898.

Grave, S. A. *The Scottish Philosophy of Common Sense*. Oxford: Oxford University Press, 1960.

Jones, O. N. *Empiricism and Intuition in Reid's Common Sense Philosophy*. Princeton, N. J.: Princeton University Press, 1927.

Rasmussen, S. V. *The Philosophy of William Hamilton*. Copenhagen: C. A. Reitzel, 1927.

Segerstedt, T. T. *The Problem of Knowledge in Scottish Philosophy*. Lund: C. W. K. Gleerup, 1935.

IV. IDEOLOGY

Books

Boas, George. *French Philosophies of the Romantic Period*. Baltimore: Johns Hopkins University Press, 1925.

Hallit, P. P. *Maine de Biran: Reformer of Empiricism*. Cambridge, Mass.: Harvard University Press, 1959.

Van Duzer, Charles H. *The Contribution of the Ideologues to French Revolutionary Thought*. Baltimore: Johns Hopkins Press, 1935.

Articles

Boas, George. "Maine de Biran," *Philosophical Review*, XXXIV (1925), 477–490.

Henrichs, Gerard. "Maine de Biran on Psychology and Metaphysics," *The Personalist*, XXXIV (1953), 124–132.

CHAPTER II

Para-Romantic Currents

Introduction: Meaning of Para-Romantic

The complexity of the romantic movement cannot escape notice, for its ramifications are to be discerned in every aspect of life and culture. It tends to extend itself and proliferate its own forms. Romanticism is not a doctrine or a movement; it is a basic insight into, and attitude toward, the possibilities of human life. What is true of romanticism in general, is also true of philosophical romanticism in particular. It takes many forms. The central movement is the passage from Kant to Hegel by way of the dissolution of the thing in itself and the construction of the system of reason. It would be arbitrary, however, to say that the romantic spirit expressed itself philosophically here and here only. Many distinct currents of speculation took their basic impulse from the romantic spirit but found their center in concerns other than the problems identified with the central movement.

To these currents, the general term *para-romantic* is applied. They receive inspiration from, but run parallel to, the central speculative movement of romanticism. The chief para-romantic currents center about the following themes: the religious theme, specifically the reconciliation of Catholicism with the modern spirit; the political theme, concerned with the evaluation of the experience of the French Revolution and the democratic institutions associated with it; and finally, the aesthetic theme, the return of art to a central role in the human spirit.

These concerns must be taken only as centers and do not exclude one another. Concerning the religious theme, at least in the early stage, the Italian philosophers Rosmini and Gioberti possess a high degree of interest which is not at all regional or geographical but is directly related to the quality of their thought. About the same center, strongly interrelated to the political concern, moves that group of French thinkers to whom the term *traditionalist* is applied—de Maistre, Lamennais, de Bonald, and others. The political concern found voice in one "imperial intellect" whom subsequent history has found it ever more

26

difficult to overlook, the Englishman Edmund Burke. England is also the scene of the development of romantic thought about principally aesthetic themes, in Coleridge and Ruskin, and, in Carlyle, about a complex of themes which touches many areas. In American transcendentalism, principally in the person of Emerson, the para-romantic currents touch their most distant geographical point.

A. *Para-Romanticism in Italy: Rosmini and Gioberti*

Para-romanticism finds representation in Italy in two figures of immense culture and sophistication of thought: Antonio Rosmini-Serbati (1797–1855) and Vincenzo Gioberti (1801-1852). Linked together in a historical complex of association and conflict so that they are not infrequently dealt with as occupying indistinguishable positions, these men are above all individuals. Equally endowed, they differ in temperament, in inward vision, in outward career. Nevertheless, they do share a common source of inspiration, the romantic ethos. They also share a common effort to bend this spirit to the service of two ideals, that of Catholicism, for both were priests, and that of the emergent Italian nation. In the latter purpose, however, they were again divided: Rosmini nurturing an ineradicable devotion to the institution of the papacy, which he served to the point of self-renunciation; Gioberti, with greater political realism, allying himself with the monarchy of Piedmont, though ultimately destined not to enjoy its favors. Philosophically, both were rich in insight, subtle in argument and strongly inclined, like the great romantics, to system building.

The roots of Rosmini's speculation lie deep in the classical Augustinian-Thomistic tradition, which had sustained the structure of Catholic doctrine for centuries. Within this tradition, his spontaneous affinity lay in the direction of Augustine. He was sensitive to the demands of his own times, however, and sought to bring the insights of this great tradition to bear on the exigencies in European thought generated by the tensions between rationalism and empiricism, romanticism and Kantian criticism. In all these efforts, however, he was guided by a single purpose: to re-create the speculative basis of Catholic doctrine in a pattern at once faithful to the old and responsive to the new in philosophy.

The work with which the name of Rosmini is most closely associated is the product of his middle years, the *Nuovo saggio sull'origine delle idee* [New essay on the origin of ideas], 1830. A work of basically Augustinian inspiration, the *Essay*, strives to meet the demands of a number of different currents in theory of knowledge. Though the notion of the "origin" of ideas figures so largely in the title, it is another notion, that of the constitutive character of the "idea of being" in human consciousness which dominates much of the work. Equally important is the notion of "intellectual perception," and it is in terms of the latter two concepts that the ostensibly central problem, that of the origin of ideas, is addressed.

It is best to begin the consideration of his project with the idea of being. This is not the easiest approach, but there is reason to believe that it will prove the most fruitful. The idea of being performs the function of the Kantian *synthesis a priori*, for Rosmini begins by accepting the Kantian dualism between the *a posteriori* and the *a priori*, the phenomenal and the noumenal orders. Like Kant, again, he recognizes the grounds of science in the latter. While Kant, however, recognizes a plurality of forms of the *synthesis a priori*, irreducible to each other, Rosmini, taking an ontologistic tack, reduces these to one, the *idea of being*.

Having conceded as much to Kant, Rosmini reverts to a strain more congenial to himself and proceeds to develop this thesis of the idea of being as the sole principle of the *synthesis a priori* in a thoroughly Augustinian idiom. This is apparent from the characteristics which he attributes to it, echoes clearly of Augustine and of Malebranche: Only this idea can be thought without reference to any other idea; at the same time, it is the idea through which every other idea is thought. The product neither of the empirical nor of the transcendental subject, it is at once a datum offered immediately by God to the intellectual subject and the constitutive principle of that subject, both ontologically and functionally.

Again, the idea of being exhibits the characteristics both of a category and of a transcendental operation. It exhibits the characteristics of a category, because knowledge takes place through the existential judgment in which being, as given in the idea of being, is predicated of things; through this process, the subsistence of the object is present and known in the judgment. As a category, the idea of being is "other," i.e., irreducible to any specific content of thought or knowledge (yet the ground of all such content). Up to this time, it had been assumed by philosophers that the idea of being, in its role as a category, had to be either a product of the empirical subject or truly "objective," i.e., the other in itself. In the first case, all knowledge would be rendered "subjective" in the pejorative sense of that term. In the second case, the "objectivity," i.e., the other in its status as object, would seem to demand that a "transcendental" subject be postulated (e.g., the *Weltgeist*). Rosmini eludes this dilemma, showing it to be ostensible and not real. The human subject is the empirical subject; at the same time, it is capable of a transcendental operation which enables it to secure universal and necessary knowledge. This transcendental operation is one with the idea of being. This idea of being, finally, is not the product of any subject, whether empirical or transcendental, but a *datum*. This datum can be referred only to the action of God. Indeed, its presence in thought is evidence of a primary order for God. It is this last point which relates Rosmini's thought to that of Augustine.

The assertions concerning the idea of being are closely related to Rosmini's conception of *intellectual perception*. It is clear that the idea of being does not, of itself, suffice to account for effective knowledge of the actual world. This world proves to be knowable only if it can be shown that sensation penetrates the realm of the idea of being and *vice versa* that the idea of being is the ground of the world of sensation. (The adversary point of view here is phenomenalism, for, according to Kant, the phenomenon is that which appears but is not, or is only for another). Sensation does indeed present the multiple forms of determinate subsistence in the real world, but it does not present them as being, but as appearance. For this reason, sensation must be informed by the idea of being. By "intellectual perception," Rosmini intends the operation by which this information of the order of sensation by the idea of being is effected.

This operation is grounded in man's constitution as a sentient and an intelligent principle. Rosmini's emphasis is on the unity of these dimensions in man's constitution. They are not independently operative faculties, sense and intellect, but every concrete act of knowing is structured by both elements in a complex, but basic, unity. There is neither "pure" sensation nor "pure" intellection; there is the concrete act of intellectual perception in which sensible perception evokes, in that "being" which is already present to the subject in the *idea of being*, determinations through which the ideas of particular things arise. Intellectual perception is not the synthesis of two previously existing elements but the complex and concrete term of a complex, concrete operation, *at once* intelligent and sensitive.

Both the notion of the "idea of being" and that of "intellectual perception" enter into Rosmini's treatment of the problem of the "origin of ideas." Strangely enough, Rosmini does not react negatively to this question; he accepts it as an authentic query, to which philosophy must respond. Ideas, therefore, seem to him (with the exception, of course, of the idea of being), to have an origin and to arise by abstraction. He chides the empiricists for confusing intellectual perception with sensation in their account of the origin of ideas; the act of reflection, through which abstraction takes place, operates not on simple sense *data* but upon objects already known through intellectual perception. By noting certain characteristics and averting attention from others, abstraction forms ideas of various degrees of generality, up to the universal. The idea of being alone is excluded from this account, for it is the presupposition and not the product of intellectual perception.

His concern with the problem of knowledge and its relation to the subject leads him to a more exhaustive study of the subject in its own right. This is the preoccupation of his *Psicologia* [Psychology] (rev. ed., 2 vols., 1850). Again, he tries to meet the demands of empiricism and idealism by passing beyond them. He refuses to resolve, as idealism does, the subject into the transcendental process or, with empiricism, to merge it into the process of sensation. He proposes, instead, a "realism of the subject." The basis of this position is his theory of the *fundamental sentiment* which is, in this order, the analogue of *intellectual perception* in the context of epistemology. The soul is the *substance-sentiment*, the intuitive sense of immanent and enacted being which generates subsistence. The reality of the subject is constituted by this sense, which is immediate, non-objective, and synthetic, drawing into unity all aspects of the subject's complex life: sense, intelligence, will. This fundamental sentiment, which generates substance, is the first and continuous experience which man has of himself, of his subjectivity and his selfhood. This sentiment always involves relationship to a body. The corporeal sentiment is thus a basic element or aspect of the fundamental sentiment. Thus Rosmini cements from within the classical idea of the composition of body and soul, making impossible that dualism which had already generated such ambiguity and doubt in modern thought. This fundamental sentiment is primitive and incommunicable; it grounds the subject in its unity and complexity. The fundamental sentiment also makes possible a restatement of the classical doctrine of the immortality of the soul: Its basis is the fundamental sentiment as focused upon the idea of being, which is apprehended and enacted and not merely contemplated. Since, moreover, the corporeal sentiment is integral to the fundamental sentiment, the body shares that constitutive immortality of the subject which the fundamental sentiment reveals.

The highest achievement of Rosmini's speculative system is his idea of the person. The subject presents two aspects: nature and person. The *nature* is the sum of the activities of which the subject is the agent, taken in their relations to each other. The perfection of the subject, in the order of "nature," is therefore determined by the number and quality of its capacities. *Person*, by contrast, indicates the unity of direction of those activities by which the "nature" is established. For this reason, "person" is associated in a special way with the will, the principle of activity. The will establishes the "person" because the will organizes and directs the capacities and activities of the "nature." It does so even more because in doing so it exhibits its own *deontic* character, that is, its orientation toward the *ought*. The person which issues from this action of the will is unique and incommunicable, for the agency of the will which establishes it is unique and incommunicable.

Rosmini is preoccupied with stressing that the unity which is proper to the person is not a merely operational or structural unity; it is *deontic*. It is constitutively oriented toward the world of value and of norms.

Somewhat strangely, Rosmini asserts that what is intended by "person" is not a seamless unity, but exhibits degrees. "Person" is implicit in all the activities of the "nature." The movement of life, especially the moral life, is toward its explication and its increment. Hence he is led to make his subtle distinction between *vita diritta* and *vita riflessa* (terms which it is impossible to translate without distortion). The moral life in its essence is the practice of the *vita riflessa,* the examined life, in a highly creative sense and hence in the *eduction* of the person.

By his *personalism* Rosmini believes that he has overcome the ethical and moral formalism of Kant. In the person, the speculative act of intellectual perception immediately translates itself into the practical judgment which becomes the nomothetic principle of action. The principle is that the truth of being, presented by the intellectual perception, inevitably draws the assenting action of the will.

Hence arises Rosmini's own version of the *categorical imperative: Be faithful to being.* Fidelity to being is immediately translated into the rule of justice, for it demands that the rule, *give to each his due,* should be interpreted in terms of the hierarchy of value and of being.

Rosmini's philosophy of right, law, and politics is developed from the ground of this notion of justice. *Right,* in the abstract, is a property of being, for *being demands to be recognized.* Concretely, however, *right* resides in the *person*. Being is most transparently present in the person and hence in the person most urgently exercises its right to recognition. What binds persons together in society is the sharing of a common intelligent principle: *ideal being.* The forms of social life fall on a *continuum* between the most rudimentary and inclusive, i.e., mere membership in the human race, and the most intimate and exclusive, the marriage relation. Civil society falls midway on this *continuum.* Civil society does not *originate* rights it only regulates the way in which they are or can be exercised. Therefore, the state must be defined as an institution which regulates the morality of human rights, while government is the concrete ordering of the rights of persons on the basis of this principle.

Personalism is also the guiding principle of Rosmini's justly celebrated educational theories. Indeed, his educational theory brings to a focus his entire philosophy: Respect the human person as the vehicle of divine light and ideal being. Education is the guided process of bringing the person to its explicit articulation and activity.

The distinctive speculative position to which Gioberti attained is commonly referred to as "ontologism." The central point in this position is his opposition to "sensism," a generic term by which he understood any doctrine which seemed to imply that in knowledge there is present to the mind, not actual being, but a modification or state of the mind itself. To this he opposed the general position that to the mind, as intellect at least, there is present being in itself, embracing the being of the mind itself. This constitutes the *principle of ontologism.* Of supreme importance is the manner in which being in itself is thought to be present. The mode of its presence is *not psychological;* Gioberti is opposed to all forms of psychologism, including that which he called "transcendental psychologism." Nor is being present only as a formal principle to be brought into the range of consciousness by a critical and analytical operation, as Kant had proposed. It is present *actively,* as constituting the mind according to the form of its own activity. This precludes the possibility that being should in any sense be the *given.* The full force of what he intends appears only when we note the specific term by which he designates the activity of mind and being in this operation. He says that mind "concreates" being. In this sense the meaning of ontologism is completed and all modes of the opposition of thought and being, whether of idealist or realist tinge, are overcome.

The doctrine of ontologism finds a first extension in Gioberti's theories of language and general aesthetics. The intuitive presence of being, in its all-inclusive infinity, is virtual rather than actual; it must, therefore, be concretely actualized under the conditions of man's existence, that is to say, it must be *expressed.* This expression *constitutes* the human "word." The word determines—that is, makes finite and concrete—the infinite being constitutively present in human thought. Expression in the word makes possible the act of reflection whereby that intuitively present being is formally apprehensible as *idea.* The concrete process of expression, in all its complexity, is language; within the scope of philosophy, aesthetics is the science of expression or general linguistics. The concrete process of language is the all-inclusive matrix of culture and institutions.

The word, considered in its *ontic* aspect as formally distinct from its expressive aspect, constitutes *mimesis:* the return of existence to being. This return is effected through the capacities of the word to establish intuitively and constitutively present being as reflectively present (hence, language is, for Gioberti, essentially logical in character). The Platonic source of the notion is manifest; so too is the transformation of *mimesis* into *methexis* by which Gioberti advances his doctrine. The word, though expressive of being, is still, as existential, in a state of alienation from it. This alienation is overcome by the gradual transformation of *mimesis* into *methexis*, expression passing over into participation. The mediating principle of this transformation is the soul. Here the neo-Platonic reminiscences are awakened; for *mimesis* as alienation is conceived by Gioberti as the descending movement from the *one* and *methexis*, the closing of alienation, as the ascent to being. These reminiscences are reenforced by the association of mimesis with the mode of existence of the sensible, methexis with the mode of existence of the intelligible and intelligence.

Gioberti's political thought possesses special interest. In his early years he responded favorably to French democratic and revolutionary thought. A stay in Paris during the first years of his political exile disillusioned him. He then turned to a position not unlike that of the traditionalists in France. Monarchy presented itself in a more favorable light than democracy, especially in view of the place Gioberti assigned religion in the civil structure of society. He developed, with specific reference to the project of unifying the Italian peninsula into one nation, the position called neo-Guelphism. This idea, which awakens medieval reminiscences, proposed that the papacy assume leadership in a federation of states to stretch from the Alps to Sicily. Gioberti was aware that a similar idea had been proposed with respect to the Kingdom of the Two Sicilies. He was aware that the effective forces for a unification of the peninsula lay in neither of these institutions but in the power which he represented, the monarchy of the House of Savoy. The policy of the latter, however, did not, at this stage, formally envisage a total unification of the peninsula but the much more limited objective of expelling the Austrian occupation of northern Italy and establishing its own hegemony over the northern third of the peninsula. Within this pattern of political strategy, Gioberti developed the complex of ideas which may be called his political theory.

At its center stands the idea of the *nation*. On the continuum of association the nation stands between the individual taken in his numerical plurality and the all-inclusive unity of the human "genus." The other modes of association which may arise among men fall along this same continuum. This continuum is an axiological ordering, for the associations stand in a hierarchical order to one another, based upon the value-range each serves. The nation occupies a central mediating position between all associations. It divides and then mediates all those which fall below it on the hierarchical continuum in the direction of *privacy* and all those which fall above it on the same scale in the direction of *publicity*, i.e., civil society. The nation is the mediating area at which privacy begins to yield place to public civil order. Prior to consciousness as a nation, all relations verge toward the private. National consciousness effects the emergence of public relations, through which private interests and associations receive a higher mediation. To this generic notion of the nation there is added the notion of the *nations*. These are the particular historical configurations which conform to the generic idea. Gioberti introduces a hierarchical order among these in turn, based on a complex set of norms. This hierarchical order culminates in the "primacy" or "primato" which makes of one nation a paradigm for the evaluation and the formation of others. On historical grounds, Gioberti assigns this primacy to the Italian nation, though recognizing that this primacy circulates historically among the nations.

What is perhaps most interesting about this idea of the nation is its relevance to the historical experience of Europe and especially of Italy. With respect to Europe, the theory appears as the rationalization of the historical fact, that the states which emerged after the Renaissance in Europe were "nation-states." The association of the idea with the Italian experience, however, brings out a more genuinely theoretical aspect of it, the thesis that the national formation of consciousness is the necessary matrix for the formation of the civil consciousness. Gioberti anticipates the remark of a later statesman after the unification of Italy on a purely political plane had already been achieved: "Now that we have made Italy, it is necessary to make Italians."

The consciousness which sustains political unity must be that complex which he called "the nation"; while finding final expression in political autonomy, it has its roots in more profound cultural, linguistic, affective, customary, etc., forms of unity. These seem to have little force; when taken together, they yield the actuality to which the name "nation" attaches. The primacy assigned to the Italian nation has less theoretical interest; it can best be understood as responding to the necessity of justifying the political aspirations stirring in the peninsula. It would be some time before Cavour would see through the myth of the nation to recognize that such aspirations need no other justification in history save the criterion universally recognized and never challenged, *success*. This realization would, in turn, provide the key to his own strategy, which was not to justify such aspirations beforehand but to present the world with a *fait accompli*.

B. *Traditionalism in France*

Para-romanticism in Italy exhibits, in early form, a conjunction between romanticism and Catholicism which will become constantly more important as the nineteenth century progresses. A powerful affinity asserted itself between these two forces, even though Catholicism strove in the name of certain of its historical positions to reduce this relationship and even to ban it, as, for example, by reintroducing the Thomistic philosophy at the end of the century. This affinity is even more clearly illustrated in the French para-romantic movement called "traditionalism."

Traditionalism may be employed in both a general and a specific sense. Used generally, the term designates an attitude of reaction toward certain historical events or revolutionary movements of culture *in the name of a complex of values transmitted by history.* This last phrase is very important, for it conveys the most distinguishing note of traditionalism, its orientation to history. The specific sense designates the movement of this general spiritual character which transpired during the period after the French Revolution and Napoleon and which represented the philosophical consciousness of the Age of Restoration. It is in this philosophical consciousness that is thus historically circumscribed that the attachment between romanticism and Catholicism manifests itself.

The major representatives of traditionalism in this specific sense are Joseph de Maistre, Louis de Bonald, and Félicité de Lamennais; to this roster may be added the lesser figures of Bonnetty, Benjamin Constant and Donoso Cortes. This specific historical movement is designated as traditionalism, not only because it advocated anew the traditional values and doctrines of Catholicism and of political legitimism which recalled the France and the Europe of pre-Revolutionary days, but, more precisely, because it elaborated, philosophically, the concept of *tradition* as the vehicle and organ of truth for man. This was in direct opposition to the exaltation of individual reason characteristic of the Enlightenment. Reason as the guide of man and rational evidence as the criterion of truth are insights to be traced to Descartes, according to Lamennais; even further, according to de Maistre, to the Baconian notion of experience. But this principle leads inevitably to skepticism because the individual reason cannot escape a universal doubt from which no countermovement of affirmation can arise. An objective criterion of truth is furnished by tradition, that is, by that complex of truths which, originating in God and communicated by God to man, are handed down through history. These truths are affirmed and attested by the *consensus omnium;* tradition in this sense may also be called "general reason" or "authority," which is social in character and to which the individual reason must subordinate itself. The organs for transmitting these truths are human institutions, especially, according to de Bonald, language, which in his view is of divine origin. These are the master ideas of the movement, to which each of the writers whom we shall briefly consider makes his own contribution and which each interprets with his own emphasis. Our attention will be limited to those who have been called its major representatives: de Maistre, Lamennais and de Bonald.

1. Joseph de Maistre (1753–1821)

The dominant motive for the thought of Joseph de Maistre is no doubt his detestation for everything the French Revolution had, in his opinion, come to represent. However, this aversion to the Revolution was not limited to the practical order of events. He was convinced that the entire enterprise of the Revolution was based on profound theoretical errors concerning the human situation, human nature, and the nature of social and political institutions. This theoretical concern gives his thought its position in the history of philosophy and leads him to elaborate the political theories associated with his name.

This aversion to the Revolution appears in de Maistre's writings, such as his *Lettres d'un royaliste savoisien* [Letters of a Savoyard royalist], 1793, and more importantly the *Considérations sur la France* [Reflections on the state of France], 1796. However, there is evidence that, like many other critics of the Revolution, he had at an earlier period been attracted to it. The *Considérations* especially reveals de Maistre's theoretical concerns, for it contains a criticism of abstract rationalism and of the social theory of contractualism which has many similarities to the criticisms of Burke. Nevertheless, he offers the opinion that the Revolution cannot be considered a complete historical aberration; it must be seen as a negative moment in history, willed by divine providence to bring into the historical purview factors which had been previously obscured. This is the notion of providence already encountered in the proto-romantic Vico: providence as the rectifier of historical process.

De Maistre traces abstract rationalism particularly to the English philosopher Bacon. To this theme he devoted a long memorial. Though the tone of this document is somewhat overwrought, the points he makes against Bacon are telling and will find their counterpoint in his own view of the human mind and the formation of culture. What he finds most open to criticism in Bacon is his celebrated theory of induction in science. Correlatively, Bacon's "technicism" comes under censure, particularly with reference to human institutions. The spirit of Bacon led, in de Maistre's view, to that exaggerated confidence in the critical and abstract human reason which came to mark the Enlightenment, generating its spirit of hostility toward history and tradition. He is also censorious of Bacon's views on language, which appear to him too nominalistic and conventionalistic. Bacon lacked any sense of the laborious growth of language through history as well as any inkling of language as transcendental, having a formative function in the process of human intelligence and not the status of a mere tool. The essay is a clue to the whole structure of de Maistre's thought.

The leisure and vantage point afforded by his position as ambassador of Savoy at the Russian court encouraged de Maistre to extend not only his political observations, so richly documented in his masterwork *Soirées de St. Pétersbourg* (1821), but also his theoretical reflections. In the important work *Essai sur le principe générateur des constitutions politiques* [Essay on the generative principle of political constitutions], 1809, he took up themes which he had raised but then neglected, such as those of his *Réflexions sur le protestantisme dans ses rapports avec la souveraineté* [Protestantism in its relations to sovereignty], 1797, and *Etude sur la souveraineté* [Study on sovereignty], 1795, and recast them into definitive form. This work contains the chief theses of de Maistre's political theory, which remain unchanged even in such later works as *Du pape*. According to this theory, the generative principle of constitutions is the precise opposite of contractualism. It is a complex principle: history and providence in a close dialectical relationship which only historical analysis can reveal. This principle yields the concrete principle of all political government, authority, which is generated by neither the abstract reason nor the historically ungrounded will but can come into existence only by the providentially guided process of history. This historical generation in turn creates legitimacy, which is the sole norm of the incidence of power and which renders all attempts to alter the form of power morally reprehensible unless arising directly from this process itself.

The principles brought forth in the *Essai* focused de Maistre's attention on the constitution of the Catholic Church. With power centered in the authority of the Supreme Pontiff, this constitution came gradually to represent in de Maistre's eyes the only form of constitution which could effectively rule mankind. This thesis becomes the concern of the work for which de Maistre is perhaps best known, *Du pape* [On the pope], 1819. The argument of this treatise may briefly be indicated in the following terms: Only the principle of authority, in sharp contrast to the principle of popular sovereignty, could prove strong enough to guide men to civil justice, because the corruption of original sin renders men incapable of self-government. Sovereignty, therefore, cannot have its origins in mankind but must be divine; sovereigns hold their power by divine delegation. Only the power of the pope is clearly and unmistakably so derived; as a consequence, it transcends the power of temporal rulers. This doctrine, in the active political order, became identified with ultramontanism. He envisaged further a European universalism based on Catholic supremacy, a point of view in direct contrast with the interconfessional universalism espoused by Czar Alexander I which led eventually to de Maistre's recall as ambassador.

From a literary as well as a speculative point of view de Maistre's masterpiece remains the *Soirées de St. Pétersbourg*, 1821. Although all of the ideas to be encountered here may be found elsewhere in his works, the form in which he brings them together, that of reasoned and urbane conversation between personages who represent various aspects of his own thought and of the points of view he is seeking to engage, adds immeasurably to both their clarity and their persuasiveness. The intransigence of *Du pape* is entirely absent as is the more labored mode of argumentation of the *Essai*.

2. Félicité Robert de Lamennais (1782–1854)

The career of Lamennais was in some sense typical of the romantic genius itself; vacillating to a degree, it still possessed an amazing coherence. After a period of youthful unbelief he returned to the Catholic faith through the influence of his elder brother Jean-Marie and like him became a priest. After two earlier efforts, one in conjunction with Jean-Marie, he composed the work with which his name is most associated, *Essai sur l'indifférence en matière de religion* [Essay on indifference in matters of religion], 1817–23, which revealed his immense talent for apologetics. A royalist and an ultramontanist in politics, in 1832 he founded the journal *L'avenir* to give voice to the interests of Catholics in the contemporary struggle of opinions and power. His record of his struggle with the Church authorities, which culminated in his second and definitive rupture with the Church, is contained in his *Affaires de Rome*, 1836–37. He became, in *Paroles d'un croyant* [Words of a believer], 1834, an advocate of an extreme, prophetic and utopian kind of democracy. His interesting *Essai d'un système de philosophie catholique* was edited by Maréchal in 1906.

The temper of Lamennais is such that it is impossible to consider his thought as a static system; only its movement can reveal its significance. It is therefore necessary to follow, however sketchily, its inner phases. These are three: 1) an early intransigent phase in which he appears as the most admant advocate of traditionalism and ultramontanism; of this phase the *Essai sur l'indifférence* is the supreme document; 2) a phase in which he becomes a champion of liberal Catholicism; this is the period of *L'avenir* 1828–32; and 3) a final phase in which he elaborates a new kind of Christianity in which social and religious themes are interwoven; the supernaturalness of Christianity is denied, religion is identified with philosophy, and Christianity itself is given a definite social meaning. Lamennais is reported to have said, almost on his deathbed, "I have not changed: I have continued." Critics are for the most part inclined to agree with him, even though the line of continuity may at times be difficult to trace. In the final developments of his thought he worked out to its most radical implications the system he had formulated in the *Essai*, especially the doctrine of the *sensus communis*.

This doctrine of common sense forms both the central thesis of the *Essai* and the line of continuity in his thought. Lamennais warns against confusing his meaning of this phrase with that, for example, of the philosophy of common sense of Reid and the Scottish school. Their notion of common sense rests ultimately on the infallibility of the individual reason; his, by contrast (and in keeping with the entire romantic critique of eighteenth-century rationalism), denies the power of the individual reason to give us certitude. The individual reason is, in his view, the source of invincible skepticism. He directs his criticism above all against the Cartesian notion of evidence, which seems to appear to the individual in complete isolation from the world and from other men. He rejects entirely the alleged value of the *cogito,* asserting that it involves a circular argument. Certitude must be sought in the *common sense;* axioms, as well as matters of fact, are recognized as true by reason of their conformity to this criterion: They recommend themselves to the agreement of all men. Lamennais assigns the transcendental function to common sense.

Lamennais immediately applies this principle of common sense to the Catholic faith. Since they rest on the very same foundations, human reason and the Catholic faith imply each other, so that one must be Catholic on the very grounds on which one is reasonable or rational. This conjunction was extended to the civil order in such works as his *Réligion considérée dans son rapport avec l'ordre politique et civil* [Religion viewed in its relations with the civil and political order], 1825–26, and his *Des progrès de la Révolution et de la guerre contre l'Eglise* [Progress of the Revolution and the war against the Church], 1829. These works were attacked by the Gallicans as challenging the privileges of the Church in France as established by the edict of 1682; at the same time, though ultramontanist in spirit, they drew the disfavor of the Church in Rome on the grounds that he confused the certitude of religion with the certitude of common sense and was endangering the carefully erected and somewhat precarious relations between Church and state in that troubled period.

From a circumstantial point of view one may declare, as Bréhier does, that to some extent Lamennais was forced to draw liberal and democratic conclusions from his principles because of the strong opposition to him in ecclesiastical quarters, Roman ultramontanist and Gallican alike. A deeper dynamic may also be discerned, however. Lamennais had a profound insight into the role that the masses must eventually play in the future of European political and cultural life; even at this early juncture, he felt impelled to pose, in however ambiguous a manner, the very basic question of whether the Catholic Church possessed the power to place itself, despite its history of aristocratic and royalist association, at the head of the masses. Viewed in this way, his thought has a very strong relevance for the whole subsequent history of Catholicism. To the question in general, it would have to be replied that in succeeding periods the Church has shown this capacity to generate a leadership of the emerging masses, but not in the form or on the basis which Lamennais suggested.

Fundamental to the liberal Catholicism of Lamennais and the men with whom he was associated in this period—Montalembert, Lacordaire and Gerbet, for example—was the close identification of the cause of Catholicism with that of liberty. Concretely, Lamennais advocated the liberation of all forms of religion and worship from the control of the state. Only then could the pure spirit of Christianity, which in his view was identical with the spontaneous persuasion of the universality of men, be released in the world. This led to a further identification which his critics, and ultimately the Church, repudiated; he tended to identify political liberation with the specific ends of the Church. In working for the one, the purposes of the other were being realized and the resources of the one were to be called upon to effect the purposes common to them. This seemed to some of his critics, as witness the encyclical *Mirari Vos* of 1832, to reduce the Church to the status of a wholly human institution, the state, and to alter her theology to a civil theology.

Under the pressure of the overt condemnation of his position, Lamennais took the next step in his continuation, that toward popularism. The documents for this last step are *Paroles d'un croyant*, 1834, and the *Livre du peuple* [Book of the people], 1838. When the leadership of the Church fails, the movement for liberation must come from within the people, the masses themselves. This is entirely possible since they possess within them that principle, common sense, which is the basis of the entire structure of liberty. In these works the style of Lamennais undergoes a remarkable change. From polemical it becomes prophetic and denunciatory; the monarchs are conspiring against the people, the evil and cupidity of the "haves" systematically alienate the "have-nots" and by design prevent the just distribution of the fruits of the earth and of labor. He predicts a kind of Armageddon between the possessors and the dispossessed. At the same time, there appears a kind of mystic exaltation of the power and rectitude of the people, as well as of the justice of their cause. The people alone could become the instrument of their own deliverance. In this effort they were not to place their trust in human institutions, in laws and constitutions; only the religious sense and the correct notion of God could be the basis of the just social order. This notion of God might well differ from that which had dominated the western mind; but the people, with the principle of common sense, would in due time generate this idea of God, which could sustain the authentic sense of religion and, through it, the just social order. At the same time, Lamennais had nothing in common with such a movement as communism, then making its first appearances. He condemned it unconditionally as a materialism which would betray the people by making them labor for ends alien to their own interests.

Lamennais was never the man to leave a task undone. He had spoken of a new idea of God which could sustain a just social order. In the *Esquisse d'une philosophie* [Sketch of a philosophy], 1840, he undertook the delineation of that idea of God. This work would seem to be a reworking of the *Essai d'un système de philosophie catholique* [Sketch of a system of Catholic philosophy] dating from about 1827 but unpublished until 1906. In this work, he rescues only the notion of the Trinity from the range of orthodox dogma. All aspects of supernatural religion are set aside: original sin transmitted to successive generations of men, redemption by Christ, and grace. In place of this mediated relation between God and man he introduces a direct imagism which some historians trace to Augustine. All men are the image of the Triune God; the task of philosophy is to identify this image. Creation is the direct reflection of the divine nature and not a mere choice among possible worlds. This imagism persists downward through all the levels of being; and being, through philosophy, moves upward again to reunite itself with the model and thus fulfill itself. This image is most clear in man, for in him are reproduced in their character and their order the very principles which constitute the Trinity: act, intelligence, and love.

Lamennais's philosophy seems hopelessly biased by its polemical and, in general, nonspeculative concerns. At the same time, it is so laced with luminous insights that it constantly attracts attention. Thus, his pages on art in the *Esquisse* of 1840 have been much admired while, even in his political theory, his emphases and predictions have been felt to carry weight. The romantic quality of his thought cannot be doubted; it inspires his idealization of the people and sustains even his elaborate theological structure of imagism. Despite the imbalances in his thought, he remains an attractive and instructive figure.

3. Louis G. A. de Bonald (1754–1840)

De Bonald has been called at once the most systematic and the most intransigent of the traditionalists; obviously these adjectives refer respectively to the more speculative and to the more practical of his concerns. In the practical area, his antagonism toward the Revolution, which he had experienced very fully in his own person, was extreme and unyielding; his entire enterprise was to restore the older order. In him the Restoration found a voice forthright enough to be somewhat embarrassing, for he apparently had little concern for the actual compromises which surround and sustain power. A member of the lower nobility, he had known exile as a result of the upheaval, during which time he had composed his earliest extended treatise the *Théorie du pouvoir politique et religieux dans la société civile* [Theory of political and religious power in civil society], 1796. On his return to France, he accepted the Napoleonic regime because it represented restoration of order and civil sanity. He rejoiced in the Restoration and became a peer of the realm under its dispensation.

De Bonald's effort to "systematize" traditionalism retains interest historically. He identifies, first, the complex of ideas underlying the Revolution; these constitute a system of interlocking notions touching God, man, the social order, etc. This complex is wholly a work of his own creation, and cannot be documented historically; it is important, however, as the frame of reference in which he worked. The chief elements of this revolutionary complex comprise: the dogma of popular sovereignty and the idea of the origin of society and authority in contract; a radical atheism which places supreme power over men in men themselves, rejecting God as its source; a radical materialism, having its roots in the prevalence of the imaginative over the rational faculties in man; and a theory of language as convention, holding that language is the arbitrarily determined sign of the thought or idea.

The ideas he opposes to this complex are contained in his most important work, *Législation primitive* [Primitive legislation], 1802. The idea of popular sovereignty is the cornerstone of that first construction; its refutation is the cornerstone of the second. De Bonald, it has been noted, exhibits his dependence on the eighteenth century even as he refutes it. From Rousseau he gets both the constitutive marks of sovereignty (unity, fixity, indivisibility), which he never questions, and its necessity, which he questions even less. His concern is to show that this sovereignty cannot belong to the people. What the eighteenth century made immanent to man he makes transcendent. Sovereignty must be sought in some other locus than the people. This transcendence of sovereignty has been called de Bonald's *social realism*. Sovereignty resides, de Bonald holds, not in the people but in God. Theocracy displaces democracy; God alone possesses the characteristics of the sovereign. The rejection of democracy implies the rejection of contractualism. Since God is the seat of power, sovereignty *precedes* society and must be *introduced* into society by an action of God, either general or specific. God introduces power and sovereignty into society by a *primitive revelation*. Through this revelation man receives knowledge of the laws by which social relations are determined; by the revelation, he receives the art of language itself.

The theory of language which de Bonald thus inserts into his *social realism* appears, from the theoretical point of view, to be the most original part of his doctrine. Man could not have invented language, any more than he could, by such an absurd act as the social contract, have invented or originated society. Since man could not have invented language, man must have received it; but he could not have received it from any other source than God. De Bonald distinguishes the faculty of thought and language from the *art* of each. The former is innate, the latter acquired. The revelation of language is only formal; it must, by the same act of revelation, have been given a content. Therefore, he concludes, an entire complex of substantive propositions—moral, religious, metaphysical—must have been revealed simultaneously with language and as part of language. This constitutes the primitive revelation. The primitive revelation is enlarged by our processes of inquiry and is transmitted by social teaching, constituting *tradition:* the elaboration and transmission of this primitive revelation by social processes.

This imparts a highly conservative historical tone to de Bonald's thought. History is conceived principally as the process by which the primitive revelation is transmitted. It differs from those romantic views of history which place emphasis on its innovational character. Similarly, he emphasizes the function of language in conveying a truth already known or determined; he does not see language and expression as the very process of molding and discovering new truth.

C. *Para-Romantic Figures Beyond the Continent*

The effects of the movement of philosophical romanticism were felt, not only on the Continent, but in England and in America. As it passed into these areas, the romantic spirit reflected the characteristics of each new environment. The specific preoccupations of the immediate cultural patterns became the matter on which the romantic spirit deployed itself. Thus, in England, the romantic spirit expended itself upon dominantly political and aesthetic concerns; in America, the concerns were predominantly moral. Obviously, it is impossible within the space available to us here to depict the full effect of the romantic speculative spirit. These pages will direct their concern to only a small number of men who do, however, have a very special right to stand in a representative relation to the whole. These are Burke and Coleridge in England and, in America, Emerson.

1. Edmund Burke (1729–1797)

Born in Dublin in 1729, Edmund Burke, by the force of his genius and the power of his massive intelligence of human political affairs, established a wide influence among the ruling classes of England and made a permanent place for himself in the history of political thought. In his entire political and social theory Burke reflects clearly the most significant features of romantic thought—for example, his abhorrence of abstract reason, his respect for history and for the organic process of growth, his regard for the immediate modes of human consciousness which cement relations among men more securely than abstract principles, and his regard for the process of historical growth as seen in the real relations of culture and society, such as custom, language, law, right. The salient features of his thought are to be found in his three discourses: *The Vindication of Natural Society* (1756), *On the American War* (a speech before the House of Commons, March 22, 1775), and his *Reflections on the French Revolution* (1790). Because of his distaste for the abstract, Burke's position is difficult to synthesize; his conclusions emerge by a process of condensation from his acute and minute criticism of concrete situations.

The Vindication of Natural Society, which has a complex structure and makes its fundamental points obliquely and by indirection, is an attack on Lord Bolingbroke's theory of religion. Burke exploits this theme to draw basic conclusions concerning the structure of political society. Bolingbroke attacks revealed religion as the basis for man's moral conduct; in its place, he suggests a "natural" religion or religion of reason. Burke constructs a parallel to this in the political order, taking the conventional arrangements of society as the equivalent of revealed religion in Bolingbroke's sense and the principles of politics dictated by abstract reason as equivalent to Bolingbroke's natural religion. Revealed religion, Bolingbroke had argued, is but a compacted tradition founded upon accident and made sacrosanct by superstition, prejudice, and inertia; so too, Burke suggests in pursuing his parallel, must be the arrangements of political and civil society. If in religion there is recourse to principles of natural reason, then there must be such recourse in matters civil and political. But the result in either case would be disastrous; the disaster, not so apparent in the matter of religion, becomes impressively evident in matters civil and political. The error lies in the principle to which recourse is had, that of abstract reason. Abstract reason applied to the political order can produce only disruption, a fact which constitutes the refutation of all rationalism in politics.

This forces a reconsideration of all the principles and procedures which Bolingbroke condemns in matters of religion. Thus, prejudice, which he sees as an unmitigated evil, is actually, Burke points out, the basis and the dynamic principle of every society, ministering to, and not impeding, the social good. To use his own example, without prejudice, social life would be as difficult as would be physical life if every breath we drew had to be the terminus of a conscious and reflective decision. Tradition, history, historical growth, with all their complex processes which escape the mere analytical force of reason, prove to be the living tissue of civil society; and it is dubious that they can be less so in matters religious. Faith in tradition and its processes is wisely predicated upon a sound skepticism toward abstract reason and toward the capacity of the individual to exercise it in a normative way.

The speech on the war in America, the Revolutionary War, is frequently considered Burke's greatest single oratorical effort. Although it did not have the effect he intended, the considerations of principle which emerge from it lift him to the highest ranks of liberal-historical-political thought (for historicism and liberalism are by no means antithetical, as this document proves). It is a plea for the historical reason and its great instrument, prudence—instead of abstract reason—in the conduct of political life. Burke states the matter in terms which are almost impossible to improve upon: "America must be governed, not according to our own imaginations; not according to abstract ideas of right; by no means according to mere general themes of government, the resort to which appears to me, in our present situation, no better than errant trifling" but according to the circumstances which history has created. This has been called by some mere contrivance, improvisation, and opportunism; in fact it enunciates what has been called the principle of "historical empiricism," the principle to which statesmen have recourse almost by instinct.

This profound insight may be summed up in a number of propositions, even though their summation allows a certain abstractness to creep in, dulling the concrete force of their argument. The first proposition may be called the *principle of concreteness;* this states that the sufficient basis for just authority and obedience can never be found in a consideration of abstract right (such as the *right* to tax, implicit in the notion of *sovereignty* to which the intransigents were appealing). Second is the *principle of historicity,* which counsels that a nation's character results from its historical and geographical circumstances. The third is the *principle that force is of little* if any *avail* in the affairs of politics and government, that, on the contrary, the one exercising power may best serve his longterm interests by curbing his immediate ambitions and his abstract claims. Fourth, there is the *principle of tradition*, reverence for precedent and for the wisdom of forebears, from which departure should be made only on the gravest grounds. The principle of tradition may be viewed as including the fifth, which counsels that the results of political action are always so complex and unforeseeable that, in decision-making, every possible enlightenment from history should be sought.

The French Revolution was of utmost importance in the history of Europe for many reasons, not the least of which is that it precipated differences which had been lurking in the superficially unruffled but deeply troubled consciousness of the eighteenth century. Burke's *Reflections on the French Revolution* is one of the greatest documents on the effects of that event in the order of ideas. In considering the views he expresses here, we must not erect a merely abstract parallel with the speech on the war in America; it is necessary to see the two in the different perspectives which qualify them. In the discourse on America, Burke was seeking the answer to the question: How should authority respond to serious challenge? In the *Reflections,* he was seeking the answer to the question: How should a state be reformed?

Burke begins by rejecting a direct parallel between the English Revolution of 1688 and the revolution in France. The concern of the former was to improve the state by eliminating its corruptions; but there was also a serious attempt to retain everything of value. This accorded with the sound principle of historical empiricism. The French might have done as much (though the opportunity for doing so had, in fact, passed by the time the *Reflections* were composed), but they preferred to act upon abstract principles, which they assumed to be universally valid, and to oppose their own reasons to those of antiquity. Again, it is rationalism in politics which draws his ire. He is unimpressed by the abstract statement of the rights of man. Real claims to rights he is prepared to uphold, for civil society is set up for the advantage of men and all of the advantages for which it is set up become his right; but in pursuing these advantages civil government must restrain the passions of men. Rights cannot be affirmed in abstract isolation from restraints. Restraints and liberties constitute a delicate balance in civil society, and this balance cannot be determined by abstract rule.

Burke looks to English experience for the clue to this balance. He discovers it in the principle of organic historical growth, which he now states in a modified form of the contract theory, in terms of a balance of interests. Society is indeed a contract—not the trivial bond some would imagine but a "partnership between not only those who are living, but between those who are living, those who are dead and those who are yet to be born." The people created by this living and historical contract is the sum total of all the separate orders and interests in society, seeking to harmonize themselves on the basis of historical wisdom. The great vice of the French Revolution is the lack of a sense of the complexity of human affairs. Its leaders, in the name of simple abstractions, are prepared to abandon the guidance of history, to renounce the prejudices and the conventions which hold society together, without inquiry into their reasons and bases. The Revolution weakened all those lesser bonds of society which actually cement it. In doing so, it transformed itself into a principle of naked force, contrary to all of its declarations. The passion for abstract equality, and for abstract principles in general, must inevitably end in tyranny, for, exasperated by the actual complexity of life, this passion has immediate recourse to force as the instrument of its will to universal betterment, thus revealing its basic unwisdom.

On the basis of these ideas, Burke has been variously claimed, now as the advocate of conservatism, now of liberalism. Little reflection is needed to show that neither designation is apt. His political wisdom goes deeper than a doctrinaire position, whether liberal or conservative. It is concrete and historical, exhibiting the best of each of these positions. As mightily as any liberal, he affirms human rights and humanity; as mightily as any conservative, he refuses to divorce these from concrete history and experience.

Burke's *A Philosophical Inquiry into the Origin of Our Ideas of the Sublime and the Beautiful,* 1757, is in a more theoretical vein. Some historians opine that this essay exercised a decisive influence on the thought of Kant in the *Critique of Judgment.* It has the same "transcendental" concern, for it centers attention upon the universality of "taste." Certain differences immediately make themselves apparent, however. To begin, this universality is perceived by Burke as actual and not as normative. Therefore, in line with his constant aversion to the abstract, he refuses to establish it by recourse to any abstract definition and undertakes a criticism of all such definitions of beauty as those which would place its essence in proportion, utility, perfection, etc. To him the universality of taste is a historical achievement of men, as complex as the achievement of order in society. He is especially concerned to place the sublime and the beautiful outside the influence of the notion of utility. He points out that esthetic love is marked by a complete absence of desire. Equally penetrating is his perception of the fact that the poetic word is neither imitative nor necessarily visive. The composition is interesting and attractive, not only for these insights, but by reason of its marked qualities of high tone, great analytical and expositive power, and abundant cultural reference.

2. Samuel Taylor Coleridge (1772–1834)

Although his chief fame derives from his poetry, Samuel Taylor Coleridge displayed an extraordinary philosophical sensibility and a capacity for hard and acute philosophical reflection. Although his writings exhibit a certain diffuseness and a rhetoricism, beneath these surface marrings abides a hard core of philosophical insights. Of chief importance for the comprehension of his philosophical views are: *The Friend* (collected in 1812 from the numbers of this periodical of 1809–10; 3 vols., 1818), *The Statesman's Manual* (1816), *Aids to Reflection* (1st ed. 1825, many thereafter), *Coleridge on Logic and Learning* (A. D. Snyder, 1929, with selections from unpublished manuscripts), and the *Philosophical Lectures* (ed. K. Coburn, 1949). Bulky manuscript remains of an uncompleted *opus magnum* survive in the British Museum and the Huntington Library in California. The features of philosophical romanticism emerge quite clearly from these pages.

Coleridge, so completely the poet, gave considerable attention to poetry's arid counterpart, logic. The first philosophical question he ever put to himself was: How do we know? He conceived the study of this problem as a "propaedeutic" to a larger study, the reduction of all reality to a single principle, which he called "metaphysics." The romantic passion for unity and system, as contrasted with empirical fragmentation, early possessed him. He exhibits the influence of the romantic philosophers in his rejection of formal logic and his characterization of the syllogism as a *petitio principii;* even more, in his insistence that logic studies the concrete processes of mind and in his distinction, above the mere classifying operation, of a unifying and organizing function and below it an intuitive apprehension. He adopts and revitalizes the distinction between reason and understanding. Understanding is no longer conceived as treating discursively the objects present by sense experience, but as entering into the constitution of the object. Placing an especial emphasis on judgment, he rejects Locke's view of this operation as the comparison of one object with another and prefers, under Kantian influence, the principle that the judgment constructs the object. Rational consciousness implies a distinction between subject and object; but the "copula" of the judgment points to a unity of reality beyond this.

While Coleridge never succeeded in the construction of a metaphysics, he does appear to have taken certain steps toward the delineation of the conditions which such a metaphysics should meet. Metaphysics means a unity and system of the whole of reality. Kant was prevented from achieving a clear view of the condition of such unity by his too-great adherence to the concept of the understanding, the principles of division, and his correlative diminution of the *ideas* of reason. In the latter, Coleridge saw the principles of the synthesis which eluded Kant; they lay within his reach. He encounters a difficulty, in that it would seem that he should define his idea of an idea; to do so, however, would necessitate conceptualizing the idea, submitting it to the very process of division and distinction from which it promised to deliver the mind. The difficulty could be met, he felt, by indicating the function of the idea rather than by presenting it as a concept. Its function is unification, specifically of particular and universal; more precisely, the idea reveals the underlying identity beneath the particularity of the particular thing. Thus, its function is synthesis from within the particular. He draws his basic example of this operation not from science but from poetry.

Coleridge exhibited, as integral to his philosophical sensitivity, a high moral sensitivity. This moral sense was itself profoundly philosophical, turning about the integrality of the self and the way it is realized. The self is the reflection of the unity of the system of the real, the moral microcosm. He rejects the empiricist view which reduces the active self to a complex of sensory impulses. Self, in his view, is, above all, unity, and the empirical view shatters this unity. The self is the universal which finds expression in the multiplicity and particularity of experience; hence, it is an idea in the transcendental sense of the term. Moral values involve the organization of the passing moments of temporal existence into a whole, representative of what is permanent in man. The self is not so much the presupposition of the moral life but its term. It is the principle of love which finally governs this moral process and not the abstract principle of law. Law can give only extrinsic unity and hence only illusory selfhood. Love fulfills the law by internalizing it, by making it a principle of actual and concrete unity.

The direction of Coleridge's political thought led to his being called "a lesser Burke." Indeed, they did follow similar if not parallel trajectories. Coleridge evinced the common note of all romantic political theory, an early enthusiasm for the French Revolution and that other infallible mark, disillusion with its result. This disillusion led first to the questioning of the Jacobin principles upon which the Revolution rested. Coleridge shares the conservative and historical skepticism toward political rationalism and especially toward its notion that political constitutions could be brought into being and sustained in their efficacy as mediating the relations of men by mere fiat of the will, on mere abstract principles. The conviction emerged that political constitutions are profoundly moral, in the sense that they bear a fairly exact relationship to the process of the formation of the self which he had depicted in his moral philosophy. As the creation of the self involved, not abstract principles, but existential motives and intentions of the will, and could be achieved, not *instanter,* but only over that extended historical process in which the moments of temporal existence are forged into a unity, a self, so society and state emerge only through the collective molding of a group, or nation, and represent the collection of the diffused life of that group into a unity sustained and defined by collective values. His was an ethical theory of the state. Constitutions seemed to him, as to Burke, moral creations of historical experience, from which they draw their power to bind and rule.

The culmination of Coleridge's philosophical thought resides in his philosophy of religion; indeed Muirhead suggests that his entire thought is a philosophy of religion. Coleridge's inquiries into religion proceed from no fixed credal bases. His object is the character of religion and religious experience in itself. Religion, he notes, "unites in its purposes the *desiderata* of the speculative and the practical being; its acts, including its events, are truths and objects of philosophical insight and *vice versa* the truths in which it consists are to be considered as acts and manifestations of that being which is at once the power and the truth." His notion of religion is dominated by his own need and desire for communion with a concrete God through the medium of prayer, a prayer which would be the synthesis and the fulfillment of every partial aspect of human action and consciousness. For this reason, the establishment of the *personal* character of God is central to his concern. A correlative concern is the establishment of the immortality of the soul; without this, religion and rational ethics alike are meaningless. Evil demands explanation. Evil cannot be begotten of God. It emerges rather through an act of the will of distinct beings in the plenitude of God's being. These distinct beings, whose essence is will, have their actuality in being one with God. It is through their willing of themselves, in the place of God, that evil emerges.

Finally, Coleridge is entirely convinced of the "naturalness of religion," not, however, in the strained sense of the rationalistic "natural" religions of the eighteenth century, opposed to "supernatural" religion, but in the sense that the "idea of God" arises by an entirely natural process within the soul and with it the desire for that union and communion with him in which religion consists.

3. Ralph Waldo Emerson (1803–1882)

In Emerson, reflecting and writing in New England, romantic philosophy reaches its farthest geographical limits. It also reaches in his thought the form of expression in which it is most clearly dominated, not by a purely speculative concern, but by a basically moral, even moralistic, concern. The works which remain most important from the philosophical point of view are: *Nature,* 1863; *Intellect,* 1841; *Experience,* 1844; and *Representative Men,* 1850; but this statement must be taken only relatively, for an interest also attaches to his *Essays* and *Journals.* Critical opinion on Emerson's status as a philosopher has been divided; thus William James praises him as the greatest American philosopher, while to Santayana he was a mystic and a dreamer. However, the balance tips in the direction of James's estimate. Emerson's transcendentalism is based on the thought of the great German romantics, such as Hegel, and anticipates the idealism of Bradley and of Royce. There are also traces of the influence of Berkeley.

Emerson's transcendentalism shares the basic romantic theme: the unification of finite and infinite. To the latter alone, under the name of God or Oversoul, reality is assigned; all finite beings are only its manifestations. They have a merely symbolic status and function. Reflection on them can lead us to contemplation and self-identification with the whole. Man is the center of the universe precisely because this operation is possible for him. Nature, by contrast, is but a metaphor for man's spirit. Man is composed of body and soul, but his body is the incarnation of God, a projection of God into the unconscious. The spirit of man is a spark of the divine fire, a particile of the universal soul. Man's task is clear; he must achieve the great return, from world to spirit and God, from finite to infinite—the classical path of the great ascent.

The center of philosophy is a moral enterprise. The individual is the highest form of reality, but the individual realizes himself only through the negation and transcendence of his empirical self. The moral law does not articulate itself in specific precepts; it enjoins only the indwelling of the universal soul in everything that exists. Our action must be measured by this and no other norm. This indwelling makes possible liberty of action, communication with other men, moral progress, and the just evaluation of nature.

Emerson's view of history is of particular interest. It is typically romantic in character and displays a great delicacy of insight. History is the work of great individuals. These men occupy a representative position because in them the testimony of the omnipresent working of the universal spirit is greatest. This notion applies for the most part to past history; and the form of historiography most congenial to it is interpretative biography. Future history becomes the realm of prophecy, in which Emerson does not hesitate to indulge. He sees in the future an ideal humanity which technical progress and consequent well-being will have made more responsive to the movements and the needs of the spirit. At the same time, Emerson levels a charge of overconcern with material and technical progress against contemporary American society. He evinces scant appreciation for science as a form of knowledge; true knowledge is provided rather by poetry and philosophy, for these retain the spiritual sense of things which science tends to becloud. Toward the end of his life Emerson somewhat altered the inner dynamic of his thought. Falling under the influence of the all-pervasive evolutionary thought, he minimized his older adherence to the Plotinian sense of the descent of the world from the one and the consequent process of return. This was replaced by a vague notion of the evolutionary movement of all being toward the absolute.

Emerson evinced a firm belief in the particular destiny of America; indeed, he affirmed, America is the last opportunity which Providence offers to mankind. The form of this destiny was a kind of social democracy, informed by a strong element of reformism. Under such a dispensation, the people of America might freely deploy and realize their liberty and the fresh forces in their veins.

Readings

I. General

Boas, George. *French Philosophies of the Romantic Period*. Baltimore: Johns Hopkins Press, 1925.

Hales, E. E. *Pio Nono: A Study in European Politics and Religion in the Nineteenth Century*. New York: P. J. Kenedy, 1954.

McClelland, J. S. *The French Right from de Maistre to Maurras*. London: Jonathan Cape, 1970.

II. Particular Figures

Antonio Rosmini-Serbati

Dewhirst, J. A. *A. Rosmini: Fundamentals of Rosminian Epistemology*. Extracts from *Nuovo saggio*. Rome: Tipografia Latina, 1962.

Feibleman, James Kern. "Ethical Variations on a Theme by Rosmini-Serbati." *Tulane Studies in Philosophy*, VI (1957), 53–66.

Leetham, Claude. *Rosmini: Priest, Philosopher, and Patriot*. Baltimore: Helicon Press, 1958.

Joseph de Maistre

Lebrun, Richard Allen. *Throne and Altar: The Political and Religious Thought of Joseph de Maistre.* Ottawa, Canada: University of Ottawa Press, 1965.

Félicité de Lamennais

Pearson, C. S. *The Politico-Social Ideas of Huges Félicité Robert de Lamennais, 1830–1854.* New York: New York University Press, 1936.

Stearns, P. N. *Priest and Revolutionary: Lamennais and the Dilemma of French Catholics.* New York: Harper & Row, 1967.

Vidler, A. R. *Prophecy and Papacy: A Study of Lamennais, the Church, and the Revolution.* New York: Scribner, 1954.

Louis de Bonald

Quinlan, Mary H. *The Historical Thought of the Vicomte de Bonald.* Thesis. Washington, D. C.: Catholic University of America Press, 1953.

Edmund Burke

Carnavan, F. P. *The Political Reason of Edmund Burke.* Durham, N. C.: Duke University Press, 1957.

Chapman, Gerald W. *Edmund Burke: The Practical Imagination.* Cambridge, Mass.: Harvard University Press, 1967.

Samuel Taylor Coleridge

Coburn, Kathleen. *Inquiring Spirit: A New Presentation of Coleridge.* London: Routledge & Kegan Paul, 1951.

Muirhead, John H. *Coleridge as a Philosopher.* New York: Macmillan, 1930.

Orsini, G. N. *Coleridge and German Idealism.* Carbondale: Southern Illinois University Press, 1969.

Ralph Waldo Emerson

Whicher, Stephen. *The Lapse of Uriel: A Study in the Evolution of Emerson's Thought.* Thesis, Harvard University, 1942.

CHAPTER III

Utopian Social Thought

Introduction

The Age of Metternich concealed beneath its shell of political and social conservatism the most profound social unrest. Its great purpose, at least at the overt level, was to undo, if possible, the work of the French Revolution; or at least to dam it up within the retaining walls of the old order through adroit diplomacy and the agencies of the police state. A greater wisdom might have counseled the futility of such an effort. The effects of the French Revolution could not be evaded, nullified, or traduced by the forces of traditionalism and conservatism. While conservatism sought to hold together the fragments of an order which had lost its historical force, the new forces of history were seething beneath the surface. The currents of social thought now to be examined belong to this wave of the future.

This new thought grasped clearly the social dimension of the French Revolution. While the most obvious results of that Revolution had been in the political order, its true character lay much deeper. It was a social revolution. An entire social order had come to the end of its historical career. At stake was an entirely new vision of the form which human society might take. The salient mark of the social thought of this period is that it struggles with the widest problems of human group relationships, among which the political proves to be but one, and, as widespread political anarchism indicates, hardly the most important. The atmosphere of the time was pregnant with thoughts of vast social reorganizations which touched every aspect of human associations, reaching to the structure of human consciousness for their motivations and projecting themselves against the vast panorama of history, past and future, to create the perspective in which they could be understood. This thought was not content with a piecemeal approach to social problems; nor did it generally view the solutions to such problems within the framework of an older order which it perceived was at least partially their cause. It was formulated in terms of the totality

54

of human associative life and was concerned, not with the solution of isolated and limited problems, but with all-inclusive issues. From the modern perspective this concern for the whole of society appears somewhat naive; however, this is the character which lends the thought of this period its peculiar quality.

Concern with the whole social fabric and the projection of the human social program against the movement of history is the first and most persistent mark of utopian social thought. Even the later systems which bitterly attacked the utopians and sternly maintained their own "scientific" character—for example, Marxian thought and its successor Soviet communism—retained this mark of the social utopianism they attacked.

Marx spearheaded the attack on utopian social thought, and his attack makes clear what *utopian* means. The basic contrast is between this type of social thought and action and that which pretends to be scientific. The utopian concern with a method of social study was minimal. The observations upon which it based its social projects were impressionistic and limited rather than orderly and inclusive. This is not to deny them great perspicacity and perceptiveness. What they lacked in method was frequently compensated for by social sensitivity and a basic empathy with the oppressed and exploited segments of society. Nevertheless, their procedures can hardly be thought satisfactory, given the gravity of the problems. The concepts with which they worked are heterogeneous and roughly formulated.

Another important characteristic of utopian thought is its conception of the means by which society might be reformed. Utopianism relied heavily on the freely exercised goodwill of men to bring about social reforms; correlatively, it tended to avoid the employment of political means, that is, the coercive forces of the state and other agencies of social control. The elements which enter into this option are many, not easy to isolate and not always in total accord with one another. The pervasive influence of Rousseau's ideas, or ideas closely associated with his name, cannot be denied—the lingering persuasion that the evil lay in institutions rather than in men and that, left to themselves, men would display an instinctive altruism and goodwill which institutional patterns inhibit to the point of atrophy. This attitude extended to the denial of the legitimacy of all coercive forms of social control, particularly those of the state. On this point the contrast between utopian thought and Marxism is especially sharp. Marx optioned early for the mastery of the political forces of a society as the first step in its social transformation. The utopians, on the other hand, relied on the principle of free private associations, removed from the coercive forces of the political arm of society.

The police state as it appeared in Europe at this time may have planted this suspicion regarding the capacity of the state to bring about social reform. Those who lived in a society where absolutism had been curbed much earlier and the processes of law were effective, like Robert Owen in England with the tradition of Bentham behind him, placed confidence in legislation. This confidence in the effectiveness of law displays a failure to appreciate sufficiently the type of social pressure and inhibition to which law itself is subject in the larger processes of society; that is, how it can be made to subserve oppressive forces and to impede reforms. Again, Marx, with his analysis of the "superstructures" of society, will exhibit a skepticism toward law which sets him in contrast to the utopians.

A final note of utopian thought is the trait perhaps most closely allied with the term *utopian* in common usage. These social thinkers employed a rude kind of model theory, familiar to social and political thought since classical times. They tended to think in terms of perfect societies as the architectonic basis for their reforms. This technique has long been familiar in social and political thought. There is, however, a difference between its use in classical thought and its use in utopian theory. In the former, model theory was conducted in terms of principles. Thus, in the Platonic Republic it is clear that Plato is practicing the Socratic art of definitions. In many of the utopians, these models take on much more concrete form; they are more "literal." This fact will connect presently with the utopians' willingness to experiment socially by setting up model communities. Neither Plato nor Marx showed such proclivity. In them, the model is a limiting and defining concept. Thus, the classless society functions only formally in Marx's thought; it cannot be shown to be the real term of his effort but only the ideal term which gives direction to current forces.

The utopians showed considerable understanding of the importance of the economic order and its influence on all social process. Despite their appreciation of it, however, their general tendency was to subordinate it to other interests and to hold that economic processes are, in their turn, subject to ethical control. They did not recognize that they have objective laws of their own, but held that they are subject to great moral and legal concepts such as justice and equity and that it is within the range of the human goodwill to order them according to these concepts. They showed some understanding of the effects of the Industrial Revolution and the strain under which it placed the institutional structure of society within which it had arisen. Many of the most arresting reforms the utopians proposed were oriented toward the correction of the social excesses and injustices which the Industrial Revolution had caused.

Utopian thought does not follow strict national lines, and it does not follow any pattern of social structure within nations. It must, perhaps, be considered principally a French phenomenon. English social utopianism, however, falls only a little behind and, for its own part, displays a moral earnestness equal to, though more subdued than, its French counterpart. Examples are also to be found in Germany; Marx, in his early career, singled them out for criticism. Indeed, if Marx is taken literally, it is possible to place Hegel among the utopians, for the Hegelian ethical state is not scientific in Marx's terms. Repercussions of French and British utopianism are to be found principally among the Americans, but also in Italy and later in Russia. The present account is restricted to some of the chief examples of utopian social thought in France and England and their repercussions in America.

A. *French Utopian Thought*

The utopian social thinkers in France may be divided into two uneven groups on the basis of their inspiration. More numerous and certainly more influential is the group motivated by secularist, laicist, and humanitarian principles and ideals. These men were the inheritors of the dissociation between religion and the moral forces of society which had been proceeding for some time. Their position in the social framework will perhaps be somewhat clearer if it is recalled that for centuries "social problems" had been the special care of the church, working for the most part through voluntary religious associations or orders. Religious orders took care of the sick, conducted schools, fed the poor. The guilds and trade groups of the Middle Ages were also active in this work and, although laicist in character, operated on the same principles of Christian charity. With the gradual "secularization" of western culture, the inspiration of social thought and work changed.

Secularization meant many things, all of which are reflected to one degree or another in the movements with which we are concerned. Most importantly, it meant the displacement of the church and the religious groups as the organs of social work. It also implied a change in the principle which inspired such thought and work. The religious motive was diminished or changed in character from a "supernatural" religious form to a purely "natural" religious sentiment; from the religion of God, presumably to the "religion of humanity." Finally the principle of charity, interpreted in an eleemosynary sense, came to be replaced by the concept of "social justice." (It should not be thought for a moment, however, that the principle of justice was absent from religiously inspired social thought, since charity has always been considered the highest form of justice from the Christian point of view.)

Religiously inspired social thought, it was argued, underestimated the importance of social injustices and inequalities; it thought them unimportant since the real destiny of man lay beyond history, where all injustices would be righted. Social thinkers of secular inspiration viewed man's career as enclosed within the "world," history in time; therefore, social injustices had to be righted here and now and could not be ameliorated with a view to ultimate deliverance from history.

The secular thinkers all had a strong sense of history, which they drew chiefly from the romantic philosophy. They conceived social progress in historical terms. Many of them, moreover, had a strong futuristic bias which expressed itself in the construction of "perfect societies" which they believed could be realized "in history." Others were "presentialists"; that is, they felt that the realization of a just order in society did not have to wait on the movement of history but could be realized immediately, if only the goodwill or rationality of men could be released. This was the inspiration of the social experiments that men such as Owen set up; they thought a just society could be realized immediately.

A second group among the utopian social thinkers retained their original religious and, specifically, Christian motivation. Among these are to be found both Catholic and Protestant thinkers. They share the conviction that justice among men eventually demands the intervention of the principle of charity; only a religious motivation is strong enough and only religious principles are clear enough to inspire and give force to just social thought and action. Catholic social thought of the period is divided. The traditionalists were skeptical of social amelioration. The "liberal" Catholics felt that a primary concern of religion must be the social welfare of men expressed in a just society. Many of the latter were very sensitive to the special kinds of problems created by the growth of modern society, problems which could be solved only if the force of religion was brought to bear upon them. In this group are also those rather lonely but highly significant figures like Lamennais, who, as we have seen, passed from the traditionalist to the liberal point of view and eventually beyond the religious sphere altogether.

Their Protestant colleagues also were awakened by the condition of society to a realization that the Christian spirit had a social mission to accomplish. They perceived the germ of the idea of the "social gospel," the conviction that the message of Jesus Christ had to be translated into terms of social relations among men in the historical conditions of the society under which they lived; that Christianity was not merely a religion of personal salvation and devotion, but a religion which found its fulfillment in a better society. These men were acute in their criticism of modern society, sincere and earnest in their efforts in behalf of its betterment in the spirit of the gospel. They could not be completely "scientific" in their treatment of problems; of necessity, they looked to the goodwill and moral conscience of men as formed by Christianity and not to some objective force of history to solve these problems. This did not inhibit great realism in their analysis of problems and in their conception of methods and projects of social amelioration.

In the following pages we shall examine the thought of some representative thinkers, first of the secularist and then of the Catholic liberal schools of utopian thought in France. The motive of religious thought in social matters will again be considered in the utopian social thought of England and its echoes in America.

1. Claude Henri, Comte de Saint-Simon (1760–1825)

Chief among the utopian thinkers of secular inspiration is Claude Henri de Rouvroy, Comte de Saint-Simon. His thought is important both in itself and for the great influence it exerted, especially upon and through the work of his successor, Auguste Comte, to whom a later chapter will be devoted. Having entered the army at any early age, Saint-Simon saw action with the French expeditionary forces under de Grasse in America and witnessed the surrender of Cornwallis. He proceeded to Mexico, where his project for a ship canal between the Atlantic and Pacific Oceans through Nicaragua attracted attention. Returning to France, he left the army to study mathematics. Although he had seen something of the American Revolution, he took no active part in its great French counterpart. With great shrewdness, he amassed a fortune by speculating in confiscated church estates. These activities earned him an eleven-month imprisonment under the Reign of Terror. This experience led him to identify himself with the common man. He renounced his title and took the somewhat equivocal name of Charles Henri Bonhomme. He lost a part at least of the wealth gained by speculation, and thereafter lived the relatively quiet life of a scholar. Although without formal education, he established relations with the learned of Paris and from them garnered much for his own reflections and projects. During this period two eventually famous men served as his secretaries: Auguste Thierry, statesman and historian, and Auguste Comte. He also enjoyed the collaboration and discipleship of two men who were to contribute vastly to the spread of his ideas and fame: Enfantin (1796–1864) and Bazard (1791–1832). So close was his association with Enfantin that their works were edited in a common edition.

Saint-Simon proved a prolific writer. Not all of his work is relevant to our interest. Writings which should be known, however, include: the two journals which he edited and in great part wrote, *L'industrie*, 1817, and *L'organisateur*, 1819; an early work, *Introduction aux travaux scientifiques du XIXe siècle* [Introduction to the scientific work of the nineteenth century], 1807, which illustrates the bent of his interests; and the three basic works on his social system, *Du système industriel* [The industrial system], 1821–22; *Catéchisme des industriels* [Catechism of industrialists], 1822; and the *Nouveau Christianisme* [New Christianity], published in 1825.

The following insight might be suggested as a nuclear idea for entrée into and orientation within Saint-Simon's thought. The Industrial Revolution was having results which were manifestly revolutionary for every dimension of man's life. It was dubious whether these effects would be salutary or harmful. Saint-Simon inclined to the view that, left to themselves, the direction of these effects was inimical to man, threatening the classical human values which are synonymous with civilization and culture. The controlling concern of his thought was, thus, not to deny the Industrial Revolution, but to insure that its effects would be salutary for human life. He did not share the optimistic view of eighteenth-century "liberal" thought. He was convinced that the intervention of human intelligence and the human ethical will was necessary to insure that these forces should serve human ends, both material and spiritual, and not destroy man. Saint-Simon also differed with such thinkers of the eighteenth century as Voltaire and Condorcet, whose thought had been characterized by a certain scorn for the past, especially for the Middle Ages, which they considered a period of unrelieved darkness.

Saint-Simon had been born a Catholic. His attitude toward the traditionalists is consequently of interest, for it casts light on certain aspects of his own thoughts. He shared something of their positive evaluation of the Middle Ages, in which the social order had benefited by the spiritual and educational authority of the clergy, in which men had been united (at least in principle) by charity, and in which the feudal lords, while exercising immense economic power, were still bound to those under them by duties of protection. He also agreed with their ideas that the social upheavals of the time could be traced at least to the Reformation. From that time, he felt, Europe, with the loosening of the medieval bonds, had been in quest of a new social order. He felt, however, that the traditionalists, with their eyes fixed too firmly on the past, underestimated the constructive resources of the present. They considered the French Revolution principally as a political event; hence, they could imagine a return to legitimacy and a restoration of an *ancien régime*. Saint-Simon saw the Revolution as economic and social in character; the political debacle was relatively superficial, and political remedies alone could not touch the underlying causes. The problems it posed could not be solved simply by evoking past accomplishments or trying to imitate them. It was necessary to muster the forces which were present in contemporary society and which would appear in the future. The forces released by industry promised an entirely new era. The great men of the present and the future were and would be the industrialists and the scientists in contrast to the unproductive men of wealth and station under the older systems. The reorganization of society which was clearly demanded had to take account of and employ the modern resources of science, both natural science and the science of man. Science must lead to development of the skills of social life as well as to technological advances.

These reflections provide a background for Saint-Simon's basic attitudes. Against this background we can examine briefly some of his eventually very influential speculative ideas.

Saint-Simon's interest in science included not only its social significance but the speculative problems posed by its nature and conditions as well. He offered a first formulation of a notion which Comte was to give more finished form, the notion of the stages of knowledge and science. In his view, science, both in itself and in its history, passed from a conjectural state to a "positive" one. The first stage was represented by the sciences which had dominated in the past: the metaphysical ideal of philosophy and the ideal of theological science. Saint-Simon did not view these as utterly reprehensible but as necessary to the internal and historical development of knowledge itself. He therefore conceives a kind of ideal and historical dialectic not unlike Hegel's, though extremely crude by comparison.

"Positive" knowledge is identified in the present with science. What makes science "positive"? Saint-Simon indicates a number of factors which enter into this character: observation, proof, verifiability by overt procedures. Also characteristic is the quality of the knowledge it imparts; "positive knowledge" is certain and demonstrable. Its certainty and demonstrability, however, do not seem to endow it with that transcendentality to which metaphysical and theological knowledge pretended. Positive knowledge, though more certain than these, is nevertheless open to revision. Saint-Simon is not entirely lucid in his account of the character of this openness. But certainly this openness constitutes one of the most valuable traits of positive knowledge and science. It is this trait which can make positive science a more sure guide in social problems than metaphysical or theological knowledge, for it can take into account historical alterations in the conditions of society.

Saint-Simon seems also to be attracted by two ideas which present a certain tension, not to say contradiction: that of the unity of all science and that of a hierarchy of the sciences. The latter rests on his not-too-critical acceptance of the view that the status of a science is to be determined by the status of its object. As man is the noblest of all objects, the science of man must necessarily take precedence over all the other sciences. The notion of the unity of science is fostered by the notion of "positive" science. Presumably, all sciences would pass through the various stages he had depicted; however, as they approach the status of positive science, it would become clear that, despite the difference of objects, they would become one under this positive character. Saint-Simon is not pellucid about the kind of unity they would possess in virtue of their positivity.

His appreciation of the social consequences of the Industrial Revolution helped Saint-Simon clarify some of the concrete relations which would eventually be subject to alteration. Chief among these, perhaps, was the value placed on the concept of work and production. Under older social systems, great esteem and social status had attached to leisure and social stratifications. Wealth was appreciated principally as securing leisure, and culture was thought to be the appanage of leisure. The position of a man in society was not measured by his productivity, and his share of the produced wealth of the society was not determined on this basis. Saint-Simon saw that all or much of this must eventually be changed, not on any specifically moral or legal basis, but simply in response to the dynamics of social change. He saw that legal and moral claims could not entirely control social changes. Productivity, work must become in the new order the basic, if not the exclusive, avenue of access to goods. People must be paid according to the wealth they produced. Obviously this would involve some change in the status of those whose position rested on other titles to goods. Work would prove a class leveler, eventuating in one class (though not without distinctions within it), the productive or working class.

The emergence of work as sole or basic title would also alter the intrinsic character of the title itself, that is, the concept of property. Property does not lose any of its classical notes in Saint-Simon, but these do receive a fresh coloring. Thus, seclusion remains as a character of property, both for goods which are consumed and those which are only used. But the degree of seclusion would seem to become limited, especially when the question of use is extended to the exploitation of goods thus secluded to generate interest—for example, rents. Saint-Simon, who had speculated in land as a young man, probably had some direct insights into what is involved here. He does not, however, believe in equality of wealth or in equal distribution of property. This view would not be consistent with the importance he attaches to work as sole basis of title. For as there must be degrees of productivity, there must be degrees of property. It is difficult to systematize Saint-Simon's views on the economic order, since he himself is not overly systematic in his development and expression of them. It would seem clear that in its economic aspects his new society would present certain features which in later periods would be thought of as socialistic; at the same time, however, Saint-Simon is a firm advocate of free enterprise and of capitalist accumulation and freedom of use as consequences of primitive title.

His reflections on the political order awaken recollections of the limited-state theories of the Manchester liberals. The function of the political arm is that of maintaining and protecting the industrial order. His evaluation of the industrial and economic aspect of society has a further effect on the political order; it regulates not only the function but the organization of the political arm of society. The value of legislation will vary according to the degree to which laws serve or obstruct the interests of industry. He assigns to industry active control of the operations of government: legislation, administration, etc. In his tripartite division of government—the house of "invention" (for the introduction of new legislation), the house of "examination" (for the critical review of such proposals), and the house of "execution"—the "industrials" dominate in every branch.

The idea of unity exercised a special fascination for Saint-Simon. It appears in the unity of science; it appears in his early concern with the unity of Europe; it appears in the class unity which he felt must eventuate from the process of industrialization. At the mature stage of his thought, this preoccupation with unity takes a new form. Two aspects of this new notion of unity are especially arresting. The first is a counterpart of the unity of classes to be induced by the progress of industrial society. The nations of Europe, in this new view, seem to be anachronistic and incongruous with the forward historical movement of mankind in society. He foresees a world unity based on the recognition of common economic interest. Within this unity, the national formations might persist in their political aspects, but their importance and activity would now be regulated by a superior principle. Peace and concord would be the outcome of the recognized community of economic interests.

Saint-Simon doubts, however, that man's recognition of a community of economic interests alone would have the power to insure peace. A higher moral or spiritual motive would have to intervene. His reminiscences of the Middle Ages enter the picture. Religion had given medieval society its unity. Religion could do the same for the present and future society. Obviously, it could not be the religion of the Middle Ages. Religion, like all else, must respond to changing times. The religion he had in mind would have to correspond to the actualities of the new society—a "New Christianity."

What gives religion its special force? It is the power to engage the higher resources of the human person. Unless these higher resources are engaged in the work of social unity, that unity cannot hold. Thus, for Saint-Simon, religion is fundamentally a social concept; it is employed as a means to promote social cohesion. Therefore, he disapproves all interpretations of Christianity which make it a force by which man escapes the social context, a force of inner release rather than of outward unity. He recognizes that understanding, intelligence, and will are not enough to achieve social coherence. This unity must rest on those resources of man which only religion can arouse: love, human sympathy, compassion, adoration. His New Christianity would in addition see that these emotions were scientifically directed. It could not work for individual and separatist ends; it must work for the ends of social cohesion. If science is to achieve all it can achieve for men, it must be motivated by compassion for the poor, a sense of brotherhood—motivations which only religion can supply; but if religion is to be enlightened, it must receive its higher guidance from science, which understands the needs and conditions of the good society. In his revision of Christianity, his purpose is to create a *civil* religion; concurrently, he tends to make society a church, in the sense that its ultimate bonds of unity are not secular but religious.

Saint-Simon showed a capacity for attracting disciples to his ideas and causes, not all of whom served him equally well. The impetus given his thought by the activities of Enfantin and Bazard were neither entirely beneficial to Saint-Simon's eventual fame nor entirely faithful to his thought. The element of cultism in these men led them to emphasize the more transitive elements of his thought. Despite a breach over the idea of the "New Christianity," Auguste Comte developed Saint-Simon's ideas most intelligently. (Comte's reputation does not, however, depend on this.) Saint-Simon's influence is to be discerned in Marx and Proudhon, in Owen, Blanc, and John Stuart Mill. He was one of the seminal thinkers of his age.

2. Charles Fourier (1772–1837)

Fourier, who exercised wide influence despite the sprawling and unsystematic form in which his ideas were expressed, published his first work, *Théorie des quatre mouvements et des destinées générales* [Theory of the four movements and the general destinies], in 1808. At this time he was engaged in business with headquarters in the industrial city of Lyons. A long silence followed until, in 1822, he published his *Traité de l'association domestique-agricole* [Treatise on domestic and agricultural association], and elaboration of the earlier work. This book was reissued in 1829 with a new title: *Théorie de l'unité universalle* [The theory of universal unity]. The same year saw an original effort, *Le nouveau monde industriel et sociétaire* [The new industrial and social world], and his last and best known work, *La fausse industrie* [False industry], appeared in 1835–36. During his lifetime Fourier drew a few followers to his ideas but failed to hold them by reason of a harshly dictatorial manner. After his death, however, his ideas found resonance in many quarters and became the basis for a number of utopian social experiments.

Fourier begins his reflections on the "social problem" with the observation that providence has introduced or established a perfect order in the material, the organic, and the instinctual worlds, but has seemingly abandoned the world of human social relations to chaos. It is incredible, however, that providence, so such in evidence elsewhere, should here be absent or in abeyance. Chaos prevails here only because man has failed to grasp the providential principle of social order. This principle, once understood, would enable man to direct social and historical process to the ends of human good, both private and public. On this principle, with nature as the model, man should attain happiness without artificial restraint of the basic passions.

Human society, however, is clearly organized on quite other lines. Everywhere, under innumerable forms, man is constricted and constrained by law, morality, religion, and custom. The unnaturalness of this restraint is clearly indicated by the fact that, in the present organization of society, work is a burden and a punishment for man. Were his nature free to follow its primitive and basic movements, it would surely prove that passion, the source of all activity, naturally translates itself into productive work which is joyous. Productivity is the condition of human progress, but work can be productive only when it is rendered attractive by being a source of joyous activity. Work will be attractive only when it conforms to the tastes and capacities of the worker, when it fulfills his natural passion for productive activity. The ideal of society must therefore be, in the view of providence, a productive group in which every man is free to choose among the labors useful to all that which is most in accord with his own propensity.

At the theoretical level, Fourier's ideas do not readily group themselves into anything like a system. Certain dominant ideas, however, are persistent and impart a certain structure to the whole. Despite his appeal to the plans of providence, Fourier seems to have given a basically materialistic interpretation to history and society. This materialism (if it can be called such) appears at two points: in his analysis of human needs and in his theory of the determination of traits by heredity. Man's needs are confined to his well-being in this world. Although he includes intellectual and other spiritual pursuits among them, Fourier makes material well-being their absolute condition and does not assign them any autonomous power to satisfy man in the face of material deprivation. According to his notion of heredity, human nature is fixed and determined in the number and interrelation of these needs; consequently, the function of society is to meet and satisfy them, not to modify them. The peace, harmony, and joy of which he spoke is identified with the simultaneous, free interplay of all these constitutive needs and interests. He was suspicious of any ethical system which envisaged some modification or restriction upon them. This suspicion expressed itself as iconoclasm toward existing moral codes and religious cults.

These ideas, which constitute Fourier's anthropology, are neither original nor impressive. Greater insight is to be found in his criticism of the existing social system. Some of his telling comments concern the capitalist mode of production, or more precisely, the mode of production which had been permitted to grow up under the early capitalism which managed the Industrial Revolution. He saw that there was no logical connection between capitalistic principles and the mode of production he criticized. Its chief fault was both material and human wastefulness. In the order of material wastefulness, he discovered that there was no established relation among raw material, expended labor, and distribution of the product. The product did not realize even approximately the full possibility of the material of which it was wrought. In the order of human wastefulness, his remarks are more pointed because here the system appears in most direct contrast and opposition to his basic insight about human nature. The capitalist mode of production squandered human potential in the actual process of work because it did not consult the principle that work can be really productive only when it is joyous. Capitalist work was the epitome of joylessness, consulting at no point the principles of human nature; it offered the individual no opportunity to follow his propensities or to express the passional bases of action within him. Hence, it stifled the productive instinct at its source. It could secure from its workers only a fraction of their productive capacity and this only by the artificial and coercive means. One of its social consequences was the social parasite, the very personification of wastefulness, who lived off the productive activity of others. Finally, the capitalist mode of production alienated the worker from his work, the most serious and socially disasterous form of waste. The worker was alienated from the product of his work, in the first instance, because under this system the product never flowed freely from his natural proclivity; he was also alienated from it in the sense that, once it had been produced, he had no natural, continuing relation to it. These are points which will be elaborated on by later social and economic critics of capitalism, such as Karl Marx.

Another social waste which Fourier saw as proceeding from the capitalist mode of production was the quality of life the great industrial urban centers had formed or were beginning to form under capitalist pressure. Capitalism needed to mobilize its workers at certain points, the factory centers. It drew them into large urban groups. Once they were there, their form of life was abandoned to sheerest chance. To the waste of its workers as workers was added their complete debasement as human beings, under conditions which did not provide for the most elemental human need for expression, privacy, closeness to nature, and spiritual space between human individuals.

Fourier, with his deep aversion to any form of coercion, looked suspiciously upon the state as an instrument for the reorganization of society. The state appeared to him rather as the epitome of the worst features of the capitalist system. It was wholly an instrument of coercion with little power to initiate anything of social value. Due to its innate servility, the state might readily lend itself to other purposes, particularly those of capitalist interests. Fourier, therefore, exhibited a kind of basic, but not highly articulated, form of political anarchism. He had an early vision of the withering away of the state. He did not advocate violent revolution against existing states, but neither did he think that the state could be converted to an instrument of social betterment and reorganization. He thought the sources of such reorganization, when they appeared, would certainly prove nonpolitical. The form of the renewed society would also be nonpolitical, completely noncoercive, and expressive of that basic freedom of action and life which is so important to man. He was tolerant of the state as it existed and of the parasitical classes as they existed; even more, he was willing to have them support him in his efforts to initiate the process of social reorganization. It is said that he published an announcement of a daily appointment hour at which time any man of wealth who was philanthropically inclined might present himself. None ever did.

The practical and structural details of the society which he envisaged absorbed much of Fourier's attention. The principle of this reorganization is quite constant: His new society must offer men something of the kind of life which his anthropological ideas indicate. One of its most obvious features reflects his criticism of the city as capitalist enterprise was transforming it. His people would be regrouped in moderate-sized villages, situated to allow physical space. Each village was to be constituted of about three hundred families, about fifteen to sixteen hundred persons, according to his calculations. These, in turn, were to be organized into three classes. These communities were to be "phalanxes." Fourier insisted that they should be situated in areas of natural beauty and that the population density should not exceed 225 to the square mile, since spatial distance is clearly essential to human dignity, privacy, and spiritual distance. He advocated birth control and colonization from parent communities as means of keeping this ratio stable. He conceived the eventual complete regrouping of the world's population in some two million such communities and even suggested that all should be under one ruler, an "omniarch," with his seat at Constantinople.

Fourier rejected egalitarian notions as inconsistent with his view of the varying natural aptitudes of individuals, which the community should cultivate. The new society would have a class structure reflecting the various kinds and degrees of capacity: capitalists, laborers, intellectuals. The only class he did not include was the priestly, for he seemed to think priests parasitic in all social conditions. Each person was to contribute to the productive capacity of the community as a whole according to his own capacity, and he was to receive a proportional share of the product of that creative activity. Every member was to be assured a certain minimum of the necessities, which included, according to Fourier's list, a private room and toilet, five modest (third-class) meals a day, sufficient clothing, tools for his work and entertainment. Fourier insisted that no one person could fulfill himself by exclusive devotion to one kind of activity; therefore, each person should participate in a number of forms of productive activity, through which he would form filiations with other members.

The persistent note in everything Fourier prescribed is the elimination of waste, material and human. This, he held, is the key both to material abundance and to human joy and happiness in the tasks of life. Fourier made no direct attack on the notion of private property. While some things were to be held by the whole community, consumer goods were to be privately held. Thus, although he prescribed life in large community dwellings, to be called "phalansteries," life within these structures would not seem to have been thought of as communal; indeed, provisions such as private rooms were explicitly made to insure the persons freedom and privacy within the common dwelling.

The range of Fourier's influence was extraordinary. He gave expression to many ideas which were "in the air" and which, once expressed, were readily communicated to those who were already disposed to receive them. His right-to-work ideas were taken up by Louis Blanc and his remarks on capitalism and its mode of production by Marx. Both of these men were influenced, not directly, but through the well-digested expositions of Fourier's thought by Victor Considérant (1808–1893) in his *Destinée social* (*Social Destiny*), 1834–44, and the journal *La phalange*, which appeared under his direction from 1845 to 1849. *The Social Destiny of Man*, a well-ordered summary of Fourier's ideas by Albert Brisbane, appeared in America in 1840.

3. Etienne Cabet (1788–1856) and Louis Blanc (1811–1882)

Cabet thought of himself as a disciple of Fourier, but other influences are to be discerned in his thought, especially Thomas More and, indirectly, Robert Owen. Cabet's ideas are attractively presented in novel form in his *Voyage en Icarie* [Voyage to Icaria], published in 1846. Here a classical genre, the utopian dream, is revived. A young member of the British aristocracy, sailing distant seas, discovers the enchanted land of Icaria. Here the Fourierian society is depicted as having already been realized. Since Cabet does not share Fourier's political anarchism, it is the Icarian state which orders all society to the ends which Fourier had enumerated. Fourier's dream of work which is joy and production which is the natural overflow of joyous work is realized; every man is assured the opportunity for employment at a task both socially useful and in accord with his major propensity. Through a beautifully managed system of state education, every child is prepared for the part he will take in society. Work is well distributed according to its kinds so that society develops no imbalances such as those exhibited by industrial society under budding capitalism. Greater emphasis than Fourier's is placed on socialist patterns of ownership, exchange, and use. Fourier's ideal of privacy and individual dignity is still maintained. A most important point is the image Cabet creates of the coercionless state. The state functions entirely by persuasion, a persuasion which is established by consulting the individual's true interest and winning his ready cooperation through his perception of the identity of his interest with the concern of the whole.

Louis Blanc deserves a place in history for his authorship of the famous formula which has become the almost universal rubric of socialist thought: "From each according to his ability, to each according to his need." Blanc is not a man of original ideas; he reflects many of the ideas of the leading social thinkers of his time, including Fourier and Saint-Simon. His overwhelming interest is practical: to bring about concrete reforms in accord with advanced social ideals. This very practical purpose is the source, interestingly enough, of the particular pattern he imparts to the ideas he had absorbed from other thinkers. For example, his practical concern leads him to assume a position closer to that of state socialism than any assumed by the other thinkers. Blanc saw the state, in the context of existing society, as the means of realizing his projects and optimistically thought that the state itself might undergo some modification in the process. Blanc shared the general persuasion of the natural goodness of man and his right to happiness and the development of his personality, and he accepted the criticism that capitalism was subject to the iron law of wages and hence must lead to the eventual destruction of the working class; therefore, he immediately conceived a practical reorganization to insure the one and thwart the other—his famous *ateliers sociaux,* social workshops. In these, men would band together to produce goods for human need according to human norms. They would unite the functions of producers' cooperatives and trade unions. Individual workshops, voluntarily organized, would eventually band together into one great federation and transform the entire method of production of society.

Blanc was practical enough to realize that such a scheme would demand large-scale financing, which could hardly be expected to come from the pockets of workingmen. At this point the usefulness of the state suggested itself to him. The state would prove the chief source of such capital through its power to levy taxes and to secure receipts from such organizations as railroads, mines, banks, and insurance companies. To make sure that this power could be wielded effectively, Blanc suggested the nationalization of all such organizations and enterprises. He formulated a fairly coherent notion of the service state, which, in contrast to the protective state of classical liberal theory, would actively intervene in the social process to insure the conditions he envisaged. This role would impose the necessity of securing funds for the financing of industrial production and agriculture, the active support and organization of the "ateliers," the nationalization of various properties, and the providing of social benefits for groups and individuals. Nevertheless, Blanc thinks of the state as transitory, a "trustee state," since it would act for the people and not in its own name. It would exercise these powers only until the people were able to exercise them without its help; therefore, the state would have to educate individuals and groups in the process of social cooperation. Interestingly, it would be preparing for its own demise, the point at which its role would prove unnecessary. Thus, the shadow of the withering away of the state falls far before Marx.

4. Pierre Joseph Proudhon (1809–1865)

Proudhon is the last important secularist utopian in France. If the crucial year 1848, so important in so many different ways, is considered the transition point between "utopian" and "scientific" social thought, then Proudhon's productive years stand astride this transition. This is symbolic, for he passes beyond the purely utopian mode and begins to approach problems in a "scientific" spirit, speaking, in his *Système des contradictions économiques,* of political economy as a "science of facts." He retains many of the utopian characteristics: rejection of religion and religious charity as mere social palliative, rejection of revolution as a means of social transformation, and elaboration of sympathy, pity, and justice as the basic traits of human sociality. But he also exhibits a sensitivity toward the facts he is dealing with, a desire to have his theories corroborated by experience and his projects orientated toward historical possibility—all marks of a growing scientific attitude.

Although lacking formal education, Proudhon acquired considerable erudition and information and formed a sharp and incisive critical capacity. In many ways, however, he never overcame the limits of his lack of formal training; thus, his attempts to employ what he thought to be the Hegelian dialectic made him an easy butt of the criticism and scorn of Marx and many others.

Proudhon was continuously productive over some thirty years. He had a facile pen, but a style far from polished. His first work, *Qu'est-ce que la propriété? (What Is Property?),* published in 1840, though slight in comparison with his other efforts, still retains an important place. It contains basic insights which he was never to relinquish. His *Système des contradictions économiques ou philosophie de la misère (System of Economic Contradictions or the Philosophy of Poverty),* 1846, contains criticism of most of the important social thinkers of his day—Saint-Simon, Owen, Blanc, etc.—and drew a caustic reply from Marx called *La misère de la philosophie* [The poverty of philosophy]. 1849 saw the appearance of his *Les confessions d'un révolutionnaire* [Confessions of a revolutionist]; 1858, his *Justice dans la révolution et dans l'église* [Justice in the revolution and the church]. His *De la capacité politique des classes ouvrières* [Political capacity of the working classes], 1865, and *Théorie de la propriété* [Theory of property], 1866, are posthumous.

Proudhon's ideas about property are the earliest of his social reflections and remain to the end the vital principle of every theory he developed. His lapidary summation of his views has been quoted innumerable times: *Property is theft.* He approached property under the technical aspect of title and discovered it to be a fictitious, if not fraudulent, title with specious legal grounds. It was fraudulent because it claimed to convey a power which it was powerless to convey and which no legal device could justify, since it violated a basic social fact, namely, that goods belong to the community. Any so-called justification of their alienation, sequestration or transfer by individuals was fraudulent in its very nature. Obviously, this criticism of property involves a criticism of the entire complex of social relations built upon it. Proudhon both perceives and develops these implications. At some points, however, he exhibits inconsistency; for example, in his consideration of the family. Unlike many other utopians, he was a strong advocate of the family as a unit of social organization and perceived that property in some way was its basis and defense; hence, he was inclined to vindicate for the family a concept which he condemned when applied to men and society generally.

His condemnation of property rested on another and perhaps more positive concept, his theory of *value*. He accepted the position generally designated as the labor theory of value: that value is created by the labor which goes into the production of the product. The link between this view and his attitude toward property should be the assertion that all work is social; Marx supplies this link, but, while it is certainly implicit in Proudhon, he does not express it in this manner. He says rather that men retain a natural title to their handiwork even after they have been paid for the work expended on it; the relation between work and its product is inalienable. In his formulation of the labor theory of value, Proudhon specified duration of labor as the exact determinant of the value resident in the product. The latent notion that all work is social expresses itself in economic egalitarianism. He holds that there should be equal sharing of production. At the same time, he recognizes that men develop different capacities; he did not, however, believe that this difference was entirely inherent, and he did not hold that it created any special kind of title. His thoughts on education do, nevertheless, include provision for the training of special talents.

Proudhon sought to formulate with some degree of clarity the notion of human sociability, for he thought that only the establishment of this notion could provide the adequate purpose of social action. He begins by isolating three elements which enter into the fabric of sociality: sympathy, pity, and justice. While these do not of themselves create sociality, they must be present in the concrete relations of men in some degree and proportionality. Thus, justice alone cannot create society; it would create a heartless machine which could serve good and evil indifferently. Even less could sympathy or pity alone effect this end. A "proportionality" created by the presence of these elements in varying situations and between different persons or groups of persons generates the property with which sociality is most directly associated. This property is *mutuality*, and it is in mutuality that sociality, properly speaking, consists. Mutuality is not an abstraction. It finds embodiment in a system of reciprocal rights and obligations which will result from the proportional operation of sympathy, pity, and justice. This system of rights and obligations will be entirely unlike any created by a process of law, for it will rest immediately and directly on mutuality and not on any abstractly defined principle which may conceal limited and oppressive interests.

Proudhon was the first man to call himself an anarchist. His attitude toward authority as structured in government and institutions is adequately conveyed by this term. While Proudhon does not seem to have distinguished very sharply between social and political anarchism, he was aware of this difference. In his own thought, social anarchism proves more limited than political anarchism. Certain social institutions seemed to him to have an entirely natural basis and hence could not be called into question, for example, the family. Toward government and the state his anarchism seems to have been complete. He questioned any title or right of the state and systems of government to the authority which they pretended to exercise over men. This challenge goes back to the nucleus of all his thought, the notion of property. Government and the state were constructs inspired chiefly by vested property for the defense of its specious and fraudulent title. They were therefore without intrinsic rational and natural foundation. If the fictitious legal notion of property were displaced and goods distributed in accord with the principles of the theory of value and of social mutuality, the need for government and the state would disappear. Indeed, in Proudhon there is little thought of the withering away of the state; since its function is conceived by him as essentially meaningless and unjustifiable, he tends to talk of it as something already displaced. Unlike Marx, he assigns it no intermediate transitional function. This obviously separates him from the scientific social thinkers, who generally advocated the confiscation of the state and its direction toward the end of social revolution and made its eventual demise a function of this process. The range and limits of his social anarchism become clearer in *Justice dans la révolution et dans l'église*, 1858. Few of the historical institutions of western civilization escaped Proudhon's criticism.

Proudhon's most ambitious and detailed projection of his ideal community from a structural point of view is given in his *De la capacité politique des classes ouvrières*. The picture is not sharp in outline. It is relatively free from the kind of group reorganization upon which Fourier lavished attention. While some of his ideas recall Fourier's concept of "series," there is nothing resembling the community living there depicted. Proudhon is concerned with the technical problems of wages, exchange, credit, etc. He has in mind a system of free credit which would avoid, on the one hand, a dictatorship of the proletariat and, on the other hand, state intervention. Mutuality would be the principle controlling the entire process. The institutional center of the structure would be the "Banks of the People"; these would make available funds for all purposes of social life, buying and selling, etc., free of the entailments of profit and interest. The strict rule would be equivalence of value given and taken. Somewhat inconsistently within the context created by this picture, Proudhon includes a free market idea; for he says that prices would not be fixed by the amount of labor involved in the product, though such labor is the sole measure of value, but would be left to the free agreement of buyer and seller. Either he does not perceive the danger implicit in the provision that wages should be equal or he does not see in wages the chief source of fluid funds for consumers' goods.

There can be little doubt that Proudhon's thought influenced Marx as well as many other thinkers. His relations with Marx contain a certain element of drama. At first, it seems that Marx thought a rapproachment between them was possible, for they seemed to occupy considerable common ground. Proudhon soon made it clear, however, that he shared little of Marx's position. Most memorable is his statement that, while capitalism might be the exploitation of the weak by the strong, communism promised only the exploitation of the strong by the weak. Especially provoking to Marx was the influence of Proudhon at the meeting of the First International; perhaps this influence was decisive in shaking Marx's faith in that organization. At the other end of the spectrum is the common assertion that Proudhon is anticipated in many of his ideas by Godwin. While this is substantially true, a very great difference in tone and mood nevertheless exists between them.

5. French Utopians of Christian Inspiration

As has been noted, utopian social thought in France had a dual inspiration, secularist-humanitarian and Christian. The latter was not always narrowly orthodox or even institutional; neither, however, was it always as extreme as the "New Christianity" of a number of philosophers. The Christian thinkers included not only orthodox Catholics such as Lacordaire, Montalambert, and Ozanam, but also some who took a freer view of the meaning of Christianity in the progress of human culture. The most outstanding of the Catholic utopians was Lamennais. His views, noted in an earlier chapter, developed to a point where he could no longer remain within the limits of the orthodox faith. Two other social thinkers of broad, historico-cultural Christian inspiration deserve to be mentioned: Buchez and Pecqueur.

Phillip Joseph Benjamin Buchez (1776–1860) was in an early stage an adherent of the "Carbonari" movement, which was social-revolutionary in character. He became converted to Saint-Simonism, but in time broke with it, repelled by the extremism of Bazard and Enfantin. In intention, he remained within orthodox Catholicism, though his development of his doctrines does not always bear out this intention. These doctrines are expounded in two principal works: *Introduction à la science de l'histoire* [Introduction to the science of history], 1833 and 1842, and *Essai d'un traité complet de philosophie, du point de vue de catholicisme et de progrès* [Sketch of a complete treatise in philosophy from the point of view of Catholicism and of progress], 1838–40. He was elected a member of the Constituent Assembly during the Revolution of 1848.

Buchez's philosophy is based on the conception of a continuous progress of human civilization through successive stages of history. The last stage in this series was ushered in by Christianity. It will be completed when the ideals and precepts of Christ, which Buchez conceives to be equality, fraternity, and charity, have been applied to the organization of human society. The historical church was originally entrusted with this mission. In his view, however, she had failed; therefore, it remained for other agents to take up and fulfill the mission. Unlike the great body of Catholic thinkers he accepted the French Revolution both as irreversible historical fact and in principle; nevertheless, he rejected violence as an instrument of social reform and progress. He advocated instead the principle of cooperation, working within the existing form of society to correct the old tendencies and to initiate new ones. He urged the formation of workingmen's cooperatives to control raw materials and the tools of production, and consumers' cooperatives for distribution. Buchez' ideas exercised considerable influence on Ludlow and other English Christian utopian thinkers.

Constantin Pecqueur (1801–1887) was at once an economist, social reformer, and philosopher. His system constitutes an original synthesis of elements derived from such different sources as Saint-Simon, Fourier, the ideology of the French Revolution, particularly its Rousseauist elements, and finally, the Bible. An advocate of collectivism, he based his ideas not on abstract reasoning but on historical necessity. In his view of historical development, presented in *Economie social* [Social economy], 1839, he maintained the independent force of ethical and religious ideas; nevertheless, he placed fresh emphasis on the role of economic elements. Economic conditions prove primary determinants in all institutional relations and systems of culture. So complete and detailed is his elaboration of this thesis, both in this work and one which appeared but shortly after, *Des améliorations matérielles* [On the improvement of material conditions], 1839, that he has been placed among the initiators of the theory of historical materialism, considerably antedating Marx. His development of such concepts as class, class consciousness, and class struggle, his view of contemporary civilization as the product and reflection of bourgeois interests, and his competent technical analysis of the process of economic exchange, all clearly anticipate the ideas of Marx and are considered to have had an important influence on the *Communist Manifesto*. Pecqueur was an excellent student of classical liberal economic theory, exhibiting competence possessed by no other French social thinker of the time. He developed an original labor-time theory, which he conceived as an essentially ethical norm.

The Christian and ethical elements of Pecqueur's thought become very evident in his constructive view of collectivist society, developed in *Théorie nouvelle d'économie social et politique* [New theory of social and political economy], 1842. Some interpreters believe, however, that the Christian phraseology merely cloaks a hard, realistic state socialism. By *collectivism* Pecqueur means state ownership and administration of all of the instruments of production and the conversion of every citizen into an employee of one national organization. His is not the aristocratic state of Saint-Simon; he exhibits a firm faith in the democratic form of government, in the ideology of liberty, and in the moral and social value of free will. He saw the danger of authoritarianism in his state socialism but refused to accept it as inevitable. In his essay *De la république de Dieu* [On the republic of God], 1844, he tried to develop a contravailing theory of voluntary collectivist associations. Historians admit with ever-growing certainty the range of Pecqueur's influence on other, better known social theorists, such as Louis Blanc, Proudhon, Marx, and Engels.

B. *Utopian Social Thought in England*

English utopian thought retains all the utopian characteristics and strikes the reader as more realistic in tone than the French. Realism here has no "metaphysical" overtones, but means a simple adherence to the facts of experience. In social thought, realism leads to preoccupation with concrete projects rather than with abstract constructions. This realistic element makes utopian social thought more experimental, more open to the kind of correction which failure in action leads one to accept. On the whole it lessens the humanitarian tone, though not the humanitarian intent, of the utopian theories and undertakings. It exhibits a curious mixture of the caustic rationalism of the eighteenth century and the peculiar quality of English romanticism. The term *radicalism* is frequently used to characterize this thought, but is in fact no more radical, either in the sense of penetrating analysis or that of extremism in its recommendations for reform or change, than the

French. Finally, English utopian social thought displays the same bifurcation between Christian and secularist humanitarian inspiration and the same ratio between them in quantity and influence, that is, it heavily favors the secularist humanitarian strain.

1. William Godwin (1756–1836)

The name of Godwin has become almost synonymous in the popular history of culture with social and political radicalism. This reputation is not entirely undeserved, for Godwin does possess an extreme and trenchant manner of stating his criticisms of the existing system and his constructive concepts. His influence was great and was especially strong in the case of Proudhon. Godwin is a striking example of the cultural passage from social thought of religious inspiration to that of secularist and agnostic provenance. An ordained minister, he became disillusioned with Christianity, especially with its capacity to influence modern industrial society. That his Christian ministry was English nonconformist makes this experience even more striking, for nonconformism had already shown a certain interest in what would eventually come to be known as the "social gospel." In his later life a certain notoriety became attached to Godwin's name because of his trenchant criticism of social mores. He found an ardent disciple in the poet Shelley, who incorporated some of Godwin's ideas in his poems, where they underwent, of course, a sea-change which did not always clarify them.

For the history of philosophy and social thought, Godwin is a man of one book, written in the white heat, or better perhaps, the cold rage, of his first disillusionment with the social power of Christianity and of religion in general. Its main outline was directly inspired by the impact of the French Revolution on the English social and political consciousness. The book is called, in typically English eighteenth-century manner, *An Enquiry Concerning Political Justice.* It appeared in two volumes in 1793. It enjoyed an immense and immediate success and began to exercise an evident influence despite its length, its prolix style and its acid tone. Some of the interest it awakened was a response to its author's unorthodoxy in religion and politics, but this can explain neither the full force of its impact nor its continued persuasiveness.

Godwin's theological orientation is immediately apparent. His work opens with a severe castigation of the Protestant doctrine of "total depravity." This portion of the work possesses little of original interest, though it sets the trenchant tone for the entire work. This paves the way for his acceptance and social adaptation of Locke's doctrine that there are no innate ideas. Godwin extends this to mean that there are no innate principles which incline man toward either virtue or vice; on the contrary, he is a creature entirely malleable to the forces of his environment. He has in mind not man's physical environment as much as his intellectual ambient. While the physical environment is important, it must be recognized that, since man is rational, the chief forces which can move him are intellectual and it is upon his rational reaction to the intellectual elements in his environment that his inclination toward virtue or vice will depend. The chief elements of the intellectual environment which Godwin identifies are literature, education, and the institutions of political justice, i.e., social and political institutions. The chief place must be given to these last institutions, for they have more far-reaching influence. Literature and education are by nature always restricted in the numbers they can reach and can affect with any profundity.

For the purposes of his discourse, Godwin concentrates on the social and political institutions, bringing them under the rubric of "political justice." He selects three for special criticism: property, marriage, and government. His remarks on the first relate him most directly to Proudhon; those on the second seem to have impressed Shelley most; and those on government connect him with the utilitarians.

Godwin's critique of the institution of property is scathing but not as erudite as that of Proudhon. He does not declare property theft, but he does hold that the distribution of goods in existing society follows a pattern which is directly contradictory to the demands of rational justice. In existing society property is correlated, on the one hand, with hereditary possessions and, on the other, with competition, aggression, and cupidity. Accumulated wealth, unrelated to need, endows those who possess it by inherited title, or those who acquire it out of acquisitive impulse and desire, with social status and power, while it leaves multitudes without the capacity to satisfy the basic needs of life. Property, as presently consecrated in legal institutions, represents, therefore, a complete distortion of what is *just*. Rational justice demands that goods be correlated with *need*. Furthermore, need should be determined only by reason and not by competitive and accumulative appetites. If this were accomplished, those attitudes and modes of activity which in the present depraved state of society are called virtues—greed, show, lust of power and place, competition, social aggression—would appear in their true light, as vices; what today is despised as vice would be seen as deprivation, denial of the just satisfaction of rational needs, both physical and intellectual. It would be a mistake to attack this depraved condition at the level of personal motivation; for it is the complex social environment which determines what men shall conceive and follow as virtue, what they shall despise and shun as vice. Only destruction of this social notion of property and its replacement by a rational conception can be effective.

Permanent, monogamous marriage, as sanctioned by Christian society, is vitiated because it has inculcated as virtue what reason admonishes us is vice. The mark of reason is, above all, independence and autonomy, self-determination. This institution, however, demands constant dependence of one upon another, constant adaptation of one person to the will and authority of another. The result is a serious deformation of the entire character. The autonomous person can find rational satisfaction in a number of directions. Moreover, the attachments which he forms with other persons do not render him dependent, but enhance his freedom and autonomy. These attachments tend of their nature to be transitory, since the dynamic structure of the person involves changes which correspondingly reorientate his relations with other persons of his own and of the opposite sex. Finally, the investment of the marriage institution with so many social prerogatives, duties, and powers, as well as so many personal handicaps, basically distorts the social structure which reason would project. Only a social revision of the institution, at the public level, can pretend to be a reform commensurate with the evil and irrationality involved.

Government, as a permanent institution in human society, suffers, in Godwin's view, all of the defects of the institutions of property and marriage plus others proper to itself. It is fundamentally an intolerable usurpation. The rational man should possess an inalienable autonomy of judgment and decision. No public power should exist which can thwart this autonomy. Government as it exists directs human energies into patterns which generate dependence, servility, and a false sense of obligation. Some justification of government as a temporary measure required by the undeveloped state of much of mankind might be found. But this justification would demand that government possess a capacity of self-limitation, that it prepare its own demise as the enlightenment of mankind progresses. Godwin is realistic enough to suspect that no government would evince this capacity.

The character of government as usurpation is underlined when attention is turned to the chief instrument of government: law. Law declares itself a surrogate for the rational decisions of autonomous men. It perpetuates this surrogacy, wrong in essence, by generating such erroneous concepts as those proper to criminal law—free will, personal guilt, responsibility—while denying implicitly what reason affirms, that human conduct is a product of social conditioning and influence. The whole of criminal law appears to Godwin a fiction. Political anarchism is the ultimate term to which a rational view of society must lead.

To counterbalance such harsh criticism of society, Godwin possessed an unbounded optimism in the fundamental rationality of man and in history as a rational process which would progressively realize the values of reason. Though reforms were obviously called for on every hand, touching the very foundations of civil society, he did not advocate violent measures. Reason and persuasion are the instruments of historical progress. Faithful adherence to these, without other intervention, would generate a society of simple abundance and order, free from the distortions, oppressions, and dislocations characteristic of present social life.

Godwin wrote many other works, but none ever reached the stature of the *Inquiry* in power of statement or range of influence. He found a congenial co-worker in the feminist Mary Wollstonecraft, the author of *A Vindication of the Rights of Women,* who became his wife.

2. Robert Owen (1771–1858)

The characteristics of English utopian social thought are realized more fully in Robert Owen than in any other figure. By comparison, Godwin remains a cold and distant commentator, following an abstract principle called reason. Owen thought, projected, and acted from the basis of his own experience, with a wealth of human goodwill, energy, and devotion. His capacity for abstract criticism is inferior to that of Godwin, but his perceptions into human nature, his willingness to transform his ideas into projects supported by his private resources and energies, his boundless optimism, which not even repeated failures and disillusionments could quench, make him a fitting representative of the best that secularist-humanitarian utopian social thought could offer.

Owen's life is important, for his later thought and activity rests upon the experience he gained in his rise from poverty to wealth and influence in industrial society. Although without formal schooling, he became, by the age of twenty, manager of a large spinning mill in Manchester. In the management of his mill his education in the nature of industrial society and human life began in earnest. Clearly the inhuman conditions which the factory system created, but over which a mere manager had no control, aroused his deepest humanitarian feelings and stirred the same energies which accounted for his material success.

When, in 1797, he went to New Lanark in Scotland as superintendent and part owner of another large spinning mill, he introduced radical modifications in working conditions with no apparent loss to the efficiency of the mill. The length of the workday was reduced from seventeen to ten hours. He abolished the employment of children under ten years of age. By a much more brilliant insight, Owen looked beyond his mill and saw the pattern of the environment. New Lanark was a typical mill town of the period with a population of about five thousand. It was dirty and unkempt; the death rate, due to heavy work loads and minimal sanitation and health measures, was very high at all age levels. Drunkenness and other forms of depravity were high in incidence and destructive in social consequences. Owen saw an opportunity to apply directly all that he had absorbed from his reading of Godwin and Rousseau about the natural goodness of the individual and the all-powerful influence of environment. He arranged the purchase of the land on which the town stood and set in motion an extensive program of renewal. The older houses were replaced by model dwellings, arranged in garden plots. Inspired by Godwin's teaching on the importance of education and also no doubt by his own early deprivation, he set up a model school and a program of education for adults. In the model school he initiated a program based on the latest pedagogical ideas, which won him a reputation in the area of infant education; singing, dancing, and other activities were given an important role in the program because they developed sensory coordination and provided the bases for more complicated skills. He set up cooperative stores in which goods purchased by the mill were resold to the workers at cost. The sale of alcoholic beverages was forbidden. He reorganized the structure of the mill corporation so that five percent of the profits would be devoted to the welfare of the workers. Jeremy Bentham became associated with him in the project, and it attracted the attention of businessmen and politicians all over the world. Without direct intent Owen had created a community in which social consciousness and paternalism were effectively interrelated. This mixture was to remain a constant element in state socialism in Europe.

Only after achievements of this magnitude was Owen led to put his ideas down in writing. In 1813–14 he published a group of essays under the title: *A New View of Society: Essays on the Formation of the Human Character and the Application of the Principle to Practice.* Though this book reflected the influence of many other social thinkers, Owen was never inhibited from taking an independent line, especially when his own experience supported him. Thus, against Godwin's political anarchism, he held that government should provide work projects of national scope for the unemployed. Against Malthus he held that the basic problem was not one of overpopulation, but rather one of production and maldistribution of goods. In 1817 he authored a report to the House of Commons Committee for the Relief of the Manufacturing Poor which won him considerable approval.

In the most famous of his works, the *Report to Lanark*, a plan involving both principles and concrete projects for a new social order received articulation. The utopian tone prevails. The theoretical principles again reflect Godwin and Rousseau as well as other influences. The supreme object of social institutions is the happiness of the individual; the influence of environment is paramount, and the chief means of social improvement is the creation of an environment to which the individual can respond creatively. Since education is the basic dynamic principle of all social improvement, its aim should be, not merely training, but character formation. The practical aspects of the *Report* recall Saint-Simon: Model communities were to be set up with a restricted number of inhabitants; the ideal was the agricultural village cultivating 800 to 1500 acres and having 800 to 1500 inhabitants; self-sufficiency was the aim of each community; and adults were to engage in agricultural and industrial activities in due proportion. There were to be many features of life in common—houses, kitchens, recreational facilities. Equal educational facilities were to be provided for all, with special facilities for the cultivation of talents of particular social value. Under these arrangements, crime would eventually disappear and coercive government would be reduced to a minimum.

3. English Christian Social Thinkers

It is a sad commentary upon the place of Christianity in our culture that so much of the social thought consequent upon the Industrial Revolution found it necessary to orientate itself about nonreligious principles. Whatever the reason for this situation, it nevertheless should not be concluded that the Christian conscience was entirely closed to the demands for amelioration of the social conditions. On the contrary, it was extremely sensitive to these demands in England as elsewhere. In these matters Christians did not hesitate to learn from those who denied the efficacy of religion; the influence of Owen, for example, was very evident among the Christian social thinkers and workers in England. The Christian response crystalized itself first in the formation, in 1848, on the morrow of the Chartist uprisings, of the Christian Socialist Movement. Its leading spirits included such eminent names as Frederick Denison Maurice (1805–1872), Charles Kingsley (1819–1875), and John Ludlow (1821–1911). Kingsley, a novelist, employed this form of expression to convey the Christian social message; thus, his novels *Yeast,* 1848, and *Alton Locke,* 1850, are social documents as much as works of fiction. The preface to *Alton Locke* was especially influential. Ludlow's *Progress of the Working Class,* finally published in 1867, was equally important.

Christian social thought was much more conservative in its theoretical aspects than the secularist and humanitarian. There was practically no direct attack on property or vested land interests. Christian theological commitments made it impossible for these thinkers to sympathize much with extreme revisions of the traditional view of human nature and its possibilities. They tended to reaffirm the traditional Christian view of man, while most of the evils consequent on the capitalist economy and the Industrial Revolution were laid to the weakness of the moral conscience of the men involved in these great social transformations. As the evils of these systems had arisen from a laxity of the moral will, they could be corrected by a direct appeal to that same faculty. All social issues were transformed into moral issues. This position proved somewhat weak in the face of the rising sciences of political economy and economic and social statistics, for these tended to show that there is a clear limit to the moral possibilities of individuals and even of groups, that social process has a certain "objective" dimension which man can master and control by understanding it. Later Christian social thought was to learn this lesson and thus to become more scientific and objective, but Christian social thought in England at this time remained quite unshakably moralistic and, under this aspect, utopian.

The leaders of the Christian social movement were as indefatigable as the secularists in the area of practical good works. Here they had a millennial tradition of active charity behind them. Unfortunately, instead of turning to it, they often tended merely to imitate the projects of the secularists and humanitarians, unmindful of the fact that these projects were a direct expression of the secularist theoretical criticism of the Christian view of man.

4. Resonances of Utopian Social Thought in the United States

At this time, the United States was still far from entering upon that vast movement of industrialization which was rapidly to place it in the forefront of the modern world economically and socially. Nevertheless, this process had advanced far enough that some thinkers here could see a certain relevance to American conditions in the thought and projects of European utopian social thinkers. The center of this movement was a group of intellectuals who were ahead of their times in their sensitivity to these problems but who lacked the basis of experience to make their arguments wholly meaningful; nevertheless, their resourceful treatment of the theme was to become an integral part of social thought in America.

The basic link between utopian thought in Europe and that in America was Fourier. An American writer, Albert Brisbane, met Fourier in

Europe in 1832 and was converted to his ideas. On his return to America he wrote *The Social Destiny of Man,* in which he summarized and commented upon the basic teachings of Fourier. The book must have touched a sensitive spot in the American conscience, for it was widely influential. "Fourier Clubs" began to appear for the discussion of the new ideas. Brisbane was commissioned by the *The New York Tribune* to write a daily article to advance Fourierism, which in these pages was linked with another of the paper's social interests, abolitionism. In 1839 the members of the Transcendentalist Club of Boston began to hold meetings for the discussion of Fourier's ideas at Brook Farm, near Boston. As this group included some of the most able intellectuals and writers of the period, its concern with these new ideas was bound to be influential. Among the members were Ralph Waldo Emerson, Margaret Fuller, Bronson Alcott, Henry Thoreau, Nathaniel Hawthorne, and others, who gave the utopian idea a variety of presentations and treatments. The most nearly philosophical treatment was that of Orestes Brownson, in his books and in the pages of the journals which he successively edited, especially in his personal periodical *Brownson's Quarterly.* Brownson was easily the most vigorous, though not the most polished, mind of the group. His reading in social and political literature of Europe was vast. Though there have been a number of studies of his thought, it still remains to be definitively evaluated in this area.

C. *The Principle of Utopianism*

The utopian principle, which can be reduced theoretically to the statement that man's social life can be entirely controlled by his own will and can be molded according to ethical ideas, has never been conclusively refuted. Nevertheless, it seemed doomed to failure by its inability to confront successfully the complex social organization which emerged in the West after the Industrial Revolution. It was destined to give way to scientific socialism: an effort to conceive social problems in "scientific" and "objective" terms and to adapt to their solution forces other than those deriving from man's conscience and ethical will. Nevertheless, the utopian attitude persists. It is realized that, while it may not be possible for man to create and sustain ideal social relations simply by an act of his goodwill and in accordance with his idea of moral good and evil, surely, lacking these, society cannot exist at all. Consequently, any attempt to contrast utopian and scientific social thought in exclusive terms cannot succeed.

Readings

I. GENERAL

Buber, M. *Paths in Utopia*. Boston: Beacon Hill, 1958.
Calverton, V. F. *Where Angels Dared to Tread*. (Regarding American social experiments.) Indianapolis: Bobbs-Merrill, 1941.
Christensen, T. *Origin and History of Christian Socialism*. Aarhus: Universitetsforlaget, 1962.
Cole, G. D. H. *The History of Socialist Thought: The Forerunners, 1789–1850*. London: Macmillan, 1953.
Cole, M. *The Story of Fabian Socialism*. Stanford, Calif.: Stanford University Press, 1961.
Egbert, D., ed. *Socialism in American Life*. Princeton, N. J.: Princeton University Press, 1952.
Evans, D. O. *Social Romanticism in France, 1830–1848*. Oxford: Clarendon Press, 1951.
Hertzler, J. O. *History of Utopian Thought*. New York: Macmillan, 1923.
Negley, G. R., and Patrick, J. Max, eds. *The Quest for Utopia*. New York: H. Schuman, 1952.
Stein, Lorenz Jacob von. *History of the Social Movement in France, 1789–1850*. Translated by Kaethe Mengelberg. Totowa, N. J.: Bedminster Press, 1964.
Talmon, Jacob Leib. *Political Messianism: The Romantic Phase*. London: Secker & Warburg, 1960.
Tuveson, Earnest L. *Millennium and Utopia*. Berkeley: University of California Press, 1949.
Ulam, A. *Philosophical Foundations of English Socialism*. Cambridge, Mass.: Harvard University Press, 1956.

II. PARTICULAR FIGURES

Cole, G. D. H. *Life of Robert Owen*. 3rd ed. Hamden, Conn.: Archon Books, 1966.
Fleisher, David. *William Godwin: A Study in Liberalism*. London: Allen & Unwin, 1951.
Lubac, Henri de. *The Un-Marxian Socialist: A Study of Proudhon*. Translated by R. E. Scantlebury. New York: Sheed & Ward, 1948.
McCabe, J. *Robert Owen*. London: Watts, 1920.
Manuel, F. E. *The New World of Henri St. Simon*. Cambridge, Mass.: Harvard University Press, 1956.
Woodcock, George. *Pierre-Joseph Proudhon: A Biography*. London: Routledge & Kegan Paul, 1956.
————. *William Godwin: A Biographical Study*. London: Porcupine Press, 1946.
Zeldin, David. *The Educational Ideas of Charles Fourier*. New York: A. M. Kelley, 1969.

CHAPTER IV

The Positive Philosophy of Auguste Comte

A. Comte and the History of Philosophy

Utopian social thought reaches its culmination and transcends itself in the philosophy of Auguste Comte. All of the basic characteristics of that current not only are present in Comte but are heightened and coordinated to a degree achieved by no other thinker. At the same time, utopian thought transcends itself, in Auguste Comte, making a conscious effort to pass into its opposite, scientific social thought, without losing any of its utopian features.

Two concepts closely allied with the name of Comte establish his place in the history of philosophy: "positive" (and its substantive form, "positivism") and "sociology." The first indicated, in an inchoate way, a path which science and philosophy were to follow for many decades and which has not been abandoned even now: the approximation of the method of philosophy to the methods of the sciences; the second projected the idea of a new science, the "science of society," which would realize in the study of men and institutions all the characteristics of "positivity" proper to science.

B. Comte's Life and Works

The name of Comte was first encountered in association with that of Saint-Simon, whose secretary he was for some years. Comte was a critic of Saint-Simon's notion of a "New Christianity." This difference marked the separation of the careers of the two men and, for Comte, the final emergence of an independent philosophical point of view.

Comte was born at Montpellier in France on January 19, 1798. Like Saint-Simon and his disciple Enfantin, Comte received the type of technical education which was rapidly threatening to eclipse the humanistic approach which had dominated higher education in France until the Revolution. This type of education reflected the influence of the Industrial Revolution and the humanitarian sentiment which, fused into the vision of a society made perfect by technological advances, imparted its spirit to the entire positivist movement. After teaching mathematics in a private capacity, Comte assumed the position as Saint-Simon's secretary, which he held until 1824. The impress of Saint-Simon's personality was indelible and the frame of reference within which Comte worked remained fundamentally Saint-Simonian. Nevertheless, by the year 1822, in the work entitled *Plan des travaux scientifiques nécessaires pour réorganiser la société* [Plan of scientific work necessary for the reorganization of society], he had begun to develop an independent line.

After his separation from Saint-Simon, Comte devoted himself completely to the elaboration of his own position. After eight years of labor —interrupted, as he notes in the "Preface personnelle" of the *Philosophie positive,* by a violent nervous crisis during the years 1826–27—the first volume of the *Cours de philosophie positive* [Course in positive philosophy] appeared in 1830; the last of the remaining five volumes was completed in 1842. Meanwhile his academic career followed an unfortunate course. He was an unsuccessful candidate for a teaching post in mathematics at the Polytechnical School in Paris and had to accept the humble post of "repeater" in the same institution; however, he lost this position by reason, it is alleged, of the hostility engendered in the academic world by the ideas he propounded in the final volume of the *Cours.*

For the remainder of his life he was supported by friends and followers. Separated from his wife, he formed a platonic bond with the celebrated Clothilde de Vaux, to whom he pays a glowing tribute in the preface to the 1890 edition of the *Système de politique positive, ou traité de sociologie instituant la religion de l'humanité* [System of positive political science or treatise in sociology which establishes the religion of humanity], which appeared in four volumes between 1851 and 1854. In this synthesis the basic religious orientation of his thought is clarified, in the sense, of course, in which "religion" is meaningful as a "religion of humanity." He expresses his own view of his accomplishment and purpose by saying that, whereas in the earlier synthesis he had transformed science into philosophy, so in the present work he is trying to transform philosophy into religion. At this time he began to refer to himself as the prophet of a new religion and composed the *Catéchisme positiviste* (*Cathechism of Positive Religion*), published in 1852. These two great syntheses carry the burden of what, in his numerous writings, is relevant for the history of thought.

A certain ambiguity invested the work of Comte. The part of his thought which had the greatest impact was his theory of science and the sciences. However, he himself considered this a secondary or instrumental aspect of his thought. His real purpose was to construct a philosophy of history. Even as he worked on it, however, the latter transformed itself into the religion of humanity with its complex apparatus of prophecy, doctrine, cult, etc. This ambiguity is a reflection of his culture, of which his works in both their strong points and their weaknesses are the fruit.

When he speaks of himself as a philosopher of history, Comte links himself with Condorcet and Bossuet. To the latter he attributes some of his own positivist attitudes toward history. He read as little as possible, since reading, contrary to Montaigne's admonition, impoverishes a man, lessening his originality and dissipating the coherence of his reflections. He specifically denies any firsthand knowledge of Vico, Kant, or Hegel. His concern with the philosophy of history and certain elements of his "religion of humanity" link him with romanticism. Even his approach to science is motivated, not by scientific concerns, but by his concept of science as the instrument for the social and moral transformation of mankind; nevertheless, his doctrine of science becomes the point of departure for the scientism of the nineteenth-century mind.

C. *The General Character of the Positivist Enterprise*

The dominant motive of Comtean positivism is not speculative but practical. Comte's ultimate purpose is the reformation of the social order. Under this aspect, his thought continues the preoccupation of the eighteenth-century mentality against which it is simultaneously in revolt. Many characteristics of the Enlightenment appear: the simplism, the belief in reformatory action, etc. While it is reformatory, the spirit of positivism is, nevertheless, conservative and anti-revolutionary. It is part of the general movement of "restoration" which found expression in the Holy Alliance and the recall of the French kings. In view of this conservatism, it is understandable why Comte would turn to such institutions as monarchy for support of the positivist program; similarly, his admiration for certain aspects of mediaeval culture and institutions becomes comprehensible. The similarity between his ideal, "sociocracy," and theocracy has been noted more than once.

While this practical aim is the dominant element in positivism, its vital core is speculative. This speculative concern, which very quickly passes into a program of educational reform, is the reformation of the human intellect and of the idea and system of the sciences, always, however, in the service of social reform. The positivist theory of science and the sciences achieves an influence quite apart from its ordination to the program of social reform, and this quasi-independent value, culminating in the projection of the "new" science of "sociology," gives Comte his standing in the history of philosophy.

This speculative concern places positivism in the line of those attempts, innumerable in the history of modern philosophy, at the reformation of the intellect, a line including the *Novum Organum* of Bacon, the *Discourse on Method* of Descartes, the *Essay Concerning Human Understanding* of Locke, *The Emendation of the Intellect* of Spinoza, etc. The common characteristic of these efforts is their concern with the human mind itself in an attempt to determine its constitution, history, and mode of operation; thence they proceed to the determination of a *method* which will reflect this constitution and mode of operation as well as the nature of science and the order and system of the sciences in which the intellectual enterprise will find realization. All of these fall within the scope of Comtean positivism. The distinctive characteristics of Comte's approach lie, first of all, in the social service to which he would direct the scientistic undertaking and, secondly, in the specific character of the positivist analysis of the human mind, the notion of science, and the order of the sciences. We must undertake to present this analysis in a concise manner, never completely separating the theories of mind or of science from the goal of social reconstruction.

D. *Architectonic Principle of Positivism: The Law of the Three Stages*

Comte considered the "law of the three stages," which is closely identified with his name in history, his fundamental discovery and the controlling principle of his system. Consequently, any consideration of his thought should begin with this law. However, the relationship between this great "law" and the other elements of his system is not direct but oblique and complex. Therefore, before considering the law in itself, one should consider the main aspects of this relation.

In the first place, Comte would seem to hold that the perception of this law is, in a certain sense, independent of all that he will have to say in his theory of science about the human mind, its mode of operation, method, etc. He indicates that this law is somehow "immediately evident." The evidence for it is immediately verifiable by any subject through an examination of his own personal experience. He asks: "Who among us does not remember, considering his own [personal] history, that he has been, with regard to the most important ideas, a *theologian* in his infancy, a *metaphysician* in his youth and a *physicist* in his manhood?" (cf. *Cours de philosophie positive*, 6th ed. [Paris: Costes, 1934],

Vol. I, p. 94). By this strange question, Comte is implying that the law of the three stages can be drawn from the retrospective examination of personal experience and that it is the law of human growth and development. In the third place, he will adopt a similar dual, and not unequivocal, attitude toward this law, science, and the sciences; i.e., the law of the three stages is in some sense established by the doctrine and procedure of science, according to his theory of science; but it is also the *law* of the intrinsic process of science itself and, finally, the architectonic principle of the encyclopedia of the sciences. This law itself cannot, according to Comte, be characterized as theological, metaphysical, or physical. It should be noted that there is no way in which this circularity could be definitively resolved in Comte's thought. It would seem to characterize every effort to isolate and identify the principles of the human mind and the notion of science; for the propositions in which such principles are stated either are themselves statements in the sciences which the human mind can produce or are, in some way, independent of them.

Apart from this consideration of the status of the law of the three stages and its multiple levels of application, it must be asked what the law itself is; i.e., how is it to be stated? As differentiated *formally,* the three stages are: the *theological* or *fictitious,* the *metaphysical* or *abstract,* and the *scientific, positive,* or *physical,* to employ the term Comte uses when he asserts that the law can be verified from personal experience. At this level, the three stages may best be distinguished as modes of explanation. That is, they differ in what is projected and accepted in each as adequate explanation for any order of experience or "phenomena." In the first, theological, stage, the human mind directs its inquiries toward the "intimate nature" of things, what they are "in themselves" or what makes them thus and not otherwise. It projects its reply to this line or inquiry in terms of "causes," principally "first" and "final" causes, and it considers phenomena the "effects" of such causes. Finally, it considers the causes in question a) above or not of the order of the effects attributable to them and in this sense "supernatural"; and b) of the order of entities, with an independent though inscrutable nature of their own. Anything in the phenomenal order is considered to have been explained when it can be referred to the operation of some such entity, and such reference constitutes knowledge and even science.

In the second, or *metaphysical* stage, which is a modification of the first or theological, *abstract forces* are substituted for transcendent or supernatural entities. These abstract forces are still true *entities,* though abstract; they are, however, immanent in the order of phenomena which they produce. Their abstractness consists in the fact that, while they do not enjoy independent or transcendent ontic status, they are, nevertheless, irreducible to any order of phenomena but instead account for all phenomena of any order. Determining an adequate explanation for the phenomena of any order consists, therefore, in assigning the phenomena of that order to such an abstract force as its principle. In both stages, the knowledge achieved through this process of explanation is ostensibly absolute; i.e., it permits no alternate explanation and applies to all phenomena of any order. This is the point which relates the first two stages and differentiates them *in kind* from the third.

The third stage is evoked in the human mind by the recognition of the impossibility of achieving absolute notions or explanations. It thus involves a basic reorientation of the mind and an essentially altered notion of what constitutes science. In this stage the mind renounces the search for the origin and destiny of the universe, i.e., of that which is, and contents itself with the discovery and study of the effective *laws* of phenomena, i.e., the invariable and unvarying successions, precedences, similarities and dissimilarities among them; its method is a careful combination of observation and reasoning. This gives rise to a fresh notion of what constitutes explanation and science. In Comte's own words: "The explanation of facts, reduced to its real terms, is now but the bond established between diverse particular phenomena and certain general facts: the number of which the progress of science tends steadly to diminish" (*Cours de philosophie positive*, I, 10).

The order among the three stages demands consideration. First of all, that order is *necessary;* Comte does not conceive any of these stages as dispensable from the structure, order, and movement of reality. The theological is the necessary condition of the metaphysical *and* the positive, and the metaphysical is the necessary condition of the positive. In the order of becoming, consequently, they are all of equal value. Their value is not equal, however, when considered from the point of view of the notion of science itself. From this viewpoint, the metaphysical and theological are necessary but of negative value. They exist only to be replaced by the later stages. Comte offers no adequate theory to explain why science, etc., must pass through the earlier stages in order to reach the positive stage, why a stage which is negative in value must precede a stage which is positive in value.

Secondly, in the order of their relations the law of the three stages is considered to apply to many levels of reality and of discourse. First as we have already noted in the first quotation from Comte, the law applies to the growth and maturation of the individual organism in its conscious aspect. It applies also to the order of science itself. Science must pass through these three stages of explanation to come eventually to the positive stage, and, as each stage has its own methods and systems of general explanatory concepts, the law governs the relations between these. Thirdly, the law applies to the social order. Three systems of social organization, ordered to the three stages of science, corresponding to the three stages of the law, can be distinguished; these are related by the same order of necessary succession and progressive disvaluation of the earlier stages.

Finally, the relation between these stages, at all levels, is *temporal* as well as *logical*. They follow in historical time as well as in idea. It is this succession in time, as well as in the logical or ideal order, that constitutes Comte's system as a philosophy of history. History itself is the temporal succession, necessary and ineluctable, of these three stages. History here is not *past* history. Essential to this temporal-ideal order is the *future*. The future is precisely the temporal locus of the ideal as ideal, i.e., of that which must be but as yet is not. It is this concept of the future which gives Comte's thought its utopian character. The future is the basic category of his thought. Positive science is the *science of the future*, not yet achieved but inevitable; the social order which he calls *sociocracy* is the *social order of the future*. His is a future, however, which is grounded necessarily in the past, neither detached from it nor violently opposed to it. Hence, his vision is essentially conservative, in contrast to the revolutionary character of many utopian theories and programs. Though it is not clearly expressed by Comte, there is present in his thought a theory of positive residues, as it may be called. This is particularly evident in the social order, for, the society of the future will contain many elements of the past; however, it will contain them in a manner proper to itself. Thus, for example, the society of the future will be hierarchical, a note exhibited by many, if not all, societies at the theological level. But in the past this hierarchy rested on a theological basis; in the society of the future it would rest, presumably, on a *positive* basis.

E. *Science and the Sciences*

It is unfortunate that the doctrine of the law of the three stages must be treated somewhat independently of the body of Comte's thought about science. Ideally, this law should be a product of science. The consideration of his theory of science and the sciences necessarily follows this somewhat abstract treatment of the law. It may be considered under the following rubrics, which are not absolute but do have a basis in his thought: a) the reformation of the intellect; b) the doctrine of *science;* c) the doctrine of the *sciences*, first in their particularity and then in their encyclopedia, as they constitute an ordered whole or constellation of the sciences. In the development of each of these topics, the presence of the law of the three stages is felt.

1. The Reformation of the Intellect

The presence of the law of the three stages is felt most clearly in the project of the reformation of the intellect, since only with reference to that law is the notion of "reformation" intelligible. Comte might well be interpreted as holding that the passage of the human intellect through the three stages is simply inevitable, the result of a kind of "natural" process which lies outside the competence of the human agent to retard or advance. With this interpretation it would be completely out of order to speak of a reformation. Also the positive program would be incomprehensible, for the positive program is based entirely upon the competence of the human mind to assess its own condition in relation to the law of the three stages and to take an active part in the process subject to that law. Hence, the notion of reformation of the intellect is entirely intelligible, and, even more important it is the central dynamic principle of the entire positivist program.

In what does this reformation consist? It must be described wholly in terms of the three stages. The reformation of the intellect consists in the conscious and methodical substitution of the order of the third stage for the second order of science and operation. The note of "consciousness" cannot be overestimated here; this transition does not simply befall the human subject, individual or corporate. The human subject *actively brings it about.* Secondly, in a certain sense the crucial step in the self-reformation of the intellect is precisely the *formulation of the law of the three stages.* The formulation of this law is the basic and constitutional step in the reformation of the intellect. The act of recognizing and distinguishing these three stages involves, as noted above, the necessity of each and the necessary transvaluation and desuetude of each of the first two stages. The human mind, in fact, releases itself from the metaphysical stage (as at an earlier stage it released itself from the theological by a similar act of recognition) and *establishes itself in the positive stage.* This interpretation, though it recognizes a value in the law of the three stages which Comte only dimly perceives and never clearly formulates, is the only interpretation which does justice to his entire enterprise and the place of this law in it.

The crucial question in the notion of the reformation of the intellect is the nature of this act of recognition, which presents two aspects. Under the first it is seen as identifying the stages to be substituted. By identifying the theological and metaphysical stages, as they are in themselves and as they relate to its own ideal and historical career, the intellect is enacting this recognition in its initial phase. This initial phase immediately gives way to another, which is Comte's whole concern. The positive stage thus discerned becomes the present state of the human subject, not as an actuality, but in programmatic form. The positive stage must now be identified and described as the program for the self-realization of the human intellect. This is an entirely self-guided enterprise. In it the human mind is absolutely positive, in the sense that it is now realizing itself in full consciousness according to the immanent laws of its own operations. The first stage in this programmatic dimension of the reformation of the intellect is the formulation of the positive doctrine of science, for science describes the positivity of the human intellect in its projective actuality.

2. The Doctrine of Science

The "doctrine of science" refers to what Comte understood science to be or, more precisely, to the conditions which knowledge has to meet in order to be *science*. Since the science he has in mind is clearly that which corresponds to the third of the three stages of his "law," his is a doctrine of positive science. Therefore, we should attempt to clarify what Comte understood by the term *positive* as descriptive of the nature, conditions, and attributes of science. It would be unrealistic to expect his doctrine to possess rigid coherence. From a twentieth-century point of view, it is filled with unexpected dissonances. It is difficult to know, however, whether these are inherent in his thought or whether they arise because our expectations of what *positive* ought to mean are not fulfilled in his text. Our purpose will be to remain as close to his own meaning as we can, but we shall not fail to note some of these dissonances, leaving their value or importance undecided.

The first concern must be to fix the notes of *positivity* as this term is applied to science. The first note of positivity would seem to be legalism. Science is the quest for the *laws of phenomena*. Here Comte is following a concept which has been common since the dawn of modern science; Newtonian physics, for example, is essentially a product of scientific legalism. Setting aside the search for "cause," it sought only to establish with the exactitude of mathematics the constant relations between phenomena. There is, nevertheless, a profound difference between the legalism of Comte's positivism and that which had preceded him. Earlier legalism had been methodological and unitary, tending toward the ideal of a single method applicable to all orders of phenomena. It tended to erase the differences among the sciences which stem from the diversity of their objects. Comte's legalism, by contrast, insists upon the irreducibility of a multitude of orders of objects; thus, he conceives a multiplicity of laws, and hence of sciences, not reducible to any unity, whether formal or contentual. This fidelity to the irreducible complexity of phenomena and, consequently, to the irreducible diversity and plurality of the sciences, adds a fresh note to the positivity of sciences. The sciences are *positive* in the sense that each is directed to a distinct order or body of phenomena, in the sense that they seek nothing beyond these phenomena but only the immanent law or laws of each order, and in the sense that they resist unification according to any abstract methodological principle.

The next important note of positivity is *phenomenalism*. Comte had been particularly impressed by certain accomplishments in the science of his day. He frequently, for example, called attention to the achievement of Fourier in the area of the mathematical theory of heat. Fourier had been successful in giving mathematical expression to the phenomena of the transmission of heat without recourse to any hypothesis concerning the *nature* of heat. This seemed immensely superior, in Comte's view, to the physics of Laplace. Laplace's mechanical theory of heat, bound up with molecular theory, seemed as objectionable to Comte as any hypothesis involving qualitative essences of the Aristotelian type. He pointed out, in reference to the work of Curvier in biology and Chevreul in chemistry, that "all the best minds of the present recognize that our studies are strictly circumscribed to the analysis of phenomena in order to discover their effective laws" (*Cours de philosophie positive*, III, 209).

The third note of *positivity* is *objectivity*. The laws of science are objective in the sense that they are wholly immanent to the order of phenomena; nothing in them derives from the presence of the subject. Comte expresses this *objectivity* when he writes that it is necessary "to transform the human brain into an exact mirror of the external order" (*Système de politique positive*, II, 382). The order which the laws of *positive* science formulate is not established by the mind; it is a reflection of the order of phenomena. He emphasizes this point by his denial, directed against Cousin, that there can be a science of psychology in the positive sense; for mind can discover its own principles or laws only by modeling itself upon the "external" order and not by any effort to grasp its own processes introspectively.

This consideration leads to a further note of positivity: *verifiability* by experience. All of the laws which the science formulate, even the laws of mind itself, are completely verifiable by experience.

The dissonances in the doctrine of science contained in the notes of its positivity are arresting, though their value is difficult to assess. One might expect that Comte's notion of science would lead in the direction of pragmaticism and technologism. On the contrary, he insists on the speculative character of science and distinguishes it sharply from the kind of knowledge identified as technical-practical. Nevertheless, the study of nature, taken as a whole, is intended to furnish a true rational basis for man's action on nature; for only knowledge of the

laws of phenomena can guide us in the active life and make it possible
to modify those phenomena to our advantage (Cf. *Cours de philosophie
positive*, I, 51). Science leads to prediction; prediction to action. Comte
tends to lay stress on this formula.

Again, in view of the emphasis upon phenomena, one might be led
to expect the development of a form of empiricism, but this does not
emerge. A form of neo-authoritarianism prevents it. If we take the two
elements which enter into science in the Comtean view—the observed
or observable fact and law—it is the law which Comte seems to place
first. Science tends not to rely more and more on observation but to dispense with it as soon as feasible; the aim becomes to reverse the movement from observation to law, into the movement from law to fact.
Science consists in laws and not in facts, even though facts are indis-
pensible for the establishment and sanctioning of laws (Cf. *Cours de
philosophie positive*, V, 600). Comtean positivism tends to increase the
rational domain at the expense of the experimental, substituting for the
immediate exploration of phenomena their provision on the basis of
law (Cf. ibid.).

Finally, this rationalistic emphasis might lead one to expect a kind
of abstract absolutism in his thought, that is, an assent to the unique-
ness and the immutability of the categories of human knowledge. The
fact is exactly the opposite. Science is, for Comte, relative. He links it,
on this basis, to a theory of the organism and its ambient, which, it
would seem, ought to be excluded by his emphasis on the objectivity
of science. He asserts that all of our knowledge is subject to two factors: the action of the ambient or environment and the reaction of the
organism. These factors can never be entirely determined, either in
themselves or in relation to each other. As a consequence, he argues,
one has to recognize the intellectual development or evolution of
humanity, subject to the evolution of the organism. The categories
of man's intellectual operations are not immutable. Successive theories
are approximations, and the best theory in any period is that which
best reflects the *ensemble* of observed facts. (cf. *Cours de philosophie
positive*, VI, 622–623).

Other discordances might be noted, but these probably suffice to
indicate, in contrast to the firm emphasis on the notes of positivity, the
elements of uncertainty which invest Comte's theory of science.

3. The Sciences and the Encyclopedia of the Sciences

The order of phenomena contains irreducible differences which
establish the plurality of the sciences in their positivity, in contradistinction to the abstract and methodological unity which earlier sci-

entific legalism had sought to impose. These irreducible differences constitute the order of objects. Orders of objects are marshaled according to the rule of the inverse relationship of complexity and generality. Complexity increases as generality decreases; generality increases as complexity decreases. This rule makes it possible to establish, without any reference to their natures, orders of objects and corresponding orders of sciences addressed to these orders of objects. In this way Comte introduces a positivist encyclopedia of the sciences and an order of the techniques to which the sciences may give rise. This interest in the technical affords a final note of positivity which effects the transition from the free movement of science as a self-contained activity with no end beyond itself, to science as an instrument for the transformation of reality and the reformation of society. This note relates Comte to those other thinkers of the period who see the salvation of society in the changes which might be brought about through the growth of technology.

Thus, the overall order of the positivist universe becomes discernible: the order of phenomena and their laws; the sciences which discover and formulate those laws, considered as particular sciences directed to specific orders of phenomena and as the encyclopedia of the sciences which traces the relations among them correlated to the relations among orders of objects; and finally the order of techniques which emerges from the sciences and which provides the instrument for the transformation of nature and of society.

The construction of the encyclopedia consists of two steps: 1) the distinction of the ideal order of the fundamental sciences, with respect to the order of objects to which each corresponds and the consequent internal structure of each science, and 2) the identification of the order, ideal and historical, which relates them to one another and constitutes the universe of scientific discourse.

Comte distinguishes six such fundamental sciences: *mathematics*, which studies quantity, the simplest and most indeterminate of realities; *astronomy*, which, *adding* to *quantity* the notion of *force*, studies *masses* endowed with *attractive forces; physics*, which, adding *quality* to *force*, studies such qualitatively diversified forces as heat, light, etc.; *chemistry*, which addressess itself to *matter* which is qualitatively distinct; *biology*, which has as its object *life*, which adds to matter the reality of *organization;* and finally, his own creation in the order of the fundamental sciences, *sociology*, which studies society as relating beings by ties independent of their organic laws. These sciences constitute a hierarchy, moving from simplicity to complexity and from concreteness to generality.

This hierarchy is the key to the encyclopedic structure of the sciences. As a consequence of these natural interrelations, these sciences can be pursued or realized as a body only in a historical order which translates the ideal hierarchical order into procedures. Thus, the mind can pass to the consideration of the more complex only by prior consideration of the simpler and less complex. From mathematics to sociology is alike an ideal, a historical, and a procedural order. This order can be verified, Comte believes, by reference to the history of the sciences. That history is the temporal-concrete-procedural development or elaboration of the ideal order existing among the sciences taken in themselves. There is nothing accidental about this order in the history of the sciences. It reflects the necessary relations which prevail among the sciences. No science can be born out of its time; no order of scientific discourse can be constructed or comprehended outside the context of the whole or outside the context of its relations to its immediate and remote antecedants and consequents. Thus, while mathematics, he notes, was known to the earliest peoples, sociology is the last flower of western thought, born only in his own day and by his own efforts. This order of the sciences is also pedagogical. It indicates the order in which the sciences can be communicated and patterned in order to form a persistent culture, transmissible from one generation to another.

While the above scheme seems fundamentally true to Comte's idea, a special note should be added regarding two sciences, one of which appears in this catalogue and the other of which is somewhat conspicuously absent from it. The first is mathematics, which appears as the first of the sciences in the order enumerated. It would seem that Comte did not entirely intend to establish mathematics as simply one science among the others. It bears a very special relation to them all and is, in itself, an encyclopedic principle. Comte sees mathematics as indeed a science which can be pursued in its own terms but also as a science which, in one manner or another, is fundamental to all of the other sciences and even to the precise formulation of the relations between the other sciences. Comte distinguishes two branches of mathematics: abstract mathematics, which is the calculus, and concrete mathematics, which is general geometry. The latter is a true natural science, founded, like all other such sciences, on observation. By reason of the extreme simplicity of their objects they can be systematized more perfectly than any others. The calculus is the more purely instrumental form of mathematics; it is, in his view, an immense and admirable extension of natural logic (cf. *Cours de philosophie positive*, I, 87).

The science conspicuous by its absence from this catalogue is psychology. Comte's skepticism toward psychology as a science has already been mentioned. It is omitted from this listing because it is not a science and cannot become one. The type of "interior observation" which ostensibly was to become the instrument for the examination of psychical phenomena is impossible for the human subject. Psychical phenomena cannot be observed in the same act in which they are realized. "The individual thinker cannot divide himself in two, of which the one reasons, while the other watches or observes it as it reasons. Since in this case the observing organ and the observed organ are one and the same, how can the observation take place?" (*Cours de philosophie positive*, I, 32).

4. Sociology

A special place must be given to *sociology*. This science is Comte's own creation. It is the science to which all others minister and for which they exist. Comte's definition of sociology in the *Cours de philosophie positive* (IV, 7) is portentous but still very significant, for in it are reflected all of the elements of positivism which have been distinguished above. The role or function of this science is to "perceive clearly the general system of the successive operations, philosophical and political, which should free society from its fatal tendency to imminent dissolution and lead it directly to a new organization, at once more progressive and more solid than that which rested upon theological philosophy." As a science, sociology must be constructed in the same manner as the other positive sciences; it must conceive social phenomena as susceptible to formulation under immenent laws. These laws make possible social prediction, though this must necessarily be more limited than in other sciences due to the extreme complexity of social phenomena.

Within the structure of sociology Comte distinguishes a social *statics* and a social *dynamics*. Of the two, statics is more fundamental; for the social order, existing in itself, has permanent organs or structures which persist even through historical change. The role of *social statics* is to identify these persistent organs and structures of society. These organs are not generated by patterns of social change, the object of social dynamics, but are ultimately the subject of social change, which can transform them, but which can neither originate nor eliminate them. Comte enumerates these permanent organizational patterns of society: religion, property, family, language, power, (spiritual and temporal). However he is somewhat unclear about the relations between them. It would seem that these are not as fixed as the organs he identifies but instead are the precise locus of social change, which is then reflected in the disposition of the permanent organs.

By this subordination of social dynamics to social statics Comte sets himself in opposition to the idealist systems of reason, to the eighteenth-century type of progressivism, and to the social evolutionists who were beginning to emerge. These other points of view all had one thing in common: emphasis on social dynamics over social statics, whether it was the ideal dynamics of the system of reason, the revolutionary dynamics of progressivist theory, or the gradualistic dynamics of evolutionary theory. The reality of society was discovered in the process of change. Its forms originated in change and were generated by history; they had no status outside history. Comte, on the other hand, discovers the reality of society in its permanent elements, the elements which are not generated by historical change and which do not change in themselves but which are presupposed as the subject of all change and progress.

Comte's own theory of social statics is the other formal dimension of his sociology. The object of this study is the movement which the permanent forms or structures of social life undergo in the realization of their inward characters and the systems of possible relations between them. All social movement consists in the effort which mankind makes to realize more fully a social structure which is ultimately fixed and given. The purpose of a social dynamics, consequently, can only be to fix the ideally possible forms of this greater organization of the basic social structures and to trace through history the actual transformations which have taken place. In his own manner, Comte too is a progressivist. History gives evidence of an actual movement, gradual but continual, toward the fuller realization of the potentiality of those fixed forms of social life. In this progressive movement, each consequent social state is the necessary result of the preceding and mover of the succeeding. "Cosmic individuals" appear, for Comte, to be the prime movers of change, but they are only the organs of a predetermined movement which, lacking them, would have found other avenues to its ends.

The progressive perfection of society does not imply that any stage in the story of human social development was inferior or imperfect. Every epoch of history is all that it could have been according to the potentialities of its time and order. If this were not the case, history would not be comprehensible. In this context, Comte, violating his earlier views, does not hesitate to have certain recourse to final causes. History is a rational *plenum* in which everything that has to happen does happen, and all that does happen is necessary and indispensable. The perfection of human social relations is the goal toward which the entire process advances, through successive stages, each perfect in itself though not perfect with respect to the end.

Comte's social statics and dynamics eventually find expression in terms of the theory of the three stages. This expression may be illustrated in terms of one of the permanent organs of social life—political society. Here the theological stage is represented by a transcendence of the "spiritual" over the "temporal" power. Though exercised by an earthly or temporal principle, political power draws its warrant from a transtemporal source, for example, from God, as in the theory of the divine right of kings. The metaphysical stage is represented by a political theory which immanentizes power in the processes of social life and considers all the phenomena of political life as deriving from the different dispositions of this force within the body politic; examples may be: the theory of classes and estates, constitutional theories, and theories of political consensus. There is no recourse to any transcendent principle. Finally, in the positivist stage the disposition of political power would be determined by the positive doctrine of science and would involve the use of political techniques developed from the positivist formulation of the laws of political phenomena. More concretely, Comte envisaged this third stage as a period in which power would be divided between the learned, who represent the "spiritual arm," and the "industrials," who represent technological advance. A balance would be achieved between them for the comprehensive control of society.

The translation of the social dynamics into the law of the three stages asserts that history is motivated by a necessary and inevitable movement toward the realization of a social order of the positivist type. As was true in the general theory of the three stages, this historical progress does not involve denigration of earlier stages. These appear as perfect, in themselves and according to their kind, and completely justified as steps toward the realization of the positivist form of political order.

While the theological and metaphysical organizations of social power belong to the past, the positivist belongs to the future. This circumstance gives rise to two necessities. The first is the employment of futuristic categories for the depiction of the positivist social order. This is not in principle difficult for positivism, since the element of prediction has already figured largely in its language; difficulties do appear, however, when these futuristic categories are to be selected. They should follow necessarily from the past and the present, but the present resides in an awareness of the possibility of alternative lines of development. The choice between alternatives is so difficult that Comte is forced to have recourse to arbitrary option. The second necessity involves the period of transition which stretches between the past and the future. An acceptable form of social and political organization for this transitional period must guarantee the passage to the desired future state. Comte finds himself advocating a dictatorship, renewing a pattern which had occurred in the Reign of Terror. Needless to say,

this dictatorship would be benevolent, both in its manner of comport-
ment and in the fact that it would guarantee the advent of the positivist
state. It would be a self-liquidating dictatorship, existing only to guarantee the advent of a situation which would be the direct antithesis of
its own character and would spell its demise. As an operating principle,
it would possess all of the hard and inevitable attributes of real dictatorship: control of the entire social process from the most inward to
the most external dimensions, from the most minute and contingent to
the widest and most permanent. Although it is clearly the logical
contradiction to the positivist vision of society, Comte advances it
as expedient.

F. *Humanity: The "Great Being"*

The social dynamics of Comte's sociology raises a very important
question. The attempt to answer this question releases in Comte those
springs of enthusiasm and mysticism which had always been present,
though they were repressed behind a facade of cold rationality. Social
statics isolates the permanent forms of social organization, which are
the subjects of social change. Society is not, however, constituted by
these permanent social forms; it is constituted by human persons living
together under the constraint of social necessity. These social individuals bear a peculiar relation to the social process, whether considered
statically or dynamically. Yet they elude inclusion within either category. The individuals do not have the permanent status of the static
forms, and they do not have the kind of future involved in the projective and futuristic categories of Comtean sociology. What, then, is the
real subject of society, both of the static forms of social organization
and of the progressive, time-ideal movement of society toward the
realization of positivist society? In terms of Comte's social, laicist, and
historistic mysticism, this subject is *humanity*: the "*Great Being.*"

What is this "Great Being"? It is the name for humanity taken as
a whole, a whole which is immanent in individuals but which at the
same time transcends them. In them it is capable of a career different
from any which they can experience individually or in any particular
collectivity. It is composed of all men actually living at any moment;
of all men who have lived and who have concurred by their actions
in the conservation and development of the human species; and finally,
all men who are not yet born and who will be called upon to build the
positivist society of the future. But it is concretely identifiable with
none of them; over and above its partial identification with them, it has
a life of its own, which they share in an oblique way but never fully.
The real history is not, therefore, the history of men in their concrete

actuality or in their concrete collectivities. The only history which matters is the history of the *Great Being*.

The history of the "Great Being," humanity, is controlled by the law of the three stages, proving anew the architectonic role of this law in the whole positivist enterprise. In this employment of the law, an inflexible determinism, already apparent at various points, becomes dominant. Institutions arise in response to specific needs of humanity; they become installed in being, ossify, and become obstacles to the progress which is the only ultimate law of the life of the "Great Being"; they eventually enter into a period of decay and disappear. In this new context, a fresh relationship, already hinted at, is introduced into the relations between the three stages themselves. The theological stage and the positivist stage have positive characteristics; the metaphysical stage can only be characterized by traits of the dissolution of the theological stage and the gradual appearance and self-affirmation of the positive stage. The career of the "Great Being" is delineated in terms of these two sets of positive traits and the single set of transitional traits thus implied.

The theological stage is divided into three periods: the fetishistic, the polytheistic, and the monotheistic. Fetishism made possible the first progressive movements of the human species toward an ordered life. It curbed man's instinctively destructive tendencies, teaching him to conserve certain objects—those of his "fetishistic attachment." Further, by restraining men from moving too far away from the sacred objects, this period taught them love of homeland and thus discouraged anarchic, non-productive, nomadic forms of life. But fetishism could not survive the gradual formation of larger groups, and the passage to the polytheistic stage was opened.

This condition of life favored the military virtues. Each army had its god, whose powers it sought to share. The sacred and divinatory arts, in the tutelage of priests, also flourished. The polytheistic state took various forms of organization, in response to various specific sets of conditions. At first it was static and conservative, with a social structure forbidding communication among the castes. Later it became aggressive, endowed with a passion for expansion and conquest. Military polytheism, in its turn, took two forms. The first was the military polytheism of the Greeks, which sought to conquer others with the arms of intelligence and beauty (though Comte does not think that Greek art was equal to its fame). The Romans turned military polytheism into a social system. In the harmony of the *pax romana* new gods were added to old as new peoples were added to the Roman power and became dependent on the City. Tolerance was the supreme principle.

But even this great edifice was destined to collapse, and in its place arose a new culture, the medieval. With this culture we pass into the monotheistic stage. Society was ruled by two powers, each firmly organized and exercising a beneficent rule proper to itself. The Church ruled men's souls; the feudal system provided the basic structure of temporal power with the feudatories forming a pyramid. This organization of society proved very fruitful in many ways. Among its achievements must be placed the glories of chivalry and the Gothic cathedrals, the poetry of Dante, and the philosophy of Thomas Aquinas. Comte cannot resist a gibe at the eighteenth-century hostility to the Middle Ages; only a blind man, he says, could fail to see its achievements and their lasting value. But even this era had to pass, and in its place arose the Renaissance, ushering in the metaphysical stage.

This stage, as has been noted, appeared to Comte to be essentially transitional. Like all transitional stages, it exhibited two inward movements: one destructive, one constructive. The destructive movement reached its culmination, in his view, in the superficiality of illuministic criticism and in the terrors of the French Revolution. Comte sees the work of positivism in relation to these movements, implying that it belongs, at least under this aspect, to the transitional, metaphysical stage. The work of positivism is to "close the revolutionary period" and, by the same token, to initiate the constructive phase of the metaphysical period, which will carry civilization into the positive age. The moral and political principles of positivism must prove the surest guides in this constructive work. The fundamental principle of positivistic morals is summed up in the adage: live for one's neighbor. The evidence of this principle is absolute: Every individual comes into the world freighted with a complex of obligations toward those who have preceded him and toward his contemporaries. He is in debt to others for everything: for material goods, for the very thoughts he thinks and the very sentiments he feels. From the social point of view, it is evident that society demands that its members love and respect each other; only thus can its further development be assured. The fundamental drive of human nature is altruistic and needs only to be developed in a positive society.

G. *The Religion of Positivism*

To overcome the anarchy in which the Revolution had left not only institutions but all social bonds and the souls of men, the morality of positivism must be fortified by a stronger principle. Here Comte enunciates a point which many others of the period, especially the "Traditionalists," also stressed: This ulterior principle resides only in religion. Only religion can provide that basic bond of sociality upon which the solidity of any society can rest. The basis of society must necessarily be a civil theology, and the inner form of every solid society must be a church, that is, a society in which the members are bound to each other and to all by the religious bond, expressing itself in civil organization. To reach its own inner goal, the positivist social order, positivism must generate this bond within itself; that is, it must become a religion.

The positive religion must have its deity. With the demise of monotheism and the development of the positivist view of man, only one deity is possible: *humanity*. Unlike the religions which preceded it, the religion of positivism is demonstrable; it rests upon positive truths and hence is binding for all. Its supreme formula is stated by Comte thus: "Love is its principle, order the basis, progress its purpose" (cf. *A General View of Positivism*, trans. J. H. Bridges, [Standford, Calif.: Academic Reprints, 1953] p. 355). The religion of positivism has its dogma, its cult, and its regimen. In respect to cult, Comte exhibits a great admiration for the Catholic Church and seeks to adapt many of its characteristics to his designs; above all it is the Catholic Church of the Middle Ages which attracts him.

Cult is in part private and in part public. Private cult in turn falls into two parts, personal and domestic. Comte even uses the theory of angelology, which provides him with the idea of the guardian angel; this becomes in his hands, no doubt under the influence of Clothilde de Vaux, the cult of the "eternal feminine," realized in the figure of the woman who is at man's side in all his enterprises. The religion of positivism also contains something faintly resembling the Catholic doctrine of the sacraments. All of the crucial moments of human life are identified and their passage is to be solemnized by a kind of sacramental ritual. At the moment of death it is the function of the "priest" of positivism to fill the dying man with the hope of immortality: continued life in the memory of posterity if his actions have been worthy. With some reference to the organization of the.liturgical year in Catholicism, Comte constructs a "positivist calendar" dedicated to keeping in memory the men who have contributed most to the benefit and progress of humanity and of the sciences.

The positivist social order takes on the form of a church; the model is again the Catholic Church of the Middle Ages. The positivist social order recalls and renews the medieval distinctions of function, class, and status. It is perhaps the first example in history of the consciously formulated "lay church."

H. *The Fortune of Positivism*

It is almost impossible today to appreciate the vast influence of positivism a century ago. During the period of the Second Empire,

Comte was known and esteemed in many strata of French society and even beyond France. Most critics assign this influence to the elasticity and comprehensiveness of Comte's thought. Much of his fame must also be accredited to the unflagging efforts of his disciples, especially Emile Littré (1801–1881) and Pierre Laffitte (1823–1903).

Littré, however, refused to follow Comte into the nebulous areas of his speculations on civil religion, considering them the product of the fatigued and disturbed mind of his master. In 1867 he founded the *Positivist Review* and in its pages insisted that the real value of positivism lay in showing that philosophy could subject itself, with profit, to the same methods as the positive sciences. He accepted the Comtean thesis of the strict relationship between social advancement and the advancement of the sciences and believed that positivism offered the only hope for the future development of society on rational lines. For him, positivism directed human efforts toward work, toward social equity, and toward international peace, by means of industry, the diffusion of science, the cultivation of the fine arts, and the gradual moral improvement of individuals and of social mores. Laffitte also founded a journal for the diffusion of positivism, the *Occidential Review,* but his work possesses little of the positive value which attaches itself to that of Littré.

In England, the positivism of Comte found advocates in Harriet Martineau (1802–1876), who translated the *Cours de philosophie positive* (1853), and in Richard Congreve (1818–1899), who translated the *Système de politique positive* and the *Catéchisme positive.* Finally, that erratic genius George Lewes (1817–1878) also lent his talents to the diffusion of positivism in England, differing from his teacher, however, in admitting the possibility of psychology. Later, while not explicitly renouncing his allegience to Comte, Lewes was to adopt many elements of the thought of Spencer.

Readings

Books

Charlton, D. G. *Positivist Thought in France: 1852–1870.* Oxford: Clarendon Press, 1959.

Evans, D. O. *Social Romanticism in France: 1830–1848.* Oxford: Clarendon Press, 1951.

Fletcher, Ronald. *Auguste Comte and the Making of Sociology.* New York: Oxford University Press, 1966.

Manuel, Frank E. *The Prophets of Paris.* Cambridge, Mass.: Harvard University Press, 1962.

Simon, Walter M. *European Positivism in the Nineteenth Century: An Essay in Intellectual History.* Ithaca: Cornell University Press, 1963.

Talmon, J. L. *Political Messianism: The Romantic Phase.* New York: Praeger, 1960.

Essays and articles
Lubac, Henri de. "Comte and Christianity." In the same author's *The Drama of Atheist Humanism*, pp. 77–159. London: Sheed & Ward, 1949.
Middleton, R. "A Reappraisal of Comte's Position in the Development of Sociology." *Sociology and Social Research*, XLIV (1960).

CHAPTER V

Philosophical Romanticism in Crisis

Introduction: Nature, Motives, and Extent of the Crisis

The crisis in philosophical romanticism which developed in the latter decades of the first half of the nineteenth century resulted from mounting tensions both within and without romanticism. The major external force generating tension was positivism, the current of thought which had grown out of the Comtean insight that philosophy could assume to itself the methods and standards of science. The major internal source of tension was the notion of system as it involves the process of the dialectic. Philosophical romanticism reached maturity in the concept of the system of reason founded on the dialectic. By definition, system based on dialectic involved the synthesis of divergent, even contradictory, elements. These elements were not passive; in themselves they possessed powerful dynamic principles moving toward autonomy. For example, the famous Hegelian synthesis of inner freedom and outer order in the political realm was essentially a labile synthesis, for the notion of liberty and the notion of authority each possess within themselves strong dynamic elements which tend to make them autonomous and dominant. Whether such a unity of divergent elements be maintained depended on the unifying principle, i.e., the dialectic. But the power of the dialectic in turn depended to a great extent on the skill with which it was wielded. In the hands of a Hegel, it gave the impression of an all-powerful instrument. In lesser hands, it proved an inept tool. The recalcitrant elements which it sought to synthesize tended to exercise the strength which each inherently possessed and to return to their autonomous status.

Various levels of motivation may always be distinguished in the dissolution of the romantic synthesis. In this context, however, only the philosophical motives are of interest. Where a philosophical motive was really present and dominant (where it was not, for example, deeply qualified by some ideological motive stemming from a practical concern, such as social reform), it proves to be always the same: a questioning of the romantic notion of what philosophy is and the manner in which it must be conducted. However, this motive was not present in all of the figures of the romantic crisis to the same degree or in the same purity. It was frequently associated, as in powerful thinkers like Marx, with other motives which in the end dominate the purely philosophical one.

The *crisis* in philosophical romanticism does not mean its *demise* or disappearance from the historical scene. On the contrary, the romantic motives in European philosophy—and culture in general—were strengthened rather than weakened by this process of crisis. In its great period philosophical romanticism was linked with logic. The unity which Hegel sought to impose upon reality through the process of dialectic was a logical unity. He struggled to make the principle of the *logos* prevail: the principle that the unity of the real is a logical unity and not a unity founded upon any other principle, such as artistic intuition, faith, etc. Kept in control by this ideal, the romantic synthesis took on classical form. Released from this control, each element in it began to assert its own autonomy and become the center of a fresh synthesis. Thus, in Kierkegaard the religious motive, which the Hegelian synthesis had sought to locate in a place and relation conformable to dialectical reason, asserted its autonomy and dominance and became a fresh center about which reality, human experience, and human discourse were to be organized (in so far as Kierkegaard would admit any such organization). Similarly, art and science, which, in the phenomenology of the spirit and in the system of logic, had been assigned roles in the representation of reality commensurate with a logical principle, asserted their autonomous and dominant claims, generating aestheticism and scientism. When the full nature of philosophical romanticism is kept in view, it must be concluded that all of these elements are phenomena within its orbit and not outside it. They are hardly comprehensible without reference to the context that philosophical romanticism supplies. Thus, it may be said that romanticism remains a dominant motive of our culture, but that the unity (a complex, multifaceted unity) envisioned by philosophical romanticism in its speculative and logical form has, through the crisis in philosophical romanticism, been replaced by a free pluralism of principles. These principles are still those which philosophical romanticism sought to hold in logical and speculative unity, but they have been released from that unity. Each has sought to become the center of a lesser unity. The multitude of points of view released in the second half of the century can thus be placed in historical context with the purpose, not of prejudging their value, but of understanding their genesis and relations in the ceaseless flux of opinions.

Of all the figures who emerge in the process of this crisis, Schopenhauer possesses the most indubitable speculative stature. For this reason, the present treatment of the crisis of philosophical romanticism may begin with his thought.

A. *Arthur Schopenhauer* (1788–1860)

The philosophy of Schopenhauer, in the popular mind, means his celebrated pessimism. If this term is to be applied to him, it must be applied in a philosophical sense, one which demands considerable speculative sophistication and has little to do with the ordinary expectations and disillusionments of life.

Schopenhauer was born in Danzig; his father was a well-to-do banker; his mother, a rather celebrated author of romances. After a youth spent in travel and polite study, followed by a desultory commitment to a commercial career, he attended the University of Göttingen. His first philosophical impressions were formed under the influence of the post-Kantian skeptic Schulze. As a consequence, the figure of Kant loomed large in Schopenhauer's thought. More than once he indicated that he considered Kant the most original thinker in the history of philosophy. In 1811 Schopenhauer was at Berlin, where he attended the lectures of Fichte. He took his degree at Jena with a thesis entitled *Über die vierfache Wurzel des Satzes vom zureichenden Grunde (On the Fourfold Root of the Principle of Sufficient Reason)*. During a stay at Weimar, he formed a firm friendship with Goethe and wrote his *Über das Sehn und die Farben* [On sight and colors] in 1816 in defense of Goethe's scientific theories. He was already at work on the book which would become the classical statement of his views, *Die Welt als Wille und Vorstellung (The World as Will and Respresentation)*, which was published in 1819. Between 1820 and 1832, in the status of *privatdozent* he offered courses at the University of Berlin but without much success. The same epidemic of cholera which carried off Hegel prematurely, in 1831, forced Schopenhauer to leave Berlin, and he settled in Frankfurt am Main. The year 1836 saw the publication of *Über den Willen in der Natur (On the Will in Nature)* and 1841 of *Die beiden Grundprobleme der Ethik (The Two Fundamental Problems of Ethics)*. His last published work was a series of essays and papers, *Parerga und Paralipomena*, which appeared in 1851.

Schopenhauer's works were not immediately well-received. He was clearly out of joint with his times; in the period of the great ascendency of philosophical romanticism he had already formulated his criticism of it. It must be admitted that these criticisms are not always inspired by speculative motives. Thus, he castigates idealism as a pharisaical philosophy, devoted not to the pursuit of truth, but to the defense of vested interests; not disinterestedly speculative, but given to the weaving of sophistical arguments to justify fixed attitudes of the state and the official beliefs of the Church. He is not too harsh with Fichte and Schelling, in whom he professes to see a certain talent. The full measure of his scorn and wrath is reserved for Hegel, whom he called a "charlatan." He spared neither Hegel's purpose, ideas, nor style. The patent exaggeration of his animosity and the plain untruth of his evaluation of Hegel escaped neither his contemporaries nor subsequent historians and critics.

Schopenhauer was devoted to freedom of thought. It was the "official" character of the regnant philosophical romanticism which repelled him. He could not tolerate the notion of a philosophy devoted to the maintenance of the political or social status quo and serving as an instrument of indoctrination. Nevertheless, Schopenhauer remains within the orbit of romanticism; even its passion for system possesses him. We shall group his main insights under the following rubrics, which are not fixed indices and justify themselves only by the order they impart: "Reality as Infinite Will"; "The World as Representation or Idea"; The World as Will; Art and Freedom; the Tragic Sentiment of Life (with due acknowledgement to Unamuno); and The Conduct of Life.

1. Reality as Infinite Will

Kant furnishes the point of departure for Schopenhauer's main line of thought, that is, the distinction between *phenomenon* and *noumenon*. The ambiguity of this distinction, in Kant's own thought, is notorious; and it is generally conceded that the interpretation given it by Schopenhauer is not Kantian. While Kant spoke of the noumenon as the *thing-in-itself*, he did not identify it with the real or the knowable; this designation is reserved for the phenomenon, for in the Kant of *The Critique of Pure Reason* knowable reality is the reality which appears. Schopenhauer reverses this order. He speaks (and he is perhaps the first to insist on this line of thought) of the phenomenon as appearance and illusion, the dream, what, according to his interpretation, is called in "Indian philosophy" the "veil of Maya." Correspondingly, the *noumenon* becomes the reality which hides itself behind this veil of appearances. (He thus destroys the basis of Kant's phenomenalism, for Kant never forced this contradistinction between *appearance* and *real-*

ity.) It is frequently pointed out that this interpretation is of Oriental derivation, for Schopenhauer was devoted to the study of Indian and Buddhist sources. The problem for him then becomes how to draw aside this veil and penetrate to *what is—the noumenon, the reality.*

Kant had replied, through the development of the successive critiques, that when the limits of pure reason had been laid clear, moral faith and the postulates of practical reason placed men in relation with the noumenal. Hegel, correcting Kant, had insisted that reason, through the logic of the dialectic, fulfilled this office. Schopenhauer rejects both of these possibilities and asserts that it is will which reveals reality to us and that it is under the concept of will that reality must be subsumed. But here a contrast which both Kant and Hegel had employed is also employed by Schopenhauer. Kant had labored to show, in the *Critique of Pure Reason,* that it is the transcendental and not the empirical reason which imparts unity to experience; Hegel, still closer to Schopenhauer's chosen field, in the *Philosophy of History* made his famous distinction between the finite volitions of man and the "astuteness of the Idea," which, while working through men, directs their wills and ideas to ends they do not apprehend. Schopenhauer takes his clue from these, distinguishing between the finite, empirical will of individual men and the infinite will. The former is surely not the category of the real; the finite and empirical will belongs to the realm of phenomenon, of illusion. It is the infinite will which denominates the real. Historians and critics assert that it is precisely this central thesis of his entire position which places Schopenhauer firmly in the orbit of philosophical romanticism. Releasing the will from the place it had been assigned in the Hegelian synthesis, he raises it to the status of the denominating and unifying principle of reality. But it is still the same *infinite* character, assigned now to will, which is the principal mark of his thought, a character wholly of romantic provenance. And if Hegel had underevaluated the individual, subjecting him wholly to the movement of the Idea, Schopenhauer had equally deflated him, assigning him wholly to the realm of phenomena, of appearance.

Schopenhauer goes on to qualify this infinite will. He finds that, lacking the sovereign principle of reason, the idea, as its intrinsically illuminating and ordering element, this infinite will is at war with itself, destroying and devouring itself. It is, to employ the romantic term, *self-alienated.* It is substantive and essential sorrow—not *anyone's* sorrow, which must always be finite and hence surpassable, but the sorrow of being itself, for which there is no remedy on the transcendental level. Yet as will—will to be, to live—reality affirms itself in and through this alienation. It is this infinite sorrow which reverberates in the sorrows of the individual empirical self. While the individual experiences this sorrow always in the finite mode of his cares and woes: need, sickness, loneliness, still in his more perceptive moments he glimpses dimly that it is not he who sorrows but being itself which is sorrowful within him.

This analysis places the empirical will, the individual, directly *vis-a-vis* that infinite will. How should it dispose itself toward that infinite will? How can it transcend the situation of sorrow and pain in which being, as infinite will, places it? The answer seems clear: by detaching itself from that infinite will-to-being which is all-sorrowful. This is the essential "pessimism" of Schopenhauer, and its essential remedy is his "asceticism." That asceticism is the negation of reality as infinite will by the finite will.

At first glance Schopenhauer would seem to be in complete contradiction to himself at this point. How would it be possible for finite will, which is appearance and non-being, to enact a negation or detachment such as he indicates? Superficially, it is impossible, and Schopenhauer nowhere indicates that he sees beyond this impossibility. But speculatively there is a possible answer. Precisely because he is, as finite and phenomenal, *non-being*, man, as individual, can elude being. To shut out being he need but retreat into himself, his own phenomenal existence. This is what he longs to do. Schopenhauer counsels just such an asceticism as the only escape from sorrow: a detaching of the finite will from the infinite, sorrowful will.

It would seem that the logical step forward from this counsel, for the philosopher, would be to offer philosophy as the "way" of such detachment. Schopenhauer does not do this. He does not conceive philosophy as a "way," but only as a mode of representation. The role of philosophy is speculative: to "reflect abstractly, universally, clearly, in concepts, the entire essence of the world, and thus, as a reflected image, to dispose it in the permanent and always available concepts of reason: this, and this alone, is the role of philosophy" (*The World as Will and Representation*, trans. E. F. J. Payne, 1958, Vol. I, Sec. 68, pp. 383–384). Philosophy counsels the way, but it does not conduct man in the way. In his own words: "It is as little necessary that the saint be a philosopher, as that the philosopher be a saint" (ibid.).

2. The World as Representation

Schopenhauer opens his chief work, *The World as Will and Representation*, with the cardinal principle of his whole system: "The world is my representation [or idea]" (Vol. I, Sec. 1, p. 3). To this principle he gives the status of a self-evident truth; it is known to everyone on simple inspection. Within his system, it functions as an axiom: All is explained in terms of it, but it is not subject to explanation or proof. In his view, the great achievement of modern philosophy is to have brought western thought to the full appreciation of this principle.

Within representation Schopenhauer distinguishes two essential and constitutive moments which cannot be separated: the *subject* and the *object*. This distinction structures knowledge in general, whether "pure" or empirical, abstract or concrete. The subject is that which knows all, but itself remains unknown; it cannot be known because under no conditions can it become the object of itself. The object is known, but it has no being save as known. This object is limited by the *a priori* forms of time and space. These, of course, do not limit the subject. The subject is outside of time and space. Consequently, one such existent subject is capable of establishing the world independently of all other subjects. If all subjects were to disappear, the world as representation would not be. These two moments are to be taken in strict correlation; their isolation leads to immedicable error: materialism, when it is the object which is established independently; absolute idealism, when the subject is treated in this fashion.

Schopenhauer takes a distinctive view of the *object*. It is entirely identical with its causal action within the process of representation. It is meaningless to speak of the being of the object independent of, and not subject to, the process of representation; nor is the object in any sense a passive element within that process. It is entirely immanent to the process of representation and within that process wholly *active* and completely identifiable with its *action*. From this assertion Schopenhauer draws two important conclusions for his system.

The first is a distinction between *intellect* and *reason* and the *intuition* of the causal relation between its objects (for the object consists wholly in its causal activity). This is the first and basic operation of mind. Reason, by contrast, is abstract and deals wholly with concepts. These are derived from intuitions of the intellect, though they are not, once so derived, reducible to those intuitions. Human knowledge moves properly at the level of reason; but the entire basis for any *certainty* it may possess lies in the intellectual intuition. At this point Schopenhauer's analysis encounters a difficulty with which he does not deal adequately: Since the basis of the concepts of reason is the intellectual intuition, but the former cannot be reduced to the latter, how can a proof be conducted at the level of reason?

The second conclusion is his celebrated identification of *dream* and *reality*, or dream and waking. Life is dream; waking and dreaming differ only in degree of intensity. But this does not deny any reality to the dream. Insofar as dream is universal, it defines the real and cannot therefore be excluded from it.

Schopenhauer's identification of the object with its causal action leads him to place great importance on the principle of causality and the process of causation. In the thesis which he had prepared for his degree, *The Fourfold Root of the Principle of Sufficient Reason,* he distinguishes four forms of the principle of causality and, therefore, four corresponding classes of possible objects. The four forms of the principle of causality or sufficient reason are: becoming, knowledge, being, and action. The first governs the relations between natural objects and determines the necessary succession of cause and effect; it yields the classes of intuitive representations, empirical intuitions of natural bodies. The second form regulates the relations between judgments; it establishes the bond between premise and conclusion and determines the forms of knowledge which man may possess, that is to say, the forms of *rational* knowledge. The third form determines the relations between the parts of time and space and, consequently, the logical relations of geometrical and arithmetical entities; it is the basis for conclusions in the mathematical sciences. Finally, the fourth form, that of action, regulates the relations between actions and the motives which establish them; motivation is that form of causality which is seen from the internal point of view of the agent of action.

These four forms of causality and sufficient reason yield the *forms of necessity* which structure the world as representation: physical necessity, logical necessity, mathematical necessity, and moral necessity. His conception of *moral* necessity involves Schopenhauer in his celebrated denial of human free will. Man's actions form a necessary system, like any other system of phenomena; hence liberty, in the sense asserted by that doctrine, is precluded. The principle of that system is motivation, which is the specific mode of the four forms of causality proper to man. But Schopenhauer's denial of man's freedom is not absolute; he is denying only that form of freedom implied in the theory of the freedom of will. Man may be free in another, higher, sense.

3. The World as Will

What this higher freedom may be, becomes clear when the world is considered as *will.* The assertion "the world is my representation," though enunciated absolutely by Schopenhauer, is actually restricted to the *phenomenal world.* He has already indicated that in its *noumenal* aspect, as it is in itself, the world is not representation but will. Under his *noumenal* aspect man is endowed with absolute freedom, just as under his phenomenal aspect his action is absolutely determined. But how is this passage from the phenomenal to the noumenal effected? If man is so absolutely enclosed in the phenomenal world and subject to its necessities, how is he to become established in the noumenal world? Schopenhauer has already supplied the basic answer to this question in his assertion that, while the object of knowledge in representation is subject to the *a priori* conditions of time and space, the subject is not; indeed, the subject cannot be, since it can never become object to itself. The test case is man's body. As body, man is wholly in nature, in the phenomenal order and subject to its necessities. But his own body is not given to man only under this form of phenomenal necessity. He also knows his body in an immediate and more interior mode: as will. Bodily movements are not merely the *effects* of the will; they are the actuality of will itself in its moment of *objectivization*. Body is the *objectivity* of will, and under this form will becomes the object of intuition and representation.

Consequently, man is endowed with the absolute freedom which is proper to the noumenal order, just as the ineluctable necessities associated with the principle of sufficient reason proper to the phenomenal order bind him absolutely. Man is absolutely determined in the phenomenal order and absolutely free in the noumenal order. Since the relation between these orders is that of appearance and reality, man is in appearance absolutely determined and in reality absolutely free.

The matter cannot, however, be dismissed so lightly. Schopenhauer has established a rather tight nexus between these orders—noumenal will and phenomenal nature. He has said that the one is the objectification of the other. Therefore, he would seem to be committed to the paradoxical assertion that absolute freedom objectifies itself as absolute necessity. This would seem to make that noumenal order itself something of an illusion. His conception of freedom, indeed his conception of reality, is seriously lacking unless he can show that there is some order in which the absolute freedom of the will is objectified. Schopenhauer maintains that the world of art is such an order. Art is the objectivization of the noumenal in the mode of absolute freedom yet with all the properties of representation.

4. Art and Freedom

In order to understand this notion of art within Schopenhauer's system, it is necessary to consider this process of objectification anew. Objectivization may be projected as a continuum, the extreme terms of which are *nature* and *art*. The dynamism of this continuum has two directions: absolute necessity as it approaches nature and absolute freedom as it approaches art. The noumenal will moves in both of these directions, seeking these diverse and opposed conditions—representation under the forms of necessity, representation under the forms of freedom. The latter corresponds directly to the inner nature of noumenal will.

Thus, the problem arises: Why does noumenal will move toward objectivization at the level of phenomenal nature, absolute necessity, when this condition is manifestly contrary to its intrinsic character? The answer must be that there is a necessity which moves the noumenal in this direction; that is to say that phenomenal objectivization at the level of nature is in some sense a necessary step toward the phenomenal objectivization of will at the level of freedom. The continuum suggested above is thus given a circular motion, a catabasis of the noumenal toward phenomenal order and an anabasis of noumenal will toward art through liberation from the objectivization of nature. This is indeed the pattern which finally emerges in Schopenhauer's thought. The most important point to grasp is the necessity involved, why it is necessary to pass through the objectivization as phenomenal nature in order to ascend to the objectivization as art.

The answer would seem to lie in Schopenhauer's notion of the "idea." The idea is the phenomenal objectification of noumenal will under the form of absolute freedom. This is the pure form of art. The idea, however, cannot be released directly by art. There is a certain dialectic of opposites involved. Noumenal will must pass through phenomenal objectification as nature because, in some way, only through this process can the idea emerge and be projected as art. Representation as phenomenal nature works out all of the ambiguities implied in noumenal will as purely noumenal. Noumenal will must pass through the representation stage of absolute necessity before the idea of itself can be achieved in art. If this were not the case, the freedom of the representational mode of art would always be spurious; i.e., it would not contain within itself the objectivization and the negation of the necessities of nature. Hence, it would seem that noumenal will must pass through this circle, that it can achieve its liberation in art only through its representation in the necessities of nature. Schopenhauer's exposition of this point of view seems clouded by one factor: his reluctance to recognize and explicate the dialectic implied in his position. The position formally expounded seems to be composed of alternatives—nature and art—which are simply juxtaposed, the relation between them left obscure.

These considerations make it clear that art is, for Schopenhauer, the supreme expression of life, the pure form of the representation of reality as will. In art, reality as will is delivered from all of those impulsive necessities with which the notion of will is otherwise freighted. The freedom of art is absolute; it frees man from even the shadows of necessity intrinsic to noumenal will and delivers him into the world of the pure idea. In art the dualism between dream and waking, which Schopenhauer had denied but did not really overcome, is finally resolved. In the absolute, free representation of art, the unity of these states is realized. The work of art is dream which is absolute reality, for it represents *what is,* under absolutely ideal conditions, subject to no constriction or necessity other than pure presence.

5. The Tragic Sense of Life

The liberation of man through art and the contemplation of the ideas constitutes the positive vision of freedom and liberty in Schopenhauer. There exists in his thought, however, another, quite distinct vision which may properly be called negative for it is reached not by the pure élan which is art but by an *askesis,* a process of renunciation. To appreciate this negative freedom, which is perhaps more important than the freedom of art since it is available to every man, we must again take a step back in the process of Schopenhauer's thought to the point at which his tragic sense of life asserts itself.

The absolute will, though *noumenal,* appears in man phenomenally, as a constant lust for life, a perpetual drive to satisfy the numberless vital needs and desires. This converts the individual into a sheer egotist; at the same time it sets up in him that elliptical movement, desire turning back upon itself, which is the source of his vital sorrow, of his sense of tragedy and futility. Since the desires which draw him on and the capacity for satisfying them with which the universal principle of life equips the individual are absolutely incommensurate, his life is doomed to be perpetually self-defeating. At the same time, the egotism in which this lust for the needs of life involves him alienates him from all other men, making him a solitary hunter, as it were. Thus, he finds himself enslaved, first, by the vital force or will which drives him on in that hopeless endeavor and, second, by the loneliness which makes him a stranger to all other men. His liberty will never be complete until he achieves release from these bonds. To meet this need Schopenhauer prescribes two ascetical courses.

The first recalls the negative way of the ancient Stoics or, some would suggest, the ascetical paths of the eastern sages. It is, in a sense, a technique of cheating the noumenal will to life in man, but without endowing him with the capacity for complete satisfaction. This path counsels the detachment from desire, its forceful limitation and denial. The introduction of a strict economy of desire, based on a principle which the individual himself options, limits that infinite desire with which the absolute will inspires man. Within this controlled economy some degree of satisfaction may be achieved. The essence of this satisfaction will be the fact that absolute will no longer dominates. This is the essence of freedom from ontological sorrow.

The second path must lead man to overcome the isolation which the egotism generated by the drive of the absolute will imposes on him. He must find a path to others and open a path for others to himself. This path lies in the understanding that all are the common dupes of the absolute will and that all individual sorrow is but the apparition of the one common sorrow which emanates from the absolute will at the level of its phenomenal existence. This knowledge breeds compassion among men in the literal sense of the term: the sharing of sorrow. But this compassion has a deeper effect. Once compassion breaks the bounds of isolation between men, the dominion of the absolute will to life is effectively negated. This negation is the complete knowledge of the servitude of the will. Only when the will has come to complete awareness of itself, is it able to renounce itself and cancel out all desire. The asceticism of denial of desire and the ethics of compassion complete the process of liberation which art initiates but which only the ethical life realizes.

6. The Conduct of Life

Schopenhauer now faces the task of deducing an effective and relevant morality from these ethical principles. He does not succeed in doing this in any persuasive manner, but the fault is not his. It is implicit in these principles. A pure asceticism cannot be reduced to a moral rule, for it lacks content. The ethics of compassion yields little in the way of guidance for life. Compassion is self-defeating in that the relations to others which it engenders dissolve into passivity and inaction. This does not prevent Schopenhauer from trying to formulate such moral rules and ideals. Resignation, poverty, sacrifice have a certain authentic ring, especially to ears which are accustomed to the words and precepts of the gospel. However, in Schopenhauer, these echoes lack completely that forceful affirmation of life which, in the Christian economy, gives them power and persuasiveness. Christian resignation is power over life and not flight from it; Christian compassion is charity, active love, not passive condolence.

7. Conclusion

Fame and influence were slow in coming to Schopenhauer, and they have never come in overabundant measure. To the degree that they did come, however, they have been abiding. His high evaluation of art won him a certain following; thus, Wagner reflects his influence during the first stages of his activity. Friedrich Neitzsche spoke of him as the true educator of the generation to which Nietzsche belonged. His "pessimism" awakened a response in many sensitive persons;

August Strindberg, for example, echoes a strong Schopenhauerian note in his plays. Perhaps the most important figure to reflect his immediate influence is Eduard von Hartmann (1842–1906) in his *Philosophie des Unbewussten* [Philosophy of the unconscious], 1869. As far away as Mexico, José Vasconcelos wrote, in his early period, that Schopenhauer, in certain of his formulae, expressed the very basic insights of the modern spirit. This list could be extended, sometimes to the most unexpected areas. An effort to develop Schopenhauer's thought along more academic lines was made by such men as Julius Frauenstädt (1813–1879), editor of Schopenhauer's collected works, and Julius Bahnsen (1831–1881), but Schopenhauer's thought did not lend itself readily to this kind of treatment.

B. *Johann Friedrich Herbart* (1776–1841)

Herbart was the most explicit critic of idealism; he developed his own theories under the rubric of "realism." Nevertheless, even Herbart did not escape the idealist influence; many of his ideas represent a special development of this position.

Herbart studied under Fichte at Jena; however, his attitude toward his teacher was extremely critical. At Berne he came under the influence of the philosopher-educator Pestalozzi and education was to remain a constant preoccupation. He taught first at Göttingen, later at Königsberg, where he succeeded to the chair of Kant. In 1833 he returned to Göttingen. His influence was marginal; nevertheless, he always remained a presence in academic philosophy.

Herbart's earliest writings are all polemics against idealism. The term *realism* first appears in an essay critical of Schelling in 1796. The influence of Pestalozzi is reflected in his *Allgemeine pädagogik* [General theory of education], 1806; his continued interest in this area is expressed as late as 1835 in *Umriss pädagogischer Vorlesungen (Outlines of Educational Doctrine)*. These educational writings had a wide and enduring influence on the theory and practice of education in Germany. His chief philosophical writings include: *Hauptpunkte der Logik* [Principal points of logic], 1808; *Hauptpunkte der Metaphysik* [Principal points of metaphysics], 1806–1808; *Lehrbuch zur Einleitung in die Philosophie* [Manual for the introduction to philosophy], 1813; *Allgemeine praktische Philosophie* [Hand book of psychology], 1816; and toward the end of his career *Allgemeine Metaphysik* [General metaphysics], 1828–29. The very titles of these works reveal the academic and formalistic cast of Herbart's mind. The focal points of his interest are logic and method, metaphysics, and ethics; aesthetics also engages his attention.

The best key to Herbart's work is his view of the philosophical task. Philosophy ought to develop a set of concepts which eliminate the contradictions of experience. It would thus arrive at the *real*. The chief characteristic of reality is that it tolerates no contradictions. Philosophy begins with a skepticism which calls into question all concepts and laws of thought which offer themselves as norms for the discernment of the real. The end of philosophy is not skeptical, for its purpose is the attainment of reality through the dialectic of the contradictions of experience in which the real lies concealed. Herbart enumerates these contradictions: unity and multiplicity; causality and succession; the self and the process of its representations; etc. He calls philosophy in this sense *metaphysics*.

Metaphysics has two moments or dimensions. The first is methodology; the effort is to discover the rules and procedures which may make it possible to reduce the contradictions inherent in experience. Within its scope falls logic, which distinguishes, orders, and relates concepts. The Herbartian logic is Aristotelian with touches of Kantianism. In his own idiom, in logic concepts have the value neither of real objects nor of acts of thought; they have force only in relation to what is thought by means of them, their objective reference. This has seemed to some an adumbration of Husserl's phenomenology. The other part of metaphysics is ontology, the elaboration of the structure of what is, insofar as this has been reached through the process of reducing the contradictions of experience. Ontology investigates the simple beings which lie beyond all contradictions and constitute the real. His name for these "simples" is "the reals." These are qualitatively distinct beings whose relations or combinations constitute the multiplicity of actual things.

Experience is the *appearance* of something which is. However, there is no evidence in experience that what *is*, *is* according to the mode of its appearance, the contradictions in appearances force the conclusion that what *is* cannot *be* according to the mode of its appearance. Hence, the task is to determine, through the penetration of appearance, what *is* and what may be its nature: secondly, to determine why what *is* manifests itself through a system of appearances which does not faithfully mirror what it is.

The locus of this complex transaction is the *concept*. The concept is a structure of presence in which the relations between what is and what appears are ordered. A concept is a principle in terms of which what is may be identified in itself and in relation to its system of appearances. Such a concept may be elaborated linguistically by means of definitions. The function of methodology and logic is the elaboration of concepts, and *logic* may be defined as the science of concepts.

This doctrine includes three elements: 1) the characterization of the real as that which lies beyond all contradiction; 2) the characterization of the order of appearances of the real; and 3) the determination of the ontological status of the processes by which those realms are ordered to each other.

The first point is covered by Herbart's theory of simple entities. The simplicity of these entities is the correlative of the complexity and contradictory nature of the order of appearances. In Herbart's words: "There exists as a matter of fact, outside of us, a quantity of beings whose simple nature remains unknown but about the internal and external conditions of which we can achieve a sum of knowledge which can be increased infinitely" (*Introduction to Philosophy*, Sec. 125). These beings are the "reals." The comparison with the "monads" of Leibnitz seems inevitable.

Herbart indicates a number of characteristics of these "reals." They are *qualitatively* distinct. Here the difference from Spinoza is striking. For Spinoza, the real must be one—substance and *its* properties. For Herbart, there is no question of one thing and its properties: there is a basic plurality of "reals." This applies to the structure of any *given* thing as well; there is not the relation of substance and accidents, but a system of appearances which are functionally related. The "reals" are absolutely immutable. They are immaterial and indestructible. These simple entities enter into syntheses, through which they constitute the world of multiple things, the "manifold" of Kant. These syntheses are not produced by any principle of diversity existing within the reals themselves, but, paradoxically, by the mere self-conservation of these simples against the possibility of perturbation from other "reals."

How do the reals relate to the order of appearances under which they show themselves in experience? Certainly the order of appearance is not "nothing," is not illusion. The appearance taken in itself must *be*, and must be *something*. Herbart assigns the order of appearances— of multiplicity, change, time, space—to *thought*. (The residual "idealism" is here manifest.) The systems of relations, etc., which structure the world of appearances are "accidental vistas" within which the reals present themselves as linked by certain relations but not as taking these relations upon themselves. These "vistas" multiply and relate the reals for thought, but do not multiply or relate them in themselves. To this order of "accidental vistas" (perspectives) belong the concepts which philosophy elaborates. The aporiae in this structure readily appear. Philosophy is based, as an enterprise, on the possibility of reaching the real through the concept. On the other hand, the concepts are considered accidents with respect to the real which they are supposed to exhibit. It is difficult to understand how the concepts can exhibit the real unless they share its properties, unless, for example, the multiplicity of the concept reflects the multiplicity of the real.

This difficulty leads directly to the third question: the ontological status of the order of concepts. One must recognize Herbart's sharp distinction between the determinations of being within the concept and empirical determinations. The concepts do not have any element of existence; i.e., they are not *entia rationis*. Their locus is intelligibility considered as an order of being. Intelligibility is the order of being in which the reals appear after the contradictions of empirical appearances have been reduced. It is a pure phenomenology. This order most clearly *is*, though its being is neither that of the changeless reals nor that of the contradiction-ridden empirical appearances. In view of his persuasion that the concepts are of this order, i.e., that they *are*, Herbart characterizes himself as a realist.

Herbart's ethics is based on "aesthetics" conceived as a general theory of values of which moral values form one species. Aesthetics concerns the judgment of value. Within this general field, the moral judgment is particularly concerned with the relations of the will. These relations are autonomous, derivative from no other order of values. They are expressed as immediately evident ideas. Herbart calls the first of these the idea of internal freedom; it concerns the relation between the will and the moral conscience which is the general form of the ethical judgment. This judgment is differentiated by reason of its content into the moral, the juridical, the political, and, finally, the inclusively societal order. Thus, ethics is the basis of an entire system of value-sciences—those involving the human will. To this corresponds another, the aesthetical in the conventional sense. This embraces the world of art, where the human will is not the chief concern but where a free association prevails between the elements of the value judgment.

Herbart's philosophy was more fortunate than that of Schopenhauer. A "Herbartian school" emerged, concerned chiefly with his psychological and educational theories. Herbart's influence is best evidenced by the fact that, as late as the last decade of the nineteenth century, it had a strong impact on such a philosopher as Benedetto Croce, who admits to a "Herbartian phase" in his philosophical development.

C. *Psychologism: Fries and Beneke*

The idealist analysis of experience had, to risk a paradox, proceeded independently of experience. Its concern had been the *a priori* and, while it might take some area of experience as its point of departure for the critical derivation of *a priori* principles, these were in fact the

product of the "pure reason." This *a priori* procedure reached its culmination in Hegel. Its concern was with the transcendental, that which
makes experience possible; therefore, its instrument and procedure
could not reasonably be subjected to the processes whose conditions of
possibility they were seeking to determine. Nevertheless, this did not
seem justifiable to many critics. It became one of the critical points at
issue in the crisis of idealism. This tendency to criticize the *a priori*
method on the ground that it had no warrant in experience for the
kinds of statements it sought to make about the conditions and possibilities of experience is what is meant by *psychologism.* Without repu-
diating the aim of idealist speculation, i.e., to determine the transcendental principles of experience, psychologism holds that this inquiry
should be based on experience and that the science of psychology is
the instrument for this inquiry.

The two most important figures in this criticism of the idealist
enterprise were Jakob Friedrich Fries (1773–1843) and Friedrich
Eduard Beneke (1798–1854). Their common point of departure is in
Kant more than Hegel. Their common purpose was not to abandon the
basic Kantian enterprise, but to perfect it.

Fries develops his ideas in an extensive series of writings, chief
among which are: *Wissen, Glauben und Ahnung* [Science, faith, and
insight], 1805; *Neue Kritik der Vernunft* [New critique of reason],
1807; *System der Logik* [System of logic], 1811; *Psychische Anthropologie* [Psychical anthropology], 1821. Of Beneke's very extensive
output, the most relevant titles would seem to be *Kant und die philosophische Aufgabe unserer Zeit* [Kant and the philosophical task of our
times], *Lehrbuch der Psychologie als Naturwissenschaft* [Manual of
psychology as a natural science], 1833; *System der Logik als Kunstlehre
des Denkens* [System of logic as the art of thought], 1842.

Fries's thought revolves about certain themes of Kantian criticism
which he considers to have been developed insufficiently or in an erroneous direction. Chief among these is the status of the *a priori* principles.
He doubted that their absolute validity for the transcendental subject
had been demonstrated by Kant. To Fries they appeared to constitute
merely a new field for scientific investigation. This investigation should
be the object of internal experience, conceived as self-observation or
introspection. He subjects the *a priori* principles to psychological
inspection and validation. Kant quite knowingly sought to avoid this
procedure, beginning his analysis, not with psychological data, but
with logical data, such as analytic and synthetic judgments. Kant had
made a great advance when he asserted for the first time that reason
had to achieve self-knowledge as the basis for its *scientific* application
to any order of objects; he had not seen, however, that unless this kind

of self-knowledge was firmly based on the examination of the psychic processes involved in scientific and other forms of knowledge, the principles ostensibly established as defining the possibility of all such knowledge would have no immediate reference to the actual processes of thought. Psychology, therefore, and not transcendental analysis, must be the instrument for the philosophical purpose which Kant had so well defined.

Beneke's thought shows a parallelism to that of Fries. Much of his schooling came from the English empiricists, and some of their basic insights carried over into his own efforts. He did not intend to negate the work of Kant, i.e., to reduce the conditions of knowledge to purely subjective levels. He recognized the validity of Kant's question concerning the transcendental character of scientific knowledge and normative principles—their universality and logical necessity. The key lay, not in a transcendental analysis, but with psychological introspection of the concrete processes of the subject. The principles which the reason uses as universally valid are to be found in psychological experience. Psychological introspection becomes the supreme method of philosophy, and psychology becomes the basic philosophical science, on which all others depend. Beneke was never inclined to accept a psychological relativism of thought. He was convinced that the principles isolated by introspection would have objective force equal to that claimed for the *a priori* principles on transcendental grounds. They would have also the advantage of being actual laws of the concrete processes of thought, subject to scientific formulation.

D. *The Dissolution of Hegelianism*

1. The Integrity of the Hegelian System

The crisis in idealism reached its culmination in the dissolution of Hegelianism. Hegelianism was the supreme achievement of philosophical romanticism; its dissolution marks the nadir. The fact that the process of dissolution could set in within such a short time after Hegel's death makes one question inevitable: What was the character of the Hegelian system, the degree of its coherence, the principle of its integrity? In Hegel's own thought the coherence of that system appeared seamless. Its rapid dissolution suggests another view; the system fell short of the coherence necessary to withstand pressures both from within and from without.

From the external point of view, Hegel's system was sustained by the powerful Prussian state system, of which it had become the "official" philosophy. This, of course, is wholly accidental and irrelevant from the philosophical point of view, but it is an element in the situation which cannot be completely ignored. Looking at the system internally, we are drawn to other factors. On the one hand there are the substantive propositions in which the content or doctrine of the philosophy is expressed. On the other hand is the method by which these substantive propositions are achieved, formulated, and maintained. In the "ideal" system, there would be perfect balance between these elements. Every substantive proposition and every relation between substantive propositions is the fruit of the method. Even more, the principles of the method can be stated within the system itself. This is the ideal of system which guided Hegel. His doctrine was the product of his method, the dialectic. The dialectic, in turn, was really the substance and heart of his system taken as doctrine, the foundation of all its other substantive propositions. Such a system would seem unshakable.

As long as Hegel lived the ideal seemed to have been achieved: A perfect coherence seemed to prevail between these elements. This coherence, as a matter of fact, was only ostensible. Its sustaining principle was not the system but the mind of Hegel. The vast erudition and culture which he brought to his task, his own mastery of the method, the somewhat ponderous but still effective rhetoric which he developed for its literary expression, and the presence of the philosopher himself conjoined to hold in union doctrine and method. This is not to deny that there exists within the system a high degree of what might be called objective coherence, that is, coherence not involving the personal presence of the philosopher. The Hegelian system remains one of the most impressive of such attempts in the history of western philosophy. In the final balance, however, the personal factor dominated. The evidence lies in the fact that the system did disintegrate—though its dissolution was not the easy process which some have asserted it to be.

Further evidence is the fact that, when the process of disintegration did set in, it followed the line of potential tension between doctrine and method. The basic fissure was opened between two groups of followers and interpreters. One group held that the doctrine was the important factor, possessed of a certain truth independent, to some degree or other, of the method by which its substantive propositions were produced. Another group saw in the method a powerful instrument but doubted that, properly employed, it would of necessity generate the propositions which made up the Hegelian doctrine. The first group retreated into what has been called a Hegelian scholasticism; the latter developed into a radical methodology in which the free employment of the dialectical method, without doctrinal commitments, became an instrument of criticism applicable in a variety of fields.

2. The Pattern of Dissolution

The pattern of the dissolution of the Hegelian system has come to be stated in crypto-political terms. It is the accepted mode to speak of a Hegelian *right*, a Hegelian *left*, and a Hegelian *center*. The origin of this rhetorical trope has been traced to a prominent member of the Hegelian left, David Strauss; in an essay of 1837 he chose these terms, drawn from the famous alignment in the French Parliament, to describe the pattern beginning to emerge within Hegelianism. This description, though purely rhetorical, does prove suggestive. The parliamentary right generally stood for the forces of conservatism, while the left stood for liberalism, criticism, and change. This pattern is reflected in the dissolution of Hegelianism. The appellation *right,* was applied to those followers of Hegel who clung to the doctrinal elements of the system, and *left,* to those who, careless of doctrine, were attracted by the dialectical method as an instrument of criticism which was free of doctrinal ties. Of course, these rhetorical designations demand to be made more precise.

The fundamental issues which opened this fissure were of a religious and a political nature. The "official" status of Hegelian philosophy rested on two bases: its apparent ability to sustain the power of the Prussian state by its political theory and the official state religion, Lutheran Christianity, by its philosophy of religion. When Hegel's personal presence was withdrawn both of these appeared questionable. The dialectic as an instrument of analysis and criticism could be turned with great ease, it appeared, against Hegel's cherished view that his philosophy represented a complete speculative justification of religion in general and the doctrines of revealed Christian religion in particular; with equal ease it could be turned against the monolithic, paternalistic, and hierarchical Prussian state conservatism with all of its social implications. The culmination of these basic divisions, it will presently be seen, appears in the thought of Kierkegaard and Marx. But the basic pattern also provides the proper context for the consideration of the intervening movements, schools, and personalities.

3. The Hegelian Center

Although we have spoken heretofore chiefly of the "right" and the "left," the consideration of the pattern of the dissolution of Hegelianism ought correctly to begin with the "center," for aesthetic reasons if no other. A Hegelian "center" really did exist with as legitimate a claim to recognition as "right" or "left." The Hegelian center stood for the integrity of the Hegelian system. It was equally opposed to any conservatism of doctrine apart from method and to any employment of the method without commitment to the received Hegelian doctrine. It stood for the *whole* Hegel.

Perhaps the most important figure of the center was J. K. F. Rosenkranz (1805–1879). He was both the editor of Hegel's works and a firm apologist for all aspects of Hegel's thought. The most bellicose of the exponents of the Hegelian center, however, was Karl Ludwig Michelet (1801–1893), professor of philosophy at the University of Berlin and author of two portentous and solemn tomes: *Hegel, der unwiderlegte Weltphilosoph* [Hegel, the unrefuted universal philosopher], 1870, and *Das System der Philosophie als exakte Wissenschaft* [System of philosophy as exact science], 1876–1881. Many of the members of the center were installed in chairs of philosophy in German universities, and from this position of vantage continued to produce, in writings and in lectures, solid expositions of the master's thought with little advertence to the challenges from various sectors of the world of culture. They will eventually be of importance again in the history of philosophy, for in the revival of Hegelian thought toward the end of the century, their works became the sources from which the knowledge of Hegel was drawn.

4. The Hegelian Right

Historians have more than once referred to the Hegelian right as "Hegelian scholasticism." This phrase has been given various meanings by various authors. Hegel thought that his philosophy offered a complete justification, in speculative terms, of the beliefs of Christianity (in their Lutheran form). The Hegelians of the right employed the Hegelian system in the same manner that the medievals had employed Aristotle and the seventeenth-century apologists had employed Cartesianism —that is, to establish the doctrines of Christianity on speculative grounds. This current was of the utmost importance, not only in Germany, but throughout western culture, for Protestant theology during the nineteenth century, wherever it took systematic form, was Hegelian in the rightist sense. It should be pointed out that the "liberal" wings of Catholic theology in the same period drew heavily on the same inspiration, culminating in the case of "modernism"; also, the revival, within Catholicism, of classical scholasticism in the figure of St. Thomas Aquinas was inspired, at least in part, as a reaction against the dominance of rightist Hegelianism. Under another aspect, it is the Hegelian left which strongly influenced Catholic modernism.

The religious membership of the Hegelian right was numerous.

Karl Friedrich Göschel (1784–1862) set the pattern in a work which had been praised by Hegel himself, *Aphorismen über Nichtwissen und absolutes Wissen* [Aphorisms on non-knowledge and on absolute knowledge], 1829, in which he maintained that a speculative justification of the supernatural could be achieved only in Hegelian terms. He maintains a similar position in an essay on the immortality of the soul. The right Hegelians emphasized this theme in response to the denial of immortality by Feuerbach, of the Hegelian left. In the controversy which developed, Friedrich Richter, Kasimir Conradi, and others took an active part, for and against the possibility of proving this fundamental Christian notion on Hegelian grounds. The periodical *Beiträge zur spekulativen Theologie* [Review of speculative theology] was founded by Bruno Bauer (1809–1882), later of the Hegelian left, probably partly in answer to the *Leben Jesu* (1835) of the left Hegelian David Strauss. During the three years of its publication this review enjoyed the collaboration of the most representative members of the Hegelian right and those most committed to the theory of the strict concordance of Christian doctrine and Hegelian philosophy: Göschel, Erdmann, Conradi, and Gabler.

The Hegelian right also defended the political theory of Hegel, the theory of the ethical state. This defense proved somewhat weaker than its defense of Hegel as the support of Christian theological orthodoxy and suffered from the attacks of Marx and others. The concept of the organic and ethical state was, however, a powerful one with considerable resilience and later found fresh expression in the political theory of the neo-Hegelians.

The Hegelian right produced a strong school of historians of philosophy, counting among them some whose works are still standard reference items of the field: Eduard Zeller (1814–1908), in Greek philosophy; the historian of modern philosophy Kuno Fischer (1824–1907); the historian of logic Karl Prantl (1820–1888); and, the most famous and enduring of all, J. E. Erdmann (1805–1892). Erdmann also produced theoretical works devoted to such problems as body and soul, creation, nature, faith and knowledge, all in the direct speculative line of right Hegelianism.

5. The Hegelian Left

From left Hegelianism flowed most of the dynamic philosophical, theological, and political currents of the second half of the nineteenth century. Friedrich Engels, co-developer with Karl Marx of the doctrine of historical and dialectical materialism, in his essay on Ludwig Feuerbach and the end of classical German philosophy, put his finger on the point which really distinguishes the right Hegelians from the left, or "Young," Hegelians. Hegelianism, considered as a *system*, as a body of doctrines, was static and conservative. However, Hegelianism considered as a method—that is, the dialectic—was revolutionary. Logically, that method implied a conception of philosophy and of reality, not as a body of fixed doctrines, but as a process. This process made it impossible to conceive any truth as final or absolute; it also made it impossible to consider any state of being, any social order, etc., as definitive and not subject to revision. The essence of left Hegelianism was the exploitation of this distinction: the rejection of the system of Hegel for the method of Hegel and the application of this method to every dimension of culture, even philosophy itself. But it is not correct to assign Engels the entire credit for perceiving this distinction. Even before him, the inner contradiction, or at least incommensuration, of Hegel's thought and the option which the "Young Hegelians" had made within it was expressed by one of themselves, Moses Hess (1812–1875), a member of the liberal opposition in Prussia under Friedrich the Fourth. Hess wrote: "It is the human spirit itself which engenders so-called truths. . . . All truths are but forms of the absolute spirit. They have nothing definitive about them; the spirit is always producing fresh truths. The future is the *only principle of all philosophy.*"

Nevertheless, it was to the past that the Young Hegelians first applied the method of Hegel. Specifically, they applied it to the history of Christianity. They maintained that Christianity, which had advanced itself as a pure system of revealed dogma, entirely immune to change and possessing an absolute sovereignty over the human intelligence, proved, upon closer investigation, to be itself a historical product of human consciousness. It could be correctly understood only as such; to transform it into a system of absolute dogmas distorted its historical truth and prevented it from developing its historical potentialities in succeeding ages, especially in the present age. This was the common thesis of such writers as D. F. Strauss (1808–1874), Bruno Bauer (formerly of the Hegelian right), and Ludwig Feuerbach. The publication, in 1835, of Strauss's work *Leben Jesu* signals the first appearance of the division between Hegelian right and Hegelian left. Strauss's viewpoint in this work is typical of that of all the Young Hegelians regarding the origin of Christianity, the criticism of its sources, and its historical possibilities of development.

Strauss takes up the point which Hess noted in the passage quoted above: Truths are creations of the human spirit and are relative to its needs. This is transposed into the realm of religion and made the clue to the interpretation of the life and teaching of the founder of Christianity. This is the *humanism* to which more explicit reference will be made in the consideration of Feuerbach. To take the gospel narrative of the life of Jesus as simple historical fact not only violates the norms of historiography but robs that gospel account—and the figure of Jesus—of its religious meaning. Religion, Strauss avers, carries the same burden of truth as philosophy, but it carries it under a different form: that of myth. While myth, for the eighteenth-century Enlightenment, for example, was essentially mendacious, for Strauss myth is essentially veridical. The life of Jesus carries profound truths for the religious consciousness of man; it carries them, however, not in the form of historical fact or philosophical proposition, but in a form proper to itself, myth. The myth is a metaphysical idea expressed in the form of an imaginary or fantastic recountal. As such, it has both a negative and a positive aspect: negative, in that it is not to be considered historical fact, though the form of its expression is historical; positive, in that it is the expression, in the conditions proper to a particular people in a particular historical situation, of a basic need of human nature. The essential character of religion is that it expresses its truths under the form of myth. So essential is myth to religion that in any particular religion all that cannot be recognized as myth must be either history or philosophy and not religion.

The story of the life of Christ is an imaginary recountal, a form under which the specific insights of Christianity are narrated; it is the Christian myth in its purity. That is why Christianity is entirely and wholly the religion of Jesus. But Strauss sees such questions as whether Jesus lived, in a historical sense, as entirely irrelevant. The principles of historical criticism make it necessary to answer such a question negatively, leading people erroneously to question the *truth* of that narrative. The truth of the Christian myth is independent of that historical contingency. To understand Christianity it is necessary to penetrate to the metaphysical truth which is expressed in that mythical form. Since that mythical form is the product of the human imagination at a specific period of its history under specific historical conditions, it is equally a mistake to view the mythical form of expression as exhausting the truth which it conveys. With the movement of history, the human imagination does not lose its power to envelop in myths the truths of religion rooted in the needs of human nature. To appreciate the truth of the Christian message it is not only possible but necessary to find new expressions of it according to the situation of man in successive historical periods. This is *not* to question the truth of Christianity as it appears in the gospel narrative in the person of Jesus, but it is absolutely necessary that the truth of which Jesus was the bearer be re-expressed in terms proper to each new age. Otherwise, a genuine religious skepticism toward that truth will emerge, for no man and no age can believe in another's myth.

What is here said of the life of Christ applies to all of the ostensible "dogmas" of Christianity. It is an error to take them as philosophical propositions, subject to the same critical principles as any philosophical propositions. These dogmas are comprehensible only when their mythical character is grasped, when they are released from the iron shroud of logic in which the dogmatic mentality encases them and are seen for what they are.

Strauss's ideas, which the other Young Hegelians shared, have had a long life; they have reappeared in a variety of forms during the succeeding century and are by no means dead today, in this age of dialectical and existential theology.

The Young Hegelians did not restrict the application of dialectical criticism to religion. They applied it to the field of politics also. They were at first sympathetic to the state system of Prussia; they saw it as a possible instrument for a policy which would transcend the limits of nationalism. However, the policy of Friedrich Wilhelm IV sorely disillusioned them, and they soon sought another fulcrum for their anti-nationalism. They directed the same skepticism toward the absoluteness of the Prussian state that they had directed toward the dogmatic form of Christianity. No political system could claim to be absolute. Every such system expresses the particular configuration of forces and interests, ideas and sentiments, of a particular people at a particular time in their history. The essence of politics is service to a given human need, and this need can be served through different forms of political organization. In looking for a positive fulcrum upon which to rest this criticism of Prussian absolutism, the Young Hegelians found a congenial body of doctrines and attitudes in communism and socialism as these were developing in France. It is at this point that Marx, who will carry the social dimension of left Hegelianism to its most extreme form, emerges to take a central position among the Young Hegelians. It was he who wrote, expressing a persuasion shared by the Young Hegelians, that the only hope for the future of Europe lay in the close union of German philosophy and socialism as it was developing in France. But before a just appreciation of Marx's thought in its Young-Hegelian phase can be formed, it is necessary to consider in somewhat more detail the thought of the member of this movement who seems to have most influenced him.

E. *Ludwig Feuerbach* (1804–1872)

Feuerbach was born at Landshut. He studied theology at Heidelberg and followed Hegel's lectures in philosophy at Berlin. He emerged as one of the most prominent and influential of the Young Hegelians. Feuerbach always remained a theologian and a Hegelian, in the sense that for him the religious problem was always central and the Hegelian philosophy, even when he had moved as far from it in intent as seemed possible, remained the frame of reference for all his speculation. He must be credited with an achievement for which Marx is frequently given the credit: the complete inversion of Hegelianism from a form of spiritualism to a form of naturalistic humanism. Feuerbach's most important works include: *Gedanken eines Denkers über Tod und Unsterblichkeit* [Thoughts of a thinker on death and immortality], 1830; *Das Wesen des Christentums (The Essence of Christianity)*, 1840; *Vorlesungen über das Wesen der Religion (Lectures on the Essence of Religion)*, 1851; *Philosophie und Christentum* [Philosophy and Christianity], 1859; and *Theogonie* [Theogony], published posthumously.

Feuerbach was the most acute, systematic and technical critic of the Hegelian system among the Young Hegelians. He attacked the system at its weakest point: the status of "nature," the "objective" moment of spirit. According to Hegel's doctrine, this moment was a moment of negation and alienation for spirit, a moment which had to be transcended and reassimilated to spirit before its rationality could become apparent. It remained dubious whether, even on his own principles, he could explain unambiguously the necessity under which spirit lay to project this moment of nature.

At this point Feuerbach performs the feat of inverting the Hegelian system. Rejecting the notion that nature is the product of spirit, a moment of its self-alienation, he reasserts (for this assertion is part of the classical patrimony of western philosophy) the primacy of nature. He recognizes spirit as only a manifestation of nature, which comes to self-awareness and the spiritual stage only in man's consciousness. This would seem to be the essence of Feuerbach's humanism: that man is the moment of consciousness of spirit in nature. This does not, of course, involve any disvaluation of spirit or any skepticism toward it. On the contrary, as the last and highest self-manifestation of nature, spirit, finding expression in man, remains the supreme value of the system.

At this point an ambiguity invades the thought of Feuerbach which proves no less destructive of its coherence than did the Hegelian ambiguity toward nature. How does man, as spirit, form a merely natural being in Feuerbach's view? Primarily by the power of thought, through which he is capable of conceiving infinite and transcendent beings. But this capacity is no guarantee of the existence or reality of those entities which the spirit in man can conceive. In other words, the highest activity of human consciousness is, for Feuerbach, essentially self-deceiving. His entire speculative system—above all, his criticism of religion in general and of Christianity in particular—rests on this ambiguity. The Marxian system, insofar as one can speak of a Marxian *system,* rests directly upon the acceptance of this same ambiguous point in the thought of Feuerbach.

The gods whom man worships are projected as real transcendent beings and superior to man in all the attributes assigned to them. In fact they are the creatures of man's thought, if not merely of his imagination. They have no reality or meaning as transcendent, existing entities. They have meaning only in terms of the human needs, fears, and aspirations of which they are born and which they express in hyperbolic tropes. This line of thought does not lead Feuerbach to take a skeptical view of religion. Religion remains for him a basic form of presence. However, it must be read, not outwardly, in terms of some transcendent, supernatural order to which man is subject, but inwardly, as revealing, more than any other mode of his presence and expression can, man's authentic mode of being, which, if not expressed in this way, would remain hidden even from himself. The religions of man are not to be dismissed or rejected; they are to be studied and understood as the supreme roads to man's self-understanding.

Feuerbach calls himself an atheist; there is no reason to deny him this appellation. His atheism, however, is not the simple negation of the existence of those transcendent beings in which man expresses his deepest desires. Atheism is for Feuerbach the highest moment of man's self-knowledge. It is the state in which man achieves at once the consciousness of his limitation and of his power. His limitation is his immersion in nature, from which he cannot, even by the exercise of his highest "spiritual" powers, extricate himself. His power is his capacity, through this very knowledge of his immanence to nature, to free himself from the shadow of the transcendent and take its attributes upon himself.

Feuerbach's criticism of Christianity lies within this framework of the general anthropology of religion. He contrasts a false and a true interpretation of Christianity. The false is precisely what the right Hegelians were trying to erect, an interpretation in which Christianity is "justified" by being made to seem conformable with the principles of the Hegelian philosophy. The true interpretation is his own, in which Christianity is understood as revealing the highest authenticity of man, the pure form of his aspirations and desires. Interpreted in the latter way, he needs to reject little of the ethical side of Christianity. What he rejects is the theological apparatus within which this pure ethical vision has become obscured. Christianity reveals its meaning and truth only when it is understood as a pure humanism.

On this same naturalistic and humanistic basis, Feuerbach developed a sense-theory of knowledge. This doctrine exhibits marked opposition to Hegel at many points, but it is not a rejection of the fundamental Hegelian rationalism. The work of reason, according to this doctrine, is to order what the senses offer. Without the senses or without the ordering reason there is no true knowledge. Within this theory, Feuerbach seemed to be moving, in his last phase, toward a materialism of the extreme type exemplified by such thinkers as Moleschott.

The vast influence of Feuerbach, however, does not rest on either this theory of knowledge or the materialism toward which it seemed to lead him. It rested on his criticism of dogmatic religion and on the vision of the human future which his naturalistic humanism seemed to open.

Readings

I. GENERAL

Dupré, Louis K. *The Philosophical Foundations of Marxism*. New York: Harcourt, Brace, & World, 1966.

Hook, Sidney. *From Hegel to Marx*. New York: Reynal & Hitchcock, 1936.

Löwith, Karl. *From Hegel to Nietzsche: The Revolution in Nineteenth Century Thought*. Translated by D. Green. New York: Holt, Rinehart & Winston, 1964.

McLellan, David. *The Young Hegelians and Karl Marx*. London: Macmillan, 1969.

Marcuse, Herbert. *Reason and Revolution*. 2nd ed. New York: Humanities Press, 1963.

Schweitzer, Albert. *The Quest of the Historical Jesus*. Translated by W. Montgomery. 3rd ed. New York: Macmillan, 1956.

II. PARTICULAR FIGURES

Berlin, I. *Life and Opinions of Moses Hess*. London: W. Heffer, 1959.

Brandt, F. B. *Friedrich Eduard Beneke: The Man and His Philosophy*. New York: Macmillan, 1895.

Chamberlain, W. B. *Heaven Wasn't His Destination: The Philosophy of Ludwig Feuerbach*. London: Allen & Unwin, 1941.

Copleston, Frederick C. *Arthur Schopenhauer: Philosopher of Pessimism*. London: Burns & Oates, 1946.

DeGarmo, Charles. *Herbart and the Herbartians*. New York: Scribner, 1895.

Delfgaauw, Bernard. *The Young Marx*. Translated by Franklin Schütz and Martin Redfern. Westminster, Md.: Newman Press, 1967.

Dunkel, Harold B. *Herbart and Education*. New York: Random House, 1969.

Engels, F. *Ludwig Feuerbach and the Outcome of Classical German Philosophy*. New York: International Publishers, 1934.

Gardiner, Patrick. *Schopenhauer*. Baltimore: Penguin Books, 1963.

Knox, Israel. *The Aesthetic Theories of Kant, Hegel and Schopenhauer*. New York: Humanities Press, 1958.

McCoy, C. "Ludwig Feuerbach and the Formation of Marxian Revolutionary Ideas." *Laval Thelogique et Philosophique*, VII (1951), 218–248.

McGill, V. J. *Schopenhauer: Pessimist and Pagan*. New York: Bretano's, 1931.

Marx, Karl, and Engels, Frederich. *The Holy Family*. Translated by R. Dixon. Moscow: Foreign Languages Publishing House, 1956.

Marx, Karl. *A World Without Jews*. Translated by Dagobert Runes. New York: Philosophical Library, 1959.

CHAPTER VI

Marx and Kierkegaard

Introduction

Karl Marx and Søren Kierkegaard are not ordinarily found in the close conjunction in which they are placed in this chapter. Therefore, some explanation seems to be in order. That explanation is simple: It is the correct historical relation. This historical relation has become somewhat blurred by the fortune, in subsequent periods, of each. Since the present preoccupation is historical, it is necessary to restore it.

Karl Marx emerged as one of the greatest, if not the greatest, social theorist of the second half of the nineteenth century. His social thought became the basis of international communism and underwent those ideological metamorphoses, at the hands of the Russian revolutionary social thinkers and of western gradualistic socialists, which are a matter of record in the history of social thought. Finally, the alleged doctrine of Karl Marx became canonized in the ideology of Soviet communism, the complex "Marx-Leninism" (today one must add Maoism) which constitutes the dogmatic element in the Soviet secular religion of the state. In this process the original Marx, the Marx of history, has been obscured. Nevertheless, Karl Marx as a philosopher remains a figure of direct interest for the history of philosophy, with a valid claim on the attention of anyone who would understand the history of nineteenth-century thought.

The developments—or better, metamorphoses—of Marx's thought begin almost immediately with his appearance on the historical scene and form a substantial part of the history of social thought. By contrast, the philosophical and theological works of Søren Kierkegaard excited little immediate interest. For a long time they remained dormant, without effect upon the central development of ideas. Only when the twentieth century was already well advanced did a wave of interest in his thought emerge as part of that larger movement ambiguously called "existentialism." Moreover, when this interest in Kierkegaard began to develop, it was not historically inspired; its basic concern was not to see Kierkegaard in his historical context. This was subordinated to other interests, primarily those centering about theological movements in the Protestant churches. This interest in Kierkegaard's thought and the use made of it were, of course, entirely legitimate. Nevertheless, part of the effect was to blur the outlines of his proper place in the history of philosophy, a place which is of considerable interest.

When this historical concern dominates, the link between Marx and Kierkegaard, thinkers ostensibly so diverse, becomes clearer. Kierkegaard and Marx represent, respectively, the extreme developments of the critical movement of the Hegelian left along the two lines of its chief concern, religion and socio-political thought. Consequently, from the historical point of view, they are related both by a principle of community and a principle of complementarity. The principle of community places both of them within the context of the Hegelian left. The principle of complementarity points to them as contributors of complementary elements of the developing thematic of the Hegelian left.

Yet it would not be entirely correct to treat them exclusively in this fashion, that is, solely as representatives of a movement or trend. Neither would it be entirely correct to suggest that this historical link exhausts the relation between them. Neither Marx nor Kierkegaard is a thinker who is *merely* representative. Each exhibits a strong speculative personality which lifts him above the mean level of the historical current to which he belongs, and in each that current finds an expression and development which endows it with an entirely new dimension and significance. The Hegelian left becomes articulate in them to a degree that it achieves in no others; they, in turn, develop this basic movement in a manner which reveals, in an entirely original manner, its possibilities and even its fatalities.

It has been suggested that there is another, more profound bond which unites Marx and Kierkegaard, or at least relates them in a manner more significant than any historical conjunctions. This bond is the primary theme of all their speculations: *man*. When they are treated from the philosophical point of view, it becomes clear that Marx and Kierkegaard have a common concern for man and the human situation. The fact that the development which each gives to this theme sets them in sharp contrast does not alter this situation. On the contrary, this contrast itself tends to heighten the significance of their thought. It reveals the alternatives concerning the nature of man which were possible for the thought of the nineteenth century; thus, it establishes a basic element in the pattern of its historical unfolding. But beyond all this, the preoccupation with this common theme establishes another direct relation between these thinkers. Together with a third, Nietzsche, they emerge as the great moralists of that century; not in the superficial sense of the study of conduct, but in the profound sense of probing without mercy the most elemental sources of man's situation and prospects, in history and beyond.

A. Karl Marx (1818–1883)

The period of Karl Marx's philosophical activity—or, more precisely, his activity which might be recognized as philosophical by conventional norms—was brief. Different dates are assigned to this period. Some authors restrict it to the decade of the forties; others extend it to the publication of the *Critique of Political Economy* in 1859. After that date, it is sometimes suggested, he abandoned philosophy for economics and social thought and for revolutionary activity. The superficiality of this view reveals itself very quickly, however, when Marx's career is looked upon as a whole. Then it becomes clear that he abandoned none of his philosophical concern in his later activity but that that activity is related to, and intelligible only in the light of, the principles he had established in the period of more formal philosophical activity. This is especially true regarding the principle of the relation of thought and action, or theory and practice, which involves in its turn the transformation of the classical image of the philosopher, realized so completely in Hegel, into the figure of the revolutionary, the philosophical revolutionary, the man who not only contemplates the world but changes it.

Marx completed his philosophical studies at Berlin some ten years after Hegel had ceased to "reign" there but while his spirit was still dominant, either directly, as in the Hegelians of the right, or as an ambivalent, father-antagonist image, as in the case of the left or "Young" Hegelians. The subject of his thesis for the doctorate, the difference between the philosophy of nature of Democritus and that of Epicurus, is thought by some to be of interest for an understanding of the historical and dialectical materialism with which his name will become associated. On completion of his studies he became a journalist, first as editor of the *Rheinische Zeitung* (1842–43), and later, after having to leave Germany because of his political views, as an editor, with Ruge in Paris, of the *Deutsch-Französische Jahrbücher* (1844). The latter publication contributed to the exchange of ideas between the Young Hegelians and French socialism and communism, an exchange of special importance in the case of Marx.

In 1843 he published his first substantial philosophical work: *Aus der Kritik der Hegelschen Rechtsphilosophie* (Kritik der Hegelschen

Staatsrecht) [Critique of the Hegelian philosophy of law], an introductory form of which appeared in the *Deutsch-Französische Jahrbücher* (1844). In 1844, in Paris, he met Friedrich Engels and entered into the collaboration which was to continue until Marx's death. Its first result appeared the following year: *Die heilige Familie* (*The Holy Family*). This work reorders Marx's relations to the other Young Hegelians; from this point he passes rapidly beyond their positions. Forced once more to emigrate because of his political ideas, he went from Paris to Brussels. Here he published, in French: *La misère de la philosophie: response à la philosophie de la misère* (*The Poverty of Philosophy*). While in Brussels he also wrote: *Manifest der kommunistischen Partei* (*The Communist Manifesto*), which was published in London in 1848. From Brussels Marx returned first to Paris and then to Cologne. In the latter city he established the *Neue Rheinische Zeitung*, which was short-lived. Again, by way of Paris, he moved to London, where he settled for the rest of his life, becoming a fixture of the reading room of the British Museum, where his favorite chair is still pointed out.

The order of the composition of his philosophically important works is not the same as their order of publication. Thus the important *Thesen über Feuerbach* (*Theses on Feuerbach*) were composed in Brussels in 1845 but not published until 1888 when Engels used them as an appendix to his own work on that philosopher. *Die deutsche Ideologie* (*The German Ideology*) was composed in Brussels in 1846 but not published until 1933 in Moscow. The *Ökonomisch-Philosophische Manuskripte aus dem Jahre 1844* (*Economic and Philosophical Manuscripts of 1844*) had a similar career. The important *Zur Kritik der politischen Ökonomie* (*A Contribution to the Critique of Political Economy*) appeared in 1859, the same year as Darwin's *Origin of Species,* and the first volume of *Das Kapital* in 1867; the second and third volumes, edited by Engels, appeared respectively in 1885 and 1894. The philosophical significance of this last work is no longer in question. Indeed, as its strictly economic relevance lessens, its philosophical interest increases. It is now recognized as a study in the alienation and liberation of man and thus is central to modern philosophical anthropology.

Any manner of presenting the thought of Karl Marx is open to criticism almost before the fact; he was a volcanic and titanic thinker, whose thoughts followed a highly individual pattern of formation and expression. The most basic feature of Marx, however, is his polemical character; all of his ideas were forged in the white heat of controversy. This provides a key to a possible ordering of his ideas in a brief presentation. We shall first try to establish the basic

lines of polemic within which his ideas take form and then move to
a presentation of what we may call his constructive ideas. This
second phase will have difficulties of its own, but a certain order may
be induced by a strict adherence to the *philosophical relevance* of
his ideas. When this point of view is followed, Marx appears as fundamentally a philosophical anthropologist, whose basic and constant
problem is *man;* and as a moralist rather than a pure humanist, for
the basic categories in which he perceives and projects the being of
man are normative (as distinct from value-neutral) categories. Super-
imposed on this basis are the particular doctrines in which he formulates the vision of man and of society with which his thought is directly
identified when the chief concern is to indicate *what* he taught rather
than to determine the problems and questions to which his doctrine
or substantive propositions (for example, his atheism and his political
anarchism) are replies.

More than one critic has undertaken the task of discovering a
basic and inclusive formula for the structure of Marx's thought. Among
the many offered, the following seems to bear up well under reference
to the documents: Marx accepts the Hegelian formula of the *unity of
the rational and the real* but only after having accepted and put to his
own use Feuerbach's criticism of the manner in which this unity had
been conceived by Hegel. The return to Hegel, after the acceptance
of Feuerbach's critique, in itself constitutes a critique of Feuerbach.
Within this formula the polemical patterns and the constructive patterns of Marx's thought appear with relative lucidity.

1. The Polemical Posture of Marx

Marx's polemical thought ultimately resolves itself into one problem: What is the nature of philosophy? His answer to this question
determines his own status as a philosopher and is the key to his
thought. At the same time, this response relates him, both positively and
negatively, to the philosophers who influenced him most directly
and extensively, Hegel and Feuerbach. The direction of this polemic
and his own attitude toward philosophy is expressed in these words:
"The philosophers have only interpreted the world in various ways;
the point, however, is to change it" (*Theses on Feuerbach*, Thesis 11,
in Marx and Engels, *Selected Works* [Moscow, 1955], Vol. II, p. 404).
While this formulation may seem to phrase the matter too smoothly
in terms of a simple inversion, the proper interpretation of this
statement does yield Marx's basic insight into philosophy and, by
way of this, into man.

What had Hegel conceived philosophy to be? It has been noted that Marx both accepted and rejected the Hegelian notion, or, more properly, came to accept it only after he had screened it through the criticism advanced against it by Feuerbach. The nub of the entire process for Marx is the idea of *pure thought.* Hegel was the philosopher of "pure thought" *par excellence;* for him pure thought and philosophy are one and the same. But Hegel is also the philosopher who creates, in the body of his own thought, the principles which refute this notion of philosophy and open the avenue to the notion of philosophy which Marx will accept.

What then is included under this rubric of "pure thought"? It is, in the first instance, thought which is alien from action, which does not express itself in action, and which is not tested by the demands of action. It is, in this sense, "contemplation," the viewing of a reality which is already fixed and established in all its basic characteristics and over which thought has no formative or trans-formative powers, but only informative or reportative ones. The world which is thus given and fixed in character is the world of appearances, the empirical world of phenomena, as present to the passive human subject. Pure thought limits itself to the quest of that *reason* (determining, explanatory principle) of which the phenom-enal world is the appearance and ends in the discovery that the phenomenon is the necessary expression, the "essential manifestation" of that reason. The bond of fixedness is thus strengthened twofold, the determination of the phenomena to reason and the necessary expression of reason in this (and no other) order of phenomena. Pure thought is essentially contemplative, and, viewed from the point of human existence, conservative: What is, *is* indeed, *must* be. Philosophy can only explicate this complex of necessity; it cannot create or transform the real. What *is,* in this necessary sense, is the measure of truth and departure from this is error. This is the root of that conservativism which Marx, together with the left Hegelians, discovers in Hegel; and it has a far deeper root than any mere adherence to the status quo in religion, politics, or social life.

What is the function of human thought in this world of pure thought? And what is the status of human action? Obviously, human thought, when it is true, merely mirrors that order of fixed reality; hence, the classical definition of truth itself: "conformity of the mind to the thing" (*conformitas mentis cum re*). What is the status of man's action? Human action is obviously illusory for it can have no *effective consequence.* Any alteration which his action might initiate must be in the way of a deformation; consequently, its value is purely negative. This is the root of *alienation* as Marx will interpret it. The world of pure thought is alien to man; it is not his world but another which he merely contemplates. Even more, his very thought and his very action are not his, since the measure of his thought, its truth, is in another and the measure of his action is in another. Hegelianism as pure thought accepts this alienation in its theory of the "Idea"; for the Idea, though it may find expression in the thought of men, and action in their wills, is always "another," working in and through them but not properly their own. The Idea is an immanent transcendence, an indwelling *other*, which merely makes alienation more profound since the stranger is within the house.

The notion of philosophy in this context of "pure thought" seems the most self-depreciating notion conceivable. Philosophy is confirmation in alienation. It is, in Marx's vulgar phrase, "cosmic onanism."

Marx first became aware of these defects in the Hegelian conception of philosophy through the criticisms advanced against it by Feuerbach. These criticisms have been noted in brief form; together they constitute the celebrated "humanism" of Feuerbach. The salient point in this criticism consists in a great inversion of the order of "pure thought." Now the world, the order of phenomena, God, the world of nature, the ethical and social orders, which for pure thought were *fixed* and *other*, are made entirely relative to the human subject; they are projections corresponding to his inward and constitutive needs and necessities. They are to be read inwardly, with reference back upon human nature, which the conformations of those projections reveal more completely and truly than any process of introspection. With this humanism, Marx is essentially in agreement, insofar as it seems to give human thought and human action reality and effectiveness, since such thought and action seemingly *account for the world*. Hence, it would seem that man is not alienated in the world of Feuerbach.

But this is only seeming, as Marx, turning his critical powers upon Feuerbach, discovers. Man, in Feuerbach, is as alienated as the subject of "pure thought" in Hegel. The world which man projects as the expression of his needs and his nature is an illusory world. This is the whole gist of Feuerbach's bitter criticism of religion. He sees religion as an illusory projection, in the figure of God, of what man himself aspires to become. It is illusory by the strict fact that through this projection, in religion as we know it historically, man in no way realizes this aspiration; in no way becomes God, by projecting the idea of God; in no way secures justice, by the projection of the historical social order; in no way secures its rationality, by projecting the world of nature. On the contrary, by these projections, man is fixed in a state of alienation more radical than that to which he fell victim in the world of pure thought; for in the world of Feuerbach there is no necessitating principle to relate man and that projected world. That entire projection cannot escape being, self-deception. The humanism of Feuerbach, by which is meant his attempt to assign to man an effective and active relation to being, does not achieve its purpose.

Marx perceives this. Thus, while accepting the humanistic effort of Feuerbach as a critical instrument against the pure thought of Hegel, he finds it necessary to extricate himself from Feuerbach. His intention may now be stated in these terms: to establish an authentic humanism which would really achieve what Feuerbach's pretends to achieve but does not. Ironically (given his criticism of Hegel), this drives him back upon the resources of the Hegelian system. Having used Feuerbach to reduce the pure thought of Hegel, he must now use Hegel to achieve effectively what Feuerbach had ineffectually attempted.

At this point, Marx again reveals his relation to left Hegelianism. He now has recourse to a distinction within Hegelianism which, as has been seen, was characteristic of left Hegelianism, the distinction between the conservative and the revolutionary elements in Hegelianism, between pure thought and the dialectic. Hegel had created the dialectic as the instrument of "pure thought"; further, he had defined it as the inner law of "pure thought." In Marx's view, he had sought to make a revolutionary principle and process into a supporting principle of a world "made and given" to man's passive and impotent contemplation. He had sought to make a principle for the liberation of man from alienation into a principle which would confirm him in that situation. Marx seeks to release the dialectical principle in Hegelianism for the constructive purpose of thought and action.

In this he indicates his affinity with the Young Hegelians, but again he rejects their procedure. Their employment of the dialectic is both ineffective and purely negative. This is the burden of his polemic against Bruno Bauer. He agrees fundamentally with them that the dialectic is a principle which might really define philosophy and make it effective as a human enterprise. His own efforts as a philosopher may be said to be contained entirely in the realization of this potential of the Hegelian dialectic.

With the critique of the Hegelian dialectic, its rescue from mis-employment, and its release for the constructive work of philosophy, the polemical phase of Marx's thought passes into its constructive phase. His criticism and correction of the Hegelian dialectic are revealed completely only in the positive restatement and positive employment of it which constitute his own philosophy. For this reason, it would be erroneous to deal with the Marxian revision of the Hegelian dialectic as belonging only to the polemical phase of Marx's thought; it is, on the contrary, the basis of his constructive thought.

2. The Constructive Phase of Marxian Philosophy

The revision of the Hegelian dialectic is the first stage in Karl Marx's constructive philosophical enterprise. In what did this revision consist? In the first place, it consists in making the dialectic a *concrete,* as distinct from an *abstract,* process. In his revision of the dialectic, Marx is threading his way warily between two abstractions, the Hegelian and the Feuerbachian. The Hegelian abstraction resided in the conception of the dialectic as the process of the Idea, of "pure thought." This pure thought, as has been noted, was entirely passive before reality; it only mirrored the world as given and could not determine it in its necessary principles. The Spirit and the Absolute cannot be the real and concrete subjects of the dialectic. The stages through which the Spirit or the Absolute is presented as passing in Hegel's thought—estrangement, mediation, synthesis—are abstract moments of an abstract movement which is without results in the order of the real. The pretended revision of the Hegelian dialectic by Feuerbach results in a second kind of abstraction. Feuerbach had made the whole order of the ideal simply a reflection of man, of his needs and aspirations, of what he called "human nature." This human nature is not, however, the reality of concrete, historically existing men, but an abstract principle common, presumably, to all men. Feuerbach's is an abstract humanism, involving not actually existing human subjects but an abstract "human nature," fixed and determined in all its aspects and presumably realized in every single human being. By this nature, the concrete, existing human being is placed in a state of alienation from himself that is strictly analogous to that which Marx has discovered in Hegelianism. The dialectic is, indeed, the form of the real for Marx and the only form under which man can understand reality; but it is the form of actually existing human subjectivity and not of the abstract Idea or an equally abstract human nature.

In the second place, the Marxian revision of the Hegelian dialectic consists in giving the dialectic an unambiguous existential locus. This locus is man himself in his concrete, existent, historical character. The dialectic is not the form of a reality extrinsic to man, but the form of a reality which he himself, in the effort to generate his own being, produces. The dialectic is thus the point of contact and unity between thought and action, for the actually existing and operating man is neither disembodied thought, impotent of effective action, nor blind dynamism. He is a concrete agent for whom all thought is grounded in the necessity of acting, both transitively and intransitively, and all action, when rational and not spastic, is grounded in thought. The dialectic is thus the basic form of human presence, and the unity of thought and action describes the inner structure, or form, of existent, human, historical subjectivity.

This "localizing" of the dialectic also indicates for Marx the real character of philosophy. It is the very opposite of the sterile speculative "pure thought" of Hegelianism. Philosophy is human existence grasped by man as subject under its basic dimensions, as thought and action, in dialectical unity as productive of the real conditions of human reality. It is only through philosophy in this sense that a *human* reality can be brought into being. Therefore, all human activity is philosophy when that activity is brought to a certain degree of consciousness of its own conditions. Marx's entire system is philosophical in this sense, for he is concerned with bringing human consciousness to that point of awareness at which its real condition will appear, at which it can finally escape from the illusion generated by "pure thought" and the metaphysics of "human nature."

The third element in the Marxian revision of the Hegelian dialectic involves a morphological change. For Hegel, the dialectic of the Idea and of the Absolute was triadic: position, negation, synthesis. Hegel had placed the greatest emphasis on the moment of synthesis, since it is the moment in which the totality, and hence the rationality, of the real is vindicated. Marx, by contrast, places the greatest emphasis on the moment of negation. The dialectic appears for him most forcibly in the necessity of negation as the basis of all dialectical movement. Every moment of synthesis is tentative; its reality can only be tested by its negation, and any negation necessarily involves an alteration in that pretended synthesis. The dialectic is, therefore, not, a conciliatory movement for Marx, as it was for Hegel, but a revolutionary movement; its central moment is not a synthesis of opposites but an affirmation of negation in the face of all pretentedly absolute affirmations.

Marx accepts the dialectic, as thus revised, as the instrument of all thought and action, of human, historical existence.

3. Marx's Philosophical Anthropology

In his revision of Hegel's dialectic, Marx had placed a new emphasis on man as concretely existent and historically operative. The dialectic is not the abstract dialectic of the Absolute, but the dialectic of concrete human existence. It is necessary, consequently, in order that his thought might go forward, for Marx to bring this human character into focus and determine what man, thus existentially considered, *is*. In what does Marx find this basic and authentic character of man? He finds it in *work*.

The basic character of the human, as distinct from all other forms of existence, of "matter," is that it must *produce itself*. At every moment its whole activity is production of itself. Thus, finally, its authentic mode of being is production of self. This process of the self-establishing of being is the radical concept of *work* in Marx and the defining characteristic of man. So basic is this insight to the whole of Marx's thought that it generates the sole lyrical moment of his expression. In depicting this notion of work as the characterizing note of man, he approximates the mood of poetry. Work is not, as has been traditionally thought, a curse or a burden for man; work is what man *is*, his proper mode of being, without which he would not be. The term of work is not, in the final analysis, to produce something other than man, some object or product alien to him, but himself in his fully human character. Only work can release man from all constriction, can raise his mode of being to its highest level, can make him creative and free. At his highest, man works without concern for mere physical need; indeed, he works truly and produces only to the degree that his work is free from such concern. The animal produces things only according to the measure and the need of the species to which it belongs. "Man, however, knows how to produce according to the measure of all species and in everything he knows how to confer upon the object the correct measure and even to form it according to the laws of beauty" (*Economic and Philosophical Manuscripts of 1844*, trans. M. Milligan [New York, 1st American ed. 1964], Part I).

Finally, work is, according to Marx, the *only* manifestation of liberty and freedom for man; and the liberty thus manifested is not empty, like the freedom of man in the Hegelian view, but full and substantial. The activity and the product of work give freedom substance and plenitude. Marx refuses to speak of an infinite or indefinite freedom. Production is always limited and conditioned by material factors and by needs already developed. These conditions act as limiting factors at every stage in individual life and in history. These conditions are not external to man; they are internal to, and constitutive of, the individual. In the initial state, before the contradictions in the social system arise, the relations which exist among men are relations among concrete individuals (ideally); they derive directly from the individual and reflect and manifest him. These are the conditions which Marx depicts in his dual myth of initial communism and the terminal "classless" society.

Here it would be well to pause and note carefully the importance of this notion of work and its relation to the individual. The only alienation which is real and meaningful to Marx and which, when it appears in history, constitutes a heinous crime against man is the alienation which separates man from work, both work as the creative, self-establishing activity of his being and work in terms of its product. Between man and work there is an inalienable relation; indeed, in the case of work conceived as the self-creating activity, this relation is one of pure identity. To introduce any principle of alienation here is to destroy the very integrity of man, his integrity as a real being. Only when this is kept in mind can the analysis of capitalism, which Marx will eventually undertake, be fully comprehended. Only when this is kept in mind is it clear that Marx's basic concern is moral: a concern for the integrity of the human principle. His indignation against the capitalist system is a moral indignation which rests upon a basic conception of the character and integrity of the human existent; it is indignation against something which violates this integrity by introducing a state of destructive alienation.

The individual existent human being is thus central in the Marxian theory of man. At the same time, however, Marx emphasizes that man is a *social being*. For him there is no contradiction in these affirmations. On the contrary, the predicate "social being" belongs precisely and directly to the individual. "The individual is a social being," he affirms (*Economic and Philosophical Manuscripts of 1844*, Part III). The ground of this assertion is the Marxian insight that *work is social* and production is a social operation. Since work, in both its intransitive and its transitive aspects, is the very being of man, taken generically and individually, and since work, of its nature, is social, it follows that man, as he actually exists, as a concrete historically conditioned individual, is social.

A number of factors generate or establish this social character of work. The first of these factors is *nature*. By "nature" Marx seems to indicate the material factor which enters into all process of production, beginning with the production of the biological basis of human life. The generation of life within nature has a social basis, the matter out of which that life is generated. For though the biological organism achieves a certain kind of individuality, it always remains closely dependent on the natural and material sources of its being, and these are common to all life, to life at all levels, and to all individuals within the membership of any species. This generation of the biological organism of man, as the basis of all his other activities, is a pure example of work, since it is productive of the very physical being of man; it is also evidence of the social character of work, for the entire process is enveloped within a matrix common to all individual living things. Nature, as the basis of the social character of work, also illustrates another aspect of work, namely, its objectivity and the objectivity of its conditions. The social character of work, deriving from its basis in nature, is not dependent upon the reflective consciousness of man and is even less a product of it; it appears simultaneously with that work and with its product. This objectivity conditions work as well as the social relations it generates in human society.

The second basis of the social character of work is the fact that it requires the cooperation of other men for the human existent to become productive as an individual. This cooperation may be conscious and reflective in various degrees, but it is always present in work and production. It is as surely present when the activity of the individual is ostensibly private (for example, scientific and artistic work) as when it is overtly public and collective. Thus, all of the private productive operations of the individual are executed by means of instruments—language, science, etc.—which are social in character, both in the sense that they are socially produced and in the sense that they are without meaning and value when conceived individualistically. The highest and most explicit form of this social cooperation is the division of labor. The division of labor may take different forms; in one instance, it may be exploitative; in another, cooperative in the full sense of the term. The form it takes will determine basically the kind of society man has. In any case, the principle of the division of labor clearly establishes the social character of work.

Finally, work is always social in its product and end. This can be seen at the level of the production in nature of the individual members of the species. The individual is a social product in the sense, first of all, that in him culminate the common and collective productive operations of nature (i.e., in the order of sex), but also in the sense that he is produced in that order for the common or social being of his species, which he in turn continues. The circularity of this relation in the order of work between the individual and the social principle is clearly illustrated here. In the cooperative work of human individuals, the end of work is equally social. A private product is meaningless. Every product is brought into being specifically as a social value and can be considered genuinely a product only to the degree to which its social value is manifest. The self is a social concept and a social value in his very being, for he labors to create and establish himself, not under the aspect of his purely private character, but as a social value. This is even more explicitly determinable in respect to the transitive product of work; here the social character of the product, residing in its social value, is clearly manifest.

Society is only the objective aspect of this social character of man. It is the complex of relations into which men enter by the process of social work. At this point, it might be expected that Marx would undertake to define society in terms of an ideal set of such relations. Eventually he will, but not at this point. To try to do so at this point would involve a regression to the abstract philosophical process of the Hegelian or Feuerbachian type. Instead, Marx remains consistent with his notion of the dialectic as a concrete historical process. He recognizes that this dialectical character invests the productive process in its material elements. The material forces of production available to man undergo a process of development. This process is not of course, independent of the intervention of conscious human activity such as science, art, etc. On the contrary, the available material conditions of work and production involve and reflect at every step the degree of cultivation of the sciences, the technical arts, and even the aesthetic sensibilities. Marx sees the specific configuration of any society at any given moment in its history as the correlative of the degree of development of the material means of production. It is not to be thought, however, that a society is consciously formed in accord with the degree of development of the material forces of production. The society is, rather, their *expression*. He writes, "In the social production which men carry on, they enter into definite relations that are indispensable and independent of their will; these relations of production correspond to a definite stage of their material power of production" (*A Contribution to the Critique of Political Economy,* trans. N. I. Stone [Chicago, 1904], p. 11).

It might be convenient at this time to point out the relevance of this assertion for Marx's relation to the social thought of his time. He constantly opposed his own social thought to "utopian" social thought. The central point of this criticism of utopian social thought lay in this: utopian social thought imagined that a social order could be erected on ethical bases, with a certain independence of the state of the material forces of production. This seemed to him meaningless. How an ethical will could maintain a social order which was not the expression of the stage of development of the material forces of production was incomprehensible. Such a society would not be a society at all, but two societies at war with each other, and one would eventually have to prevail. The one which would eventually prevail, in his view, was precisely that which would express the stage of the development of the productive forces. An ethical system has no matter in which to express itself save in those relations which arise in correlation to the stage of material production; it has no normative force save in relation to them since the whole being of man is expressed and realized in the activity of production.

Despite this opposition to "utopian" social thought, Marx's thought is itself dominated by an ethical ideal. This will become more apparent when we speak of the "classless" society, which is incomprehensible save as the complete vindication of Marx's initial ethical insight that work is the pure form of man's self-creative freedom.

It is impossible at this point to resist the temptation to express, even at the risk of doing so abortively, some notion of what the ideal society would be for Marx. It does not seem that this ideal society ought to be expressed in the negative terminology of the "classless society." Rather, it would seem more precise to say that Marx has a vision of a point in the development of the material means of production at which a society would emerge organized upon the purely cooperative form of the division of labor. In it his complex interweaving of the individual and the social character of work would find complete expression. The free creative work of the individual would find full social realization, and the society would support the individual as the perfect expression of itself. To appreciate the force of this ideal, it is necessary to follow Marx through the critique of capitalist society by means of which he formulates it.

4. Alienation

The concept of "alienation," like the dialectic, is part of the Hegelian inheritance of Marx. Like the dialectic, moreover, it undergoes a reinterpretation at Marx's hands and in the same direction, that of concretion. Alienation as it appeared in Hegel seems to Marx to partake of that same abstract character which had invested the dialectic, but he considers the concept far from meaningless. On the contrary, he tends to give it a prime importance in his analysis, especially in the earlier and more philosophical phases of his thought; however, he accepts the concept only after it has undergone a process of concretion, of being made to refer to a moment in the concrete historical development of the relations of men in society.

In order to appreciate the transformation of this concept in Marx and the use he makes of it, we should perhaps fix more clearly the sense assigned it by Hegel. Hegel develops and employs this notion in the last pages of his *Phenomenology of the Spirit*. Here "alienation" is used to designate that process by which the Idea, which is self-consciousness, posits itself as *object to itself* and hence as *other to itself*, in order to return to itself by the process of mediation. This moment of otherness (which, it should be noted, is not pure otherness, but the otherness of something which is, in its nature, self-identical) is the moment of alienation. Hegel's own words are important:

> The alienation of the Self-consciousness posits, of itself, *thingness*; hence, this alienation has not only a negative but also a positive meaning. And it has this meaning not only *for us* or *in-itself*, but also for

Self-consciousness itself. For Self-consciousness, the negative character
of the object, the self-disengagement of the object, has a *positive* meaning. Self-consciousness *knows* the nothingness of the object, because
Self-consciousness alienates itself from itself. In fact, in alienation, it
posits itself as object; or, by reason of the infrangible unity of *being-
per-se*, posits the object *as itself*. On the other hand, there is in alienation also that other moment in which Self-consciousness takes back into
itself that alienation and objectivity, thus remaining identical with itself
precisely in its *being other*. [*Phänomenologie des Geistes*, ed. Glockner,
VIII, 602–603]

One may readily see why Marx felt impelled to castigate this as
abstract. However, he did not fail to appreciate the basic insight, which
had, in his view, only to be transposed into the concrete order of the
historical process of society in order to appear in its full meaning.

Marx has reached the conclusion that man is social by reason of
the nature of the work which constitutes him and that this sociality
takes concrete historical form as *society* in correlation with the degree
of development of the means of production. He therefore turns to the
concrete existent society in which man finds himself at present. It is
here, and not in an abstract Self-consciousness, that he finds the true
subject of *alienation*. Alienation is the historical condition of man under
the existing form of society, which he calls *capitalistic*.

What is it in capitalistic society which generates this condition of
alienation, of man divided in his innermost being? The answer is clear:
Alienation derives from the basic element, i.e., the relations of men as
a consequence of their relation to the means of production in the
present state of development. The basic relation which should prevail
in society (note that the "should" emphasizes the basically *ethical* character of Marx's analysis) between man and the material conditions of
production is that of *operator-instrument*. In capitalistic society this
relation is directly inverted. Man, from being master, becomes *instrument;* the material means of production become *master*. In this situation man is completely *other to himself*, completely alienated, in the
Hegelian sense.

What, precisely, is it in capitalistic society that produces this
alienation? The reply of Marx awakens a Proudhonian echo. This
alienation is the result of a specific social relation between men and
the means of production, namely, private property. Ownership of the
material means of production makes it possible for the one who claims
this form of title to withdraw the product of the worker and make it
the exclusive appanage of a person or group. When this condition prevails, in Marx's words: *"It is no longer the worker who employs the
means of production, but the means of production which use the
worker.* Instead of being consumed by him as the material elements of

his productive activity, they consume him as the aliment of their vital process . . ." (*Das Kapital,* Buch I, Abschnitt III, Kapital 9, in *Werke,* ed. H. J. Lieber and B. Kautsky Vol. IV, p. 348, italics Marx's). Private property transforms man from an end to a means, violating the great ethical principle which Kant had enunciated, that the human person may never be used as a *means,* but must always be respected as an *end.* The process of production, which by nature has the character of instrument, is transformed into an end in itself. Man is made to serve the process of production, which is proposed as an absolute value in itself. Man is valued only as he serves the productive process; his character, needs, and aspirations as man are ignored. Again Marx's words cannot be improved upon: "Production produces man not only as a commodity, the human commodity, man with the character of a commodity; it produces him, conformably to this character, as a dehumanized being both physically and spiritually" (*Economic and Philosophical Manuscripts of 1844,* Part III). It is to be noted that for Marx, especially during his earlier and more strictly philosophical period, this alienation is to be deplored above all because of the division it brings about and the wound it inflicts in the very being of man. He has insisted on the integrity of man, and he has insisted that the elements involved in this integrity are man's relations with nature and with other men. These relations should unite and fulfill man in society and in the fruitful exploitation of nature for the purpose of increasing the quality of human existence in the individual and the group. Instead, in capitalistic society, organized about the principle of private property, man is rent asunder in his very being; he is separated and isolated from nature and from other men. Man comes to look upon himself as an object, as the instrument of an impersonal process. This manner of viewing himself, forced upon him by the manner of existence in this society, violates his very sense of his own being. In the very process of producing his life, he is alienating his life, handing it over to another principle, presenting it as an object for the use of another. His life becomes a kind of living death, a self-annihilation in the name of a foreign and exploiting title (cf. *Economic and Philosophical Manuscripts of 1844,* Part III).

Marx isolates private property as that element in the structure of capitalist society which directly produces the alienation of man. How does private property do this? Marx does not develop the process of this alienation with the same explicitness that he achieves elsewhere. It may perhaps be treated in the classic terms of the theory of *title.* A title is a *claim.* In the Marxian view there is a direct relation between man and his work. It is not so much that his work and the product of his work *belong* to man, but that they *are* man; they enter into his constitution. This statement must be understood, of course, in relation to what Marx has to say about the derivation of the social character of man from the social character of work. The only mediating principle is society, but, since man is social, this is seen not as an alien mediation but as a self-mediation between man and work, a mediation in the same sense that the body is an automediation of the self in the individual. Private property alienates man by introducing a situation of claim that is not sustained by the analysis of man, work, and society. This false claim is concretely identified with the claim of a specific person or body of persons to exclusive possession and use of the material means of production and the product itself. Obviously the material means of production *belong*, in the Marxian analysis of the character of work, to society as a whole and not to any specific individual or group. There is no principle in his analysis on which such a property claim could be advanced. From his viewpoint such a claim necessarily appears as a direct contradiction of the concept of work and the social character of man. Hence, every such claim must be considered spurious, fictitious, and lacking all basis in principle.

But there is another aspect to this problem. No group in society advances the claim implicit in private property purely on the basis of exclusive sequestration and use of work and its products, including men as workers. The claim is advanced in capitalistic society on an ideological basis; this ostensibly makes the claim implicit in private property a characteristic, not of the group which is its beneficiary, but of the productive process itself. Its adherents hold that only under the conditions of private property can the productive process function. It is against this ideological view of private property that Marx, as a social scientist and economist, protests. As a philosopher, he is incensed against the human consequences of this mode of thinking and operating in society. That is to say, as a social scientist, he is concerned to show that the productive process not only *can* function independently of the principle of private property, but must function more freely and fruitfully when that principle is removed. As a philosopher, he is concerned to show that that principle ought to be rejected and removed because it is destructive, in its consequences, of the integrity of the human person in his relations to himself, to other men, and to nature. These two themes are always closely interwoven in Marx's thought.

5. Communism

The same dualism which characterizes Marx's critique of private property also invests the final constructive element of his thought, communism. Communism may be conceived as a socio-economic system; as such, it preoccupies Marx as a social scientist and economist, constituting his solution to the basic problems of society in that order. Communism must also, however, be considered as an ethical ideal; it is as such that it preoccupies Marx in his more specifically philosophical character.

What is the nature of communism in the ethical-philosophical context? It is clear that for Marx, since man is a social being, constituted of relations mediated by work and production, any attempt to characterize man concretely must be made in relation to the state of society, or better the states which social life historically assumes. It is possible for Marx to speak, in the terms of classical ethics, of the perfection of man; but for him this perfection cannot be exclusively a matter of individual or private concern or effort. It cannot be achieved through the conception of morality, religion, or philosophy as a "way." The perfection of man is a social concept, and its effectuation is a social problem involving the transformation of the forms of society by means of the transformation of the economic structure which is its basis. The ethical perfection of man will depend on the kind of society he can achieve. This, in turn, will depend on his organization of the material means of production.

Capitalist society appears in the Marxian analysis as fundamentally amoral or immoral. It directly destroys the ethical integrity of human life in its individual and social dimensions. It plunges man into an alienation which robs him of all human and spiritual character. If man is to advance ethically, in the direction of the ideal of integrity with self and others through work, it is clear that the capitalist form of society must be altered. It is useless to preach moral betterment to individuals or groups; it is useless to think, as did the utopians, of improving society through moral effort while leaving its objective structure untouched; it is useless, with religion and philosophy, to offer the individual or groups within society a way of escape from their actual conditions of human debasement, since such escape can only be illusory. The individual cannot develop in any direction save that which his society permits or fosters. Men cannot be free in a society which enslaves them; they cannot be whole in a society which fragments them; they cannot be integral in a society which sets them against themselves. Neither can any kind of action, save that directed precisely toward the transformation of society, be effective ethically. Therefore, the great ethical imperative of Marxian thought is the transformation of capitalist society, beginning with a transformation of its economic basis. Communism is the name for the direction of that transformation. It designates a state in which man, on the basis of a transformed economic system, will be restored to himself, his alienation healed; in which his relation through work to self, others, and nature will be restored to integrity. This is communism as an ethical ideal and as it appears at the most profound level, philosophically speaking, of Marx's thought.

Yet, unless its concrete constitutive elements can be specified, this statement of communism runs the risk of appearing a pure abstraction, no less than the Spirit or the Idea of Hegel. Chief among these elements, as all-conditioning, is the economic transformation which Marx associates with the notion of communism. This transformation has a dual aspect: the elements of capitalism to be rejected and the elements of communist society which are to replace them. Chief among the elements of capitalist society to be eliminated is *private property*. This, as we have seen, is the root of the alienation of man from himself which makes capitalist society an immoral and inhuman contrivance. With private property will be abolished all particular claim or title to the product of work based on any other principle than the inalienable relation between worker and work. Private ownership will be replaced by the only possible moral, and hence juridically approvable, title: work. Since work, however, is social, it is obvious that the primitive title to the product of work cannot be assigned to the individual, *qua* individual; i.e., abstracted from the society in which his particular work is accomplished. Primitive title to the product of work can only be assigned to the society.

At this point Marx is in danger of becoming himself the victim of the abstraction of society as being distinct from or in opposition to the human beings as workers who compose it. If he were to fall into this trap, a new form of alienation would arise, worse perhaps than that which, in his view, infected capitalist society. This, it would seem, is precisely that type of alienation which would later appear in the "totalitarian" societies which emerged under the banner of Marxism. Marx is alert to this danger and seeks to avoid it. To the extent that he sees it and manages to avoid it, he cannot be called the progenitor of those later forms, though they claim to originate in his doctrine.

Marx is not in intention totalitarian. For him, society is only the sum of the concrete persons, the workers, who compose it existentially. Therefore, the primary and primitive title to the product of work does not belong to society as an abstraction. It belongs to society as the concrete collectivity of the workers. The specific problem is the manner in which collectivity and individual, group and subgroup, are to be mediated. It is necessary to find a formula by which the primitive title may be redistributed among the numerically distinct individuals.

At this juncture Marx would seem necessarily to have recourse to some ethical principle to insure this mediation. Had he had such recourse, he would, of course, have fallen into the position of the uto-pian socialists. Such ethical, juridical, or political principles, moreover, would have to be fixed *a priori*, and this too would have been in direct contradiction to his own principles. For Marx, there was only one pos-sible way for the scientific character of his socialism to be vindicated. The principle of mediation would have to be of the economic order. Since all other structures and principles are derivative from the eco-nomic, a principle of mediation from any other order would also have to be derivative. This would demolish the entire structure of his thought. He seeks, therefore, an economic formula for communism which will replace the principle of private property in capitalism. Strictly speaking, the development of this economic formula belongs to the history of economics; for the history of philosophy, it is enough to indicate the relationship of these principles to the general Marxian position as an ethical structure.

Marx provides this formula in two ways. The first is by his analysis of the manner in which capitalistic society, in its purely economic structure, generates, by its inner contradictions, the communist eco-nomic structure. From the point of view of the present issue, this is a *via negativa,* although it is completely in accord with his doctrine of "historical materialism." The second manner in which Marx seeks to provide this formula is by his "labor theory of value." This must be recognized as the positive address to this problem.

How does the inner movement of capitalist society necessitate, according to the doctrine of historical materialism, the emergence of the communist society in its purely economic basis? Marx begins this analysis with reference to a principle advanced by the classical liberal economists, Adam Smith and David Ricardo: the *value* of any product is determined by the *amount of labor* necessary to produce it. Abso-lutely speaking, this would imply that the whole of the product should be returned to the source of the labor necessary to produce it. In the capitalist society, however, the notion of profit and the accumulation of *capital* (surplus value) intervene. The capitalist (personifying the pro-cess) interjects himself into this relation and proceeds to return to the laborer or worker only a *part* of the product of his work, as wages, or purchase price of his labor. The rest the capitalist appropriates to him-self, or expropriates from the worker, as *surplus value,* the source of capital. Thus, the very substance of the capitalist economic system rests on exploitation, the unprincipled appropriation from the worker of a portion of the product of his labor and its diversion to the purposes of the exploiter, who is protected and justified by the principle of private property. The capitalist returns to the worker a strict purchase price of his labor which is calculated by an entirely inhuman measure as the amount of sustenance necessary to maintain the worker at a certain level of productivity.

This process results in the two basic phenomena of the capitalist system which Marx criticizes most vehemently, ostensibly in purely economic terms but always with a humane and ethical preoccupation: the *accumulation of capital* and the *progressive impoverishment of the worker*. Marx, in accordance with his "scientific" claims, formulates these phenomena as "laws": the "law" of the accumulation of capital and the "iron law" of wages. According to the first, wealth as surplus value and capital tends to accumulate more and more in the hands of a few; according to the second, there is always an attempt made to reduce the amount of the product to be returned to the worker as the "price" of his labor. But the movement of these two laws is such that, sooner or later, a point will necessarily be reached at which the workers will turn to "expropriate the expropriators," taking upon themselves all of the functions of power and destroying the capitalist system from within. Thus, the capitalist system tends to produce, within itself and by the movement of its own logic, its contradiction or negation; it does this, not in abstract terms, but in the completely concrete terms of a revolt of the workers intended to claim that portion of the product of their labor which has been taken from them. Thus communism is for Marx not a mere abstract ideal but a concrete situation which capitalist society by its own dynamics will, eventually and necessarily, produce within itself.

This account still does not answer fully the question proposed: What is the economic formula for the redistribution of the social product of labor? Marx meets this question by his own formulation of the labor theory of value. In this formulation, Marx reveals his dependence on the same utopian social thinkers upon whom he had expended so much criticism. His labor theory of value has the effect of renovating the classical socialist formula: to each according to his needs, from each according to his powers. In the communist society a situation of actual, not abstract or *a priori,* justice will emerge in which this formula will be realized in the transactions of economic life. The powers and the needs of the individual will be mediated at every point by the social character of work and its product.

As we have noted, the actual working out of this formula in economic terms belongs to the history of that science. What is most important from the philosophical point of view is the effect of communism upon that state which Marx has identified as alienation. It brings about the complete reintegration of man, the complete healing of that radical alienation introduced by the separation of man from his own constitutive process, work, and its product and, in the last analysis, his own being. Communism, by the complete abolishment of private property and all of the phenomena of social life which are concealed under this term, heals the trauma which that principle, or pretension, had generated both in society and in the personality of the individuals composing society. In communism, labor becomes again what it ought to be, the personal and autonomous activity of man and the instrument or means of solidarity among men. Communism brings "the complete, conscious return of man to himself, as social man and as human man" (*Economic and Philosophical Manuscripts of 1844,* Part III). Thus communism appears in the full character which Marx, as a philosopher, is seeking to assign to it and to achieve through it—the complete vindication of the dignity of man as individual and the pacific solidarity of man in society.

This brief treatment does not pretend to a complete presentation of Marx's thought. It has concentrated on one point, Marx as ethician, as moral thinker, which we believe to be the heart of his character as a philosopher. Not everything of philosophical interest in Marx has been touched on here. In the course of this work we shall have occasion to treat Marx's thought at two other points: his doctrine of "historical materialism," in the context of the "materialism" of the nineteenth century, and the development of the theory of "dialectical materialism" by his friend and co-worker, Friedrich Engels.

B. Søren Kierkegaard (1813–1855)

Unlike Marx, Kierkegaard was without immediate influence in his times. A considerable period passed before his thought found, in the movements of existentialism and existentialist theology, a resonance in any way reflecting its originality and profundity. Consequently, Kierkegaard is regarded primarily as the precursor of existentialism, and his ideas are interpreted in this perspective. This poses a problem for the historian of philosophy, whose first concern is to see a philosopher's thought in its historical context; for, in the theory of the history of philosophy, no man is essentially a predecessor; he is a thinker in his own right, a man of his own time. His subsequent influence, the interpretation subsequent thinkers give to his thought and the use they make of it, is always of interest, but it cannot be seen as central to any philosopher's own speculations. Thus, to take a more glaring example, it is an obvious mistake to find Marx principally in the interpretation given his thought in contemporary Soviet "Marx-Leninism." The latter must indeed concern the historian, in its own time and place, but he must be careful not to substitute it for Marx. Thus, in the case of Kierkegaard, his influence on existentialism is important and must be considered in its proper place, but that interpretation must not be substituted for his own thought and his own insights in their own historical time and setting.

To meet this problem, the present treatment will take the following form. It will try to see Kierkegaard in historical focus, in his own time and place. His thought will again occupy our attention when existentialism appears, and its interpretation of him will be considered. In this way, both aspects of Kierkegaard will be given just consideration, but any confusion between them will be avoided.

A second problem for the historian of philosophy is the great importance given by some of his best commentators to the biographical basis of Kierkegaard's philosophy. The biography of a philosopher is never without interest, but it varies in importance with different philosophers. With some, like Kant and Newton, it would seem to have relatively slight importance; with others, like Pascal and Newman, it is highly illuminating. Even when it is judged illuminating, however, care must be taken not to reduce a philosopher's thought or, more accurately, the philosophical interest and value of a man's thought to a facet of his biography. Indeed, it may even be said that a man's thought begins to acquire genuine philosophical interest and value only when it transcends his biography. When the case of Kierkegaard is considered, it is immediately clear that he belongs to that group of thinkers whose biography is greatly illuminating. At the same time, in his case this value has been exaggerated. As one historian, Abbagnano, puts it, the investigations into Kierkegaard's life have reached the point of becoming not only useless but indiscreet (cf. *Storia della filosofia* [2nd ed. 1963] III, 182). Nevertheless, even Abbagnano does not deny the basic importance of the biographical element. The solution adopted in the present text will be, on the one hand, to state as simply and as clearly as possible what, by general consent of the best Kierkegaard scholars, that importance is and, on the other, to rely as little as possible on the biographical element in the analysis of his thought and to stress those points on which it reaches universal relevance.

A final problem in addressing Kierkegaard's thought is the selection and ordering of the elements of his thought according to their philosophical interest and value. Kierkegaard must be considered primarily a religious thinker; even more precisely, he is an apologist for the Christian religion. He is also a perceptive psychologist of religious experience, which he tends to make equivalent with significant experience as such. His philosophical reflections arise within this context. It is necessary consequently to limit the perspective within which his thought can be considered. A decision as to which elements are truly philosophical must be ventured. There must inevitably be a great divergence of opinion on this point. Every interpretation must justify its own selection and emphasis. The point of view or perspective which will dominate in the present treatment has already been indicated. Kierkegaard will be considered in the perspective of left Hegelianism, because in this perspective his philosophical insights are revealed most clearly. An even more precise focus may be achieved. Kierkegaard's thought will be considered as the rectification of center and right Hegelianism; that is, the Hegelianism which devoted itself to the demonstration of the power of Hegel's philosophy to offer a complete rational justification of Christianity.

The entire thrust of Kierkegaard's thought derives from his denial of this assertion, from his counterassertion that the Hegelian philosophy spells the complete dissolution of Christianity and religion itself, and from his need to work out an apologetic which would not only prevail against the Hegelian influence but which would establish Christianity on intellectual bases consonant with its own character and the character of human existence. Kierkegaard nevertheless accepts the Hegelian conditions of apologetics. He does not retreat into mysticism in an effort to justify the Christian experience and dispensation but remains on common ground with Hegelianism because his apologetic is speculative and philosophical. However, he will challenge the very notion of speculative thought and of philosophy involved in Hegelianism. His thought gains considerable interest because, like Marxian philosophy, it represents a crisis in the very theory of philosophy, the notion philosophy has of itself.

The order to be followed in the treatment of Kierkegaard's thought emerges readily from these considerations. After a consideration of his philosophically relevant works, we shall indicate the biographical basis of his intellectual activity. We shall then be concerned with his critique of Hegel and Hegelianism (although the space available will not permit a careful distinction as to the direct object of his attacks—Hegel or right Hegelians). The purpose of this examination of the critique of Hegelianism will be, not to justify Hegel, but to discover the emerging master-lines of Kierkegaard's procedure. Finally, Kierkegaard's constructive analysis of human existence and the manner in which Christianity responds to it will be considered.

1. Kierkegaard's Writings

Kierkegaard wrote in Danish, a language which has not figured largely in the philosophical tradition of Europe. The standard complete edition of his works in that language is that edited by A. B. Drachmann, J. L. Heiberg, and H. O. Lange: Søren Kierkegaard, *Samlede*

Vaerker, 20 vols., Copenhagen, 3rd ed. 1962–64; a new Danish edition, under the editorship of N. Thulstrup has been in process since 1951. A complete edition of his works in German translation is available: Søren Kierkegaard, *Gesammelte Werke*, 26 vols., Dusseldorf and Cologne, Eugen Diederichs Verlag, 1950–62, while a new English translation following the text of the Thulstrup edition is also in process. A complete English edition of the works, under the direction of D. F. Swenson and W. Lowrie, Oxford, 1940–62, is available and translations of individual works and anthologies have also appeared.

Of greater interest is the matter of the order which prevails or should prevail among this vast literary output. To determine this order, or indeed to infuse it, has been a constant concern of scholars. Perhaps the most satisfactory organization, by reason of its basis and of its inclusiveness, is that offered by one of the most indefatigable of Kierkegaard scholars, Cornelio Fabro.

The basis of this ordering is Kierkegaard's duality of method, the "indirect" and the "direct." "Indirect communication" is the term applied to the writings which Kierkegaard published under a plethora of pseudonyms, and "direct communication," those to which he signed his own name. The first constituted the greater and the better known portion of his work, for the pseudonyms become a problem in the interpretation of his work and thought. Fabro excludes from this ordering and treats as preparatory the two earlier works: *From the Papers of One Still Among the Living* and the dissertation which Kierkegaard presented to the university in 1840, *On the Concept of Irony.*

The body of Kierkegaard's writings under the category of "indirect communication" is further divided into three "cycles": a) the Regina cycle, b) the "Philosophical Intermezzo," c) the Christianity cycle. The components of these cycles are signed with a variety of pseudonyms. The most plausible reason advanced for the employment of these pseudonyms is that they are intended to develop situations which Kierkegaard could not assume as his own and which he therefore transferred to ideal personages created by his own imagination. A second account finds their root in the psychological state of Kierkegaard, that "prevention of commitment" which prevented him from identifying even his own personality unambiguously and which had its speculative complement in the notion of "possibility" as this notion underlies his concept of the "self" or "ego." Of these two accounts, the first is too banal to detain our interest; the second will necessarily find elaboration when the concept of "possibility" is considered more carefully.

The "Regina cycle" is so called because it uses the theme of his rejection of marriage with Regina Olsen, a major event in his biography, as the basis for his speculative reflections. The cycle comprises (with pseudonym adjoined): *Either/Or* (Victor Eremita), *Fear and*

Trembling (Johannes de Silentio), *Repetition* (Constantine Constantius), all dating from 1843; the *Concept of Dread* (Virgilius Haufniensis), 1844; *Stages on Life's Way,* including *Guilty or Not Guilty* (Frater Taciturnus), 1854.

The "Philosophical Intermezzo" comprises principally two theoretical essays over the name "Johannes Climacus": *Philosophical Fragments,* 1844, and the monumental *Concluding Unscientific Postscript to the Philosophical Fragments,* 1846. In this cycle are also included the *De omnibus dubitandum est,* 1843, which has been translated into English as *Johannes Climacus* (trans. T. H. Croxall, 1958): *On Authority and Revelation: Book on Adler,* and *The Dialectic of Ethical or Ethical-religious Communication,* both of 1847.

The "Christianity cycle" has one pseudonymous author: "Anticlimacus." To this cycle are assigned the "masterpiece" *Sickness Unto Death,* 1848; the *Training in Christianity,* 1850; and *For Self-Examination, Judge For Yourselves!,* 1851–52. *The Book on Adler* and *The Works of Love,* 1847, are both candidates for inclusion in this cycle, for it is impossible to make these cycles absolutely self-contained.

"Direct communication" is represented by *The Point of View for My Work as an Author,* published posthumously by his brother Peter in 1859, and *Edifying Discourses,* which in the English translation occupies four volumes. Here also are placed the ten parts of The Moment, the review which Kierkegaard published during 1855, the last number appearing posthumously, and the numerous polemical articles published during 1854–55. The greatest and most continuous document of direct communication is the diary (in English translation; *Kierkegaard's Diary,* ed. Peter P. Rohde, trans. Gerda M. Andersen, 1960).

Obviously, not all of these writings are equally important for the consideration of Kierkegaard's philosophical thought; at the same time, none can be definitely banished from such consideration. In addition, the lesser works, many of which have also been translated into English, can be consulted profitably on various points. (A useful list of the English translations is to be found in Walter Lowrie, *A Short Life of Kierkegaard* [Princeton University Press, 2nd paperback ed. 1965]; the exhaustive listing is: Jens Himmelstrup: *Søren Kierkegaard International Bibliografi,* 1962.)

2. The Relevance of Kierkegaard's Biography for an Understanding of His Thought

The salient feature of Kierkegaard's life which is relevant to his philosophical thought seems to be the sense of dread, of a menace, at once formless and terrible, under which it was passed. He speaks of a "terrible earthquake" which took place at a certain point in his life and compelled him to alter his attitude toward the world (*Diary*, II, A 805). He casts this threat in the form of a guilt which rested upon his whole family, a chastisement of God which had descended upon it and which condemned it to disappear from the earth, like an effort of the powerful hand of God which had not succeeded. At several points in his works, he speaks of a "thorn in the flesh" which he had been condemned to carry. What this terrible threat, this terrible event, this thorn in the flesh, might have been has preoccupied the attention of many scholars and biographers of Kierkegaard. The extent to which these inquiries and speculations have gone may be indicated by two recent studies of Kierkegaard by R. Magnussen: *S. K. set udefra* [Søren Kierkegaard's external appearance], Copenhagen, 1942, and *Det saerlige Kors* [The particular cross of Kierkegaard], 1942, in which it is asserted that this "thorn in the flesh" is to be identified as a defect of formation and physical appearance. This is similar in many ways to an earlier tradition that his deficiency was due to an accident in early life which left him deformed and hypersensitive. These assertions have been thoroughly refuted by the eminent German student of Kierkegaard, Theodor Haecker, in his essay *Der Buckel Kierkegaards* [Kierkegaard's deformation], 1947. The truth seems to be that this sense of some imminent or eventual disaster was spiritual and not physical. His student days seem to have been marked by an equanimity of character, marred only by certain eccentricities. At the same time, there began to emerge strong conflicts between Kierkegaard and his father. These remain obscure in character, but most evidence points to a growing difference over the religious and spiritual life. Kierkegaard began to grow restive under the domineering pietism of his father and to experience interior conflicts centering about the problems of sin, guilt, providence, and the saving power of Christianity. These struggles seem to have reached a culmination at the time of his father's death in 1838. It is then that he speaks of the "great earthquake." In this context the earthquake would apparently consist in the scandal he experienced from Christianity by reason of the contrary movements of attraction and repulsion which it awakened in him. Christianity seemed, on the one hand, to wreak havoc with the nature of man and with the self while, on the other, it seemed to offer the only "radical cure" for the "mortal sickness" with which sin afflicted man. That in some way not entirely clear to us all of this deep commotion of spirit involved the father-son relationship seems well-established. Some critics and commentators have emphasized this by pointing out Kierkegaard's use of the Abraham and Isaac figure in various contexts in his writings.

The psychological effect of this sense of menace upon Kierkegaard seems to have been a paralysis of decision. Under its shadow he seemed unable to muster the power to choose any of the basic alternatives which weigh every life. Though graduated in theology and prepared for the ministry, he proved unable to take up a charge; though apparently attached to Regina Olsen by a sincere and even profound affection, he withdrew his promise of marriage. From the point of view of his philosophy, a wavering relation has been set up between this spiritual disturbance and its psychological effects, and the concept of "possibility," of existence as "possibility" and of the self as "possibility." In subsequent pages, this notion, central if not absolutely fundamental to his thought, will be examined. However, no pretense will be made of solving the riddle of its relationship to these spiritual and psychological factors; only its speculative character and function will be considered.

That the root of this inward commotion of spirit was indeed just what Kierkegaard had indicated—a restiveness before the orthodox pietistic form of Christianity—seems to be further established by the harsh contest which broke out between Kierkegaard, Bishop Mynster, and the latter's successor, the philo-Hegelian theologian Martensen. The Bishop had been a close friend of Kierkegaard's father, and Kierkegaard himself had originally expressed a sincere affection for the prelate. This affection turned to disaffection, apparently because the Bishop failed to defend Kierkegaard from an attack launched against him in the *Corsair*, a humorous journal published in Copenhagen, and further, an article of his own seemed to place Kierkegaard and the editor of that journal, one Goldschmidt, on the same spiritual plane. The full measure of Kierkegaard's disaffection, revealing its much deeper sources, was released after the Bishop's death against his successor, Martensen. Kierkegaard brought all his ironic and polemical powers to this attack (counterattack, in his view) in the articles published in the periodical *Øjeblikket* (The Moment) in the middle months of 1855. But it became very clear that Martensen was only the occasion, not the real object of these articles; the real opponent was the entire Protestant conception of life, religion, and Christianity as Kierkegaard had come to know it through institutional associations and theological studies. This fact brings us to the threshold of Kierkegaard's intellectual undertaking, which, as has been suggested, involved a complete reexamination of the character and power of Christianity.

3. Kierkegaard's Critique of Hegelianism

Viewed in its strictly philosophical character, Kierkegaard's thought begins with his critique of Hegelianism. This theme preoccupies him constantly and is diffused throughout his most important works. Passages of special force and significance are to be found in the *Concluding Unscientific Postscript,* which Fabro has called the only work of the nineteenth century which can really challenge the triumphant march of the Hegelian logic. Important polemical passages against the Hegelian system are also to be found in the *Concept of Dread,* in the *Sickness Unto Death,* and throughout the volumes of the *Diary.* We may ask at what precise point Kierkegaard makes contact with the Hegelian system. The answer to this question has already been indicated in a cursory manner. The point of contact between the thought of Hegel and that of Kierkegaard is extreme right Hegelianism. It is against this position that Kierkegaard musters all the force of his logical, critical, and literary skill, and the thrust of his criticism carries him to the heart of Hegelianism itself: the concept of logical necessity as the supreme principle of the unity of the real and the guarantee of the identity of the rational and the real.

Right Hegelianism took as its special concern the central Hegelian thesis that Christianity had found, in the Hegelian system, its complete philosophical justification; that the effort, which may be said to have begun with St. Paul, had, in the Hegelian system, found its final success: the justification of faith to reason. This was undeniably the end toward which Christianity, as a culture taking up into itself the Judaic and the Greek strains, had striven throughout its history. The fundamental insight of Christianity, as a culture, had been that these two moments, faith and reason, could not remain autonomous, contradictory, and exclusive moments of the human spirit; that they had to have some necessary relation which, while preserving the authenticity of each and reducing neither one to the other, would unite them in the integrity of the human spirit, of human consciousness. Hegel recognized that every great theological-philosophical synthesis of the past: the Augustinian, the Thomistic, the Malebranchian, the Spinozan, had offered itself before the bar of western culture in this form. (The Spinozan must be included, for, despite its specific exclusion of the Christian element, in its *cultural form* it belongs in this order, and the influence of Spinozism on the formal structure of the Hegelian system of reason is well established by Hegelian scholarship.) For this reason, Hegelianism offers itself as a fulfillment of this millennial aspiration of western Christian culture. The Kierkegaardian counterassertion is that the Hegelian speculative justification of Christianity and of the religious life, the life of faith in itself, is an illusion; that it is, in fact, the complete annihilation of the moment of faith and of religion.

In what way had the Hegelian system achieved (imagined it had achieved, Kierkegaard will say) this rational justification of religion?

The answer to this question has been suggested in the section of this work which treats the "System of Reason" in philosophical romanticism and specifically in its Hegelian form. The contention of the system of reason, in all of its forms, had been that reality is a *whole*, sustained by a single principle of unity which both *establishes* and *synthesizes* all distinctions—the distinctions of noumenon and phenomenon, of unity and multiplicity, of the moments of consciousness themselves, of necessity and liberty, of universality and individuality, of essence and existence. The various forms of the system of reason had identified the principle of the unity of the real in various ways: as aesthetic, as moral, as pure dynamism, etc. The special mark of the Hegelian form of the system of reason was that it adhered strictly to the classical insight that the unity of the system of the real is *logical*, that the bond of the system, relating all differences, is *logical necessity;* that whatever is, must be. It affirmed this of the whole, of all of the differences included in the whole, and of all of the relations prevailing among the differences themselves and between them and the whole. Rationality is logical necessity. "The rational is the real and the real is rational." This classical Hegelian rubric becomes transparent when the Hegelian notion of the system of reason and its principle is understood.

It is also the contention of Hegelianism that earlier attempts at the logical synthesis of the real, which had polarized about the moments of faith and reason, had fallen short of success, while its own effort, in principle, was successful. The reason for the failure of the one and the success of the other is of the same order: the *logical*. The failure of earlier systems was due to a unilateral adherence to the logical *principle of contradiction*. The Hegelian critique of the principle of contradiction must be clearly understood. It in no wise involves a rejection of this principle; it consists wholly in a recognition of its intrinsic limitations. The principle of contradiction is a valid principle of abstract differentiation within the system of the real. Its function, however, is exhausted in the process of differentiation. It has no power of concrete synthesis. This in turn is the fundamental limitation of classical, syllogistic logic: It sought to turn the principle of contradiction into a principle of concrete synthesis. The intrinsic limitations of the principle resist this effort and, consequently, rob syllogistic logic of the demonstrative force to which it pretended. Reality can never be grasped as a system if the principle of contradiction is taken as the supreme logical principle. On the contrary, reality must appear as a welter of immedicable and unmediatable abstract dualities. Just as the distinctions established on the basis of the principle of contradiction are abstract, so the syntheses to which it pretends are abstract. A science built on the principle of contradiction will be an abstract science (an example, according to

Hegel, is mathematics). Such a science can never be speculative and philosophical, for speculative and philosophical science is science of the concrete real—in the last analysis, of the existent.

The basic achievement of Hegelianism, upon which the validity of its entire enterprise rests, is the discovery of a logic beyond the principle of contradiction. This is the *dialectical logic*. The dialectical logic of Hegelianism must be conceived as the completion of the logic which rests upon the principle of contradiction. It embraces, justifies, and transcends the logic resting on the principle of contradiction. It can establish the character of the sciences constructed by that logic, while excluding them, on the basis of their intrinsic abstractness, from the encyclopedia of the philosophical sciences.

The logic of the dialectic follows an order of its own. It is concrete. Its movement is the movement of reality itself. It has two basic moments, inseperable from each other: opposition and synthesis. The process of negation (opposition) in the dialectic differs *toto caelo* from the correlative operation in the logic of the principle of contradiction. Negation in the dialectic discovers or lays bare, through the process of *differentiation,* the grounds of the *unity* of the real. It prepares the way for the transformation of the unity of the real from an undifferentiated, and hence irrational, unity to a unity which is grasped in *principle*. The establishment of the unity of the real in principle rests on the prior establishment of differences and the prior discovery of these differences, not as immedicable contradictions, but as grounds of higher unity. Thus is the system born, and its sustaining principle is the dialectic, whose stages of position, negation, negation of negation, and synthesis are not abstract movements but movements of the real itself in concrete logical character. In this process everything which can be said of the dialectic must be said of the real, of what *is,* for the meaning of *to be* is discovered within the dialectic; even further, authentic being is established *by* the dialectic.

The system of the real is consequently, as constructed by the dialectic, a system of *logical necessity.* Whatever *is,* in the authentic sense established by the dialectic, *must* be. Even further, its authenticity is this necessity. This necessity alone makes for the security of the philosophical proposition; it is the pure expression of this concrete logical necessity. This logical necessity is the meaning of the copula in the philosophical proposition. It affirms that what is asserted, *is,* in the complex sense that it *cannot not be* and that it cannot *be* other than it is. The system of reason is a system of logical necessity, but it is *not* the contradiction of possibility. (This is a point of cardinal importance with respect to the Kierkegaardian critique.) The abstract opposition of possibility and necessity (reintroduced by Kierkegaard) is excluded from the dialectic. The logical necessity of the dialectic is grounded in and is the fulfillment of concrete possibility. The moment of possibility is immanent and intrinsic to the movement of the dialectic; it is what is precisely indicated by the moment of opposition or differentiation. Possibility outside the order of this opposition within the dialectic is abstract. Concrete possibility, "real" possibility, is a moment of the dialectic intrinsic to the order of logical necessity. The real, as logical or rational (in the sense of the dialectic), is the order of possibility-necessity in a concrete logical relation.

What is offered here is not, obviously, a complete exposition of the Hegelian logic; this presentation does touch the points necessary for understanding (and even, perhaps, for evaluating) the Kierkegaardian critique. But a further point must be considered before Kierkegaard's critique can be addressed directly. In what way was all this applied to the task of the speculative justification of Christianity by Hegel and right Hegelianism?

The specific task of that apologetic for Christianity was to overcome the (apparently) immedicable opposition between *faith* and *reason*, between revelation and science. As it had existed in previous systems, this opposition had been interpreted as a *contradiction*. In a world governed by logical necessity as established by the principle of contradiction, faith and revelation appeared as *absurd*. At the same time, the reference of faith and revelation was held to be a real order; i.e., Christ is really God, and the proposition of faith is an affirmation of this reality. In analogous language faith and revelation might be said, on the basis of this same logic, to be the affirmation of the reality of the impossible. Thus, the unity of the real, demanded by the exigencies of truth, was riven. The essence of the Hegelian apologetic was the denial that the opposition between faith and reason, philosophical science and revelation, is an opposition of contradiction and the affirmation that this is a *dialectical opposition*. As a dialectical opposition, it is the establishment of the grounds of their unity—their *dialectical* unity. At the same time, it is an affirmation of the real possibility of revelation and of the synthesis of faith and reason in the system of the real.

Further still, within the system of the real as established by the dialectical logic, the moment of revelation and the moment of faith are necessary (not gratuitous) moments in the career of the Idea. There is no *either-or* here; it is a *both-and* which prevails. But neither is this *both-and* an unordered relation. There is a strict order of necessity between faith and reason. Each is a logically necessary moment of the Idea. Each is autonomous in its affirmation of the real, in the sense that the mode of the affirmation of the one never contradicts or excludes the other; on the contrary, the affirmation of each is the ground of the affirmation of the other, though in no wise reducible to it.

Only one point remains. If the Hegelian apologetic is to be complete, it must also establish that the Christian revelation is unique; i.e., that only one revelation is logically possible and that the Christian revelation in Jesus Christ is that one revelation. This aspect of the Hegelian dialectic belongs to Hegel's philosophy of history, where this proposition is maintained: that the Christian revelation is at once necessary, actual, and unique.

It is against this system of ideas that Kierkegaard takes up arms, and no historian of philosophy would suggest that the attack he launches against it is either trivial or negligible. Indeed, there are some who would say that the full force of his critique of Hegel is not to be felt in the area of apologetic, but in that area of much greater interest to the history of philosophy, the notion of philosophy itself. The Kierkegaardian attack on Hegel, these writers assert, has changed the notion of the nature and the condition of the philosophical enterprise. If this is true, Kierkegaard ushers in the post-Hegelian age in the history of philosophy, from which there is no turning back.

In its architectonic form, Kierkegaard's critique of Hegel may be expressed in the following manner: Hegel is guilty of one of the classical fallacies long since pointed out by the Aristotelian logic; that is, *petitio principii*. Aristotle had described that fallacy in the *Prior Analytics* (I, c. 24, 41b): "there is postulated the conclusion which it had initially been proposed to demonstrate." The conclusion to be demonstrated is the unity of the real, its character as system. But at every point in the Hegelian construct it is clear, according to Kierkegaard, that this unity is already presupposed. As a consequence, its demonstration is specious; and the Hegelian system remains a vast postulation and the dialectic a vast operation in *vacuo*.

Kierkegaard singles out with great acumen the precise point at which he considers that fallacy most evident: the notion of logical necessity. The force of logical necessity as the unitary principle of the real is made evident in the Hegelian formula, whatever *is, must be, cannot not be,* and *cannot be other than it is.* In Kierkegaard's view, the force of this principle is to subvert, or more precisely perhaps, invert, the order of necessity and possibility. In the Hegelian system, possibility is always derived from necessity. Possibility can be asserted of anything only as a consequence of its actuality. If there were any possibility outside of necessity, the entire system would be dissolved, and reality would be returned to its original chaos. Anything which, though it *is, need not be* would fall outside the system. Even more, the presence of one such instance would make the system a vast irrelevancy. It would be clear that the relationship between the actuality and the possibility of that existent could not be logical necessity; logical necessity would exclude the possibility of its not being. Kierkegaard maneuvers the entire Hegelian system in such a way that its validity becomes entirely dependent on a single question—namely, can an instance of existence be indicated in which the possibility is antecedent to the actuality in the sense that, though that existent is, it *need not be?*

Not only can such an instance be indicated, Kierkegaard affirms, but such is the only instance of being and existence immediately present to us. What is this instance? Kierkegaard answers: the individual, existent, human person, the singular human subject, *hic homo.* He is such that his possibility of non-being is the very mode in which he grasps his existence. This individual, as subject, is the only immediate instance we know of "what is," *in actuality.* Whatever, consequently, we hope to be able to say about *what is* and its conditions, must be related to and based on this sole instance of immediately given existence. To the *whole* of the Hegelian system, Kierkegaard opposes, on basis of absolute equality, the *singular.* Dramatically, he expressed the wish that on his tomb there be inscribed as an epitaph: "That Individual."

At this point, Hegel and Kierkegaard stand in complete opposition. At the same time, there is revealed here the great affinity between them. Kierkegaard accepts the speculative task from Hegel in its entirety as Hegel conceived it. This task is to relate the singular, in all its singularity and its contingency, to the Absolute. Hegel sought to do this by way of logical necessity and the dialectic. Having rejected this method, Kierkegaard, confronted by the same task, must find another method consonant with his conception of the singular as unmediatable possibility and contingency.

The establishment of this affinity between Hegel and Kierkegaard brings us to the threshold of Kierkegaard's constructive speculative work. By way of anticipation it may be remarked that Kierkegaard discovers the clue to this task in Christianity itself: in the revelation of God in Jesus Christ, which is, in the last analysis, the whole of Christianity. The Christian revelation indicates that the relation between the contingent existent and the Absolute can be established only on the initiative of the Absolute (not, as in Hegel, by human thought) and that it can be accepted by man only by an act which is the complete antithesis of the Hegelian dialectic: *the leap of faith in the face of the absurd.* But even here, all elements of abstractness must be eliminated. This act can take place only in the direct confrontation of the individual human person in his complete self-identity, his complete selfhood, and Jesus Christ. The whole of Kierkegaard's philosophical thought is but the attempt to determine the process involved in reaching this moment of confrontation. It should be noted, however, that in this confrontation it is, from the speculative point of view, the Hegelian problem which Kierkegaard resolves.

A controversy has long existed among students of Kierkegaard as to the order and unity of his thought. Some have held that it is a radical violation of his thought to impose any strictly logical order upon it, that he is fundamentally an inspirational and lyrical thinker whose ideas must be followed in the order of their appearance in his works. Others, like Jolivet, have pointed out that Kierkegaard himself was conscious of a definite unity and order in his work and spoke of it again and again. In the present view, this controversy seems somewhat academic. A certain order has already been discovered, we would submit, in the comparison between the speculative tasks of Hegel and Kierkegaard. The order flows from the task itself. Kierkegaard must find his way from the pure radical possibility of the existent human subject to that ultimate moment of confrontation with the absolute in its form of pure absurdity—its incarnation in the historical person of Jesus Christ. It is a difficult itinerary and one whose course could not readily be plotted beforehand; its motto had, perforce, to be that of Newman: one step enough for me. But these steps do emerge and lead one to another and finally to that supreme moment of confrontation and faith toward which all has been moving.

These steps may be indicated briefly and will provide the plan of the brief exposition which will be attempted in the following pages. They are: existential thinking; the meaning of possibility; the stages on the way; dread and despair; sin; faith; the "problem of Lessing" or confrontation with Christ. Two points ought to be noted about this order: 1) It is not offered as the order of Kierkegaard's writings, but as an expositional order that seems clearly suggested by them; 2) this order responds to the quest for the speculative character of his thought; it does not exclude other orders responsive to other demands.

4. Existential Thinking

The failure of Hegel was due to his trust in *pure thought*. Pure thought is the source of the illusoriness of the "system." It seduces man into believing that he can deliver himself from the contingency of existence by regarding it from the abstract point of view of the Absolute Spirit or Idea. He is led to lose sight of his actual existential plight and surrenders himself to the illusion of logical necessity which pure thought weaves for him. Kierkegaard's first constructive speculative effort is, consequently, to discover the alternative to pure thought, to establish man's authentic form of thought as existent. He finds it in existential thinking.

We may note, in passing, the similarity on this point between Kierkegaard and Marx. The latter too had fixed on "pure thought" as the radical flaw of the Hegelian system. He had insisted that an alternative to pure thought had to be found, as he found it in *class consciousness*. Here the similarity ends. The class consciousness of Marx and the existential thinking of Kierkegaard are poles apart. The penetrating critic Lukacs, himself a Marxist, has pointed this out at great length. While defending class consciousness as the only authentic alternative to the "pure thought" of Hegel, he excoriates existential thinking as a malady more deadly than the affliction it sought to cure.

What are the salient traits of existential thinking? It is, first of all, the thought, the *thinking,* of the *singular, individual, actually existing* man, the "man of flesh and bone," as Unamuno was to call him. Pure thought pretended to be transcendental, the thought of the Pure Idea. Truth met the objective and transcendental conditions of thought. Its marks were universality and necessity; it found expression in and sustained the world of common experience, the objective modes of discourse like science, and the transcendental choices of a formalistic ethics of duty. Against all these, existential thinking stresses the *subjectivity* of thought and of truth. Thought is an operation which the singular existent carries out in his own person and in his own name, not in the name or under the aegis of transcendental principles. For pure thought truth is transcendental, objective. It is *other* and hence alien to the singular, concrete thinker. It is a norm to which his thought must conform, in which it must lose itself. "The truth," Kierkegaard states by contrast, "is a truth only when it is a truth for *me.*" Truth is not a condition in which I conform my thought to another or to an abstract, transcendental, universal, and necessary principle; it is a condition in which I discover myself most completely and am, for the first time, identical with myself, or simply, *myself.*

It is not the mere numerical individuality of the singular which is at stake in existentialist thinking; numerical individuality is purely abstract. The concrete singularity, the subjectivity, of the human existent is involved. This subjectivity makes of thinking, not a contemplation, as it surely was and must be for "pure thought," but a participation and a suffering, a passion and an ordeal. Truth is not in propositions but in the existential state of man as he lives through the terrible quest for the reality of that condition and feels the full force of it upon himself; for instance, when he comes to know, as Unamuno will point out, not that all men are mortal, but that he himself must die. This will become especially important for Kierkegaard when he considers the "truth" of Christianity. This truth has little or nothing to do with the "truths" of Christian doctrine as expressed in dogmas and propositions. The latter are born of the subjugation of Christian truth to "pure thought." The "truth" of Christianity can be "known" only as it is lived by the singular, existent human subject, as it becomes his truth and the form of his life. From this viewpoint, Christian truth is not different from, but the utmost extension of, existential truth, the fruit of existential thinking.

While this emphasis upon existential thinking as the product of the singular, existent human subject, according to the conditions of his existence and not according to the illusory transcendentality of pure thought, is certainly justified and in complete accord with Kierkegaard's texts, there is a point of greater speculative interest which is sometimes overlooked. This is the modality of existential thinking. The modality of pure thought was necessity, and in this it was consistent with the entire tradition of western philosophy, which had recognized without dissent that significant philosophical discourse must be in this mode. One need but recall the famous analysis of Plato and the figure of the "line" in the *Republic* to reassure oneself on this point. All other modalities were held to be in some way either dependent upon or ultimately reducible to that mode, and the truth value of the various modes of discourse—science, rhetoric, poetry—was measured with reference to the paradigm of discourse in the mode of necessity. In projecting the notion of existential thinking, Kierkegaard is suggesting that the authentic mode of philosophical discourse is not necessity but possibility, that the human condition can be expressed only in the mode of possibility.

It is obvious that the entire quest of western philosophy for the "nature" of things and of man himself, as expressed in discourse in the mode of necessity, is called into question. It would not have been too revolutionary if it had merely been suggested that discourse in the mode of possibility might indeed possess significance and even significance which escapes discourse in the mode of logical necessity. How many times had it not been suggested that the avowal of love, the response to nature in poetry, the persuasion of the orator, possessed meaning, indeed expressed meanings which eluded the philosopher? However, it had never been seriously suggested that the discourse of philosophy could itself be in any other mode than that of necessity. The whole of model logic has its anchor in logical necessity. Kierkegaard is suggesting that this entire persuasion had been in error; even more, he is suggesting that the proper mode of philosophy must be possibility and not necessity. This is the declaration which alienates him from the classical notion of philosophy. Existential thinking, therefore, is philosophical thought in the mode of pure possibility. The "paradox" and the "scandal" (to employ terms which he favored) in this affirmation can escape no one, nor can the latent possibility that either Kierkegaard has worked a radical revolution in western philosophy or has placed himself outside its pale, thus disallowing his philosophical pretensions.

The last notion which remains to be explored in connection with existential thinking is that of "existential reflection." This idea can be fixed best if considered in relation to perception. Kierkegaard discusses it in relation to the manner in which the singular existent apprehends the being which he is. In the first instance he may be said to "perceive" that being, his own existence. In perception, however, that existence seems to possess a kind of necessity, derivative from the immediacy of perception. The existence of the singular has for the singular the necessity of the immediately (without mediation) apprehended. What is given immediately (without mediation) in perception *must be*, in the sense that it cannot be and not be given in perception. This is a property of perception which many philosophers have defended in the course of history and upon which many have rested the certainty of affirmations about the external world. The speciousness of this necessity in Kierkegaard's view seems readily apparent. In perception the existent is present to itself under the two aspects of subject and object; it is present both as the object which is perceived and as the perceiving subject. Being, however, falls between the two. They become a pair of other-reflecting mirrors, and the being of the subject is lost in the regressive perspective. The being of the object in perception is being-for-the-subject; the being of the subject is wholly the presence of the object. Of neither can the initial necessity be affirmed without qualification. Perception is therefore specious *in its unmediated necessity;* the singular existent cannot truly apprehend his being in this fashion.

That being may, however, be apprehended truly through "existential reflection." In this process, the existent apprehends himself, not as a "what" (object-being for another) but as the "how" of that which perception speciously presents. The character of his being as an existent is here revealed to him truly, for the response to this "how?" possesses no element of logical necessity. There is nothing in human existence—the actual, concrete existence of the human, singular subject—which, under existential reflection, generates the affirmation of that existence with logical necessity, or with logical necessity excludes the affirmation of non-being as an essential ingredient of that existence. In existential reflection the singular existent is seen as what it really is, *pure possibility*. This matter may be stated in another manner. Between possibility and actuality there is a relation of non-being. There is nothing in the possibility of the existent which necessarily involves his actuality; there is nothing in his actuality which excludes an implicit non-being.

In this way, under existential reflection, the human singular constitutes the complete refutation of the Hegelian system. He is the single instance of that being whose very actuality involves the possibility of its non-being and whose status as possibility not only is not derived from its actuality but is in contradiction to that actuality. The moments of possibility-actuality are governed by the law of contradiction and hence separated as being and non-being. No dialectic can synthesize them.

If Kierkegaard might be said to have, employ, or advocate a specific method, it would be existential reflection. It cannot be said, however, that he ever formally established it as a method, though it may be said that many of his statements become more transparent if they are interpreted as the results of existential reflection.

5. Possibility

The concept "possibility" has so forced itself to the forefront of attention in the examination of Kierkegaard's thought that it clearly demands explicit and direct consideration. It would be convenient had Kierkegaard developed, in some single passage of his works, an exhaustive and coherent statement of all aspects of his insights into this notion and had then proceeded to employ the concept in his other writings in strict accordance with this statement. Needless to say, no such statement is forthcoming. On the contrary, Kierkegaard presents at least two accounts of possibility and he does not employ them consistently.

Possibility is, first of all, the very form or structure of man's existence. These terms, *form* and *structure*, have so many other associations that one is reluctant to use them without qualification in this context. Thus, for example, both terms tend to exclude that complete openness to existence which Kierkegaard is clearly trying to convey, because both *form* and *structure* imply, in their historical associations, a limitation upon the openness of possibility. Thus, in those systems in which "possibility" is denominated from "act," the limit or range of possibility is clearly prescribed. Similarly, structure implies a certain organization of possibility which would limit the openness of existence. Hence, the terms are employed with caution. What is most clearly intended is that, under existential reflection, existence appears as a completely open field of possibility to which Kierkegaard will not hesitate to apply the romantic term *infinite*. As the "form" or "structure" of existence, possibility is the source both of *anguish* and of *despair*, each of which derives its specific character and quality from its relationship to possibility. When we come to consider what might be called a definition of *possibility*, the inconsistency in Kierkegaard's employment becomes more apparent.

Thus, in *Sickness Unto Death* we come upon the definition of reality as the "unity of necessity and possibility." However one construes this expression, it would seem to be inconsistent with the notions developed in relation to existential reflection and the structure of existence revealed by it. There, actuality and possibility were opposed as being and non-being; that is, by a complete and radical contradiction. The Hegelian could accept this definition without qualms. Any system which conceives of the reality of change as the Hegelian system does could certainly subscribe to this notion of possibility but always within the pattern of necessity, not in the stark opposition in which Kierkegaard has previously set them. This conception of possibility has given some encouragement to those interpreters who, like Fabro, would like to discover in Kierkegaard a position called "ontological realism," for every "realism" certainly demands a necessitarian basis such as this definition of possibility conceivably could supply. Still the definition seems out of joint with the overall pattern of Kierkegaard's thought and suggests a rationalistic reminiscence rather than an insight proper to himself.

Kierkegaard's most serious effort to come to grips with the notion of possibility is to be found in the *Philosophical Fragments*, "Intermezzo." Here he contrasts his employment of the term both with that of Aristotle and with that of Hegel. Referring to the *De Interpretatione*, he suggests that Aristotle errs by considering the necessary as itself possible; but since the possible *can* not be while the necessary *cannot* not be, he is forced to postulate a changeless possible over and above the possible as subject of change. The status of that changeless possible seems ambiguous to Kierkegaard and amounts only to saying "not impossible." Aristotle would have been better advised simply to have excluded the possible from the necessary and the necessary from the possible. The whole of this argument, it should be noted, turns about the notion of change, and it would not seem too much to say that the treatment does not do justice to Aristotle's preoccupation with this problem.

In like manner, Kierkegaard criticizes the notion of possibility he finds in Hegel. The necessary, Hegel avers, is the synthesis of the real and the possible. This seems to Kierkegaard to involve a basic confusion. If by their synthesis the real and the possible were to form the necessary, they would become something absolutely opposed to their original character: that which excludes becoming, i.e., the necessary. He goes on: "the necessary does not become," while "becoming is never necessary." The necessary cannot change because it is always in relation, and in a constant relation, to itself. The necessary, by definition, *is*. But possibility is always involved in change and in non-being, in its own non-being, its own partial annihilation. For when one alternative is realized, the other, which was equally possible, is annihilated; at the same time, even that alternative which is realized is annihilated as possible. The passage offers many difficulties to the interpreter of Kierkegaard; but it does seem consistent with what has emerged under existential reflection, namely, actuality and possibility are opposed as being and non-being; possibility seems, therefore, the coming to be which, even in coming to be, remains non-being and does not transpose to *act*.

This impotence before *act* remains the essence, so to say, of possibility. Act is the shadow of the absolute under which the concept of possibility in Kierkegaard takes form, for act is possibility whose actuality is necessary. It is the pure antithesis of the possibility which he discovers in human existence. The presence of act, of the absolute, of the necessary, thus remains the dialectical element in Kierkegaard's analysis of possibility. His analysis of existence in terms of possibility remains linked to the classical metaphysics of Pure Act.

6. The Stages of Existence

In the preceding paragraphs we have treated the notion of possibility abstractly; in doing so we have obviously violated a basic principle of Kierkegaard's thought, for which abstractness is the nemesis of truth. His doctrine of possibility is seen in its positive and concrete character in his exposition of the stages on life's way, the stages of existence. Here without question we are at the center of Kierkegaard's positive speculative construction within the framework of which all of the specialized concepts such as possibility, anguish or dread, desperation and sin, and, finally, faith find their place.

Taken in itself, and somewhat independently of the special concern of the history of philosophy, the doctrine of the stages of existence in Kierkegaard possesses the greatest interest. It reveals him as a master of the spiritual life in the great tradition of Christianity, though with accents entirely his own. The "stages on life's way" bear resemblances both to the "itineraria" and to the "classes of men" and "states of soul" of the venerable literature of Christian spirituality. Great interest would attach, for example, to a comparative study of these stages and the doctrine of the "Spiritual Exercises" of St. Ignatius of Loyola. Kierkegaard gives to this venerable pattern an interpretation which has no literal antecedents. From the point of view of the history of philosophy, this doctrine is of interest principally as it deepens the notion of possibility as the very being and non-being of human existence.

We may begin the consideration of the stages on life's way, the stages of existence, by advancing an all-embracing question: What is the architectonic movement of the stages, whence do they move and whither, from what state to what condition does the traversing of the stages transport the human individual existent subject? By the stages on life's way the individual human subject is brought, through a deepening sense of himself as possibility, to a pure confrontation with himself and eventually with the Absolute in its absurd manifestation in the person of the historical Jesus Christ, the man who is God. By these stages the human soul is brought to its knees—first through the recognition of its own nothingness, then through the recognition that the essence of its nothingness is the longing for the absolute, and finally through the realization that the Absolute is present and available to it, not under any form which the human mind itself may construct, but under a form which it must recognize as palpably absurd. Thus the ultimate recognition of its own nothingness, and at the same time the release from that nothingness into the absolute, takes form in an act which is at once complete self-annihilation and complete fulfillment: the act of faith. In this way Kierkegaard reaches by his own tortuous route the identical goal toward which Hegel had striven, the simultaneous annihilation and fulfillment of human contingency in the Absolute. But for Kierkegaard the absolute is not the Idea of reason, but the historical figure of Jesus Christ, the ultimate scandal of reason but the savior of the human existent. Kierkegaard's apologetics for Christianity is indeed complete, for Christ is the only answer to man's ontological hunger for God; he is fullness of being which is the antithesis of nothingness.

Within this architectonic movement, the doctrine of the stages develops. Central to this development is the notion of interiority. Here again, through the selection of this classical term of Christian spirituality, Kierkegaard's subconscious alignment with the entire tradition is made evident. As might be expected, he gives a meaning to this term which, while evincing profound affinities with its classical employment, still is entirely his own. *Interiority* for Kierkegaard means a dual movement of the spirit. The first is in the direction of an ever-deepening sense of human existence as pure possibility, groundless being which by this fact is pure non-being and absolute liberty. It involves the necessity of educing all forms or limitations of this pure possibility as without logical grounds, on the basis of pure choice or leap. The second, simultaneous movement is in the direction of the ever-deepening hunger for the absolute as the overshadowing presence of being, against which the pure possibility of human existence is projected. The "interior man," a hero of Christian spirituality from the beginning (for he is found present in St. Paul), is, for Kierkegaard, the man who is completely present to himself as pure possibility and absolute liberty, that is, as pure nothingness. In that nothingness he discovers the positive kernal of his authentic self: his need and hunger for the absolute, for God. Growth in interiority is the principle of continuity among the stages of life's way.

Within interiority itself, two movements may be distinguished. The first is the development of interiority against the foil of the world. Again the echoes of the ancient spirituality are awakened in every line of Kierkegaard. The interior man is man driven into the wilderness, leaving the haunts of men: Christ driven into the desert, Benedictus seeking his mountains, Bernardus his valleys, Ignatius the lonely cave of Manresa. The outward spatial isolation from the world is the symbol of the inward movement toward the self. In this movement, the spirit is led by the belief that the plenitude of being, which was first sought in the world, may be found within the self. But this expectation is doomed to disillusionment. A further movement of interiority awaits it—the discovery that the self, in which the fullness of being was sought, is itself nothing. The final stage of interiority emerges only when this disillusionment with self is reached. It is the dim apperception that the fullness of being is an absolute other from which the self, in its nothingness, is separated by an absolute abyss, the unbridgeable gulf between being and non-being. The fullness of interiority reveals that the only possible meaning of the self is that absolute other, from which it is alienated by its own non-being. Toward that absolute, the self can make no effective movement of the heart or the head, either by will or by reason. The words of Christ are ominous: "Who by taking thought may raise his stature by a cubit?"

Thus, interiority includes three essential elements, the basis of Kierkegaard's whole religious ontology: the presence of the self to the self as pure nothingness, the recognition by the self of the absolute other as the whole meaning of the longing for being which is the essence of its nothingness, and finally, the recognition by the self that by reason of its nothingness it is impotent to make any movement toward the other, that every such movement recoils upon it as a mockery and only increases the desperate sense of its nothingness. The nothingness that is the human subject would take possession of that absolute other, consume and possess it, make it its own. But how will he do so? By an *act* of his will? By an *act* of love? By an *act* of reason? Of thought? Of pure thought? The mockery in each such gesture is manifest in the notion that the subject which is nothingness can *act* at all. The human subject is pure wanting, pure waiting, pure desire, all passion, all suffering, all expecting, never acting. If ever the absolute comes to the nothingness which is man, it must be on the initiative of the absolute and in the form which the absolute selects, indifferent to the demands, the expectations, and the conditions of human existence.

To each of the moments of interiority there corresponds, in Kierkegaard's analysis, a definite tonality or quality; a specific manner, so to say, in which the nothingness of the subject, the void which is human existence, is felt and apprehended. There are three dominant modalities: dread, desperation, and sin. Dread is the modality of interiority when interiority is defined against the foil of the world. It is the qualitative apprehension by man of his situation in the world and before the world. Unlike fear and similar states, which refer to some definite object, dread refers to nothing in particular, nothing precise. It is the pure sentiment of possibility. Man in the world lives in possibility as the dimension of the future. His life in the world, as evidenced in Kierkegaard's portrait of the aesthete, is continually protracted toward the future, toward some expected event or good or pleasure or even some hoped-for relief. But the possibilities which open out before man as he is in the world, whether specified in terms of power, wealth, learning or whatever, carry no guarantee of realization. Under a veil of illusion they offer themselves as possibilities of pleasure, of happiness, of victory. As human possibilities, they offer no assurance of fulfillment; indeed they conceal the alternative possibility of disaster, misery, and, finally and inevitably, death.

But it would be mistaken to think that Kierkegaard regards dread as something which man should shun. On the contrary, it is the first quickening sign of spirituality or interiority, the first assurance that man is not entirely lost to and in the world. It is a sentiment which the spiritual man recognizes and welcomes as a sign of interior life, as opposed to the specious life of illusory expectation which the world offers him. The spiritually weak man, the man who, as St. Ignatius would say, is all "effusio ad exteriora" seeks to conceal this dread from himself; he wraps himself, as Jacob Wasserman says, in the "world's illusion" (cf. *The World's Illusion*) and feigns an optimism which he does not feel or which, if he does feel it, is but a sign that he is spiritually dead or not yet awakened to life. Kierkegaard describes the state of life in which dread arises in his portrait of the aesthete and aesthetic existence, but his counsel to the aesthete is not to shun dread, but to seize and embrace it.

The modality or tonality of interiority as defined against the self, as resting upon the disillusionment with self, the recognition of the nothing which the self is, is *desperation*. This, for Kierkegaard, is the "mortal sickness," the sickness unto death, which, paradoxically, is also an opening upon life. Desperation is that sickness which is proper to the human personality and which renders it incapable of realizing itself. Under this aspect, it is the constituent possibility of human existence which contains within it no principle of actualization, which moves backward upon nothingness with the same degree of assurance that it moves toward fulfillment. Before the self, the human existent may take either of two attitudes, but the tonality of desperation is proper to both. He may seek to be himself, that is, to recognize and embrace the nothingness which is his essence as possibility; when he does, desperation is identical with this recognition. For to be oneself is to despair of oneself, and this is an authentic mode of being proper to the human self. But, by contrast, the self may turn away from itself; a man may seek not to be himself. When he does so, desperation is still his lot. For how will a man not be himself? How will nothingness be being? To despair of oneself is to "live the death of the self," that is, to come to the nothingness of the self whether by way of seeking and embracing it or by way of escaping and denying it.

As in the case of dread, it would be wrong to suppose that desperation is something to be shunned. Like dread, it is to be embraced as an evidence of spiritual life. Indeed, it is the sign that the soul has reached a deeper level of interiority, that it has been delivered in a certain sense from a deeper illusion, namely, the illusion that the self can yield the being which the world promised but could not realize. It is a stepping stone from which the leap into a higher sphere of spiritual being may be possible. A man may believe that, though the world is all illusion, certainty, being, a fortress against death, abides in his own self. Desperation, which rests upon a perception into the deceptiveness of this persuasion, delivers him from a second illusion more profound than the illusion in which the world enshrouds him.

Sin is the modality of interiority when interiority embraces, not only the nothingness of the world and of the self, but the total nothingness of the human subject before the absolute being which defines that nothingness, i.e., before God. The soul is in sin, the soul is sin when it stands before God. This statement is true, yet it is not adequate for Kierkegaard's insight. Kierkegaard's conception has little to do with the older notion of sin as the voluntary transgression of a given moral law. He entirely ontologizes sin, that is, redefines it in terms of man's state of existence. Sin is a situation of existence, a degree of interiority to which man attains, or a condition he discovers on attaining a certain degree of interior vision. As a state of existence, sin would seem to have two elements or dimensions. The first is properly ontological; it resides in the recognition by man of his own nothingness and the further recognition that his nothingness has a positive core: the need and demand for the absolute other. The nothingness of man in sin is the absolute otherness of God. In this sense, sin, like dread and desperation, is not something to be shunned; indeed, there is no meaning to saying that it might be shunned. It is what man is, and the degree of interiority to which he has attained in the religious state of existence testifies to this fact. Indeed, he can really only be himself when he accepts sin as his absolute state before God. For man to reject sin would be to reject truth and God himself and to plunge into the most profound illusion of all. The rejection of sin is the crime of Lucifer, who would make himself equal to God. Sin is man's actual state before God, and to deny or reject it would be the most terrible of crimes.

The conception of sin has a second and a deeper aspect. Sin is the desperation of not having faith. This means, in basic ontologocial terms, a failure to recognize the absoluteness of the absolute other. This recognition is proper to that degree of interiority at which sin, is revealed as the ontological condition of man. To the absoluteness of the absolute other must belong the possibility of coming to the sinner. The sinner, man, has no right or power to deny this power to the absolute. But such a denial would be the essence of sin in that further sense which rests on the ontological meaning of sin. The desperation of sin is the denial by the nothingness of man of the absoluteness of the absolute, which he has recognized as the whole positive meaning of his nothingness. For in our nothingness God is witnessed as all.

This second dimension of the notion of sin leads us directly to the consideration of Kierkegaard's notion of faith. Obviously, the concept of faith is complex. Its basis in the human subject seems clear. The ground of faith is the dual recognition of the absolute in that degree of interiority whose tonality is sin. The absolute is recognized, relatively, as the being of which the nothingness of man is the other and that which gives meaning to the nothingness of man. The absolute is recognized further specifically, or positively, as *absolute*. This second aspect of recognition is the basis of faith in man. It is only the basis, not the actuality of faith, for faith can never be an act of man; it cannot have any beginning or origin in him. It cannot be any movement of his toward the absolute, but only his openness to the absoluteness of the absolute. Faith is waiting, but not waiting for anything specific; it is simply the proper attitude of the existent toward the absolute other.

What then is the actuality of faith? It is the movement of the absolute other toward the openness of the existent; more specifically, it is the power which the other gives to the existent to recognize the form of the absolute other as it advances upon the existent. Faith is wholly the work of the absolute other. Man has no power to have faith; he cannot dictate the conditions of faith, nor its object. Any such attempt would be a vain effort to encompass the absolute in terms of the finite, or non-being, and would be the deepest sin. Faith comes from the absolute. It is the manner in which the absolute comes to the nothingness of the existent (if it comes at all, for it is manifestly free not to come since it is absolute). Finally it is the power with which the absolute endows the nothingness of the existent that it might bear the weight of the absolute as it chooses to reveal itself.

The great separation between Hegel and Kierkegaard is clearly manifest here, despite the common purpose of their thought, the justification of Christianity. The condition of man at the highest reaches of Hegel's philosophy must be for Kierkegaard the purest form of sin and the complete destruction of the condition of faith. For as Kierkegaard sees it, the human spirit in Hegel takes on the form of the absolute and defines for the absolute, from the ground of the mind's finiteness, the condition of its absoluteness. Hegelianism must seem to Kierkegaard the very abyss of godlessness, the giddy peak of humanism from which man can await only the dreadful plunge into the darkness of complete disillusionment. For Hegel reveals to God what God is, the conditions on which he may speak and act, the meaning which his words and actions may have. He would make God the slave of logical necessity, thus stripping him of his divinity. For Kierkegaard, the attitude of man is complete openness, waiting, before the absoluteness of the absolute other. Whether the absolute other comes, whether it reveals itself, what is the form of its revelation, whether the human existent has the strength to bear the revelation of the other—all these are questions out of the range of the existent.

7. Revelation in Christ

All of these considerations bring Kierkegaard directly to the central issue of Christianity, which is Christ Jesus. There is no escaping the problem. Christ appeared in history, in time, in finite being, under the pure form of nothingness, that is, the form of man, and subject to all the conditions of that situation. Nevertheless, he said, "I am God," and he demanded that man believe in him as God. He demanded of them faith, that is, the bearing of the absolute under the form in which it chose to reveal itself. It is the essence of absurdity to conceive that the absolute would reveal itself in this, the weakest of all forms. It would be absurd to demand that reason so abase itself as to assent to this possibility, without seeking to bring it into the orbit of its own conditions. It is absurd to think that the absolute would come into time and among men in this form of a poor carpenter, in an inferior culture, to follow a career filled with inconsequences and to end finally upon the tree of ignominious crucifixion. Yet this is what is demanded by Christ of history.

What is the possible attitude of sinful man before this demand? The possibilities are terrifying. The only authentic possibility is faith. But faith is not in the power of man. Man cannot by his own power assume the weight of this absurd self-revelation of the absolute. Reason must decry it as a monstrous pretense or seek by a monstrous dialectic to bring it down to the level of rational comprehension and necessity. The imagination is staggered and can form no image which could make this revelation tolerable. The heart of man would embrace it if it dared, for the heart, of all the powers of man, is most inured to absurdity. But it dare not, for, of all the powers of man, what other is more prone to self-delusion?

The only possible disposition of sinful man before the self-presentation of Jesus Christ as God and savior is that of Abraham, the spiritual father of us all, before the divine command to sacrifice his son Isaac. What is that movement of Abraham? It is not a justification of the divine command, for who will justify the Lord? Neither is it an assent, for one does not assent to a command. It is obedience, that is, the recognition of the absolute Lordship of the Lord, the absolute freedom of the divine other. The Christian before Christ neither reflects, nor discourses, nor reasons; he does not even love. He obeys. His obedience is his faith, in pure and living form. But not even this obedience has its origin and source in himself. This power to obey is the power of the absolute other in him. The faith of the Christian, by which he bears the self-revelation of God in Christ, is not the Christian's faith, but Christ's. The Christian believes and obeys in fear and trembling; in fear and trembling lest, assumed as his own, his very faith and obedience may pass over into their opposites. By faith the Christian empties himself entirely to take up Christ; filling up the absolute void and nothingness within himself with the revelation of the divine and absolute other.

But what transpires in faith? All that Kierkegaard dared hope and all that Hegel dared to accomplish. The unreality, the nothingness of the finite and contingent is dissolved; it is replaced by the absolute being of that which must be. Everything that is, is revealed as that which must be. But that "must be" is not the command of logic or pure thought. It is the free movement of absolute being, whose every movement must be since it is all that is. Faith accomplishes all that the laborious dialectic could not accomplish. But this was only to be expected, in Kierkegaard's view; for the dialectic is the work of man, faith is the work of God.

Surely it would be the acme of fatuity to assay a judgment of value between Hegel and Kierkegaard. On purely historical grounds, Kierkegaard would seem to be the denial of philosophy, Hegel the ultimate dissolution of faith, but, on deeper grounds, so easy a disposal of the matter is impossible. The reality of the human spirit is too complex for such simple solutions. Hegel and Kierkegaard alike respond to profound demands of that spirit: the one to bring everything under the sovereign sway of reason, the other to recognize the utter nothingness of man and his works and, on the basis of this recognition, to seek authentic being in some transcendent principle or power. Every man who is at all "interior," in Kierkegaard's sense, must feel the conflicting tensions of these two demands within himself and must feel as well how impossible must be any easy or one-sided relaxation of those tensions.

Readings

I. KARL MARX

Books

Adam, H. K. *Karl Marx in His Early Writings*. London: Allen & Unwin, 1940.

Berlin, I. *Karl Marx*. New York: Time, 1959.

Bernstein, S. *Beginnings of Marxian Socialism in France*. Revised ed. New York: Russell & Russell, 1965.

Bober, M. M. *Karl Marx's Interpretation of History*. 2nd rev. ed. New York: W. W. Norton, 1965.

Carmichael, Joel. *Karl Marx: The Passionate Logician*. New York: Scribner, 1967.

Cornu, A. *Origins of Marxian Thought*. Springfield, Ill.: C. C. Thomas, 1957.

Delfgaauw, Bernardus. *The Young Marx*. Translated by Franklin Schutz and Martin Redfern. London: Sheed & Ward, 1967.

Garandy, Roger. *Karl Marx: The Evolution of His Thought*. Translated by Nan Apotheker. New York: International Publishers, 1967.

Hunt, R. N. C. *Marxism Past and Present*. London: G. Bles, 1954.

Jackson, John H. *Marx, Proudhon and European Socialism*. New York: Collier Books, 1962.

Kamenka, E. *Ethical Foundations of Marxism*. New York: Praeger, 1962.

Lefebvre, Henri. *The Sociology of Karl Marx*. Translated by Norbert Gulerma. New York: Pantheon, 1968.

Lewis, John. *Life and Teaching of Karl Marx*. New York: International Publishers, 1965.

Lobkowicz, Nicholaus, ed. *Marx and the Western World*. Notre Dame, Ind.: University of Notre Dame Press, 1967.

Essays and articles

Avineri, Shlomo. "Hegelian Origins of Marx's Political Theory." *Review of Metaphysics*, XXI (1967), 35–56.

————. "The Non-European World in Marx's Philosophy of History." *Iyyun*, XIX (1968), 12–27.

Blakeley, Thomas J. "Salient Features of Marxist Theory of Knowledge." *Boston College Studies in Philosophy*, I (1966), 155–174.

Fromm, Erich. "Marx's Contribution to the Knowledge of Man." *Praxis*, V (1969), 55–64.

Gilson, Etienne. "The Idea of God and the Difficulties of Atheism." *Philosophy Today*, XIII (1969), 174–205.

Greger, A. James. "Marxism and Ethics: A Methodological Inquiry." *Philosophy and Phenomenological Research*, XXVIII (1967–68), 368–384.
Hammen, Oscar. "The Young Marx Reconsidered." *Journal of the History of Ideas*, XXXI (1970), 109–120.
Hodges, Donald C. "The Détente Between Marxism and Linguistic Philosophy." *Praxis*, III (1967), 578–591.
Hyppolite, Jean. "The 'Scientific' and the 'Ideological' in a Marxist Perspective." *Diogenes*, LXIV (1968), 27–36.
Lobkowicz, Nicholaus "Karl Marx's Attitude Toward Religion." *Review of Politics*, XXVI (1964), 319–352.
Rotenstreich, Nathan. "Theory and Practice in Marx." *Iyyun*, XIX (1968), 1–11.
Tucker, Robert C. "Marx and the End of History." *Diogenes*, LXIV (1968), 165–174.

II. SØREN KIERKEGAARD

Bibliography

Himmelstrup, J. *Søren Kierkegaard: International Bibliography*. Danish and English. Copenhagen: Nyt nordisk forlag, 1963.

Books

Arbaugh, G. E., and Arbaugh, G. B. *Kierkegaard's Authorship: A Guide to the Writings of Kierkegaard*. Rock Island, Ill.: Augustana Library, 1967.
Carnell, E. J. *The Burden of Kierkegaard*. Exeter, England: Paternoster Press, 1966.
Channing, Pearce M. *The Terrible Crystal*. New York: Oxford University Press, 1941.
Collins, J. *The Mind of Kierkegaard*. Chicago: H. Regnery, 1953.
Diem, H. *Kierkegaard's Dialectic of Existence*. New York: Edinburgh, Oliver & Boyd, 1965.
Dupré, Louis. *Kierkegaard as Theologian: The Dialectic of Christian Existence*. New York: Sheed & Ward, 1963.
Garelick, H. M. *The Anti-Christianity of Kierkegaard*. The Hague: M. Nijhoff, 1965.
Hohlenberg, J. E. *Søren Kierkegaard*. Translated by T. H. Croxall. New York: Pantheon, 1954.
Lowrie, W. *Kierkegaard*. New York: Oxford University Press, 1938.
_____. *Short Life of Kierkegaard*. Reprint. Princeton, N. J.: Princeton University Press, 1965.
Price, G. H. *The Narrow Pass: A Study of Kierkegaard's Concept of Man*. New York: McGraw-Hill, 1963.
Roos, H. *Søren Kierkegaard and Catholicism*. Translated by R. M. Brackett. Westminister, Md.: Newman Press, 1954.
Sponheim, Paul Ronald. *Kierkegaard on Christ and Christian Coherence*. New York: Harper & Row, 1962.
Thompson, Josiah. *The Lonely Labyrinth: Kierkegaard's Pseudonymous Works*. Carbondale: Southern Illinois University Press, 1967.
Ussher, A. *Journey Through Dread*. New York: Devin-Adair, 1955.

Essays and articles

Allison, H. E. "Christianity and Nonsense." *Review of Metaphysics,* XX (1967), 432–460.

Blanshard, Brand. "Kierkegaard on Faith." *The Personalist,* XLIX (1968), 5–23.

Collins, J. "Faith and Reflection in Kierkegaard." In the same author's *Three Paths in Philosophy,* pp. 7–85. Chicago: H. Regnery, 1962.

Gerber, Rudolph. "Kierkegaard: Reason and Faith." *Thought,* XLIV (1969), 29–52.

Gill, Jerry. "Kant, Kierkegaard and Religious Knowledge." *Philosophy and Phenomenological Research,* XXVIII (1967), 188–204.

Johnson, H. A., and Thulstrup, N., eds. *A Kierkegaard Critique.* International symposium. New York: Harper & Row, 1962.

Kainz, Howard K. "Ambiguities and Paradoxes in Kierkegaard's Existential Categories." *Philosophy Today,* XIII (1969).

Mackay, Louis. "Philosophy and Poetry in Kierkegaard." *Review of Metaphysics,* XXIII (1969), 316–332.

Mourant, John A. "The Place of God in the Philosophy of Kierkegaard." *Giornale di Metafisica,* VIII (1953), 207–221.

Sontag, Frederick. "Kierkegaard and the Search for a Self." *Journal of Existentialism,* VII (1967), 319–328.

Stack, George. "Concern in Kierkegaard and Heidegger." *Philosophy Today,* XIII (1969), 26–35.

PART II
THE AGE OF BOURGEOIS
NATIONALISM

Introduction

Periodization has always been one of the most difficult tasks of historiography. Yet, it might be argued, it is an unnecessary task which historiography fecklessly assumes. For the movement of history itself, if sufficiently attended to, suggests such demarcations spontaneously. The historiographer has but to observe and follow.

Certainly this would seem to be the case in the history of western philosophy as it advances into the nineteenth century. The period of the dominance of romanticism and of the great ideal of the Hegelian speculative system is brought to a natural close, but by no means expunged from history, by the appearance of two new intellectual forces: modern science in general and, in a more particular way, the concept of evolution.

The strong development of science, in all its aspects—empirical, theoretical, and technological—during this period, coupled with the extension of the results of the Industrial Revolution, gave rise to the movement of positivism. The essence of positivism resided in the principle, or perhaps more accurately, in the ideal, of the ever-closer approximation of philosophy in its models and its methods to the concepts and procedures of science. This is by no means a new idea. On the contrary, from its inception in western culture, philosophy and science have been closely linked. However, in past ages it was philosophy which served as the model of what constituted scientific knowledge and might, therefore, claim a nomothetic status in the world of knowledge. What is new in the positivism of the nineteenth century is the reversal of roles between philosophy and the "natural" sciences as these had developed during the previous centuries. As the natural sciences achieved an ever greater autonomy in method, procedure, and model of knowledge, they began to assume a normative role with regard to philosophy itself. Positivism may be said to be the culmination of this trend, when it came to be openly asserted that this autonomy and normative role of the natural sciences was complete.

A distinction must be drawn, however, between positivism in a serious and limited sense and what might be called romantic positivism. The latter was at times by far the more eloquent and persuasive, though at the same time the least solidly founded. The rhapsodic scientism of a Taine, of a Renan, of an Ardigò, escapes the limits of the soberer forms of the same doctrine or attitude. One of the most difficult tasks of the historian is to keep these two strains apart and to distinguish and counterevaluate their claims.

The second of these forces which induce a natural articulation and, hence, periodization in the flow of philosophical inquiry in the nineteenth century, evolution, presents quite a different case. It is certainly an influence far more powerful than the scientistic ideal of positivism. Evolution, it must be said, worked as forcibly on the imagination as upon the scientific and philosophical proclivities of nineteenth-century man. The ideal of science and of the approximation of philosophy to its model opened up few fresh perspectives to the mind. The concept of evolution seems to open them in every direction and in every field of investigation. Under its powerful influence a veritable renaissance, a new ferment in thought, appeared. But it was an ambiguous and cloudy ferment. From the small and restricted basis in Darwin's first formulation of the evolutionary theory, it mushroomed to the vast range of the cosmic evolution of a Fiske. There was relatively little self-discipline within the ambit of this concept. It seemed capable of infinite exploitation, and of bearing the weight of unlimited matter and insight. Something of the fresh enthusiasm with which it invested the intellectual life may still be felt in such doctrines as the neo-evolutionism of a Teilhard de Chardin in the mid-twentieth century. It was to be some time before a measure of discipline, of self restraint, would be felt within the ambit of this concept itself—but not before it had already given occasion for strong reactions in the direction of the great speculative movements, the dream of the system of reason which had preceded it.

CHAPTER I

The Empiricism of John Stuart Mill

Introduction

John Stuart Mill is one of the most representative thinkers of his age and, after a century, still commands attention. He embodies all the prominent traits of Victorian England, both admirable and lamentable. Though philosophy was his avocation, his achievements in this discipline readily placed him in the forefront of the intellectual life of his age. He draws into fresh focus utilitarianism, positivism, and romanticism but is not dominated by them. He employs them as the basis of his own views, which exhibit in their best light all of the characteristics of English, as distinct from continental, speculation.

A. *Life, Philosophical Influences, Chief Writings*

Son of the utilitarian stalwart James Mill, he was educated under the personal direction of his father, according to principles formulated by his father and inspired by that doctrine. At the age of sixteen, he entered the service of the East India Company, in which he achieved a brilliant career; this in nowise, however, impeded his study and writing.

The first philosophical influence upon Mill was the utilitarian doctrine formulated by his father and, more authoritatively, by Jeremy Bentham, whose works he studied from his fifteenth year. Under the double burden of an intense program of study and a budding administrative career, about the year 1826 Mill suffered a severe spiritual crisis, some indications of which he supplies in his *Autobiography* (completed in 1873). This crisis shook his faith in the utilitarian doctrine and, for a time, inclined him toward a kind of activism, but his speculative bent was too strong to be deflected for long. During this period he came under the influence of the continental positivism of Comte and Saint-Simon. However, the mystical and imaginative forms which Comte gave to his vision of the "new humanity" repelled Mill, and the rigid authoritarianism of Comte's political system went against the grain of Mill's innate devotion to liberty. A further cause contributing to his crisis was his contact with romantic philosophy in the attenuated form found in the writings of Coleridge and Carlyle. Mill never seems to have mastered romantic philosophy of the Continent, a fact attested by the confused account he gives of Kant and other German thinkers in his mature work on Hamilton's philosophy.

It would be inaccurate to say that this crisis detached Mill completely from utilitarianism; on the contrary, this doctrine continued to be the foundation of his thought. He did, however, achieve a certain perspective upon utilitarianism which enlarged, not only his personal vision, but that of utilitarianism itself. He emerged from this experience sounder than he had entered it, as is shown by the greater personal accent he was able to impart to his thought and his increased openness toward other points of view. He now believed that while Bentham's method had been empirical, his empiricism reflected little experience of life. Mill's own ideal is covertly announced in this judgment: an empiricism as wide as life itself.

Among the works of Mill which most directly interest the historian of philosophy, his two-volume *A System of Logic, Ratiocinative and Inductive*, 1843, looms largest. *The Principles of Political Economy*, also in two volumes, appeared in 1848 and the famous essay *On Liberty* in 1859. The authoritative and critical essay *Utilitarianism* was published in 1863 and the vast study *An Examination of Sir William Hamilton's Philosophy* in 1865. Lesser, but not for that reason less interesting, works are: the early *Essays on Some Unsettled Questions of Political Economy* (written in 1830–33 but not published until 1844); *Considerations on Representative Government*, 1863; *The Subjection of Women*, 1869, and the four volumes of *Dissertations and Discussions, Political, Philosophical and Historical*, published between 1859 and 1875. The year of his death, 1873, saw the publication of his *Autobiography*. He died in Avignon, where he had gone in his retirement. Three essays on religion: "Nature," "Utility of Religion" and "Theism" appeared in 1874.

B. *Mill's Logic*

The influence of positivism upon Mill's thought is clearest in the logical doctrine; at the same time, it is here that he most clearly distinguishes his own position from that of continental positivism and indicates his basic principle: radical empiricism. Comtean positivism took its point of departure in facts, but only to press on to laws, which, once formulated, could be systematized and solidified into dogmas. In contrast, the purpose of Mill's logic is to dissolve the basis of all forms of absolutism in science and to establish every truth, principle, and demonstration on empirical bases.

His first concern is the rejection of metaphysics and the reduction of the principles heretofore considered metaphysical to their empirical grounds. It is generally contended, he notes, that the existence of matter or of mind, of time or space, cannot be demonstrated but can be known only through an immediate intuition. The operation and validity of such an intuition would, by definition, fall outside the scope of examination. However, logic is precisely the science of proof and evidence. It can have nothing to do with metaphysics and immediate intuition. All truths, even principles, are empirical. The propositions for which immediate evidence had been claimed, and which provided the basis of metaphysical speculation and system building, are not to be rejected, but are to be traced to their own empirical origin before they can authentically be used by philosophy. The so-called truths of reason, or essential propositions, are purely verbal; they assert of a thing to which a name is assigned only what is implied by calling them by that name (nominalism). What have in the past been called axioms have been suggested by observation; the conclusion that two straight lines cannot enclose a space follows only on the observation of a straight line in experience. Even the principle of contradiction is nothing but one of our first and most familiar generalizations from experience.

Such a procedure would seem to lead Mill to the same kind of skepticism that Hume had reached in his analysis of similar propositions. But Mill denies that this is the necessary term of the process he has undertaken. On the contrary, in his view it would now be possible for the first time to guarantee to human knowledge the degree of validity which belongs to it in view of its empirical bases and origin. Since every universal proposition is a generalization from fact and observation, the fundamental problem of *induction* and the fundamental task of his logic is to justify such generalization and to determine its processes. One explanation might be total enumeration, the exhaustive observation of all the facts. But this is obviously impossible in any natural, i.e., not artificially created, situation. Moreover, as he admits, it is sometimes possible that the generalization may rest on a single observation. Mill, therefore, does not follow this line, but finds the ground and guarantee of the validity of such generalizations in the principle of the uniformity of nature. This principle rests in turn upon one law, the law of causality. This law, which asserts that every fact must have a beginning and a cause, asserts by this very fact that it is itself a law, and therefore that everything must have a law. The principle of causality is thus the basis of every generalization, of all inductive process, and enables us to recognize a constant and necessary order in nature.

Is this not admitting by the back door what he expelled by the front? Is not the principle of causality, or that of the uniformity of nature, of the same character as the self-evident principles which he has already rejected? Mill does not think so. The fact of causality and the uniformities in nature which it supports or makes possible are attested by observation. These principles, which support induction, are themselves the product of induction. We would never have arrived at the notion of causality, in the philosophical sense of the term, as the condition of all phenomena, had not many cases of causation or many partial uniformities of succession previously become familiar to us. The uniformity of nature, resting on the principle of causality which expresses it, is, therefore, the result of a simple induction by simple enumeration.

It would seem that Mill has now become involved in a manifest vicious circle. How is it possible to make the validity of induction itself depend on an induction? Mill believes not only that he can dispel the suspicion of circularity but that he can show that this is the only possible procedure. He proceeds by a renewal of the ancient attack on the theory of the syllogism. Making the validity of induction depend on an induction will seem circular only if the theory of the syllogism is taken as the point of departure. This theory holds that the universal truth which forms the major premise is the real demonstration, even the *cause*, of the particular truths which may be deduced from it. All men are mortal is the demonstration, the logical cause, of the proposition that Socrates is mortal. But Mill believes he can demonstrate precisely the opposite view. The major premise not only is *not* the proof of the particular propositions or conclusions, but is established by one and the same kind of evidence. All men are mortal is not the basis for asserting that Socrates is mortal; but our past experience of morality justifies our inferring, together, the general truth and the particular fact, with the same degree of assurance for each.

Mill's critics see things somewhat differently. In their view, he makes a fatal confusion in his use of the concept of law by blurring the distinction between law as fact and law as norm. Beneath this distinction lies a distinction between kinds of necessity. The law as fact possesses the necessity of fact. But logic and science are directly concerned, not with the necessity of fact, but with normative necessity which establishes the necessity of the necessity of fact itself, i.e., why the facts should be as they are and not otherwise. This latter necessity is not a fact but a principle and norm, and would not seem to be attainable by any process of induction such as Mill suggests. Thus, his entire undertaking falls under the shadow of profound doubt.

C. *"Metaphysics": The Examination of Hamilton's Philosophy*

At the beginning of the *Logic*, Mill had exorcised metaphysics and all its works. In his examination of Hamilton's philosophy, however, he becomes involved in this type of speculation in its knottiest form: the existence and nature of the external world. Hamilton's philosophy offered a challenge which Mill, apparently, could not reject. Hamilton sought to repristinate the doctrine of the Scottish school: the immediate perception (perception not mediated by an idea) of the reality of the external world. Mill's task, therefore, in the strict order of speculation, is to show that the external world could be entirely accounted for, in its status as external, by the means he had outlined in the *Logic*.

Mill was placed at a disadvantage by Hamilton's references to Kant and German romanticism. While he should have set aside these references and tried to address Hamilton's project in its native innocence, he could not do so without seeming to shirk part of the engagement. But he soon made clear that he had little or no grasp on the Kantian critical philosophy or its romantic developments and worked with an interpretation of them which was clearly inadequate. Justice to Mill demands that the portion of his work involving the interpretation of the German schools be bracketed and his criticism of Hamilton be considered, as far as possible, in its own terms.

In addressing the problem presented by Hamilton's philosophy, Mill takes his clue from Hume: He has recourse to the laws of association. What is it that we mean to assert, he asks, when we assert that the world we perceive is *external* to us? We mean that there is, in our perceptions, an element which exists even when we are not perceiving or thinking of it; an element which existed before we perceived it or thought of it and which will continue to exist after we have ceased to perceive or think of it. Even further, we intend to assert that there exist things which have never been perceived or made the object of thought and which may never be perceived or thought of. When, in the past, philosophers discoursed about substance, they meant, upon final analysis, precisely this. The material object which is present to us in actual perception is constructed, as Hume had indicated, through processes of association. But these processes extend beyond the present moment, our present sensations, and the objects constructed of them. They enable us to pass beyond, into the domain of possible sensations or possibility of sensation, which is the obvious context of our present perception. Of course, the world cannot be limited by any principle to the objects actually present in the present moment of sensation; the world includes, as well, an infinite range of possible sensations. It includes all the sensations which past experience assured us could be experienced in the present moment of perception and also the indefinite and limitless range of sensations which might be experienced under conditions unknown to us.

When this vast context of possible sensation is considered, it is readily seen that the present moment and its perceptions are partial and transitive. By contrast, the world of possible sensation presents an aspect of permanence, for the possibility of sensation is a permanent possibility. The range of possible sensation, therefore, presents itself with the same characteristic with which the external world has always been endowed by classical philosophy, the property classically assigned to substance: permanence. The world of possible sensation constitutes a kind of permanent substratum, a range of permanently possible sensation, evoked on the basis of past and present actual sensation and perception. This range of permanently possible sensation meets all the requirements for the definition of the external world. In its construction there is no need to have recourse to direct intuition to transcend actual experience, as Hamilton and the tradition which he represented maintained. Mill is so persuaded of the adequacy of this response that he believes that the same procedure can be applied to that other principle which Hume had dissolved: spiritual substance, "soul." But upon addressing this problem more closely, he discovers that it presents difficulties which he had not anticipated, especially those involved in the notion of a series of sensations and the notion of the possibility of sensation which would know itself as such. For this reason, he was prepared to let the problem of the self and personal identity remain in a theoretical limbo, accepting the fact but venturing no theoretical explanation of it.

D. *Ethical and Political Ideas*

Nowhere is the influence of Mill's own spiritual experience and his personal reflection upon the utilitarian position more clearly evident than in his thoughts on ethics and the social and political order. He gradually modifies the abstract individualism and libertarianism of earlier utilitarian ethics and its belief in inflexible laws of economic and political life in the direction of a greater sense of human solidarity and the power of the ethical will to infuse in those laws a humane quality.

Mill never abandons the hedonic and individualistic bases of utilitarian ethics, but he came to see both in a wider and more flexible context. Thus, he is led to place special force on the claims of universal happiness in the utilitarian calculus. He supplements Bentham's intellectualistic analysis of this principle with a fervent vindication of the claims of social feelings. Instead of a mere calculus of external consequences, he makes the motive force of this idea nobility of will and mind, introducing a fresh moral elevation into the entire discussion. With respect to the denomination of pleasures and pains, which enter into the structure of the concept of happiness, Mill introduces the consideration of the *quality* of pleasure in opposition to Bentham's quantitative notion. This gives him a decided advantage in refuting the charge that is frequently leveled against the utilitarians of reducing virtue to a mere form of pleasure-seeking. The introduction of the qualitative aspect of pleasure takes Mill beyond the hedonistic limits of utilitarian ethics, and pleasure itself is no longer the basic criterion.

In like manner, abstract individualism and liberty, the pure autonomy of the individual, prove not enough. The individual acquires more and more stature in his relation to others, either in direct interpersonal relations or in the more diffused and anonymous relations of social life. Liberty is inevitably modified; it becomes, not the liberty of pure autonomy, but the liberty of responsible action in view of a good (interest, pleasure) involving many, but depending for realization on the direct action and decision of the individual. In a word, Mill's ethics strongly reflects that experience of life which he had detected as lacking in his great mentor Bentham.

In his theory of political economy, the same tendency is apparent. He had inherited from his utilitarian predecessors, Smith, Malthus, and Ricardo, the idea of the inflexibility of economic and social laws, that they operated independently of all influence of the human ethical will but nevertheless made for the maximum of common good. It gradually became clear to Mill from the social conditions surrounding him, especially as they touched the distribution of wealth, that the beneficence of these laws could not be taken for granted. This inevitably caused him to doubt their inflexibility. He was led to a compromise. He was willing to recognize their inflexibility with regard to the *production* of wealth, but he came to hold more and more firmly that the distribution of wealth could be modified and better ordered through the intervention of the ethical will, employing concepts of justice and equity. In this line of reflection Mill is led to entertain a high degree of tolerance toward socialism, a doctrine which had been anathema to Bentham and Smith. For Mill the choice between individualism and socialism depends on one consideration, namely, which system shows the greatest capacity to assure the greatest possible sum of human liberty and spontaneity. He withheld adherence to socialism, chiefly because of his concern to safeguard individual liberty under all circumstances. This was for him a sacred fortress, immune to all invasion of authority. Nevertheless, he consistently supported a whole series of measures, which, through state intervention, would make for the more equitable distribution of wealth and the improvement of social conditions.

In political theory Mill is inclined to modify his own basic individualism and the radicalism of earlier utilitarianism. While it had led some of the more extreme members of the movement to the brink of anarchism, in general that radicalism had identified utilitarianism with democracy, in the sense of majority rule. Such democracy seemed to follow logically from the abstract individualism and libertarianism which they espoused, for it was a mathematical theory of majority to which these doctrines seemed to lead. Mill saw that the qualitative differences among individuals could not be overlooked in the projection of an ideal political order. This persuasion imparted an aristocratic propensity to his political thought. Bentham had wanted the legislator to be the simple mirror and instrument of the will of his constituents; Mill came to think of him, rather, as the intelligent interpreter of his constituents' needs, who must inevitably find himself, at times, at odds with their own interpretation of those needs. Political science and concrete political order ought, therefore, to explore and realize the conditions under which the best might rule. Against the notion of a free electorate, he was consequently prepared to defend the notion of a pluralistic voting structure in which superior education and other qualities would receive the added weight and consideration due them. His essay on representative government and his miscellaneous political writings record the inner tensions and the growing clarity of his reflections on this important problem.

E. *Religion and Experience*

Mill's reflections on the problems of religion hold considerable interest since they exemplify both his own speculative power and the attitudes of his times. He shared Comte's view that religion for western man had need of a profound renewal, but he dissociated himself from the form which the "religion of humanity" tended to assume in positivist doctrine. His own purpose was to assure the humanization of religion, making it serve the ends of humanity by bringing it within the limits of experience. Nevertheless, he feels that the argument for the existence of God which Kant had called cosmological is without value; matter and force, having no beginning, have no need of a cause. At the same time, Mill denies the validity of those arguments which appeal to the *consensus gentium* or to the moral conscience. He inclines only toward the teleological argument for God's existence, and that only to the degree to which that argument can be given a strictly inductive form.

The God to which the teleological argument might, in this inductive form, eventually lead would still differ markedly from the God of Christianity. He would be neither omnipotent nor omniscient, and his governance of the world would reflect these limits. Nevertheless, such a God would possess the value of utility. He could become the basis of a religion of humanity, capable of inducing men to limit their individualistic inclinations and giving them some sense of cooperation with the invisible Being from whom all good flows. This cooperation would, presumably, find reflection in the structure and process of social life.

F. *Liberty*

Perhaps the most lasting testimony to Mill's moral elevation as well as his speculative power is the essay on *Liberty*. Stylistically, it is Mill at his best, uniting the strongest qualities of his mind and pen: clarity, eloquence, the power of logical argument, polemical skill, and, withal, a profound humility (not usually associated with his character) which shines out in his intense concern for the truth. Its doctrine cannot be called original, but, in such an area, who can say that originality is the final value? What the essay does achieve is a clearly defined presentation of a complex of ideas about the nature of human liberty which had been taking form over a long period and which in Mill's mind came into powerful focus. This idea of liberty provides the theoretical basis of liberalism in its classical sense. It is Aristotelian, in the ethical sense, since it seeks to find the middle way between anarchistic and egotistical individualism on the one hand and the stultifying transcendence of the collectivity on the other. This notion of liberty is ethical, even moralistic, in tone, but its most imposing consequence is in the order of human social relations. It might be summarized by speaking of the social consequences of the autonomous, but socially sensitized, conscience. Man is free, and only from his freedom can values arise; but he has the freedom to serve an end higher than himself, an end which touches all. In that autonomous conscience and will, expansive power finds its adamant limit, and social good its lasting guarantee.

Readings

I. GENERAL BACKGROUND

Appleman, P., et al., eds. *1859: Entering an Age of Crisis*. Bloomington, Ind.: Indiana University Press, 1959.

Halévy, Elie. *The Growth of European Radicalism*. New printing. Boston: Beacon Press, 1966.

Houghton, Walter. *The Victorian Frame of Mind, 1830–1870*. New Haven: Yale University Press for Wellesley College, 1957.

Young, G. M. *Victorian England: Portrait of an Age*. London: Oxford University Press, 1936.

II. MILL'S LIFE AND EDUCATION

Ellery, John B. *John Stuart Mill*. New York: Twayne Publishers, 1964.

III. EXPOSITION AND EVALUATION OF MILL'S THOUGHT

Books

Anschutz, R. P. *The Philosophy of John Stuart Mill*. Oxford: Clarendon Press, 1953.

Berlin, Isaiah. *John Stuart Mill and the Ends of Life*. London: Council of Christians and Jews, 1962.

Cohen, George. *The Categories of John Stuart Mill*. New York: Columbia University Press, 1965.

Plamanatz, John. *Mill's Utilitarianism and the English Utilitarians*. Oxford: Blackwell, 1949.

Essays and articles

Aiken, Henry D. "Utilitarianism and Liberty: John Stuart Mill's Defense of Freedom." In the same author's *Reason and Conduct*. New York: Knopf, 1962.

Hall, E. W. "The 'Proof' of Utility in Bentham and Mill." *Ethics*, LX (1949).

Magid, H. M. "Mill and the Problem of Freedom of Thought." *Social Research*, XXI (1954).

CHAPTER II

Nineteenth-Century Evolutionary Philosophy

Introduction

If the problem were set of determining what concept of nineteenth-century speculation must be called most diffused and influential, the choice must inevitably fall to the concept of evolution. Extensive diffusion and wide influence do not, of course, in themselves constitute any evidence of the philosophical or scientific validity of a concept. On the contrary, such influence and diffusion is a cultural phenomenon; under this aspect it must correctly be assumed to be nonphilosophical in most of its manifestations. The essential paradox is that, even as a cultural phenomenon, the effectiveness and influence of the theory of evolution derived, to a great extent, from its claim to be philosophical in character.

As a matter of fact, the concept is of a mixed genealogy. The first suggestion of the concept appears in the area of economic and social statistics. It was then developed in a biological context and there received its classical formulation. Thence it was quickly, but not always critically, extended to man, both as a biological species and as an intelligent principle; to society and politics; to art and religion. In the process of this extension in all directions, an effort was made to lift the concept to a genuinely philosophical level. In this effort the direction given to thought by romanticism was an important aid, particularly since romanticism made the concept of teleology speculatively respectable again in the atmosphere of nineteenth-century science. It should be noted, however, that any effort to derive evolution directly from romantic philosophy, and specifically from the concepts of the dialectic and of spirit, must ultimately prove fallacious.

Since it is with the attempt to lift this concept to the philosophical level, and in this way to make it a universally effective principle both in the order of existence and in that of science, that the present chapter must be concerned, it is best to begin the discussion of evolution at the point where its philosophical stature begins to emerge.

To grasp this point, it is necessary to realize that the concept of evolution, as it aspired to philosophical stature, implied an alternative to the concept of nature which had, until the nineteenth century and well into it, dominated European thought. This concept of nature was based, ultimately, on the notion of causality. Despite the long critique of the principle of causality, beginning at least with Locke and Hume, the concept had not lost its hold upon the European mind. On the contrary, it had simply undergone a series of metamorphoses corresponding to the phases of the critique which had been brought to bear upon it. Comte's positivism illustrates this fact well. Comte was successful in his attempt to reintroduce the notion of science as the quest of *verae causae*, true causes; at the same time he had modified the notion of cause to make it conform to the critique it had undergone and to the exigencies of his own program. Mill's doctrine of causality also illustrates this characteristic of European thought. The most serious criticism of causality had not been that of empiricism, however, but of romanticism, which had distinguished the area of natural necessity from that of freedom. The force of the evolutionary doctrine was that it introduced an alternative to the notion of causality into nature itself.

It has become something of a fashion, though one grown stale by now, to compare effective alterations in the course of the history of thought to the Copernican revolution. Kant applied the simile to his own thought, and it has been applied by others to the thought of Charles Darwin, in whom the evolutionary theory found its first systematic expositor. As the Copernican revolution extended the view of the cosmos, infinitizing it, transforming the possibilities of cosmology and altering its basic concepts, so the doctrine of evolution introduced an extension and transformation of the view of organic life.

Up to Darwin's time, no general law expressing a universal interconnection of origin and development in the organic world had been formulated. Kaspar Wolff (1733–1794) and Karl von Baer (1792–1876) had proven that the single organism passes through a series of transformations or stages of development from the embryo to the perfectly formed individual, noting at the same time that there is little resemblance between the two terms of the process. Spinoza, Hartley, and James Mill, in their psychological studies, had pointed out that the individual undergoes a psychic development, governed by the law of association, in the process of which psychic forms arise differing profoundly from the initial state. Montesquieu, in the *Spirit of the Laws*, and the historical school which sprang from him and which flourished in France and Germany after the great Revolution, had suggested a kind of development in political and social structures. Finally, the romantic philosophers, more than any who had preceded them, spoke in terms of development, laying stress on the unity of the whole through the stages it underwent in its passage to integrity.

A significant difference, however, separates these earlier employments or statements of the notion of development from that which Darwin was to advance and which philosophical evolutionism was to foster. This difference may be illustrated by the quandary in which romantic philosophy had found itself. At the heart of the romantic conception of phenomenology, there had existed an ambiguity as to whether the process through the stages of that system of appearance to the unity and presence of the whole in the Idea must be conceived as a logical passage only or as a process in time as well. The emphasis which romantic philosophers, especially Hegel, tended to place upon history suggests that the temporal dimension of the process did not escape them; theoretically, however, the ambiguity was never effectively resolved. Evolution, on the other hand, conceives this process directly and primarily in terms of temporal development and succession; it projects the transformations of biological forms which it conjures through a time process.

There is a second difference, perhaps even more important than the first. In its earlier forms, especially in romantic philosophy, development had been conceived as a free, creative process; for this reason it had been contradistinguished, sometimes sharply, from natural process, which was characterized by necessity. In evolutionary theory, on the other hand, the time process of development, which is discovered by Darwin in the area of biology and is then projected into other areas as a key to their comprehension, is conceived in terms of nature and of natural necessity. As a consequence, one of the crucial questions which will plague evolutionism as a philosophy will be that of human freedom, while one of the most significant of the evolutionary constructs, that of Bergson, has for its precise object the union of these characters of creativity, or freedom, and evolution.

Nevertheless, some precedents for the Darwinian concept are to be pointed out. Examples of natural developmental processes had been suggested by the theories of Kant and of Laplace concerning the evolution of the solar system from an initial gaseous state according to definite physical and chemical laws; a similar case in geology is Lyell's account of the origin of the present form of the earth's crust, in which he had recourse only to physical and chemical laws which he conceives to have been operative at every state of that process just as they are operative at present. Darwin's theory, in its initial form, before it was extravagantly extended to become a philosophical principle from which no dimension of reality might be exempt, was in this tradition. Addressing itself to the world of organic nature and postulating a temporal succession of forms of life through natural and necessary causes, it tried to establish a unitary law which would account for all these transformations. At the same time it attempted to point out specific causes operative under this law.

Even the notion that different organic forms and species had been produced by natural causes was not without precedent. A. R. Wallace (1823–1913), for example, had questioned the fixity of the Linnean tables by indicating such transformations, though always in the area of rather inchoate and ambiguous forms of life. As a consequence, it becomes clear that Darwin's real achievement lay, on the one hand, in the clarity and formal character in which he stated this law, as a unitary law, and, on the other, in the fact that he indicated specific efficient causes. This truth is sharply pointed up by the fact that, a few years before the appearance of *The Origin of Species,* Herbert Spencer had employed the evolutionary hypothesis in the first edition of his psychology, but only as a hypothesis. And it was Spencer, profiting by Darwin's work, who was to press most vigorously the philosophical career of the evolutionary idea, extending it in every direction.

Like the world which it depicted, the evolutionary idea itself may be said to have had a history; that is, it too passed through ideal-temporal stages of formation and development. The first of these is its virginal statement in the context of the descriptive morphology of organic forms, by Darwin himself. The second is its extension and elevation from this limited area into a universal, or at least extensive, principle of fact and explanation, verifiable in the most varied areas; this point, of course, marks the beginning of its philosophical career. Finally, there is the stage in which an effort was made to unite the two great forms under which the notion of development had been advanced: those of freedom and creativity and of natural necessity. These stages are best studied in their most eloquent exponents; the first and second, respectively, in Darwin and Spencer; the third, ultimately, in a separate chapter on Bergson, the philosopher of "creative evolution."

A. *Charles Darwin and the First Form of the Doctrine of Evolution*

Charles Darwin was born February 12, 1809. After unsuccessful attempts to study medicine at Edinburgh and theology at Cambridge, in 1831, in the capacity of recorder, he joined the crew of the *Beagle,* which was about to set out on an around-the-world voyage for the exploration of fauna and flora. This voyage lasted six years and was to reveal to Darwin both his own interests and his real powers as an observer and student of living nature. In 1839 he published the results of this voyage of observation in his volume *The Voyage of the Beagle.* The data here gathered and presented constitute in great part the empirical basis of his theory. His basic observation may be said to have been that fauna of the same genus but of different species are observed to inhabit different environments. This suggests that a common form had undergone specific differentiation under the influence of environmental conditions and for the purpose of adaptation. This supposition leads to the basic question to which evolutionary theory in this form is the suggested answer: How are the forms and qualities which enable plants and animals to survive in their specific environments developed and preserved? (It is scarcely necessary to point out that the terms *genus* and *species* are used in the sense in which they appear in the classificatory sciences of nature, as in the Linnean tables, and not in any metaphysical or logical sense.)

The reading in 1838 of the work of the economist Malthus on population appears to have marked a crucial juncture in the formation of Darwin's thought. Malthus advanced the view that living beings, specifically men, tend to multiply in a ratio which swiftly outstrips the possible means of sustenance. This being the case, Darwin reflected, only two ways appeared open to the reconciliation or adjustment of form and environment: struggle or cooperation among living forms. His option was for struggle. (The other possibility, cooperation, was to be adopted by another great evolutionary thinker, Prince Kropotkin [1842–1921], in his work *Mutual Aid,* 1902.) Life is and must be struggle according to Darwin. The individual or group which possesses or can acquire or generate an organ or faculty which corresponds to the environment, and which at the same time is lacking to or cannot be acquired by other forms or individuals, is more likely to survive in a common environment than those not so endowed. By that individual, or within that group, the work of the propagation of life will be carried on, while forms lacking these capacities of adjustment to environment will tend to die out. At the same time, however, he noted that within a common environment a diversity of forms may better exist than a multiplicity of one form, for by this variation more dimensions of the environment may be exploited. Or again, if the environment changes, the power to change with it is the principle of survival. In this way it becomes clear to Darwin that variation and the power of variation is the great principle of the survival, multiplication, and propagation of life.

About 1845, Darwin began to put this theory into expository form, but he desisted for lack of sufficient factual data. He turned, instead, to investigations which might supply this lack. The work of formulation and presentation was resumed in the middle fifties and appeared in the memorable year 1859 as *On the Origin of Species by Means of Natural Selection.* (This was the year, it may be recalled, of the appearance of Marx's *Critique of Political Economy,* and the simultaneity gave rise to the extraordinary remark of Marx that he and Darwin had completed similar discoveries in different orders.) *The Origin of Species* was followed by a list of other works, developing and extending the field of application of the principles here formulated. The most significant of these are *The Variation of Animals and Plants under Domestication,* 1868; *The Descent of Man and Selection in Relation of Sex,* 1871, and *The Expression of the Emotions in Man and Animals,* 1872. In an *Autobiography* prepared three years before his death in 1882, he recapitulates the stages of his career and the formation of his ideas with the clarity and candor which mark all his works. This autobiographical statement was published in a work prepared by his son Sir Francis Darwin, *Life and Letters of Charles Darwin, Including an Autobiographical Chapter,* 1887.

In the development and exposition of the doctrine of evolution there emerge certain key phrases which indicate the pivotal junctures of the doctrine, and it is wise to concentrate attention upon an understanding of these phrases. The first of these is the phrase "struggle for existence." This enunciates the basic relation which exists between the individual or the species and, on the one hand, its natural environment (that is to say, the natural forces under which it lives) and, on the other hand, other individuals or species. This relation can also be expressed by saying that environment is always complex; that it consists of or includes not only natural factors, such as climate and sources of sustenance, but also other living creatures which compete within the same natural environment. It is clear that in this wide and complex sense the term *struggle* for existence can be understood only figuratively, at least in that dimension in which it involves the individual or species and the natural environment. It means simply the interaction of natural forces, as the examples which Darwin himself cites make abundantly clear. Plants on the edge of a desert may be said to be *struggling* for existence; but, in fact, whether they can exist is simply a question of available water supply. Two branches of the same tree may be said to be "competing" for the sap which flows from the bole through both; but this is simply a matter of the mechanics of plant nutriment. When the notion of environment is extended to include the presence of other individuals and species, the figure of speech takes on an added dimension but does not become literal.

Strictly speaking, the only situation in which a struggle for existence could take place is among men, for presumably men alone of the animal kingdom possess reflective judgment and will. However, since the Darwinian theory addresses man only insofar as these dimensions of his being can be reduced to unreflective reaction and interaction, the figure of speech remains a figure. What then does the phrase "struggle for existence" actually mean? It would seem to mean that there is a relation of incommensurability between all the factors which constitute a natural situation; as a result of this incommensuration, there is constant variation in the overall configuration of that situation. This is as well illustrated by the change of seasons as by any other natural phenomenon, such as the extinction of an individual or a species. Darwin means, simply, that some individuals and some species persist while others vanish, and that the cause of this phenomenon is to be found in some factor of variation in the natural situation.

It must be added that he sees these variations, not as abstract types which may recur, but as an irreversible series which cannot be repeated. Therefore, he seeks to describe the positive character of this series. Thus, it would seem that evolution is a positivist theory in the Comtean sense of the term, for it is concerned with relations between phenomena; but it lacks the legalist dimension of Comte's positivism since its generalizations are simply observations and not laws. Some individuals and some species persist, change, and develop; others perish. This is fact. The explanation consists in fixing the factors influencing or determining the one result or the other, not in abstract, legal patterns, but in unidirectional narrative sequence.

The second phrase which is pivotal to Darwin's exposition and which it is consequently necessary to comprehend is "natural selection." In itself this is as much a figure of speech as the earlier phrase, "struggle for existence," since it expresses in dynamic, volitional, and valuative terms a process which, on the postulates of Darwin's own thought, is wholly natural and necessitated in character. Natural selection is the converse of the notion of the struggle for existence. It evokes the same concrete image, that is, the fact that some individuals and some species persist while others perish. Now, however, the figurative emphasis is thrown, not on the individual or species imagined in dynamic and volitional relation to its environment, but on the image of an agent, nature, which determines a pattern according to which persistence and extinction appear. The image evoked is that of a selective, valuative, and volitional factor, nature itself, supremely efficacious, which determines this pattern. But in its concreteness natural selection is nothing but the account of those factors whose variations bring about the central phenomena of persistence and extinction.

The influence of Darwin's doctrine or theory rested as much upon its scientific character as upon any of its actual statements. The doctrine of evolution was looked upon as a triumph of the scientific method, which had been centuries in process of formation, and, in a sense, a vindication of that method. For this reason, Darwin's method of inquiry is of basic interest.

This method of inquiry illustrates, in an exceptionally clear manner, the stages of the inductive method which the methodologists of the nineteenth century (John Stuart Mill, for example) sought to establish and to develop. The first stage of this inductive method was observation, the collection of fact, experience, whether open and casual or controlled and induced. The growth of Darwin's theory seemed to illustrate this stage abundantly and even brilliantly; he was above all an observer, a collector of data, and a man of amazing keenness and discernment. Even if the theory of evolution had never been projected on their bases, the descriptions of *The Voyage of the Beagle* and the factual matter adduced in the expository portions of *The Origin of Species,* as well as in his other works, would have remained impressive and of permanent value. This dimension of his work will continue to be one of its chief claims to lasting attention. Such descriptions, even when their adequacy or accuracy is eventually impugned, retain their importance because they mark a step forward in this speciously simple, but actually very difficult task of observation.

The second stage of the inductive method, as its theoreticians have expounded it, is the constructive phase, the formation of hypotheses. This stage too would seem to be clearly, and even brilliantly, illustrated by Darwin in the formation of the theory of evolution. This hypothesis was, as has been seen, suggested in its simplest and germinal form by Malthus' thesis on population, and it remained essentially an extension and universalization of that thesis. Its importance lay in the manner in which it was projected as the interpretative frame of reference for a whole new area of observation. The root of this extension is a vast similitude, metaphor, or analogy between the narrower area of Malthus' concern and the whole vast empire of life in nature. The very vastness and daring of the metaphor, however, is a source of strength and power and recalls to mind what has been said many times about the scientific imagination and the affinity which seems to exist between the procedure of the scientist and that of the artist.

Finally, what theoreticians recognize as the third stage of the inductive method, verification, appears to have eminent exemplification in Darwin's work. Verification is essentially the reconfrontation of the hypothesis with facts of the same order as those by which it was suggested and with reference to which it was first formulated. This reconfrontation has a double value; it reflects both upon the hypothesis and upon the observed data. In the light of the hypothesis, the latter take on a new quality and significance. Depending on the impact of the facts, the hypothesis either passes to the status of principle or vanishes into the thin air of myth. The process of verification demands techniques of its own, and Darwin shows himself an adept and scrupulous master of them. He proves this adeptness by the skill with which he varies the conditions of the confrontation to draw out the various aspects of the hypothesis, to reveal its strength and its weakness; and he makes clear at every step that it is the hypothesis and not the data which is on trial.

The facts to which he has recourse in the process of verification are worthy of consideration and fall into four general classes. The first is the evidence of domestication or artificial selection (as opposed to natural selection) as practiced by English breeders for generations; this evidence is presented in the opening chapters of *The Origin of Species,* as well as in *The Variation of Animals and Plants under Domestication.* The second class comprises those facts which exhibit the relationship between extinct species and those still in existence; as a rule the extinct will be shown to be lower forms of existing groups. The third class of facts is concerned with the geographical distribution of species. Finally, the correspondence which is found to exist between the fetal stages of animals which, when they reach maturity, exhibit radically different features suggests to him the deeper implications of the hypothesis.

That the theory of evolution is subject to grave limitations is recognized by Darwin before all others. For example, he is quick to point out that this hypothesis has no relevance for determining the first origin of the variations for which he is trying to account. As a consequence, he seems to cut off, from the beginning, many of the "philosophical" extensions of the theory which were later to be attempted and to which he also, in a later phase, lent his support. This is clearly evidenced by a letter which he wrote to Huxley shortly after the appearance of *The Origin of Species.* In it he writes, "You have . . . hit on the one point which has greatly troubled me; if, as I must think, external conditions produce little *direct* effect, what the devil determines each particular variation?" In this way, he was led into recurrent doubt about the value to be assigned to environment; his later thought seems to assign a constantly increasing efficacy to this factor.

But it must also be noted that he tended to emphasize that the theory of evolution is concerned, not with the origins, but with the effects of variations in the process of natural selection and survival. Darwin further recognized that the theory of evolution has nothing to do with the question of the first or absolute origin of life; this is simply a more forceful statement of the fact that it is not even concerned primarily with the origins of variations. Such a question, since it is not a matter of observation, cannot be the object of explanation by hypothesis. In proceeding thus, he shows himself more cautious in the use of hypothesis than Newton, Kant, and Laplace.

Finally, he rejected any association between the idea of evolution and that of progress, an association which was to be advanced and exploited by those who sought to transform the doctrine of evolution into a philosophical principle. This association was based on the assumption that the evolutionary process represented an uninterrupted movement toward "perfection" in living forms. Such a continuous process was obviously not the object of observation and must consequently, in Darwin's view, fall outside any explanatory scheme which his hypothesis might supply.

Although he showed himself sensible to the intrinsic limits of his theory, Darwin was not wholly invulnerable to the temptation to extend his hypothesis to orders of fact other than those upon which it was first formed. The idea of this transformation did not suggest itself directly to Darwin, who must be considered conservative in all matters of ethics, religion, and social theory. It was suggested by the fact that the first and most bitter objections to the theory were made on the grounds of its supposed ethical and religious consequences, while other persons, like the materialist Duhring, rather ruthlessly exploited it to their own ends, involving just such "consequences." Thus, Darwin felt that he was challenged to test his position with respect to these further extensions—to protect his own position as much as to develop such extensions. The intermediary step in the process of extending the theory was the composition of the *Descent of Man*. In this work he refused to recognize that any special or distinctive forces might have come into play in the evolution of man as a biological species; man was, on this level, continuous with the whole range of organic life. From this point, the extension of his theory into all areas of human conduct and behavior, including the ethical, the religious, the artistic, and the social, seemed much easier and much more natural.

In his own ethical theory Darwin belongs basically to the school of Shaftesbury, Hutcheson, and Adam Smith, the school of "moral sentiment." However, the manner in which he brings the evolutionary hypothesis to bear upon the idea of moral sentiment changes it significantly. The moral feeling is, for Darwin, the characteristic which most clearly sets man off from all other forms of life. Nevertheless, he refuses to believe that this sentiment is removed from the process of natural formation which is considered within the framework of the evolutionary hypothesis. There is, therefore, moral evolution as well as biological; this was a theme which many other writers were to take up and extend. Furthermore, Darwin suggests that the phenomenon of the moral sentiment, in its most direct manifestation the phenomenon of sympathy or life in community, is itself a factor in biological evolution; that is to say, in the process of natural selection in the service of survival. For the effect which natural selection looks to is not merely the good or the continuity of the individual but that of the species or kind; to this the moral sentiment of sympathy and life in community directly ministers.

In the religious realm, the attitude traced by various critics and exponents of evolution is that which has come to be known as agnosticism. The roots of the association between evolutionism and agnosticism lie in the fact that the theory of evolution is offered as an explanation in a given order and is prohibited by its intrinsic limits from raising the question of the origin of that order. Huxley was to emphasize this dimension of the complex of ideas centering about evolution, and Spencer, in his turn, was to contribute to it.

For Darwin himself, the problem and the situation seem a bit more complex. He tended to adopt a middle course which was later to become somewhat fashionable among theologians. This was the position that the creative act (assuming such), since it is not subject to the kind of explanation involved in the whole structure of the theory of evolution, must have been a single and determinate act and that the process of evolution and its law is subsequent to that absolute inception. This position has the advantage of being agnostic in principle while not incurring the religious opprobrium attaching to that term. It is agnostic in principle, since, by denying any continuity between the process of natural organic life subject to the law of evolution and that first act by which an absolute beginning was induced, it declares that the character of that absolute beginning and the inceptive act, as well as its agent, must remain essentially unknown and, in the frame of reference of the theory, unknowable.

At the same time Darwin entertained serious doubts concerning this point of view which were, in the main, moral doubts. Like John Stuart Mill, he found it difficult to reconcile the sufferings and discords of man's world with the idea of a providential God. He could not bring himself to believe the proposition advanced by some theologians who were eager to exploit his theory, that natural selection was a means in the hands of God. This seemed to him to be repugnant to the notion of God's benevolence. He therefore leaned strongly to a more absolute agnosticism than that which first suggested itself to him on the basis of his own theory, an agnosticism which was prepared to assert the simple givenness of the observable world and to recognize questions concerning the origin of the given world or its purpose and end as essentially spurious. But this is not Darwin's last word. He is at times prepared to suggest, as Kant did in the *Critique of Practical Reason*, that the opposition between mechanism and teleology is one of those distinctions which we are logically compelled to set up but which we would be overly presumptuous to transfer from the order of our thought to that of objective existence.

On all these points, there is reason to hesitate in calling Darwin an evolutionist. He is, above all, an inquiring mind, characterized more by doubts and questionings than by assertions in any apodictic mode. Others were less hesitant and cautious than he.

B. *Herbert Spencer and the Extension of the Doctrine*

Herbert Spencer, it will be recalled, was mentioned earlier as having anticipated Darwin's notion of evolution, especially in suggesting its possibilities as a universal principle of explanation in the realm of science and of order in the realm of actual existence; that is, as both a scientific and an ontological principle. It gradually becomes clear that the central figure in the effort to raise the concept of evolution to philosophical status is not Darwin but Spencer. This impression is fortified when we reflect on how half-hearted and tentative Darwin's efforts in this direction were. In the extension of the notion to man— not merely as the biological species *homo sapiens* but in his social and ethical dimensions and in his activity as an artist and a discerner of values—Darwin's thought falters into doubt and hesitation. That of Spencer, on the other hand, proceeds with great confidence and vigor of mind. His display of dialectical, expositive, and argumentary skill and his omnivorous erudition held the English-speaking world of ideas in thrall for a period of thirty years or more, not only in his native England but in America as well. Indeed, his reception was even warmer and less critical here than at home. He stands as that marvel of marvels, a best-selling philosopher, for some of his works outsold contemporary novels and books of devotion and travel on both sides of the Atlantic Ocean. During his lecture tour in America, he was received as little less than a prophet.

Herbert Spencer was born in 1820 at Derby, England. His father was a self-educated schoolmaster; as a consequence, he was addicted to the notion of self-education, just as many rich men who have accumulated their wealth by their own efforts are forever after addicted to the ideal of the self-made man. His son Herbert was in time to become an outstanding example of both the marvels and the inherent shortcomings of the ideal of autodidacticism. All he knew he had learned by his own efforts; he was at once the master and the prisoner of his own erudition and his own ideas. His father seems to have intended that his son should also become a schoolmaster, but young Spencer's propensities led him into science and engineering. For a time he earned his livelihood as a civil engineer for a number of English railroads. At the same time, however, he maintained an interest in political and social problems. The first articles from his pen were devoted to problems of government. They foretold the position he was later to assume as the outspoken exponent of a doctrine of social laissez-faire which he justified, not, as had Adam Smith, by an appeal to statistics, but on the basis of the theory of evolution. His first contact with the idea of natural development, an idea germane to the evolutionary hypothesis, seems to have come by way of his reading of Lyell's *Principles of Geology,* which had appeared in the years 1830–33. He seems to have turned to this work in conjunction with his interests in railroad engineering and the problems of roadbeds.

In his first important work, *Social Statics,* 1850, he advances as the basis for social studies an analogy between the structure of society and that of organisms. This was an image which was to remain constant with him, which he was to extend freely into every field of interest, and which was to make him, in political theory, the outstanding exponent of the "organismic" theory of the state that was so influential at the end of the nineteenth century.

His earliest interpretation of this analogy was teleological. He conceived of the process of organic development as directed toward some ideal end. He owed this phase of his thought to Coleridge and, through him, perhaps to the romantic philosopher Schelling. He was later to abandon this teleological interpretation, however, as lying beyond the limits of any empirical verification. He came to content himself with merely indicating development wherever it might be observed, rather than seeking to divine its ideal term. The strict form in which the empirical rule of development was to be formulated by Spencer was suggested to him by his acquaintance with the work of Harvey in embryology, of Wolff in anatomy and of von Baer in physiology. This rule proclaimed that development went from the homogeneous to the heterogeneous. To this he was to add presently that natural movement was from the simple to the complex and from the disparate to the organized. This was to be a rule by which development, as empirically observed, might be measured.

In 1852 he undertook in a short essay to compare the evolutionary and the creationist doctrines as general hypotheses, principally with reference to the structures and forms of organic life. He concludes that only the evolutionary hypothesis is able to account for presently observable forms.

In 1855 he published his *Principles of Psychology,* which passed almost unnoticed at the time but which was eventually to become one of his most influential works. The labor expended in the preparation of this work was to prove basic to the development of his theory of evolution, for it led him to the remarkable conclusion that the form and content of individual consciousness could not be explained by the experience of the individual. In this way, he moved away from all earlier forms of empiricism, which had assumed the experiential self-sufficiency of the individual; in order to account for the individual consciousness, he was forced to refer to the process of the formation of consciousness in the species, a movement which seemed to dovetail very naturally with his earlier notions of evolution and development. The notion of evolution and development was thus extended from the material to the mental, into the sphere of consciousness, and with it was extended the notion of environment, which is the functional variable in evolution.

This analysis of psychological experience seems to have first suggested to him the idea of a "philosophy of evolution," a general explanatory system of reality in terms of this concept. The first sketch of this evolutionary philosophy was presented in the work *Progress: Its Laws and Causes,* published in 1857. In this work there appears for the first time the formal statement of the theory of evolution as a movement from homogeneity to heterogeneity. Shortly after the appearance of this work, Darwin's *Origin of Species* appeared (1859). It fitted readily into everything that Spencer had been thinking along these lines, and he was to receive it enthusiastically as offering a whole world of fresh evidence for his view. He now looked forward to a systematic exposition of the evolutionary philosophy.

1. Religion and Science

Spencer begins his systematic formulation and exposition (to be called in its entirety the *System of Synthetic Philosophy*) with the problem of knowledge in the form, not of general epistemology, but of an inquiry into the limits and nature of the scientific method. He comes to a conclusion which has been met many times in the history of philosophy, namely, that science is the only genuine knowledge but that it is subject to intrinsic limitations. This is eventually to become the basis of a doctrine with which the name of Spencer is associated: the doctrine of the "unknowable," a doctrine which will place him in the forefront of nineteenth-century religious and philosophical agnosticism.

In Spencer's exposition, religion and science appear as rivals and antagonists. Religion invades the realm of science, offering pseudo-solutions to problems over which science alone can shed illumination; at the same time, science takes as its legitimate field of inquiry the area of religion and religious experience as continuous with man's natural empirical life. Spencer holds, much in the vein of Comte, that religion seeks to give a total theoretical explanation of existence in terms of extra-existential and extra-empirical causes and forces. Thus, for Spencer, belief in ancestral ghosts becomes a primitive form of theology. The only difference between lower and higher forms of religion is the subtlety of the extra-existential and extra-empirical principles to which appeal is made. Religion ends in mystery. It appeals to revelation in order to overcome the gap between the world as it is open to experience and the causes which are assumed by religion to account for and explain it.

It might be supposed that, by contrast, science would be advanced as the perfect antithesis of religion, guilty of none of the mystery-worship of the latter. This is not the case. Spencer alleges against the most fundamental scientific concepts the same charges which he brings against religion and theology. These concepts have pretended to reveal the innermost being and structure of the world; but from the point of view of valid knowledge they have failed as much as the revelations and myths of religion. The concepts of science—such as time, space, matter, etc.—can have meaning only insofar as they are given a radically empirical sense; that is to say, only insofar as they are names for experiences and not for principles which are assumed to lie beyond, and to account for and explain, experience.

Spencer thus postulates a radical empiricism and a radical phenomenalism at the very outset of his philosophical journey. He scorns "metaphysical" science as much as mythical theology. He calls the object against which this agnosticism is directed the absolute or the unknowable, whether it be in a religious or a pseudo-scientific form. He is not content, however, to say that the unknowable or the absolute is a merely negative concept. The assumption of genuine science must be that there *is* more than science can *know*. This follows from the procedure of science itself, which, in distinguishing, defining, and analyzing, must assume that there is something which is distinguished, defined, and analyzed. This constant appears, first, as the mere content of knowledge but, more intimately, as power, such power as suggests itself as constituting the life within us. This power, shorn of all of the particular predicates which would qualify it, must be asserted simply to *be*.

Spencer is hopeful that he may compose the differences of religion and science by defining the true area of knowledge. Both religion and science, he is confident, must come, in time, to recognize that the innermost essence of the world is unknowable but that we can know, scientifically, the manner in which this nature reveals itself in the world of our experience. The dissension between religion and science must disappear when the proper form and limits of knowledge are determined.

2. Philosophy as Unified Knowledge

Science, Spencer holds, is concerned above all with unity, the unity which underlies the manifold forms of the phenomena which present themselves in experience. The particular sciences seek this unity in the special areas of experience. Philosophy, by contrast, seeks the unifying principles of all experience. Philosophy will not be content, however, to be but a synthesis of the laws of the particular sciences; it will consist in the effort to discover certain truths or laws from which the unifying laws of the particular sciences may be deduced, from which the axioms of mechanics, physical and psychological principles, and social laws might all be derived. This is the Spencerian concept of philosophy as unified knowledge—not a quantative unity, it will be noted, but a formal and legalistic unity, established on its own grounds and transcending, epistemologically, the unity of the particular sciences which are derived from it.

Philosophy begins with a provisional acceptance of the validity of those fundamental assumptions on which all thought is based. This provisional acceptance must, however, be justified by reference to experience. The validity of an assumption is measured by its agreement with all other assumptions; truth is, therefore, an axiomatic system which consists in the perfect correspondence between our representation of things and our presentation of them. The complete coherence between any single assumption and the system of assumptions leads finally to that unity of knowledge in which science in the fullest sense consists. Underlying the whole of scientific thought, however, is what Spencer calls the "primordial act." This is the act by which we discover that things resemble other things or differ from them. This act is not subject to refutation, for in the process of refutation the primordial act is reaffirmed. This is why he calls it "primordial." Since similarity and difference are simple cases of the general class of relations, the primordial act consists in thinking by relations, and not through the "essences" of things. Since similarity and difference are but special cases of relations, there must be others, two of which Spencer indicates as sequence and coexistence.

The basic experience underlying all concepts, however, is force. In the sphere of inner and outer experience, force is the ultimate concept to which we must always return. Force is primarily a dimension of inner or subjective experience; it is the primary analogue on the basis of which we form our concepts of all else. This aspect of Spencer's position resembles metaphysical idealism. The objective elements of experience are assumed to be of the same character as those of inner experience, since the inner experience is known directly. This concept of force is the basic, unitary concept of all science. It is identical with the absolute, which he thinks underlies all phenomena. In this line of reasoning, the first and most basic unitary principle of science must be the principle of the conservation of force. This principle cannot itself be demonstrated; it is assumed and reaffirmed in any effort at demonstration, since all thought is relational in form and relations are always manifestations of the basic force.

From the principle of the conservation of force, Spencer infers that motion always follows the course of the greatest attraction or the least resistance. All motion is periodic or rhythmical, as attraction ebbs and flows, and all phenomena undergo a process of development and dissolution which is determined by the ebb and flow of force. In this manner, Spencer is led from the problem of the unity of knowledge to the notion of philosophy as the philosophy of evolution.

3. Philosophy as the Theory of Universal Evolution

The demonstration that all inquiry is based on one assumption, the conservation of force, is not sufficient, in Spencer's view, to establish the unity of knowledge. There must be one all-inclusive law to which it can be shown that all phenomena are subject. He has shown, on the basis of the assumption of the conservation of force, that every order of phenomena is subject to a movement of development and dissolution; that is to say, an evolutionary movement. Each special science is concerned with this movement in the order of phenomena to which it addresses itself. The task of philosophy lies in the establishment of a general law of this movement. If this is possible, the basic assumption upon which the unity of science rests will be vindicated and ratified in a universal law.

All development, he holds, exhibits with greater or lesser clarity a definite set of characteristics. Spencer had first described evolutionary movement as a passage from homogeneity to heterogeneity. This is too vague. He therefore analyzes this general movement into three more specific stages: concentration or integration, differentiation, and determination. By the first, concentration, Spencer means a stage in which there is a simple combination of elements which previously had been scattered or unrelated. Examples of this from different orders of phenomena might be: a cloud forming in the sky before a storm; the assimilation, by living tissue, of the elements scattered in the environment; the formation of generalizations or concepts from perceptions; the collection of individuals in social groups under some compulsion such as defense or forage. This initial stage is followed by differentiation. Differentiation is a continuation of the process of concentration within the mass that has been separated from the environment. Thus, different functional centers, still within the matrix of the whole, are formed in the living organism; in the development of the solar system, on the Kantian hypothesis, nuclei are formed. The differentiation of the organs of sense within the living organism and the emergence of estates or classes within the social body illustrate the same process. The final stage is determination. Spencer defines determination as the emergence of order between the centers of differentiation within the larger, homogeneous masses affected by simple concentration. It is the passage from chaos to order, from a collection of centers of concentration and differentiation to an order of relation among those centers. This is the crucial step in evolution, for it is what distinguishes evolution from devolution. In the latter, the first two stages are present but not the third.

Evolution as a general law is established in two ways. The first is by induction. It is shown by the comparative observation of phenomena that such processes as those described actually do transpire. The second is by deduction from the law of the conservation of force. In this way the unity of knowledge is maintained.

Spencer examines the evidence for this general law in all the areas of the system of the sciences: in biology, in psychology, in sociology, and in ethics. In the area of biology, he seems most at home, for it is here that the notion of evolution had its inception. His basic exposition of biological evolution is independent of that of Darwin. Organic forms arise under the combined influence of inner and outer forces. Following the general law of development, one must suppose that some constant or uniform outer influence induced concentration. Diversity of inner pressures or forces then brought about the concentrations characteristic of the stage of differentiation. Determination then arose between these centers in response to both outer influences and inward tensions.

Spencer accepted Darwin's theory wholeheartedly. He differs in some matters however, especially those dealing with the problem of the transmission of acquired characteristics. If acquired characteristics could not be transmitted, he did not see how specification, e.g., the origin of species, could take place. In this dispute, he directed his objections, not so much against Darwin, who was somewhat undecided on the point, but against such Darwinian biologists as the German Weismann (1834–1914). This question of acquired characteristics is especially important in the psychological and sociological areas of application.

In the application of this concept to psychology, Spencer is particularly preoccupied with the problems of consciousness and knowledge. He takes a position contrary to the tradition of English empiricism and the laws of association, which are too mechanistic for him. The inward life of consciousness in general has a more complex structure than can be accounted for by mechanistic hypotheses; it moves toward the formation of "wholes" of experience and in this follows the general pattern of evolution: concentration, differentiation, determination. With respect to the theory of knowledge, Spencer attacks the tradition of empiricism because it ignores the fact that the matter of experience is taken up and developed in a definite manner and because, lacking a criterion of truth, it leads to skepticism. The organizing principle of knowledge, Spencer believes, is somewhat akin to the *a priori* of Kant, since it cannot, like the *content* of sensations, concepts, etc., be derived unambiguously from experience. This formal principle is the criterion of truth which he seeks, for it alone measures the way in which the matter of experience is developed. Also, it is identical in its articulation with the law of the stages of evolution in general. Spencer rejects the appellation "Kantian," which some critics, in view of the presence of this *quasi-a priori* principle, imposed on him. He held that, eventually, the origin of *all* dimensions of thought lay in experience. *Eventually* meant "in the total view of the evolutionary process."

It is a favorite axiom of Spencer's that societies *grow* and are not *made*. This view of sociology is in line with the general view of evolution. There must first be concentrations of individuals, but these concentrations must be under the pressure of some constant force in the environment. He is opposed to all forms of the contract theory of the origin of society. The basic analogy upon which he relies is that between society and the living organism. The individuals are the cells. The cells, grouping themselves about various functional centers, constitute the organs of society; the diversity of function is essential to their formation. Nevertheless, he recognizes a very considerable difference between the living organism and a society. In the former, the parts exist for the good of the whole. In the latter, the whole exists for the good of the parts. Thus, in political theory he is deflected from the totalitarianism which is implicit in his basic analogy and defends a theory marked by the restriction of political power and the subservience of the state to the good of lesser groups and the individual. The line of argument by which he comes to this view is not wholly consistent either with his conception of evolution or with the basic analogy between the organism and society; he appears to be subverting these to the service of a previously determined view of the political and social order.

The task of determining the highest type of human life is the task of ethics, not of sociology. The goal of evolution is the production of the perfect type of man, not the perfect type of society. This is consonant with Spencer's subjection of society as a whole to the service of its parts, to the individual. He distinguishes between an absolute ethics and a relative ethics. Here again a comparison with Kant and his distinction between the categorical and the hypothetical imperatives has been suggested. An absolute ethics presupposes a perfect life in a perfect society. In the actual course of evolution, there can be only approximations of the absolute ideal. As a result, all practical ethics is relative. This fact, however, does not dispense the philosopher from the task of determining the principles of an absolute ethics.

If we examine the different stages of man's ethical development, it will be clear that they exhibit the same characteristics as the three stages of evolutionary development. The ethical life shows greater concentration, differentiation, and determination than the unethical life. The construction of the perfect type of human life must be based on the principle of benevolence. This assumption is obviously gratuitous on Spencer's part. It is an *a priori* principle, as was the principle of duty in Kant. Although Spencer tries to show that, in the general framework of evolution, the principle of benevolence can also be derived from experience, his line of argument is not held to persuasive. In general, it may be said that, in its contents the ethics of Spencer, the ethics which is the goal of evolution, combines elements of the ethics of sentiment and sympathy of Smith and the pleasure and utility doctrine of Bentham and the Mills. As an instrument for the construction of the absolute ethics, supplying its formal principle, benevolence possesses the same value as the principle of utility; it enables the philosopher to take the "long" view beyond the immediate effects of action. But it seems clear that in this construction Spencer deserts the field of evolution, as he had defined it, to engage in formalistic theory construction.

The *System of Synthetic Philosophy* remains, when all else is taken into account, the most considerable monument to the nineteenth-century effort to construct a philosophical edifice on the principle of evolution. Its success or failure is a matter of differing modes of valuation. Its impress on the history of thought was strong.

C. *Elaborations of Evolutionary Philosophy*

Although Spencer's elaboration of evolutionary theory was, from the cultural point of view, the most influential (eventually, though not immediately), it was by no means the only such effort, nor, speaking absolutely, the most brilliantly conceived. There were others, too numerous to mention in full, but the most impressive cannot go unnoted.

The most noteworthy is, without doubt, that of Thomas Huxley (1825-1895). As a professor of natural history and physiology at London, Huxley's chief interest in Darwin's theory was scientific and professional. He was inevitably drawn to develop the ostensible philosophical implications of the theory. In doing so, he displayed no slavish adherence either to Darwin's thought or to the "system" which Spencer was elaborating during the same decades. Moreover, Huxley possessed literary and expository powers which were greater than those of either of his contemporary evolutionists and rapidly established him as the most fluent and learned disseminator of this complex of ideas. His work *Man's Place in Nature*, 1864, won a wide and immediate audience, and his eloquent lectures, delivered in all parts of the world, strengthened the impression engendered by that work. These lectures were collected and published in a number of volumes: *Lay Sermons*, 1870; *Critiques and Addresses*, 1873; *American Addresses*.

Although his arguments rested on scientific bases, his interests were clearly philosophical. On physiological grounds he described mental processes in terms which recalled the eighteenth-century materialists: Thought is an "epiphenomenon" of the brain. But he rejects the characterization "materialist" on the basis of Hume's sensationalism, to which he subscribed (cf. his work *Hume*, 1879). He speaks of Hume as the "prince of agnostics." His own agnosticism consists in abstaining from every judgment as to the "ultimate character" of reality. He holds that it is sufficient for scientific purposes to see matter as the ultimate foundation of phenomena, without, however, excluding the possibility that matter is itself a phenomenon of mind. In the phenomenal order, evolution is the sole principle of explanation. It applies not only to nature but to the realm of ethics, though in a different manner (cf. *Romanes Lectures on Evolution and Ethics*, 1893). Ethics arises initially by natural impulse but develops a normativity of its own which cannot be reduced to the struggle for existence which prevails in nature. Huxley holds that the dignity of man, the highest of values, is itself the product of ethical evolution.

The vast scholarly production of the German biologist and philosopher Ernst Heinrich Haeckel (1834-1919) is usually divided into two

parts, a strictly scientific part and an enthusiastically speculative portion. The spirit of the latter (alone of interest here) is a dogmatic positivism ready to extend the discoveries of science into the basis of an
all-inclusive philosophical world view. For Haeckel, the guiding principle of scientific research and discovery and of speculative elaboration
on that basis is evolution. In his *Generelle Morphologie der Organis-
men (General Morphology of Organisms)*, 1866, he first extends Darwin's theory to all life, from the simplest forms to man. The fundamental biogenetic law (ontogenesis is a brief and rapid recapitulation of
phylogenesis) is transformed, at his hands, into the "law of substance"
(Substanz-Gesetz), which becomes in turn the only true cosmological
law which embraces the chemical law of the conservation of matter
and the physical law of the conservation of energy. Cosmic evolution
is the result. In words recalling the monism of Spinoza, he says that
matter, as infinite, extended substance, and mind, as sensient and
thinking substance (energy), are the two attributes or fundamental
properties of the all-comprehensive and divine essence. In infinite
space, matter, without beginning and without end, is animated by an
incessant movement, developing itself in successive evolutionary processes. Evolution itself results from the condensation of matter into
innumerable centers; their destruction by shock produces the energy
necessary for further evolutionary developments. With this doctrine
Haeckel thinks it is possible to resolve the "seven enigmas" of Du
Bois-Reymond, to combat religious "superstition," and to introduce the
enlightened reign of science and philosophy, in which the work of
science would be conducted to its ultimate conclusions. Haeckel too
possessed the gift of dissemination, for one of his works *Die Welträtsel*
[The world-enigmas], 1899, achieved "best seller" proportions.

Lloyd Morgan (1852–1936) represents an evolutionism of somewhat different quality but no less inclusive range. It has been called a
spiritualistic or mentalistic evolution (in contrast to the materialistic
monism of Huxley and Haeckel). One of his works, *Emergent Evolution*, 1923, achieved very authoritative status. In Morgan's view, physical and psychical events are not connected by any causal relation;
nevertheless, they are not separable. Every physical event is *also* a
psychic event; the inverse is also true. Monism, whether materialistic or spiritualistic, is therefore impossible. The evolutionary process
reflects this complexity at every stage. This process is in no way mechanistic; it is, on the contrary, emergent, creative. (Morgan acknowl-
edges his debt to Bergson.) Each successive stage of the evolutionary
process is incapable of being reduced to a preceding stage and equally
incapable of being explained as the result of the merely mechanical
laws operative at an earlier level. Each stage gives evidence of irreduc-

ible, emergent novelty; and each new form exhibits the dual aspects, physical and psychical, in a relation not duplicated on any other level. The presence of this element of novelty makes the evolutionary process *progressive*. Life is one of the supreme examples of emergent novelty in creative evolution, and consciousness is a further element of novelty within the evolutionary process of life. Finally, Morgan breaks the link between evolutionary thought and religious agnosticism. The increment of value in the evolutionary process (progress) demands the postulation of a divine being who guarantees that progress.

Earlier it was noted that Spencer and the evolutionary doctrine in the form in which he expounded it had a significant influence across the Atlantic, in the United States. Some have ventured an estimate that this influence was greater than Spencerian evolutionism ever achieved in his native England. The chief engineer of this cultural transfer was the American William Jay Youmans (1838–1901), editor, with his brother Edward, of the *Popular Science Monthly*. He edited some of Huxley's works for this American publication, but was especially close to Spencer and organized Spencer's successful American lecture tour. The current of evolutionary thought which he thus helped to introduce into the American cultural scene was to remain influential and effective for a long time and in many fields.

Of the countless names associated with evolutionary thought in America, that of John Fiske (1842–1901) may be taken as especially representative, not because of the intrinsic value of his thought but because it very clearly reflects the immediate impress made by evolutionism, in its philosophical aspects, on American culture. His principal work, *Outlines of Cosmic Philosophy*, 1874, exhibits the same systematizing zeal as the work of Spencer, the same yearning toward a *Weltanschauung* which dominates Haeckel. A touch which will become typically American, where the application of evolution to the social field is especially insistent, is Fiske's concern to establish a social "physics." This would be a science at once natural and historical. The world of man and that of nature share a common life. Matter as such does not exist; there are only various grades of life. The cosmos is an organism which evolves in time, though its beginning and end are wrapped in impenetrable shadows. Like Morgan, Fiske rejects religious agnosticism. God is the eternal energy by which all things are produced, the force which operates in our life, both physical and psychical, and at the same time in all the activities, organic and inorganic, amid which we live. Fiske's speculations, which have been called "romantic naturalism," gradually loosened his ties with Spencer's thought, though he always remained faithful to the fundamental principle of evolution.

Readings

Books

Eiseley, L. *Darwin's Century*. Garden City, N.Y.: Doubleday, 1958.

Glass, B., et al. *Forerunners of Darwin: 1745–1859*. Baltimore: Johns Hopkins Press, 1959.

Goudge, T. A. *Ascent of Life*. London: Allen & Unwin, 1961.

Greene, J. C. *Darwin and the Modern World*. Baton Rouge: Louisiana State University Press, 1961.

Gregory, W. K. *Evolution Emerging*. 2 vols. New York: Macmillan, 1951.

Himmelfarb, Gertrude. *Darwin and the Darwinian Revolution*. Garden City, N. Y.: Doubleday, 1962.

Hofstadter, R. *Social Darwinism in American Thought*. Rev. ed. New York: G. Braziller, 1955.

Huxley, J., with Hardy, A. C., and Ford, E. B. *Evolution as a Process*. London: Allen & Unwin, 1954.

Huxley, J. *Evolution, The Modern Synthesis*. London and New York: Harper & Brothers, 1942.

Lowe, Victor. *Understanding Whitehead*. Baltimore: Johns Hopkins Press, 1962.

Tax, S., ed. *Evolution after Darwin*. Chicago: University of Chicago Press, 1960.

Essays and articles

Collins, J. "Darwin's Impact on Philosophy." In the same author's *Three Paths in Philosophy*, pp. 135–189. Chicago: Regnery, 1962.

Ellegard, A. "Darwin's Theory and Nineteenth Century Philosophies of Science." *Journal of the History of Ideas*, XVIII (1957), 362–393.

Fisch, M. H. "Evolution in American Philosophy." *The Philosophical Review*, LVI (1947), 357–373.

Mandelbaum, M. "Darwin's Religious Views." *Journal of the History of Ideas*, XIX (1958), 363–398.

CHAPTER III

The Neo-Kantian Revival

Introduction: General Meaning of the Term

As the name indicates, this movement constitutes a serious attempt to return to the philosophy of Kant as a fresh starting point of philosophical inquiry which could meet the exigencies of thought in the second half of the nineteenth century. The movement itself, however, has a starting point which both distinguishes it from the Kantianism of the "epigones" who continued the direct line of Kant's thought and defines precisely what the neo-Kantians thought valuable in criticism and what they sought from it. This starting point is the experience of positivism.

Neo-criticism is, in the first instance, a reaction against positivism. This rejection is not simple, however. Neo-Kantianism rejects positivism as "dogmatic," but it accepts the positivist idea of mathematical-physical science as the model of knowledge. As a consequence, it tends to consider philosophy as the critical inquiry into the conditions which make such knowledge possible. Romantic philosophy could not serve that purpose because it had diverted philosophical inquiry from its *critical* task and led it into the enterprise of system-construction. But Kant had isolated the critical problem as the special task of philosophy. The return to Kant was, therefore, a natural movement of reorientation.

However, this return was not easy. Many interpretations of Kant were offered which frequently were incompatible with one another. On the whole, the neo-Kantians failed to realize all the possibilities which were latent in Kant's philosophy; their reaction against positivism often led them to place an excessively narrow interpretation on his thought. Though they constantly protested their intention to return to Kant himself, their real concern was to find in his thought an instrument for confronting contemporary problems; inevitably, they bent his thought to their purposes.

Neo-Kantianism was primarily a German movement. Within Germany it gave rise to a number of distinct currents and even to two recognizable "schools"—that of Marburg and that of Baden. However, it also had significant resonances in England, France, and Italy and even, with the emigration of Ernst Cassirer, one of its last great representatives, in America.

A. Chief German Currents and Schools of Neo-Kantianism

It is always difficult to pinpoint the beginning of a current of thought. In the case of neo-Kantianism a particular event does offer itself as a starting point: the 1865 publication of *Kant und die Epigonen* [Kant and the epigons] by Otto Liebmann (1840–1912). The chief merit of the work, as a starting point of the movement, was that it coined the motto: Back to Kant. Liebmann systematically examined the thought of each of the greatest German figures in the decades intervening since Kant: Fichte, Schelling, Hegel, and Schopenhauer, as well as Herbart and Fries; at the end of each chapter, he reiterated: *Back to Kant.* Liebmann's own contribution to the movement will be noted when the metaphysical current of neo-Kantianism is examined. In addition to the metaphysical, the chief currents are: the realist, or realistic, represented chiefly by Riehl; the psychological, represented by Leonard Nelson; the logical current, developed chiefly by the Marburg school; value theory, developed by the school of Baden. Finally, Georg Simmel follows an individualistic line which is sometimes called the relativistic current.

1. The Realist Current

The realistic current of neo-Kantianism finds its best expression in the writings of Alois Riehl (1844–1924). Chief among these works are: *Der philosophische Kritizismus und seine Bedeutung für die positive Wissenschaft* [Philosophical criticism and its meaning for positive science], a vast work in two volumes and three parts, which appeared between 1876 and 1887; and *Zur Einführung in die Philosophie der Gegenwart* [Guide to contemporary philosophy], which appeared in 1903. Throughout his numerous writings, Riehl's theoretical and polemical position remains constant. He was strongly influenced by the work of Hermann Helmholtz (1821–1894), physiologist and physicist, who had employed a realist interpretation of Kantianism in his own scientific investigation and whose work is consequently accounted by some as the very first manifestation of neo-Kantianism in Germany. Because the effects of light and sound on man depend on the way his organism reacts, Helmholtz considered sensations as signs produced in our organs by the action of external forces. These signs are not copies of external objects; they do not reproduce the characters of those objects; nevertheless, the signs have a relation to the objects, since the same object, under the same circumstances, evokes the same sign in the consciousness. This relation makes it possible to determine the laws of external processes, the regular succession of causes and effects. Hence, it may be concluded that the laws of the "real" world are reflected in the law of signs.

The realism involved here is readily apparent. Riehl made Helmholtz' analysis the point of departure for an interpretation of Kant in which the realistic elements of his thought are emphasized in contrast to all idealistic interpretations. The thing in itself, far from being "dissolved," as had been the case with Jacobi and the other initiators of the romantic movement, was taken as an indispensable concept for philosophy, the only concept which prevented the dissolution of knowledge into a pure play of illusion. Riehl emphasized Kant's position that only the *form* of knowledge can be derived from the subject. Knowledge always presupposes a *content* given in the senses. This is true, even though it is recognized that this sensibly given content cannot become experience and knowledge without the intervention of the organizing and constituting intellect and the *a priori* forms. The proper function and office of philosophy, if it would achieve scientific status, is to develop a "theory of knowledge"; that is, to determine both the processes by which knowledge is constituted and the objective validity of knowledge.

The conditions of knowledge as a given process are met concretely by the natural sciences. They constitute the model-exemplars of achieved science. It is with regard to the natural and exact sciences, therefore, that the task of philosophy must chiefly be pursued. Yielding to the abstractive process involved in the methods of the natural and exact sciences, Riehl holds that the real must remain unknown in its *qualitative* aspects; only logical and arithmetical, or mathematical, relations can possess objective validity. Since values involve the qualitative dimension of the real, philosophy, as a science, must remain indifferent to them; it does not for this reason, however, deny them or their importance in man's life. It must simply recognize that the perception of values is not a purely cognitive process but implies relations of affective participation and production.

A further aspect of Riehl's "realism" is his concern to recognize the individual as the sole locus of cognitive processes and to avoid attributing an ontological status to transcendental processes (as Hegel, for example, seems to some to have done). The complex of *a priori* principles do not constitute a kind of unique consciousness outside and above individual men who are involved in concrete knowing; those principles constitute rather a system of coordinates to which all knowledge in the concrete must be referred and which is logically, but not chronologically, prior to that to which it is applied.

2. The Psychological Current

Just as the realist current in neo-Kantianism found its best expression in Riehl but its initial impulse in the physiologist Helmholtz, so the psychological current, whose major representative is Leonard Nelson (1882–1927), receives its initial impulse from the psychologist, physicist, and philosopher Fries (1773–1843). Indeed, so close is this dependence that the position which Nelson developed, and which for a time wielded considerable influence, is sometimes referred to as the "neo-Friesian" school. The philosophy of Fries is Kantianism interpreted psychologically. Since every act of knowledge is a psychical function, Fries held that it should be possible to reduce the theory of knowledge, and indeed the whole of philosophy, to a science of psychological experience. What was for Kant "transcendental" is for Fries psychological in character; hence, he is convinced that his psychological recasting of the critique of knowledge both continues and corrects Kant's insights.

Nelson edited the four volumes of the new series of the "Abhandlungen der Friesschen Schule" [Review of the Friesian school] between 1904 and 1908 and published his earliest writings in its pages. The work which first signals his own constructive phase of thought, however, is *Die Unmöglichkeit der Erkenntnistheorie* [The impossibility of the theory of knowledge]. The impossibility of this theory resides in the fact that it pretends to construct a transcendental criterion for the validity of knowledge, that is, a criterion which would be independent (functionally and valuatively) of the concrete psychological processes in which the actual transactions of knowledge (perception, reflection, etc.) take place. Kant is correct in recognizing that experience cannot be reduced to pure immediacy but, to be constituted, must involve the critical, i.e., self-grounding, moment, the moment in which its own presuppositions and operations are laid bare. However, according to Nelson, this moment need not fall outside the critical analysis of the psychological processes in which knowledge takes place. Therefore, in line with what Fries had already attempted, his purpose is to account for Kant's "transcendental" principles within psychological limits.

His attempt to do this illustrates in a very clear way the strange commixture of Kantian and positivistic attitudes which characterizes much of the thought of the neo-Kantian movement. True to the legal-istic tendencies of positivism, Nelson seeks to translate all the tran-scendental principles, both of sensibility and of intellect, into psycho-logical laws. Only the concrete psychological processes have any real ontological status. Their transcendental dimension is formulated in terms of "laws" by the critical analysis of these concrete processes. But what, in turn, is the status of these laws? Are they purely descriptive or normative? What part do they play in the construction of experi-ence? What must be accounted for is the unity, the system, of experi-ence. It is here that the Kantian exigency is clearly felt by Nelson. Those laws could in no wise account for the unity of experience, its "transcendental" aspect, if they are interpreted as merely descriptive, in generalized terms, of the concrete cognitive processes as these take place in individual subjects. He must, therefore, with Kant, assign them a normative or regulative function. Once he has done this, how-ever, it no longer seems possible to deny them some status in being; they become again the regulative principles of experience. As such they cannot be derived from experience in the way in which, following Fries, he had tried to derive them. He is forced, therefore, to draw closer to Kant's original position—that these principles are operative within experience, though not derivable from the direct, but only from the critical, analysis of experience, as its formal, regulative principles.

Nelson's analysis adumbrates a point which Husserl will later enlarge upon, namely, the foibles of all forms of "psychologism." At the same time, his analysis makes clear a basic failure of the Kantian position, namely, its failure to account adequately for the ontological status of the transcendental. Nelson's thought holds a certain histori-cal interest, for it exhibits in their incompatible complexity elements which later reflection will have to disengage and relate in more viable ways. He foreshadows both the criticism of psychologism, which is the basis of Husserl's phenomenology, and the ontology of Heidegger, one purpose of which is to define the status in being of the transcendental. Nelson went on to develop his ideas in a more systematic way in his two-volume work *Die neue Reformation* [The new reformation], 1918. His ideas enjoyed a considerable influence for a time, not only among philosophers, but among some theologians and psychologists. This influence rapidly diminished, however, during the period between the two world wars.

3. The Metaphysical Current

The attitude of Kant toward metaphysics, it is well known, consti-tutes one of the most difficult exegetical points in his thought. Under one aspect, he conceived the whole critical enterprise as the "prolegomena to any future metaphysics"; hence, while denying that a viable metaphysics had yet been achieved, he seemed to recognize that that achievement would represent the natural term of philosophical effort. By the doctrine of the thing-in-itself and of the antinomies of pure reason, he seemed to have made the metaphysical enterprise impossible from the ground of pure reason. In the critiques of practical reason and of judgment, he seems to have taken a "leap" toward metaphysics by speaking of a noumenal dimension of knowledge in these orders, thus seemingly undermining metaphysics as a genuinely speculative work resting on pure reason.

Considering these complexities it must be asked, what can a metaphysical interpretation of Kant's thought mean? In the view of Liebmann and Volkelt, the two most representative figures in this current of the neo-Kantian movement, the reply to this question seems clear. It is part of the general program of neo-Kantianism: Back to Kant. It means a return to the initial effort or projection of Kant's thought, the one which seemed to encounter defeat in the *Critique of Pure Reason*, namely, the construction of metaphysics on a *critical* basis. The metaphysical current takes on the appearance of an effort to fulfill Kant's original intention; at the same time, it would seem to offer a reply to all of the fumbling efforts of romantic philosophy to realize the positive values of Kantianism, to put an end to the "phenomenalistic" interpretation of Kant (resting on a pure agnosticism toward the thing-in-itself), and, finally, to offer a valid alternative to the dominant positivism in all areas of scientific knowledge and speculative thought. But this still is not enough. What would this critical metaphysics be in itself? In principle, Liebmann and Volkelt offer an answer. It would be a critical science of the noumenal, of the nonempirical and absolute (not merely transcendental) ground of experience, in both its contentual and its formal aspects.

The crucial part which the first work of Otto Liebmann, entitled *Kant und die Epigonen*, 1865, played in the emergence of the neo-Kantian movement has already been noted. The net result of this work, philosophically, was negative. It pointed out a task to be accomplished. The fulfillment of this task constitutes the theme of all his other works. Among the most important of these are: *Über den individuellen Beweis für die Freiheit des Willens* [On the individual demonstration of the freedom of the will], 1866; *Über den objektiven Anblick* [On objective conception], 1869; and *Zur Analysis der Wirklichkeit* [For the analysis of reality], 1876. In these works Liebmann elaborates the basic problems of Kantianism in his effort to fulfill the metaphysical project which lies at the basis of criticism. He conceives this task as the construction of a systematic synthesis in which the demands of criticism and metaphysics would be reconciled and met. The basic demand of criticism is that the human conditions of knowledge always be recognized and respected; no science, metaphysics included, may move outside the sphere of human thought and representation. The basic demand of metaphysics, on the other hand, is that the knowledge reached under these conditions transcend the conditions as to both the object known and its mode of being known. The object must be known not merely under the conditions of its "appearance" but under the conditions it enjoys in itself, and the mode of the knowing must be, not relative, but absolute. In the opinion of some critics, Liebmann's "synthesis" is incoherent; his thought oscillates between these two sets of demands without achieving any real unity. But the exigency he seeks to meet is clear enough and serves to mark the direction of the metaphysical current of neo-Kantianism. That he achieved no definitive results goes quite without saying.

Among the most relevant of the many writings of Johannes Volkelt (1848–1930) may be named his *Kants Erkenntnistheorie nach ihren Grundprinzipien analysiert* [Kant's theory of knowledge analyzed in its basic principles], 1879 and *Möglichkeit der metaphysik* [Possibility of metaphysics], 1884. Much of his speculative thought is developed in the process of reflecting on the main philosophical movements of his times. The romantic thirst for the absolute remains strong in his thought and is possibly the key to its many complexities. He pursues the same object as Liebmann, i.e., the fulfillment of the metaphysical project of Kantianism, but he does so independently. In an autobiographical statement he says that it is his purpose to pursue the metaphysical direction of Kant's spirit, despite all the official refutations of that direction.

His objective is the construction of a "critical" metaphysics, to which he gives the outlandish title "trans-subjective subjectivism." He finds a basic tension within human thought which provides the opening to the "trans-subjective" realm: certainty of the proper process of human thought and the tendency to reach a "trans-subjective" certainty. This trans-subjective certainty takes the form of the recognition of logical necessity and of the principles of causality, universality, legality, etc. This recognition secures a "trans-subjective minimum": i.e., the admission of other minds, the continued subsistence of trans-subjective entities. But metaphysics is not, in his view, limited to this "minimum" based on scientific grounds. It must advance hypotheses about universal principles of reality and lead eventually to the absolute in the orders of both being and knowledge. In the philosophy of religion, in ethics and in aesthetics, he pursues the same goal. In this last, as in the philosophy of religion, the exigency of the absolute is very strong. Reality, he maintains, is the self-realization of absolute value, while absolute value and absolute self-consciousness coincide. Artistic creation supplies us with an analogue according to which we can grasp the process of creation in the absolute or cosmic spirit. Religion is the metaphysics of the absolute spirit. The absolute spirit is the positive and rational basis of the world; there is opposed to it, however, a negative and irrational principle which is coeternal with it and which is the metaphysical basis of evil and sorrow in the world and of the tragic sense of life. From these observations it will be apparent that Volkelt's final assertions far outstrip his initial proposal: to erect a critical metaphysics. Nevertheless, in principle, all of his thought is controlled by this basic intent.

4. The Marburg School

Among the currents of neo-Kantianism named above there appeared the *logical* current. This direction of the development of Kant's thought became the preoccupation of a group of thinkers who, collectively, formed the Marburg school. The founder of the school and its central figure was Hermann Cohen (1842–1918). His most distinguished collaborators were Paul Natorp (1854–1924) and Ernst Cassirer (1874–1954). In addition to its concern with the logical development of Kant's thought, this school was very prolific in works in the history of philosophy that are noted for their wealth of erudition, perceptive interpretation, and speculative relevance. Cassirer was to distinguish himself especially in this direction.

As in the case of the "metaphysical" current, we may ask, before considering the thought of the representative men of the Marburg school, what is meant by the "logical" development of Kant's thought. This development may be characterized negatively by saying that it is the direct opposite of the psychological development offered by Fries and, after him, by Nelson. These sought to bring the cognitive process wholly within the orbit of the knowing subject. The logical development, by contrast, is objectivistic and seeks to transcend the conditions of subjectivity. The logical development may also be characterized by contrasting it to the "metaphysical" development. The latter sought to establish the trans-subjective basis of experience and to encompass the noumenal order within the range of knowledge; it sought a meta-empirical basis of experience in the absolute being of the object. The logical current of development does not range that far. It seeks to establish the objectivity of knowledge not on any "metaphysical" basis but on logical bases—that is, on the logical processes revealed by the critical analysis of cognitive experience. The isolation of these logical elements permits the philosopher to identify the "thinkable objectivity." This objectivity has nothing to do directly with empirical objectivity, i.e., with the objects of experience or the "things" of nature. These latter are but particular determinations of the former. Some critics have called this current the Platonizing current in neo-Kantianism, for it seeks to isolate the logical object of thought and sees the object of experience in some elliptical relation to that logical objectivity.

Most important, however, in the context of the history of philosophy, is the understanding of what the thinkers of the Marburg school thought could be accomplished by this line of development of Kant's thought. At least some of the advantages which they envisaged may be indicated. Theirs is, for example, the most frontal attack on the dominant positivism; their Kantian-Platonic logicism is, in fact, almost a direct antithesis to the postulates of positivism. On the basis of this logical development of Kantianism, it seemed possible to reestablish the methods of the positive sciences. Again, this logical objectivism presented an adamant front to the all-enveloping subjectivism both of positivism and of idealism. The object was again placed in the forefront of cognitive experience, not merely the empirical object with its positive determinants but, as has been noted, the logically grounded object with which science could be directly concerned. Finally, and as a mark of the persistent influence of positivism, the logical idealism of the Marburg school seemed again to close the door on all metaphysical enterprises, for the whole of the knowable content of experience could be contained within the formal limits of logical possibility and objectivity with no necessity of venturing into the perilous areas of metaphysical assertion.

Hermann Cohen, the founder of the school, developed his thought in a wide range of writings. His earliest works were in the history of philosophy, whence the continuing interest of the school in this order of studies. He was a student of Plato, and there can be little doubt that much of the inspiration for the logical development of Kant stems from this interest. In the course of his historical and analytical studies he had promised an "original" treatment of the main problems of philosophy. He fulfilled this promise in the three parts of the massive *System der Philosophie: Logik der reinen Erkenntnis* [Logic of pure knowledge], *Ethik des reinen Willens* [Ethics of the pure will], *Aesthetik der reinen Gefühls* [Aesthetics of pure feeling]. These three parts appeared in 1902, 1907, and 1912, respectively. This monumental achievement was immediately recognized in its full worth and received careful critical evaluation. It became, naturally, the basic document of the logical development of Kantianism which characterizes the Marburg school.

Cohen recognizes three valid philosophical sciences: logic, ethics, and aesthetics. The image of the original Kantian trinity obviously falls heavily upon his thought. Of these three, logic is completely autonomous and serves in turn as regulative of the other two. Here the inner tensions of the Kantian trinity are overcome. Logic concerns the realm of pure knowledge. By pure knowledge Cohen means the knowledge of the logical conditions of objective knowledge of real objects. For him, the model of this knowledge is given in the physical-mathematical sciences; as a consequence, at times his logic comes to be too exclusively the logic of these sciences. However, in the *Ethics* and *Aesthetics* he seeks to counterbalance this tendency. Within the area of the logic of pure knowledge, his first concern is to eliminate all subjective elements from thought and knowledge. Knowledge is knowledge of the object; thought is reduced to its objective content. Even the terms by which idealism, for example, sought to characterize subjectivity— terms like activity, self-consciousness, consciousness—are given a logical objective meaning or definition by Cohen. The transcendental unity of thought, of which Kant spoke, is, for Cohen, the unity of scientific consciousness. Consciousness in general is the category of possibility; and logic, ethics, and aesthetics are all brought within this category, for they study, respectively, the possibility of the exact sciences of nature, the possibility of moral action, and the possibility of sentiment in general and of the sentiment of the beautiful in particular.

Cohen rejects the Kantian notions of intuition and of thought as synthesis. Intuition is rejected because it would cause thought to have its principle in something external to itself. The notion of synthesis, which involves the manipulation of a given, is replaced by the idea of *production.* The principle of thought in its objectivity is not a *datum* but an *origin,* not something given it from without, but an inner, constitutive process and moment of thought itself. The production of which he speaks is obviously a purely logical process and that which it produces is the principle of the possibility of objects, i.e., their logical possibility. The form of this act of logical production is the judgment, and Cohen distinguishes four classes of judgments: laws of thought, judgments of mathematics, judgments of the mathematical sciences of nature, and judgments of method. The minute investigation of these in all their aspects preoccupies the philosophical science of logic, in the course of which the logical conditions of all possible objects are determined productively.

The object of ethics is the realm of "ought to be" (*Sollen*). "Oughtness" is the rule for the practical use of reason. Willing consists only in the ought; where there is no ought, there is no will, only desire. By way of the ought (duty), the will conquers a realm of authentic being. Ethics is a science, a "pure" science, only as it considers the ought, duty, as the condition of the possibility of will.

Cohen's aesthetics is humanistic. If the work of art is not to be reduced to the pure materiality of its medium, it must be a representation of an ideal and, precisely, of the ideal of human perfection, which is love. Aesthetics as a pure or philosophical science is concerned with the possibility of sentiment as the desire of this ideal of love and the possibility of the representation of this ideal in a material medium.

Cohen's thought is robust and dynamic, rich in both content and allusion. Whatever the limitations critics have alleged against it, they have unanimously recognized it as the great monument of neo-Kantian thought. As such it remained a constant source of inspiration and insight to his collaborators and to many thinkers who were not immediately within the orbit of the neo-Kantian movement but who possessed many affinities with it, such as Edmund Husserl.

Like Cohen, Paul Natorp laid the remote preparation for his important contributions to neo-Kantianism in his erudite and penetrating historical studies. Chief among these was the work *Platos Ideenlehre* [Plato's doctrine of ideas], 1903, in which, again like Cohen, he sought to establish a positive relationship between the Platonic Idea and Kant's *a priori* forms. Thence he went on to develop his own concepts in his most important critical and speculative works: *Die logischen Grundlagen der exakten Wissenschaften* [The philosophical foundations of the exact sciences], 1910, and *Philosophie: Ihr Problem und Ihre Probleme* [Philosophy: its problem and its problems], 1911. He laid even greater stress than Cohen, if that were possible, on the priority of the exact sciences as the model of all knowledge and on the necessity of penetrating to the *a priori* bases of these sciences, i.e., the bases which render them logically possible.

The task of philosophy, for Natorp, is to study the work of thought from a logical rather than a psychological point of view. Logic is the only path to reality; for the logic which Natorp has in mind is not a formal logic (as was later to be developed) but a transcendental logic in Kant's sense, one which lays bare an *a priori* structure which conditions the *possibility* of all experience of the real. Reality is not something independent of thought but something which arises in and through thought. The term of the investigation and labor of thought he called *Tatsache,* the fact, which encloses the real; taken in an absolute sense, this *Tatsache* is unattainable, but by scientific investigation it can always be more closely approximated. In Natorp's thought, the *Tatsache* displaces the thing-in-itself of Kant, bringing it (though never completely) within the scope of thought. As such, the *Tatsache* corresponds to Kant's "transcendental object" (a concept which will recur with even greater force in Husserl's phenomenology).

In his efforts to determine the logical foundations of the exact sciences, Natorp develops a theory of mathematics which is substantially in line with that offered by Kant. He holds that mathematics and logic do not differ in their fields of investigation, but rather in the purposes with which they investigate the same field. Mathematics undertakes the development of particular logical structures; logic seeks to penetrate to the systematic unity of all such particular structures. Minimizing Kant's emphasis on the place of intuition and following the discoveries of Cantor, Dedekind, and others, Natorp holds that number is a concept of relation and can be grasped independently of the intuition of time and space. Time and space (and here he is closer to Kant) are not logically necessary structures, nor are they mere empirical data, but conditions of the possibility of experience. The passage from spatial-temporal structures to the realm of physics is effected, according to Natorp, by the development of the concept of energy. Here his argument has a rather remote Aristotelian resonance. What varies in time and space, he says, cannot be in its turn time and space but must be something "substantial," of which the various entities which submit to physical measurements are particular determinations. But energy must not be conceived as a thing, nor even as a force. It is essentially the possibility of a relation. In like manner Natorp gives particular attention to establishing the bases of psychology as an exact science; but he recognizes that it can never attain stable, necessary, and rigorous laws, because it is the attempt to objectify the subjective, a necessarily inconclusive operation.

Like Cohen, Natorp recognizes ethics and aesthetics as the other legitimate members (in addition to logic) of the encyclopedia of philosophy. His ethics is the logic of the "ought," which he views as no less objective than the realm of pure being. The *a priori* principle of ethics is duty, which has as its objective content the good of mankind as overriding the good of the particular individual. The idea of humanity also provides the principle of religion and of politics for Natorp, while art, in his aesthetic theory, appears as the process of representing this transcendental ideal of human perfection to the senses.

Ernst Cassirer is the representative of the Marburg school of neo-Kantianism best known in the English-speaking world. His period of exile eventually led him to America, where he became associated with Yale University and where he composed several works of considerable influence on his new environment, the most important of which is his *Essay on Man*, 1944. His American sojourn also led to the translation of some of his works into English, including his massive *Philosophie der symbolischen Formen* or *Philosophy of Symbolic Forms* (German, 1923–29; English, 1953–57). Like other members of the school, Cassirer wrote many works in the history of philosophy, all of them eminently laudable—for example, the influential *Individuum und Kosmos in der Philosophie der Renaissance* (German, 1927; English translation, 1935). A complete bibliography of his German works as well as the English translations is given in *The Philosophy of Ernst Cassirer,* a collection of critical essays by various authors, edited by P. A. Schilpp, 1949.

With an early study of Leibnitz, Cassirer drew close to the position of the Marburg school and undertook his analysis of the problem of knowledge in modern thought. The aspect which most impressed him was the emergence and dominance of the concept of "measurability" of the sensible datum, involving its transformation into a numerical symbol. He traced the importance of this transformation in the development of modern physics by way of the dissolution of the concept of substance and its replacement by that of function (*Substanzbegriff und Funktionsbegriff* [The concept of substance and the concept of function], 1910). Algebraic symbolism lies at the basis of the sciences and gives rise, not to a physical symbolism, but to a methodological one. The importance of the symbolic process in the theory of the sciences opened to Cassirer the wider problems, to which he was to devote his most original efforts, of all human activities conceived as the creation of symbols and symbolic systems. This is the theme of the work most closely connected with his name: *The Philosophy of Symbolic Forms.*

In his *Essay on Man* Cassirer says that the philosophy of symbolic forms takes its point of departure in the presupposition that, if there exists a definition of the nature or essence of man, it can be understood only as a functional, and not as a substantial, definition. The central function which enters into this definition is that of symbol creation. Through symbols man creates the world of culture which releases him from the limits of natural and passive existence. Kant's influence may be seen in Cassirer's view that symbols are purely formal and *a priori,* receiving their content from sensible experience but ordering such data on transcendental grounds which appear only through critical analysis. Symbolic activity generates not only cultural unity but the unity of the human person through the generation of symbolic memory. Scientific symbolism always remained central for Cassirer, but in the later decades of his life he gave increasing attention to the other forms of symbolic activity—myth, language, art, and historiography. Eventually, despairing of unifying these orders of symbols definitively, he seems to have accepted a kind of symbolic pluralism embracing all these forms, and he contented himself with identifying the pure symbolic function only in a strictly formal way.

5. The Baden School

The two greatest developments of German neo-Kantianism, it has been pointed out, were the school of Marburg and the school of Baden. It is important to know what they had in common and in what they differed. The common element was the revival of Kant's critical point of view, especially with the purpose of determining the possibility and validity of knowledge on grounds independent of the subjectivistic and psychological processes involved in all knowledge. The school of Marburg, as we have seen, pursued this problem specifically with regard to the sciences of nature and took scientific knowledge as normative for all knowledge. The school of Baden, by contrast, undertook this problem in the more difficult area of the knowledge of *values*. Its purpose was to work out a theory of values which would place in relief their possibility and validity independent of psychological conditions. For this reason, the school of Baden is sometimes referred to as the school of value theory. But the programmatic and methodological symmetry which exists between it and the school of Marburg and which places them both clearly within the orbit of the neo-Kantian undertaking should not be overlooked. The most representative figures of this school were Wilhelm Windelband (1848–1915) and Heinrich Rickert (1863–1936). A brief review of their thought will reveal the salient features of the school.

Windelband is perhaps most widely known as the author of a history of philosophy constructed on problematic principles, *Lehrbuch der Geschichte der Philosophie* [Textbook of the history of philosophy], first published in 1892, with many subsequent revisions. But his interest in the history of philosophy already reflects his original and personal preoccupations, which were to be ·expressed in *Präludien* [Preliminary discourses], 1884.

Windelband conceived philosophy as the critical science of values. The most important term in this definition is *critical* because it indicates the method which is to be used in the study of values. The notion of the critical method sends his thought immediately back to Kant, the initiator of the critical method in philosophy. But the notion of *value* is also born within the critical method of Kant. For Kant, distinguishing clearly between the psychological processes involved in the pursuit of truth and truth as the *value* informing all knowledge, called attention to the notion of value itself. Therefore, the critical method is intrinsically, and not merely in an applied manner, related to values and the determination of their possibility and validity. The *value* of truth, according to Kant, is not determined by anything external to knowledge (e.g., the object) but by an internal rule of thought itself;

similarly all values are determined by such internal rules, and the object of philosophy is the identification and determination of the rules which define value and values.

This analysis is orientated basically toward the Kant of the *Critique of Pure Reason,* for it is there, according to Windelband, that *truth* as *value* is placed in greatest relief. But truth, while remaining the paradigm of value, does not exhaust the order of values. These include, Windelband goes on (again following in Kant's footsteps), values of *action* or *moral* values, which Kant had treated in the *Critique of Practical Reason,* and values of sensitivity, which had been the object of the *Critique of Judgment.* Thus the basic trinity of values is reconstituted: Truth, Good, and Beauty, and it is the critical determination of their possibility which concerns the philosophy of value as Windelband conceives and practices it.

Windelband formulates this entire problem again as the problem of judgment. Philosophy does not concern itself with judgments of fact. It is concerned with value judgments—"this thing is good" (or true or beautiful). Such judgments necessarily involve reference to the judging subject. Every valuative judgment is, therefore, the reaction of a subject to a content of representation, and the three great avenues of such reaction are thought, action, and sentiment. The content of the representation (and here Kant's direct influence is clear), is given by sensible experience, but the reaction, the formal element, is determined by the subject. Here another and further distinction is necessary. The reactions of individuals, simply as individuals, to the contents of such representation do not obey the regulative principle of value but, to a certain degree at least, follow natural necessity. The problem of value arises only when such judgments of value aspire to a universal status, aspire to be valid for all possible subjects of such reactions and claim to define the norm for such reactions.

On what principles are such universalistic and normative aspirations or pretensions based? Windelband replies that they rest upon the determination of an ideal necessity, distinct from natural necessity, and that such ideal necessity is attained by the *normative* consciousness of man, the object of which is being as *Sollen* (ought to be) and not as *Mussen* (is by natural necessity). Philosophy is the science of this "normative consciousness." Its purpose is to determine *a priori* the rules of normative consciousness in their ideal, and not merely empirical, character. These rules will tell men what ought to be judged good, true, and beautiful and will constitute the constant norm to which actual or merely empirical reactions (such as: "I prefer this," "I like this," "I want this") are to be referred for judgment.

Heinrich Rickert developed his views in very close relation with those of Windelband. However, he does not simply repeat the teachings of Windelband but seeks to extend the analysis which Windelband had initiated. Windelband, had been concerned with the *logic* of the judgments of value, the universal principles on which such judgments can be made. Rickert continues this interest, but he adds to it the problem of determining the *classes* of values. In this latter enterprise he has sometimes been accused of a certain scholasticism; it cannot be denied, however, that this problem is already implicit in the earlier one and demands clarification, even though it may be argued that, since the content of all judgments of value comes from an essentially indeterminate principle—that is, sensibility—any such classification would be empirically valueless. Rickert's reply is foreseeable; the very function of rules of value is to place a limit or impose form upon the indetermination of sensible representation. Thus, the problem of classification is rendered all the more imperative.

The two aspects of Rickert's concern are represented by his two most important works, *Die Grenzen der naturwissenschaftlichen Begriffsbildung* [The limits of naturalistic conceptualization], 1896–1902, and the *System der Philosophie* [System of Philosophy], 1921. The first of these works again surveys the ground which Windelband had explored. Knowledge means *judgment,* that is, acceptance or rejection, approval or disapproval. It means, therefore, recognition of a *value.* But, while the value which is the object of a sensible valuation (such as the pleasure taken in an immediate object), is valid only for the immediate and individual subject of that pleasure, the value with which the judgment is concerned *ought* to prevail for all such empirical and individual subjects and in all cases of such reaction. The truth of the judgment of value consists in this "oughtness." It is this ideal realm of *ought* that philosophy is concerned to identify and delineate. However, Rickert adds a significant reflection of his own. It is not enough to leave these two worlds distinct and opposed: the *is* and the *ought* of value. The relation between them demands exploration. This relation can be established only by a phenomenology of the act of evaluation which creates a realm of *meaning* in which the bearing of the *ought* upon the merely empirical reaction is made clear and that sharp dualism between *is* and *ought* becomes closed in principle. Only this realm of meaning can mediate between the opposed elements of that dualism.

In the *System der Philosophie* Rickert undertakes his classification of values. He distinguishes six domains of value: logic, the domain of the value of truth; aesthetics, the domain of the value of beauty; mysticism, the domain of the value of impersonal sanctity; ethics, the domain of morality; erotics, the domain of happiness; and religious philosophy, the domain of personal sanctity. To each of these domains he assigns a corresponding *good,* respectively: science, art, unity in the whole, free community, community of love, the divine world. He also assigns a relation of that value to the subject, respectively: judgment, intuition, adoration, autonomous action, unification, devotion. Rickert was hard put to defend this structure against the sarcastic criticism launched against it; he replied with some asperity in a polemical work titled *Die Philosophie des Lebens* [The philosophy of life] directed against Nietzsche, James, Simmel, Dilthey, Bergson, and others. The crucial point is clear: His critics stood for the illimitable character of the source of values—direct, vital experience; Rickert stood, at this point, for a second order necessity that imposed formal limits on this "illimitable" for the purpose of reflection.

Rickert's most important contribution would seem to be his distinction between the sciences of nature and the sciences of mind or spirit. This distinction cannot be said to be his by original title, but he labored well at it and it was a distinction which was to have considerable fortune and effect. It was noted earlier that the logical current in neo-Kantianism had taken the physical-mathematical sciences as the model of all forms of knowing. The value-theorists did not entirely abandon this, but they felt very keenly the limitation it imposed upon their own task, a limitation which must eventually appear arbitrary and under which they became restive.

The distinction rests upon the contrast, destined to become ever more pronounced, between nature and history. The sciences of spirit involve the dimension of history, which is essentially absent from the sciences of nature. Rickert reduces this distinction to a contrast of method. The natural and the historical sciences differ, not in object, but in method. The same empirical object may be viewed under diverse aspects as nature or history. It becomes *nature* when regarded from the point of view of the universal, *history* when regarded from that of the particular. In other words, the single object is of interest to the sciences of nature only as it illustrates a universal law, but it is the sole object, in itself, of historical inquiry. Still, not all particulars are of historical interest but only those which possess a special value. The task of history is to select and identify such value-laden facts, employing the criterion of the values of culture and civilization. This does not mean that the historian passes judgment upon events in the name of values; it means that he reconstructs the event in its full character because it possesses value. Values are in history, but they are not historical. History realizes values which are eternal, values which it does not create. This point of view, as will presently be seen, differentiates Rickert's position from all forms of historicism.

Georg Simmel (1858–1918) exhibits many features in his numerous writings which bear a marked affinity to the problems and concerns of the Baden school, with which he is sometimes associated. More properly, however, he would seem to belong to the current called historicism, and thus he will be discussed in the chapter bearing that title.

B. *Further Resonances of Neo-Kantianism*

Though the men and schools already discussed represent the chief elements of the various currents of neo-Kantianism, its influence was quite widespread both within and outside Germany. In this process of expansion the movement frequently became associated with other points of view which clouded its initial perspective; frequently, however, it took on new aspects which enriched its procedures and concerns.

In Germany Bruno Bauch (1877–1942), for a long period editor of the important review *Kantstudien,* made an excellent contribution to the movement in his monograph *Kant* (1911). In this work he shows affinities both to the Marburg school: in his concern to diminish the Kantian dualism between intuition and judgment and in his view of knowledge as an infinite progress of thought toward experience in its concrete determination, and to the Baden school: in his interpretation of the *noumenon* as a rule of value for our judgments. Another German thinker, Hugo Münsterberg (1863–1916), was the first to carry the influence of neo-Kantianism across the Atlantic to America. His *Philosophie der Werte* [Philosophy of value], 1908, reflected many of the features of European neo-Kantian thought and attracted favorable attention on the American scene. An American philosopher, Wilbur Marshall Urban (1873–1952), took direct inspiration from Rickert in many of his writings and gave a theological direction to the value theory of neo-Kantianism.

In France, the return to the philosophy of Kant advocated by Charles Renouvier (1815–1903) must be considered as independent of the parallel movement in Germany and, in its own right, equally rich in themes and speculative power. Renouvier's avowed intention was to continue the critical work of Kant, though he also professed to accept positivism's limitation of knowledge to the laws of phenomena in the conviction that this limitation was in line with Kant's own thought. He took the fundamental principle of criticism to be the reduction of all reality to representation and rejected all forms of metaphysics because it rested upon an unwarranted distinction between representation and reality. The thought of Renouvier bears some affinity with that of the Baden school through his interest in the problems of history. Like the Baden school he rejects all forms of historicism because the values which are realized in history are not the creations of history but transcendental principles. (Cf. *Introduction à la philosophie analytique de l'histoire* [Introduction to the analytic philosophy of history], 1896.)

Another very eminent French thinker is rightly placed within the orbit of neo-Kantianism, although his thought is such that it attains a speculative independence of all schools and movements. This is Léon Brunschvicg (1869–1944). Of his many works *Les étapes de la philosophie mathématique* [The stages of mathematical philosophy], 1912, is perhaps the best known and most widely esteemed. Brunschvicg is especially felicitous in his formulation of the role of philosophy. Its aim is "knowledge of knowledge" in the sense of Kantian criticism. Its object is thus *integral knowledge*. In scientific knowledge mind and object confront each other, but, in philosophy, mind seeks its own reality, the possibility and forms of its own operations. The stages of the development of mathematical philosophy signal, in his view, the liberation of the mind from the closed horizon of representation; they are the stages by which mind subordinates experience to itself.

Resonances of the neo-Kantian movement are to be discerned both in England, in such men as Shadworth H. Hodgson (1832–1912), Robert Adamson (1852–1902), and George Dawes Hicks (1862–1941), and in Italy, in Antonio Banfi (1886–1957) and Antonio Aliotta (1881–1964). While all of these figures exhibit considerable agility in the cultivation of the neo-critical point of view, in none of them does the level of speculation rise to the point where it merits special analysis or presentation.

Readings

Books

Dussort, Henri. *L'école de Marbourg.* Paris: Presses Universitaires de France, 1963.
Rickert, Heinrich. *Die Heidelberger Tradition und Kants Kritizismus.* Berlin: Junker & Dunnhaupt, 1934.
_____. *Wilhelm Windelband.* Tübingen: Mohr, 1929.
Rosmarin, T. W. *Religion of Reason: Hermann Cohen's System of Religious Philosophy.* New York: Bloch, 1936.

Essays and articles

Adickes, Bauch, Driesch, Windelband, et al. "Otto Liebmann: Festschrift." *Kantstudien,* XV (1910). (This entire volume is devoted to the philosophy of Otto Liebmann.)

Cassirer, Ernst. "Hermann Cohen." *Social Research,* X (1943), 219–232.

————. "Neo-Kantianism." In *Encyclopaedia Britannica,* 14th ed., XVI (1930), 215–216.

————. "Paul Natorp." *Kantstudien,* XXX (1925), 273–298.

Cohen, M. R. "The Insurgence Against Reason." (Regarding Rickert.) *Journal of Philosophy,* XXII (1925), 120–123.

Collingwood, R. G. *The Idea of History.* (Regarding Windelband, pp. 165–170.) Oxford: Clarendon Press, 1946.

Collingwood, R. G., Schiller, F. C. S., and Taylor, A. E. "Are History and Science Different Kinds of Knowledge?" (Regarding Rickert.) *Mind,* XXXI (1922), 426–466.

Gurvitch, Georges. "La Theorie des valeurs de Heinrich Rickert." *Revue philosophique,* CXXIV (1937), 80–85.

Hendel, C. W. "Preface," to *Philosophy of Symbolic Forms,* by Ernst Cassirer. New Haven: Yale University Press, 1957.

Henry-Hermann, Grete. "Nelson, Leonard (1882–1927)." In *Encyclopedia of Philosophy,* V, 463–467. New York: Macmillan, Free Press, 1967.

Natorp, Paul. "Kant und die Marburger Schule." *Kantstudien,* XVII (1912), 193–221.

Rickert, Heinrich. "Alois Riehl." *Logos,* XIII (1924–25), 162–185.

CHAPTER IV

The Neo-Hegelian Movement

Introduction

As the nineteenth century entered its third quarter, positivism seemed clearly to be the master of speculative philosophy. However, its mastery was never as extensive nor as firm as appearances suggested. Its rule was something like that of the Ottoman sultans, as Gibbon characterizes it: holding a loose rein in order to hold one at all. Beneath the sway of positivism a vast speculative restlessness stirred. Evidence of this has already been noted in the neo-Kantian revival, in the doctrines of historical materialism, which were fundamentally idealistic and dialectical, and in the thought of Kierkegaard. Above all, the image of classical German idealism never lost its fascination. Despite the violent attacks to which it had been subjected, despite the many flaws it exhibited in its structure, the great speculative edifice of classical German idealism offered the closest approach yet achieved in history to the fulfillment of the basic speculative aspirations of western thought.

To grasp the real in its totality and in its ideal principles had been the abiding aspiration since Plato and had been the unspoken paradigm of all the great speculative systems. Classical German idealism seemed to come closer to this ideal than any of its predecessors and certainly closer than any of the philosophies which had leveled criticisms against it. And it was Hegel who seemed to mark the zenith of this achievement. All of the strongest traits of classical German idealism seemed to find their highest development in Hegel. Little wonder that, when the restlessness which stirred beneath the uncertain suzerainty of positivism began to seek centers about which to crystallize, the philosophy of classical German idealism, and especially of Hegel, should offer one of the most promising and secure of such centers. The

247

neo-idealist or neo-Hegelian movement which began to take form in the third quarter of the nineteenth century is evidence of this attractive power of the Hegelian system.

A distinction must immediately be made between a revival of Hegelian philosophy and a revival merely of Hegelian and idealist scholarship. Hegel's thought, and that of the other idealists, never ceased to be the object of the inquiries of scholars. But this type of inquiry is not speculative; it views the philosophical systems of classical idealism from without, making no effort to identify their relevance for contemporary problems or to develop them in this direction. This is not the case with the neo-Hegelian movement. While resting on a scholarly mastery of the sources of German idealism and especially the Hegelian texts, this is a genuine attempt to revitalize idealist thought, to arrive at its life-giving principles as a speculative system, to indicate its relevance for current problems, and to determine its capacity to meet and displace the impositions of the ascendant positivism.

One might expect that a return to the tradition and achievement of classical German idealism would have its strongest center in Germany. This is not the case, for the prime motive force of the Hegelian renewal was anti-positivism, and the ascendency of positivism was strongest, not in Germany, but in England and France. As a consequence, it is in England that this movement first finds its center. From England it inevitably radiates to America, where it provided the chief philosophical sustenance until the advent of pragmatism and the instrumentalism of Dewey.

The second area of its flowering was Italy. The Italian philosophical tradition through Rosmini and Gioberti had already developed strong alliances with German idealism. With the emergence of the antipositivist movement in such men as Spaventa and Vera, these alliances were renewed and strengthened by the establishment of more direct contact with the German sources, particularly Hegel. A considerable segment of French thought, in the effort to lift the weight of positivism, took a similar course, as it was to do again later when it sought, in Hippolyte and others, leverage against phenomenological existentialism. Finally, the continuing stream of Hegelian scholarship in Germany itself inspired efforts to renew the speculative vitality of the idealist tradition. This geographical distribution, with its accompanying ideal and cultural bases, will provide the pattern for our present treatment.

A. *Neo-Hegelianism in England and America*

The remote preparation for the neo-Hegelian movement in England and America lies in the romantic renewal in literature. The poets Samuel Taylor Coleridge (1772–1834) and William Wordsworth (1770–1850) drew much of the inspiration for their essays in literary criticism and, in the case of Coleridge, philosophical speculation from the philosophy of Schelling. Coleridge's *Biographia Literaria,* 1817, is an especially important document of this influence. In Thomas Carlyle (1795–1881) the same interests found a more robust (though not, for that reason, more sensitive or more competent) exponent; in some of his early essays and studies it was his direct purpose to make German romantic literature, freighted with the spirit of German idealist philosophy, known to the English public. In *Sartor Resartus* (1834), he combined satire on contemporary society with an exposition of his own philosophical principles, which directly reflected the spirit of German idealism; the axis of this long essay is the distinction between phenomenon and noumenon. His work *Heroes and Hero Worship,* 1841, takes its theme from Fichte's conception of the incarnation of the Absolute Spirit in historically decisive human personalities. Underlying his famous treatment of the French Revolution, in the book of that title, is a grasp of the German idealist view of the philosophy of history; one discovers in it traces of the Hegelian concept of history as the history of the Idea, whose agents, to their weal or woe, are the great figures of the historical drama. It would seem just to note, however, that Carlyle, with his robust English sense of the importance of the individual, gives great personalities more decisive power in determining the course of history than does Hegel.

In America, Ralph Waldo Emerson (1803–1882) performed a like office of preparation (though this office does not by any means exhaust his function in American cultural history). His first acquaintance with German idealism was made though contact with Carlyle and other figures of the English romantic revival during an early sojourn in England. These influences suggested to him the lofty edifice of his own speculation, to which the name "transcendentalism" came to be affixed. In such essays as *Nature,* 1836, *Representative Men,* 1850, *Compensation,* 1841, and countless others, he takes up the idealist themes, giving them an impress all his own, fraught with a spirit which could only have appeared and flourished in the exhilarating and expansive atmosphere of the New World.

Emerson's fundamental conviction was that all nature, all reality, is the theater of action of a superior force or principle to which he assigns the name "Oversoul" or God. The sovereign law of man's life is conformity with this power. The world, Emerson writes in his most famous essay, *Nature,* proceeds from the same spirit whence man's body proceeds; it is an inferior and more remote incarnation of God, his projection into the unconscious. But it differs from our bodies in an important aspect: it is not subject to our will; its order is inviolable to us; it is the ever-present testimony or witness to the divine spirit, a fixed point to which we may refer in our aberrations. Human liberty does not consist in withdrawing from the world and the necessity which dominates it but in recognizing the rationality and the perfection of that necessity and in living in conformity with it. Here the most important principle of German idealism rings out: the identity of the rational and the real.

This period of remote preparation is succeeded by one of more proximate preparation that is quite different in character. The romantic thinkers found in German idealist thought only a spur to their own reflections and speculations; they were not directly interested in mastering its sources or expounding its principles. The new figures in the movement have, by contrast, the understanding of the romantic sources themselves as their direct concern. In this way they laid the scholarly foundations for the movement, without which its direct influence in the world of philosophy would have been scant. This work took two forms: the translation into English of leading works of German philosophers, especially Hegel, and the writing of expositions and commentaries on German idealist thought.

Two outstanding examples from the second category may be cited. In 1865, James Hutchison Stirling (1820–1909) published his *The Secret of Hegel*. Despite the cynical remark of one critic that never had a secret been so well kept and despite the fact that it possesses little originality, this work is important in the course of the movement, for it marks the beginning of a direct study of the Hegelian texts by English scholars with a definite philosophical purpose. Stirling formulates this "secret" in an obscure and cryptic manner; it is the "tautological reciprocity of the logical concept which is in itself concrete." This formulation can yield an intelligible interpretation which makes it clear that Stirling had indeed come close to Hegel's thought in one of its most important aspects: the "concrete universal." This involves the delicate problem of the relation of the idea, in its transcendental clarity, to the concrete and chaotic facts of experience and the thought of individual minds. Stirling saw that this was not, as some interpreters would have it, a one-sided process which destroyed the individual in its autonomy, but a reciprocal relation and process such that the order of the particular becomes intelligible through its relation to the universality of the idea, while the universality of the idea, otherwise abstract, receives its existential fulfillment in the particular. Stirling rightly links this to Kant's original statement that the concept without the sensation is empty and the sensation, save through the concept, blind. The most important point in the present context, however, is not Stirling's particular interpretation of Hegel, but the office which his work performed in the process of the movement. Stirling's later works added to his scholarly standing, but none establishes him in the history of nineteenth-century thought as does *The Secret of Hegel*.

To this scholarly and expository preparation for the neo-idealist renewal in England, Edward Caird (1835–1908) contributed three outstanding works. During his tenure at the University of Glasgow, he published first *A Critical Account of the Philosophy of Kant*, 1877, and some years later *The Critical Philosophy of Kant*, 1889. Together these works constitute the most extensive critical exposition of Kant's thought published in English up to that time. Between the publication of these two works on Kant, he published his important work: *Hegel* (1883–86). Through these works Caird established himself as one of the "founding fathers" of the neo-idealist movement in England. From today's point of view many criticisms might justly be leveled against his treatment of both Kant and Hegel; above all perhaps is the fact that he tended to subordinate their thought to his theological interests. His own chief speculative concern was the philosophy of religion, which he treated in his course of Gifford lectures during the 1891–92 term and published in 1893 as *The Evolution of Religion*. From this point of view, he was continuing the tendency of the Hegelian center. More important from the present point of view is the fact that these works displayed an ample, direct, and exact knowledge of the texts of his authors and that he saw their philosophies, not only in their own historical context, but as the key to the solution (or at least more enlightened treatment) of urgent problems of contemporary thought. In this way he set the tone, to a great extent, for the active and creative aspect of the neo-idealist movement.

A number of the more important and influential translations of the German idealists which were also preparatory to the movement may be cited. At Oxford in 1874, William Wallace published a translation of Hegel's *Logic*, comprising the section of that title in the *Encyclopedia of the Philosophical Sciences*. Wallace prefixed this translation with a "Prolegomena" of considerable perceptiveness. In 1894 he published, also at Oxford, a work entitled *Hegel's Philosophy of Mind;* this constitutes the translation of the third part of the same *Encyclopedia*. In 1886 W. Hastie published the *Philosophy of Art*, translated from the *Lectures on the Philosophy of Art*, while in 1895 E. B. Spiers published a translation entitled *Philosophy of Religion*, which was drawn from Hegel's lectures on that theme. In 1896 R. B. Haldane published a translation of Hegel's *History of Philosophy*, and in the same year appeared a translation by S. W. Dyde of the *Philosophy of Right*, perhaps Hegel's best wrought work. J. B. Baillie brought out a translation in 1910, destined to see a second edition in 1931, of Hegel's crucial work *The Phenomenology of Mind;* mention ought also to be made of Sibree's version of the *Philosophy of History,* published in 1878. These translations made the main body of Hegel's work available in English, and, while serious reservations may be expressed about their accuracy, their influence cannot be doubted or overestimated.

These translations merely offered the instruments for the development of the speculative interests of neo-Hegelianism. The elaboration of idealist speculation, centering chiefly about Hegel's views, may conveniently be considered under three headings: 1) logic, 2) dialectic and cosmology, and 3) ethics and political theory. Hegelian theories of art, of history, and of law constitute more muted, but no less important, themes, the last enjoying a close relation to the theme of ethics and politics.

In the development of the logical thought of Hegel and neo-idealism, Baillie and Wallace are the most representative figures. Baillie's contribution resides chiefly in two works *The Origin and Significance of Hegel's Logic,* 1901, and *An Outline of the Idealistic Construction of Experience,* 1906. The latter work actually constitutes a paraphrase of Hegel's *Phenomenology of Mind* which is complementary to Baillie's translation of this work and intended to present its chief ideas in an expository form. Nevertheless, the work is not entirely without original insight, for Baillie is constantly influenced in this paraphrase by the elements of his own cultural background, which tend to enter subtly into his interpretation of Hegel. In his work *The Logic of Hegel* (1873; 2nd ed. in 2 vols., 1892–93), Wallace brings together a number of works dealing with the development of Hegel's thought, especially his logic.

More important than the mere indication of their titles is the direction and purpose of the development of Hegel's logic which these writers represent. This logic satisfied two needs which were considered especially urgent in contemporary thought. The first was a release from the prevailing positivism, with its inevitable reductivistic tendencies. Positivism seemed to invalidate whole areas of human experience, challenging especially religious, artistic, and ethical values by reducing all to naturalistic processes. But this release could have no speculative value unless it could be shown to rest upon a valid philosophical method. The logic of Hegel seemed to supply this instrument and hence to make possible the satisfaction of the second need: a theoretical "construction of experience" within which provision would be made for all those areas whose validity positivism seemed to threaten.

The abiding influence both of the Kantian criticism and *apriorism* and of the romantic, and especially Hegelian, ideal of system can be discerned in the notion of "construction." This construction was to answer two questions. The first is Kantian in tone: How is rational discourse in these areas of value-discernment possible? The second is in the spirit of Hegel: What is the substantive reality and interrelatedness of the processes of consciousness within which value structures, including nature itself as a moment or phase of spirit, arise? These dominant purposes and aims control the study of the Hegelian logic, and of the Kantian criticism as well, within the ambit of neo-idealism.

The dialectical and cosmological preoccupations of English neo-Hegelianism and neo-idealism are best represented in the vigorous thought of John McTaggart (1866–1925). His thought is developed in a series of studies, the earliest of which is *Studies in the Hegelian Dialectic* (1896; 2nd ed. 1922). This was followed by his *Studies in Hegelian Cosmology*, 1901; *A Commentary on Hegel's Logic*, 1910, and his supreme personal speculative effort, *The Nature of Existence*, 1921–27. McTaggart is notable for his purely theoretical preoccupation and is perhaps the most truly speculative of the English Hegelians. In the first of his works he enters into a vigorous struggle with Hegel's thought, of which he is no merely passive transmitter. After analyzing the dialectical process, he finds it necessary to impugn the basic principle of Hegel's thought, the rationality of the real. The real does not reveal itself in the dialectic in all its rationality, for the dialectic reveals points of contingency, the most important of which is sensibility. The data of sense, without which the categories are empty (the Kantian reminiscence is clear), always remain contingent. Here is the chief point. Hegel's system is closed: infinite mind in its own process. McTaggart, instead, sees the dialectic as the process of finite mind seeking to transcend itself. For him the dialectic remains open and with it the process of reality itself. Thus, he admits a futuristic dimension into the closed "eternal presentialism" of the Hegelian system.

In his *Studies in Hegelian Cosmology* McTaggart's reflection centers about the status of the *self* or *I*, the individual existent consciousness. Hegel, it will be recalled, had been accused of assimilating the individual consciousness (as it may be verified in the consciousness of the individual subject of experience) into the absolute consciousness of the Spirit and the Idea. McTaggart seeks to show on the basis of an analysis of knowledge that this cannot be the case. On the one hand, there seems to be nothing outside the self, as its object of knowledge; on the other hand, the self distinguishes between itself and all that it knows. Hence it follows, in McTaggart's view, that the self, and not the Absolute, is the fulcrum of the real. The Absolute is the unity among selves which are, in their turn, eternal. McTaggart is concerned to determine the nature of the unity which the Absolute can supply; he finds that it can be unity neither of knowledge nor of the will nor of emotion. (Here the divisions among the *systems* of classical German idealism come to mind as the obvious framework of McTaggart's dialectical treatment.) He finds this unity can be only *love;* none of the empirical forms of love, however, but a cosmic love which overcomes all dualities in a complete equilibrium.

McTaggart's *Nature of Existence* is a robust and imposing work. The first volume consists of an exhaustive analysis, principally on *a priori* grounds, of the general meaning of the notion of existence; the second volume seeks to determine, in the light of the conclusions of the first, which aspects of the universe may be recognized as real. The first volume arrives at a theory of *substantial pluralism:* The *universe is* the substantial relational unity of all substances. In the second, he denies *reality* to time, matter, sensation, and every form of thought of which perception is not the constitutive moment.

The ethical and political themes in English neo-Hegelianism are most amply and representatively developed by Thomas Hill Green (1836–1882) and Bernard Bosanquet (1848–1923). Green's chief work, *Prolegomena to Ethics,* was edited and published posthumously by Bradley. During his own life Green had published only a few articles and his "Introduction to Hume" for the first and second volumes of a collection of Hume's works. Green's important *Lectures on the Principles of Political Obligation* were published with a preface by Bosanquet in 1895. Green was acutely aware that neo-Hegelian speculation could not be a mere reconstruction of Hegel's thought; it had to be an original synthesis in which the elements of the British philosophical tradition would be accorded full due. Green's critique of Hume is basic to his own position. He holds that consciousness cannot be resolved into a unity of perceptions or ideas, as Hume maintains, for the relation between those perceptions or ideas cannot be understood. The subject of knowledge must be outside the ideas, because it perceives them, and outside succession, because it perceives succession. This leads Green to the Absolute or unique subject, which is universal and eternal. Such a subject, he holds, is the unspoken assumption of all forms of naturalism. Individuals are, in his view, but the *vehicles* of this unique consciousness and subjectivity.

The ethical point of this epistemological problem immediately becomes evident. Man is a moral subject precisely as he is a vehicle of this eternal consciousness. This status sets up in him a basic tension between the immediate consciousness (empirical) of his merely given existence and that eternal consciousness. The latter offers itself as the goal and term of the former. Without this tension man would not be moral; he would be but an animal existent, without normative or ethical dimensions. This tension between the immediate and contingent and the absolute and necessary is distended along a *temporal* con-

tinuum which is history. It thus gives birth to the idea of moral progress. Since this tension is distributed among a plurality of subjects
which possess that absolute as a unitary goal, the good is social. Green
thus achieves an insight into the complex moral, social, historical, and
progressive unity of mankind to which Royce will presently give the
name the "Great Community."

Bosanquet is generally considered closer to the original Hegel than
many of the other neo-Hegelians. His early interests, corresponding to
his Oxford period, were chiefly logical and are documented by such
works as *Logic, or the Morphology of Knowledge,* 1888. The ethical
and political works correspond to his middle or London period. The
chief of these are *The Principle of Individuality and Value,* 1912, and
Value and Destiny of the Individual, 1913. His chief work in political
theory, *The Philosophical Theory of the State,* 1890, was without
doubt his most influential work. His interests later broadened to include aesthetics (*History of Aesthetics,* 1892, and the more original
Three Lectures on Aesthetics, 1915) and religion (*Civilization of
Christendom,* 1893, and *What Religion Is,* 1920).

It is immediately evident that Bosanquet, despite his allegedly
greater proximity to Hegel, is also responding to the necessity of
achieving a synthesis between Hegel and the English tradition. This is
clear from the tension which exists in his ethical and political thought
between the status of the individual and that of society, more particularly, the state. In the status he assigns to the individual, Bosanquet is
closer to the English tradition of individualism, for, under the ethical
aspect, the individual retains supremacy both as subject of ethical
action and as concrete ethical value. Consideration of the conditions
for the objective realization of value leads Bosanquet to the belief that
they cannot be fulfilled through individual action alone. They demand
a social context, woven of the threads of right and obligation. Only in
that context can values, and specifically the value which resides in the
individual human person, be realized.

In the social context, it likewise becomes evident, it is necessary to
have a principle of guarantee for values, for the validation of the tissue
of relations of obligation and right. In modern society this office falls
inevitably and naturally to the state. With this conclusion Bosanquet
draws closer to the position offered by Hegel in his *Philosophy of
Right.* The tension is not as great as might at first be supposed, for in
Bosanquet's view as it was in Hegel's, the office of the state as political
guarantor is still moral. There is no evidence in his thought either of
the amoralism of the state traditionally ascribed to Machiavelli, or of
that more recently ascribed to the totalitarian state of whatever ideological provenance.

Competence rather than brilliance was the mark of the English neo-Hegelians. To this generalization Francis Bradley (1846–1924) is a manifest exception. His work stands out for its speculative brilliance as well as for its clarity of vision. The movement may be said to have reached its acme in his writings. His chief works appeared in sober and steady procession: *Ethical Studies*, 1876, *Principles of Logic*, 1883, *Appearance and Reality*, 1893, *Essays on Truth and Reality*, 1914. In addition, he was the author of many important shorter studies. Although his thought is rooted in the principles of Hegel, he showed himself at every point an independent mind, and in his greatest work, *Appearance and Reality*, he reached a personal position which transcends this relationship. He clearly distinguished the enemies he was to combat; they were: hedonism in ethics, psychological associationism in logic, and naturalism, as a theory of first principles, in metaphysics.

In *Appearance and Reality*, he extends this view to include in metaphysics that panlogism which (rightly or wrongly) had come to be generally ascribed to Hegel. This panlogism led to an absolute immanence. Bradley isolated the weak point of panlogism in the theory of relations. Panlogism presupposes an entirely adequate proportion between the Absolute and the system of its appearances in experience, which derives from the correspondence of the Idea to itself in the concrete mediation of human thought. But Bradley holds that while, in line of principle, one must hold with Hegelianism that the Absolute *is* the system of its appearances, this is true only in a general sense. Concretely, there is a basic incommensurability between human thought and the Absolute. Hence, immanence is replaced by the dualism of immanence and transcendence, which becomes central for Bradley. All later essays in neo-idealism have their point of departure in Bradley's reflection, at least in the sense that all must reckon with him.

These are the most representative figures of the English neo-Hegelian current, but they are supported by others, hardly less deserving of mention. Among these we may single out the eminent Platonic scholar and moralist Alfred Edward Taylor (1869–1945), whose *Elements of Metaphysics*, 1903, exercised wide influence. Seeking the mediation which Bradley seemed inclined to deny, he conceived the Absolute as a society of individuals teleologically ordered to unity; this society finds concrete realization in human society, in its moral articulation. Here we have the basic idea which the eminent American idealist Royce will develop in the form of the Great Community. With Taylor may be ranked J. H. Muirhead (1855–1940), who distinguished himself both as the historian of English and American neo-idealism and as an ethical and political thinker of great perceptiveness. Finally, to give the roll call a certain fullness, there may be mentioned, without expatiating on their individual contributions, D. G. Richtie (1853–

1903), J. S. Mackenzie (1860–1935), and R. B. Haldane (1857–1928).

In America, the remote ancestry of neo-idealism in transcendentalism has been noted; the relation is illuminating, but not explicative. Schneider, in his masterly treatment, speaks of "desperate naturalism" as the more immediate background of the idealist revival. This naturalism was the more or less spontaneous expression of the necessity of adapting to an environment dominated by nature in its more immediate forms and not highly mediated by culture. The desperation of some of the most vocal exponents of this naturalism, such as William G. Sumner and Henry Adams, stemmed fundamentally from its incapacity to satisfy the requirements of a more rigid and perceptive philosophical reflection on man's condition. (It is very questionable to include, as Schneider does, Santayana in this list of "desperate naturalists.") Idealism presented itself as an alternative to this naturalism; and, Schneider remarks, while its growth was almost imperceptible because so gradual, it worked a veritable revolution in American culture and gave new status to philosophy. This transition was accomplished by a succession of academic teachers of philosophy whose individual works are not brilliant but who wrought the change by the combined effect of their efforts: L. P. Hickok (1798–1888); one of his disciples, C. E. Garman (1850–1907); George Holmes Howison (1834–1916); and many others.

In a later and more articulate phase, this neo-idealism flowered into a number of "schools." Among these were the Philosophical Society of Saint Louis, of which the promoter was William T. Harris (1835–1909) and the organ was the *Journal of Speculative Philosophy;* the American Academy, which published its own journal; the Concord Summer School, which attracted many first-rate talents; the Davidson School, whose promoter was the very active Thomas Davidson; and finally the Ethical Culture Society, whose prime mover was Felix Adler. It can justly be said that no important figure in American thought was left untouched by this movement. An outstanding example is John Dewey. Destined to be the great promoter of instrumentalism and a renascent naturalism, he received his first formation in this movement and based his earliest essays in philosophy upon it. Nevertheless, it must be recognized that here one is treating basically a cultural movement, whose interest for the history of philosophy is oblique. From the point of view of speculative thought, and original and genial philosophical power, the neo-idealist movement fulfilled itself and perhaps transcended itself in the thought of Josiah Royce (1855–1916), who may justly be taken as its historical representative.

Royce was a restless, prolific, and expressive mind. The list of his published writings encompasses many titles. But little purpose would be served by a listing. In this brief account, we will touch on some of the important features of his thought, the problems and perspectives which successively and progressively occupied him until he reached his final personal vision. These chief points will be mentioned: truth and the Idea (the foundation of all idealism); the nature of the Absolute; God; fidelity as the basis of morality; the Great Community. It is needless to point out that this order of treatment is eclectic and expository. Royce's thought can be treated in other and perhaps better ways. However, in these points, we believe, the essential Royce will appear.

Royce's view of the Idea and of truth establishes the basic principles of his idealism, from which he never departed despite all the further process of his thought. He distinguishes between the *internal* and the *external* meaning or significance of an idea. The adjectives are admittedly inadequate and even somewhat deceptive, since they place the argument in the context of an inner-outer dichotomy which is really alien to it. The external meaning of an idea is its reference to an object, a reality, or at least a *significatum* external to and different from itself; emphasis on this aspect gives rise to the idea of truth as conformity of the idea to the object. Royce shows that this is not adequate. The only object which can measure the truth of the idea is the object to which the idea, taken in itself, refers. Immediately the question of the internal meaning of the idea arises. When considered in this way, the idea appears as an *instrument* for selectively designating objects elected by the process of ideation. Ideas are true, therefore, somewhat in the sense that instruments are good. (The influence of James, one of Royce's teachers at Harvard, seems evident here.) As its instrumental character indicates, the idea is not merely an intellective, contemplative process; it is a process of will. It has an end which is the measure of the validity of the idea. The idea seeks this end in the object. But the end is not something other than the idea; it is the realization of the idea, its complete and explicit determination. Hence, Royce sees the idea as will which seeks its own realization. The Hegelian echo is clear here, despite the instrumental language. The idealism of Royce is determined as the immanence of the idea, and of its world, to itself. The criterion of truth is not to be sought externally, but in the nature and the process of the idea itself.

Royce is referring, of course, to the idea in its transcendental, and not merely empirical, aspect. Here the germ of the Roycean notion of the Absolute is to be found. That Absolute is not an abstraction; as will, it is transcendental and concrete, at once infinite and particular. He tries to fix the grounds of this character of the Absolute, as will and idea—or better, idea (necessarily transcendental) which is will—by recourse to mathematical theories of the infinite as then being advanced

by such thinkers as Cantor and Dedekind. The text for this is the supplementary essay he appended to the first volume of what is perhaps
his most important work, *The World and the Individual,* 1900–1901.
The mathematical infinite is a self-representative system, that is, one
which contains itself as its own part. The Absolute is such a system:
an Absolute Self, which necessarily represents itself in an infinity of
individuals. Thus, the world and the individual enter into relation to
constitute the idea.

Royce goes on, however, to try to determine the intrinsic character
of this Absolute. In this effort he relies on certain ideas of Charles
Peirce. He makes use of the Peircean idea of interpretation to establish
the order of the Absolute, in both its transcendental and individual
dimensions, as *spiritual.* Peirce saw interpretation as a third cognitive
process along side, but to a certain degree independent of, perception
and conception. It turns to objects which cannot be brought under
either of these other processes; such an object, in Royce's view, is my
neighbor, another person. He cannot be reduced to a perception or a
universal concept. He can neither be perceived (like a sensible content) nor conceptualized. He must be interpreted. He is, in fact, a
sign. The object of interpretation is a sign; not merely an abstract or
formalized sign, but such a sign as the neighbor is: a sign which concretely exists and points to a world which it expresses and which can
only be attained through its interpretation. The universe, Royce concludes, is a system of signs. The process of interpreting the universe
as a system of signs leads to the view of the universe as a community
of spirits, or spiritual beings in itself; the universe is therefore spiritual. This is the view which Royce develops in his work *The Philosophy of Loyalty,* 1908. He finds this view illustrated in and supported
by the metaphysics and moral doctrine of Christianity, and in idealism
he is prepared to find, correlatively, the philosophical support of Christianity (*The Problem of Christianity,* 1913). This view of the Absolute
as the world-individual complex will receive further development in
the idea of the Great Community.

It may justly be said that the problem of God is not a special problem with Royce but his whole problem. The doctrine of the Absolute,
especially as developed through Peirce's theory of interpretation, provides the key to the question of God's existence. God is the Absolute,
when the Absolute is grasped in its true character. The arguments for
the existence of God are identical with the arguments for the reality
and the intrinsic character of the Absolute. The Absolute *is* because
the finite, in all its forms, as evidenced by experience (the individual,
error), *is;* the meaning of the finite (its *internal* meaning) is the Absolute. But, as the argument from interpretation proves, this Absolute,

like the finite exemplified in my neighbor, the other as person, is concrete and spiritual. It is the Absolute in this sense which is God. So runs the basic current of Royce's thought on this point as developed in various texts from *The Religious Aspect of Philosophy*, 1885, to *The Conception of God*, 1897.

The ethics of loyalty is perhaps the aspect of Royce's philosophy which is most widely known. It is the theme of his important work *The Philosophy of Loyalty* and of many references throughout his other works. The key to his concept of loyalty seems to lie in his basic notion (derived ultimately, perhaps, from Schopenhauer) of the idea as self-representing and self-fulfilling will. As will, the basic endowment of the idea is freedom; and the expression of freedom is choice. Freedom as choice makes it clear that no moral imperative external to the will can be its norm; its norm must be within itself as free choice. As moral, will must choose, and it must adhere to its choice. This is the essence of loyalty.

It is equally clear, that the choice of the will which is also idea cannot be merely itself in its limited, empirical, circumscribed reality. This would violate its character as idea, which includes by definition the transcendental dimension. The object of choice is always a transcendental object. (At this point, many interpreters catch a Kantian echo.) Hence, loyality is not a self-enclosing principle, a principle of egotism or mere self-consistency, but a transcendental principle which links the empirical will with the entire community of spirits which constitute the Absolute. The basic moral link with that community is loyality to our own free choice in its transcendental implications. Loyalty thus appears as the supreme transcendental moral principle, the correlative of freedom, the foundation of the moral self, and the fundamental bond of community between all finite spirits and between finite spirits and the Absolute. It is in turn the key to the idea of the Great Community.

There can be little question that the idea of the "Great Community" is one of the noblest to appear in western thought. The fact that it cannot be considered entirely original, but finds many prototypes in the history of philosophy, does not detract from its appeal but in fact strengthens it. The Great Community, it is safe to say, has ideal affinities with the Republic of Plato, with the City of God of Augustine, and with the Mystical Body of Christ in theological thought. It is the actuality of that community of spirits of which God is both part and the whole and of which, through God as Absolute, all individual finite members are, in their turn, both parts and the whole. It is a real community, not in the sense that it can be found realized anywhere at any point in history, but because it possesses in itself eternal verity. It is the real community even if no community in history corresponds to its model; indeed, its reality may even be measured by the deviation of historical societies from its norm. It is the transcendental unity of men through God on the basis of the ontological principle of the Absolute and the moral imperative of loyalty. Royce contends, however, that the realization of this community is a historical and empirical imperative as well; and, in some of his later writings, he ventures suggestions for its realization. While these suggestions must inevitably be pronounced utopian and unrealistic, this is not their measure. They can only be measured with respect to that ideal and eternal community which he logically, lucidly, and persuasively expounds.

While Royce certainly represents the acme of the neo-Hegelian movement in America, other significant voices were not lacking. Especially worthy of note are those who represented a more spiritualistic and personalistic tendency than is to be found in Royce. One of these we have already had occasion to mention: G. H. Howison (1834–1916). He felt that Royce's idealism tended to liquidate the finite individual personality in the infinite Self and even to annihilate the personal character of God. By contrast he developed a pluralistic idealism which laid emphasis precisely on those factors he found wanting in his colleague (cf. *The Conception of God,* 1897). William Ernest Hocking (born 1873) represents even more forcibly the movement in the direction of spiritualism and personalism, though at the same time he stands for an identification, probably influenced by Creighton's objectivist idealism, of the Absolute with nature. His important work *The Meaning of God in Human Experience* (1912) brings into focus all of the complex strains of thought which influenced him but which he molded into a very personal viewpoint, dominated by the reality of God as supreme mediating existence. Finally we should mention the very able, subtle, and critically alert presentation of the entire idealist position achieved by Brand Blandshard (b. 1892) in his two-volume *The Nature of Thought,* 1939: For Blandshard, the development of thought is a process creative of a system in which all is included and perfectly determined. This absolute totality is reality itself, and thought comes to it by successive stages, each of which constitutes an advance in unity, coherence, and integration.

B. *Neo-Hegelianism in Italy*

After England and America, Italy provided the widest field for the development of the neo-Hegelian movement. One of the most important figures of this movement, Benedetto Croce (1866–1952), both in his autobiography, *Contributo alla critica di me stesso* [A contribution to the criticism of myself], and in some crowded pages of his important *Storia d'Italia 1871–1915* [History of Italy from 1871–1915], depicts the cultural background of this movement. Croce singles out as the most important conditioning factor the development of an extreme positivism, represented by Roberto Ardigò (1828–1920), but he notes as well an unhealthy nationalism in philosophy, which demanded to be counterbalanced, if not entirely eliminated, by a return to the transcendental and universalistic point of view so clearly presented by idealism. The cultural effect of positivism was the signal for a revolt against it. In the richly speculative, critical, and artistic cultural atmosphere of Italy, positivism moved like a desiccating wind from the African desert, withering artistic expression, philosophical speculation, and the moral vigor of the cultural classes. To the Italian idealists positivism seemed a radical distortion in the fundamental line of development of western philosophy, which, in Croce's words, had always been the philosophy of spirit, of mind and self-consciousness.

The most exhaustive account of the background of Italian idealism is given, not by Croce, but by his colleague Giovanni Gentile (1875–1944) in his three-volume *Le origini della filosofia contemporanea in Italia* [The origins of contemporary philosophy in Italy], 1917–23. The development of the idealist movement in Italy may be divided into two phases, the line of demarcation between them being the emergence of the thought of Croce as a decisive cultural force with the founding of the review *La critica* [Criticism] in 1901–1902. The most important figures of the first phase are Bertrando Spaventa (1817–1883) and Augusto Vera (1813–1885). The dominant figures of the second phase are Croce and Gentile. In the thought of the latter thinkers, it should be noted that the contesting of positivism and the restoration of the idealist tradition constitute but subordinate themes. Both were minds of great power and originality who demand separate treatment, which will be accorded them in Volume V, (Part II, Chapter II). Here will be selected for notice only specific aspects of their thought which contributed to the neo-idealist movement.

Augusto Vera is dismissed by Abbagnano in his excellent *History of Philosophy* as a modest but typical Hegelian of the right with theistic and Catholicizing tendencies. This treatment seems excessively harsh, although it is impossible to claim anything but historically illustrative importance for his thought. Vera devoted himself to two main tasks: the translation of Hegel's principal works with commentary on them and the speculative consideration of certain central problems of Hegelianism. He identified these problems as: the relationship between the Idea, the human spirit, and history; the autonomy of the individual human person, and especially his liberty, as the basis of the moral order; the status of nature and the sciences of nature in Hegelian thought. His purpose was to preserve the transcendence of the Idea and the effective liberty of the individual human subject. Finally, continuing Hegel's own effort, he sought to reconstruct the whole of the Christian, and specifically Catholic, edifice on idealist, as opposed to scholastic, bases.

Bertrando Spaventa (who was distantly related to Croce) is generally looked upon as the real protagonist of neo-Hegelianism in Italy at a time when the voice of positivism was unchallenged. Two dominant concerns are also discernible in Spaventa's thought. The one is historical, the other speculative. The historical concern is to draw Italian philosophy out of its provincial isolation and to bring it again, as in the days of Bruno, Campanella, and Galileo, into the central and advancing currents of European thought. In seeking to do this, Spaventa developed a theory of the history of philosophy which, today, might not sustain critical examination but which was molded to his immediate purposes. His speculative concern is the reconstruction of Hegelianism. His interpretation of Hegelianism, very rich in Fichtean and Kantian overtones, was destined to have considerable influence in the idealist revival in Italy, especially, through Jaja, on Gentile, and, through the latter, on the later spiritualistic and personalistic movements. He speaks of a "rectification" of Hegel, which consists principally in restoring the *Phenomenology of Mind* to a central place, dislodging the *Logic* from its dominant position. In this way he was striking at the alleged panlogism of Hegel and bringing his thought closer to the position of a philosophy of existence. His most interesting and influential works are *La filosofia italiana e le sue relazioni con la filosofia europea* [Italian philosophy and its relations with European philosophy], edited and published by Gentile in 1908 and *Scritti filosofici*, also edited and published by Gentile, in 1901.

Croce steadfastly rejected any characterization of himself as a Hegelian or his philosophy as a form of Hegelianism. He sought to base his *absolute historicism* upon an understanding of the central direction of the whole of western philosophy, with special reference to the thought of the Renaissance and of Giambattista Vico. Nevertheless, the criticism and interpretation of Hegel constitutes a central and persistent theme in his critical writings, and there can be no doubt that the results of this criticism and interpretation entered directly and constitutively into his own speculative edifice. Three works of Croce on Hegel are especially relevant: *Ciò ch'è vivo e ciò ch'è morto nella filosofia di Hegel* (*What is Living and What is Dead in the Philosophy of Hegel*), 1907, the *Saggio sullo Hegel* [Essay on Hegel], 1913, and, written toward the end of his life, the *Indagini su Hegel* [Investigations concerning Hegel], 1952; however, the numerous references and brief treatments of points of Hegelian thought scattered throughout his writings cannot be ignored.

Croce's evaluation of Hegel can be reduced to two chief points, one positive, the other negative: 1) Hegel is the great restorer of the philosophy of spirit and hence of the central line of western philosophical speculation (although he finds a predecessor in this in Vico); 2) Hegel made grievous errors in his analysis of the life of the spirit, and chief among them were the lingering elements of transcendence, the incomplete enucleation of the constitutive moments of spirit, and the overemphasis on the dialectic of opposites to the neglect of the architectonically more important *dialectic of distincts*. Each of these errors Croce rectified in his own "absolute historicism," a system of absolute immanence which establishes the aesthetic and economic (utility) moments of spirit on an equal footing with the ethical and logical moments, and in the reconstruction of the whole life of spirit on the architectonic principle of the dialectic of distincts. In addition, it might be added, he effected a singularly lucid rectification of the enterprise of the "philosophy of history," so closely associated with Hegel, in his work *Storia come pensiero e come azione* [History as thought and action], 1938 (translated as *History as the Story of Liberty*).

The "actualism" of Gentile, like the "absolute historicism" of Croce, is an original and autonomous speculative construction. Nevertheless, elements of the criticism of Hegel and the Hegelian tradition and of their reconstruction enter into the intimate constitution of that philosophical position. Gentile gave a positive value to Spaventa's interpretation and reconstruction of Hegel's thought, both in his work on the origins of contemporary Italian philosophy, noted above, and in his introductory essays to Spaventa's works. Nevertheless, he reserved his own thoughts, which appear most strikingly in his work *La riforma della dialectica hegeliana* [The reformation of the Hegelian dialectic], 1913. Gentile criticizes Hegel for limiting himself to a dialectic of the *pensato* (the object of thought), that is, of the concept of reality as that which can be thought. He should have proceeded to the dialectic of the *pensante* (the thinking principal, the pure act of thought). The subject of thought is always, to be sure, subject of an object, for every act of thought is necessarily the thought *of* something; but the object of thought—be it God, nature, the self of the subject or of other selves —has no reality outside of the act of thought. Gentile's own philosophy stems directly from his "reform" of Hegel; it is, above all, the theory of the spirit as pure act of thought, in which every vestige of the substantiality of the subject of thought is overcome and eliminated. In addition to the work noted above, the two chief documents of Gentile's reconstruction of idealism are *La teoria generale dello spirito come atto puro* [The general theory of the spirit as pure act], 1916, and the *Sistema di logica come teoria del conoscere* [System of logic as theory of knowledge], 1917–22.

C. *Other Manifestations of Neo-Hegelianism*

The neo-Hegelian movement as such plays itself out, as we have noted, in the Anglo-American and the Italian theaters. Nowhere else did the revival of interest in Hegelianism take on the coherence which would permit it to be identified as a movement. This is not to say, however, that this interest did not exist elsewhere. On the contrary, interest in the Hegelian philosophy has never actually faded; moreover, certain very contemporary movements of thought, such as existentialism and phenomenology (especially as these closely relate to each other in the "phenomenological ontologies" of the existentialists), have given a direct stimulus to this interest. No one today is a Hegelian, but no one today is unresponsive to the influence, however remote, of Hegel's thought. Here we may list but a few contributions, all of them dating from the Second World War, to this widespread renewal of interest in Hegel's thought and its derivatives.

Jean Hyppolite must be numbered among the most prolific and perceptive contributors to the contemporary interest in Hegel. He has written a number of important items on this theme, especially *Genèse et structure de la phénoménologie de l'esprit* [Genesis and structure of the phenomenology of mind], 1946, and *Introduction à la philosophie de l'histoire de Hegel* [Introduction to Hegel's philosophy of history], 1948. His later study *Logique et existence* [Logic and existence], 1953, is a revolutionary approach to its theme. Also in France there appeared Jean Wahl's study *La malheur de la conscience dans la philosophie de Hegel* [The unhappy consciousness in Hegel's philosophy], second edition 1951, which establishes the link between Hegelianism and existentialism. In Italy important studies have continued to appear, such as those by Enrico de Negri: *Interpretazione de Hegel*, 1943, and *I Principi de Hegel*, 1949; and that of Gennaro: *La rivoluzione della dialectica hegeliana* [The revolution in Hegel's dialectic], 1954, and a number of others. In Germany there is Karl Löwith's masterful study *Von Hegel zu Nietzsche* [From Hegel to Nietzsche], second edition 1950, and W. R. Boyer's *Zweichen Phänomenologie und Logik* [Between phenomenology and logic], 1955. In England, G. R. G. Mure contributed two excellent and perceptive studies: *Introduction to Hegel*, 1941, and *A Study of Hegel's Logic*, 1950, while in America there has appeared Emil Fackenheim's interesting study *The Religious Dimension in Hegel's Thought,* 1967. These titles constitute but a very few of the numerous works that are each year dedicated to Hegel's thought in its relevance to contemporary trends.

Readings

Books

Barrett, C., ed. *Contemporary Idealism in America.* New York: Macmillan, 1932.

Cotton, J. H. *Royce on the Human Self.* Cambridge, Mass.: Harvard University Press, 1954.

Ewing, A. C. *Idealism: A Critical Survey.* New York: Humanities Press, 1933.

Haldar, Hira-lal. *Neo-Hegelianism.* London: Heath, Cranton, 1927.

Harris, F. P. *Neo-Idealist Political Theory.* New York: King's Crown Press, 1944.

Jones, H., and Muirhead, J. H. *Life and Philosophy of E. Caird.* Glasgow: Maclehose, Jackson, 1921.

Lofthouse, W. F. *F. H. Bradley.* London: Philosophers Library Series, 1949.

Marcel, G. *Royce's Metaphysics.* Chicago: H. Regnery, 1956.

Muirhead, J. H. *Bernard Bosanquet and His Friends.* London: Allen & Unwin, 1931.

————. *The Platonic Tradition in Anglo-Saxon Philosophy.* New York: Macmillan, 1931.

Royce, J. *Lectures on Modern Idealism.* New Haven: Yale University Press, 1919.

Saxena, Sushill Kumar. *Studies in the Metaphysics of Bradley.* New York: Humanities Press, 1967.

Smith, J. E. *Royce's Social Infinite.* New York: Liberal Arts Press, 1950.

Stirling, A. H. *James Hutchison Stirling: His Life and Work.* London: T. F. Unwin, 1912.

Tallon, H. J. *The Concept of Self in British and American Idealism.* Washington, D.C.: Catholic University of America Press, 1939.

Warren, W. P. *Pantheism in Neo-Hegelian Thought.* Scottdale, Pa.: Mennonite Press, 1933.

Essays and articles

Blandshard, B. "Francis H. Bradley." *Journal of Philosophy,* XXII (1921).

Bradley, A. C., et al. "Bernard Bosanquet: 1838–1923." *Proceedings of the British Academy,* X (1923).

Cohen, Robert S. "Ernst Mach: Physics, Perception and the Philosophy of Science." *Synthese,* XVIII (1968), 132–170.

Hoernlé, R. F. A. "Prof. Baillie's Idealist Construction of Experience." *Mind,* XVI (1907).

————. "On Bosanquet's Idealism." *Philosophical Review* XXXII (1923).

Luther, Arthur R. "W. E. Hocking on Man's Knowledge of God." *Philosophy Today,* XI (1967), 131–141.

Mead, G. H. "The Philosophy of Royce, James and Dewey in Their American Setting." *International Journal of Ethics*, XL (1930).

Montague, W. D. "Prof. Royce's Refutation of Realism." *Philosophical Review*, XI (1902).

Schiller, F. C. S. "The Present Phase of 'Idealism.'" *Mind*, XIX (1910).

For figures in Italian neo-Hegelianism see Volume V of the present work and the entries *sub nomine* in the *Encyclopedia of Philosophy* (New York: Macmillan, Free Press, 1967).

CHAPTER V

The Origins of
Modern Spiritualism

Introduction: The Meaning of Spiritualism in Philosophy

A certain ambiguity attaches to the term *spiritualism* as it is employed in philosophy, and this is true especially in the English-speaking world. To illustrate: Henry Sidgwick, in the article under this term in the *Encyclopaedia Britannica,* confuses it with spiritism and discourses on preternatural phenomena; and a similar confusion infects the corresponding article in Baldwin's *Encyclopedia of Psychology and Philosophy.* This confusion tends to obscure the discussion of an important current in contemporary philosophy, which is, with phenomenology and existentialism, the most important movement on the European Continent. For this reason a few sentences to clarify its meaning will surely be useful.

The French philosopher Maurice Blondel, generally recognized as a leading spiritualist philosopher, was reluctant to apply the term to his position because he found that, on its first appearance in the eighteenth century, it had been associated in a pejorative sense with pseudo-mysticism. Victor Cousin is counted the founder of modern spiritualism since he found the term so apt that he chose it despite such associations. Thus, he wrote in *Du vrai, du beau et du bien* [On the true, beautiful, and good], 1853: "Our . . . doctrine . . . is spiritualism, this philosophy, as solid as it is ample, which beginning with Socrates and Plato was diffused through the world by the Gospel, which Descartes has stated in its severe form. . . ." And he continues: "This philosophy teaches the spiritualism of the soul, freedom and responsibility . . . moral obligation, disinterested virtue . . . and God as author and type of mankind. . . ." Rhetoric aside, Cousin was here sketching faithfully both the historical provenance and the theoretical scope of this philosophy. Benedetto Croce put the matter more succinctly perhaps when he said that the history of philosophy has always been the

268

history of the philosophy of spirit and that it could not be otherwise.

Speaking historically, the genealogy of spiritualism is even more impressive than Cousin suggests. To Socrates and Plato may justly be added every major name in the classical philosophical tradition. Aristotle surely belongs here, for his *physis,* as it appears in man, clearly possesses that element of *interiority* which is the hallmark of spiritualism. Christianity gave the greatest impulse to spiritualist philosophy, not by introducing a new problematic, but by placing the classical problematic in a fresh light. St. Augustine, whom modern spiritualists without exception accept as their progenitor, gives clearest evidence of this. In St. Thomas this tradition is given a firmer architectonic structure by emphasis on the Aristotelian elements, though Thomism, by reason of its excessive cosmologism, is unsympathetic to many modern spiritualists. A strong rectifying force to Thomas is Bonaventure, as Gilson shows in his fine work on that figure. Cousin cites Descartes, and rightly; Descartes's reaffirmation of the interiority of being, through the *cogito* and its metaphysical consequences, remains one of the pillars of modern spiritualism. To his name must be added those of Malebranche, Berkeley, and Leibnitz, while the idealist systems must be recognized as the greatest precontemporary evidence of spiritualistic florescence in philosophy.

The identity of spiritualism is established, however, not through association with great names, but by the speculative tradition it perpetuates. Spiritualism does not have a specific problematic; it shares that of classical western philosophy. It represents rather a basic theoretical orientation from which it addresses these problems. This may be illustrated with reference to that ultimate problem of all speculation: being. Spiritualism is best characterized by its address to the fundamental issue of man's access to being. That access lies, in the view of spiritualism, not in the exploration of nature, but in man's penetration and phenomenological reflection upon his own interiority. The great admonition of Augustine is essential: "Noli foras ire, in te ipsum redi." Man is the primary paradigm of being.

When man considers what it is for him *to be,* consciousness emerges as the most generalized form of being. To be, for man, is to be conscious. But consciousness is ambivalent: Janus-faced. By reason of its intentional structure, it turns man's attention upon the object. But the object cannot establish consciousness, i.e., supply its necessary ground; the object is negation, i.e., what is *for* consciousness but is not consciousness itself, what the knowing subject *is.* Consciousness, however, also turns itself upon itself as self-consciousness. But the being present to itself in self-consciousness is not present there as an *object.* It is present as pure self-generative process, in which both subject and object merge. In Gentile's term, it is present as *autoctisis*, self-positing act. Being as present to itself in *autoctisis* is what is meant by spirit. Spirit is the all-encompassing category of what is, for all being can be denominated only by way of spirit.

Autoctisis is the purest form of spiritual activity, of spiritual life and being. It is not, however, a solipsistic act. Though this act is first revealed in man, as the act of his self-establishment in being, it does not close him in upon himself in an absolute immanence. Rather it opens him to all being, to the being beyond himself, to transcendence. Modern spiritualism finds that the analysis of spirit in the moment of *autoctisis* involves the self-transcendence of the spirit in two directions: vertically, toward God, and horizontally, toward the world of other spirits and of objects (nature). Contemporary spiritualism thus differs from the spiritualism of classical idealism, which tended toward absolute immanence, though not on the humanistic level but on the level of the Idea. It also differs thus from the thought of Croce, which is both immanentistic and humanistic.

The concept of spirit which emerges in contemporary spiritualism is very close to that depicted in Pico's *On the Dignity of Man.* Man is the center, the all-mediating presence. All being receives its denomination through his mediation. This does not enclose him within himself, however, for the mediatorial act is a self-positing and a self-transcending act; even more precisely, it transcends itself in the act of self-positing. Whatever is, as affirmation, is spirit. Even that dimension of being which is called matter, and which is negation in its pure form of otherness to spirit, is spirit and affirmation with relation to spirit, through which alone matter is posited as negation. The *reality* of the material is spirit, as is the reality of all that can be said to be.

This is a position which has been reached in modern and contemporary spiritualism only through a long and laborious process, not continually progressive but marked by hesitations, deviations, even retrogressions. It is this process which concerns us in this chapter. We shall consider it in two phases: 1) that which extends from the spiritualist aspects of ideology to the thought of Bergson; and 2) post-Bergsonian spiritualism, that is, contemporary spiritualism in a stricter sense. The first phase will form the content of the present chapter, and the second will be dealt with in Volume V of this series (Part II, Chapter V; for Bergson see Volume V, Part I, Chapter VIII).

A. *The Origins of Modern Spiritualism in Germany*

A certain justice dictates that the consideration of the origins of modern spiritualism begin in Germany. The situation of German philosophy in the first half of the nineteenth century was especially sensitive. On the one hand, the massive movement of Hegelian thought threatened to overwhelm it; on the other, the development of the sciences exposed it to the pressures of an emergent scientific positivism. No third possibility seemed to offer itself. Nevertheless, in this very impasse the first movements of spiritualism are to be discerned.

One of the thinkers in this initial movement of spiritualism is Immanuel Hermann Fichte (1796–1879), the son of the celebrated Johann Gottlieb Fichte. Schooled in the thought of his father, Kant, and Hegel, he shows a reasoned indebtedness, though a firm independence, toward the first two but reserves a rather hostile attitude for Hegel. In the tradition of idealism he first conceived philosophy as system construction; he entitled this overall effort *Grundzüge zum System der Philosophie* [Groundwork for the system of philosophy]. The systematic aspect is not important; far more interesting and significant is the affirmation of the spiritualistic point of view which emerges in the first volume: *Erkennen als Selbsterkennen* [Knowledge as self-knowledge], 1833. Self-consciousness is the principle, the center, and the end of philosophy; it consists in an auto-orientation of consciousness in which it becomes aware of its own originative endowments. Philosophy is the theory of consciousness, which is omnipresent.

Somewhat along the pattern of Hegel's *Phenomenology of Mind*, Fichte delineates a history of consciousness as it moves toward self-consciousness. This history exhibits four epochs: consciousness as natural datum; the Self as the subject of representation; the Self as the subject of thought, of which God is the absolute object; finally, the emergence of Self-consciousness in its plenitude. In a way this is the history of *autoctisis*, the self-generation of spirit, conceived as the dialectical immanentization of the moments of the other. The second volume, *Ontologie*, 1836, develops an *ontology* of the eternal forms of the real. Their basis lies in the plenitude of self-consciousness, whence they are engendered by a dialectic of transcendence. The realms of being are generated theoretically by the self-knowledge of consciousness or spirit. The third volume is considered most important for the history of spiritualism. *Die spekulative Theologie* [Speculative theology] develops the idea of God as the supreme personal unity of the real and the ideal. The crucial point, however, is that the transcendent being of God is established on the analysis of man's self-consciousness, not on a naturalistic basis, thus setting a pattern which will persist throughout later spiritualism. The culmination of his thought is to be found in *Der neue Spiritualismus* [The new spiritualism], 1878. Here the spiritualist traits noted above are developed, with a new emphasis on their humanistic concreteness.

Rudolph Hermann Lotze (1817–1881) is known chiefly as the author of the three-volume work *Mikrokosmos* [Microcosm], 1856–58, which carries the significant subtitle *Ideen zur Naturgeschichte und Geschichte der Menschheit: Versuch einer Anthropologie* [Ideas for a naturalistic history of mankind: quest for an anthropology]. His thought is polarized about two concerns: respect for the physical sciences and concern for religion and for humanistic values in general. Pursuing these concerns, he sought to reconcile nineteenth-century mechanism with a theistic spiritualism which would respond to man's needs.

Already in his *Metaphysik,* 1841, he had firmly outlined the principles of his proposed synthesis. There he acknowledged the value of mechanism for an understanding of the physical world, as he was also to do for the psychic world in his *Medizinische Psychologie* [Medical psychology], 1852; but he opposed its extension and generalization into an inclusive metaphysical principle. Instead, he suggested an "idealistic teleology" in which, Platonically, he affirms the good as the supreme principle which generates and organizes all movement in the universe. The spiritualistic bent of his thought becomes apparent when, bypassing the question of its substantiality, he affirms the spirituality of the soul on the evidence of the unity of the self, a unity which eludes all mechanistic analysis and reduction.

These themes are elaborated in *Mikrokosmos.* The universal connection of things according to a mechanistic principle is acknowledged, but only as a matter of *fact.* It explains nothing and cannot itself be explained until the conditions which make the fact *possible* are established. Science can establish the fact; philosophy must concern itself with the establishment of the possibility as a principle by recourse to principles not available to science. The chief of these principles is "idealistic teleology." Its evidence is the unity of self-consciousness. The apprehension of the self is the paradigm for the penetration of the essences of things. This course of thought terminates in the affirmation of an unequivocal theism: "The true real, that which is and ought to be, is not matter and even less idea, but the living personal spirit of God and the world of personal spirits which he has created" (*Mikrokosmos,* Vol. III, p. 616).

Eduard von Hartmann (1842–1906) was a man of one book: *Die Philosophie des Unbewussten* [The philosophy of the unconscious], published in 1869 when he was twenty-seven. None of his other numerous writings won him anything like the attention aroused by this first book. He was very conscious of the antecedents of the spiritualism he advocated, noting especially the *absolute spirit* of Hegel, the *will* of Schopenhauer, and the *unconscious* of Schelling; to these he added an indebtedness to Leibnitz and even to the scientific positivism of his day, since he held that the evidence for his spiritualism was drawn from the natural sciences and that the method of demonstration employed is inductive. The principle which emerges from the synthesis of these sources is an *absolute spiritual unconscious.* This principle reveals itself in man and other living things as *will;* but the *idea* is an equally irreducible aspect of the activity of the unconscious. Will generates the *that (dass)* of the world; the idea, its *something (was).* Pessimism and optimism are both to be affirmed; as *dass,* existence, the world is evil and sorrow, for it springs from an irrational will; as *was,* essence, it may, due to the rationality of the idea, be released from evil and sorrow and realize the finality of the world. The fulfillment of the ideality of the world is the principle of the generation of consciousness. The process of consciousness emancipates the idea from its servitude to the will. But this is a limit-process; it can never eventuate in an existential state of the absolute. God is the name of the process as a whole. As absolute spirit, the substance of the world, God is unconscious. At the same time, he is the motive principle of the passage toward consciousness. He is thus both beginning and end.

The structure of von Hartmann's thought was feeble, and, as a consequence, his authority declined swiftly. His place in the development of modern spiritualism seems assured, however, because his thought represents a phase through which spiritualism had to pass in order to arrive at a clear understanding of itself. This phase was the positing and the elimination of the unconscious as a moment of the life of spirit. Von Hartmann did more than even the later Freudians to make clear to spiritualism that the idea of spirit as the unconscious is a naturalistic residue.

Some historians have suggested that Rudolf C. Eucken (1846–1926) belongs, not among the spiritualists, but among the vitalists. This point was made in the speech of presentation when he received the Nobel Prize in 1908. Properly, however, the term *vitalist* is reserved for those who take life in its biological manifestation as the paradigm of being. This is not true in Eucken's case. The concept of life is indeed central to his thought, but it is life in its spiritual manifestation with which he is concerned. It might be said that his contribution to the formation of modern spiritualism lies in his emphasis on the concept of life, not as mere biological process, but as value-creative activity. This point of view was developed in a long series of works of which perhaps the most important are: *Die Einheit des Geisteslebens in Bewusstsein und Tat der Menschheit* [The unity of the spiritual life in the consciousness and activity of mankind], 1888; *Die Lebensanschauungen der grossen Denker* [The vision of life in the great thinkers], 1890; *Der Wahrheitgehalt der Religion* [The truth-content of religion], 1901; and *Grundlinien einer neuen Lebensanschauung* [Basic lineaments of a new vision of life], 1907.

Eucken's position is centered in the insight that existence is without meaning if its only concern is material values and the external relations between men in society. It takes on meaning only when it acquires spiritual value. The process by which it acquires such value is his whole concern.

The basic concept with which he works is *life*. He distinguishes two levels in life: the biological and the noological. At the first level, man's life is bound closely to nature; at the second, it possesses a capacity for producing a world of spiritual content, of values. A danger, however, attends this distinction. When man is viewed only at the first level, his liberty and creative power escape notice; when only at the second, spirituality, interiority, value, run the risk of becoming subjective. His "noological" method is intended to avoid this danger; this method would unite liberty and objective truth by closing the caesura between man and the life of the cosmos. Cosmic life has its own conditions, and man must, through spiritual discipline, rise to that life in order to achieve the fullness of his own nature.

Man is not an absolute creator. He achieves creative power through union with the life-force of the cosmos. All of man's achievements in the spiritual order: science, philosophy, art, religion, society, are the work, not of isolated individuals, but of mankind in union with the sovereign and total power of cosmic life; man makes this life his own.

The higher life of the spirit is not a substantial thing. It is an inward operation which takes place in the interior forum of man's consciousness. Here lies his evidence that the true movement of man's life is union with the divine life-force of the cosmos. This striving, in its purity, is religion. Still, Eucken resists all temptation to pantheism; he maintains a purely theistic view of God and, while seeing him as the life-force of the universe, never identifies God and the world. For this reason, Christianity appears to him to be the highest manifestation of the spiritual and religious life. His is a Christian spiritualism. Nevertheless, he places little importance on the doctrinal content of Christianity, stressing instead its capacity to liberate the creative forces of life in man through vision, charity, and fellowship.

A lesser, but still significant, figure of German spiritualism is African Spir (1837–1890). The most important of his many writings is *Denken und Wirklichkeit* [Thought and reality], 1873. Spir's thought seems to some critics to present, in somewhat exaggerated form, all of the characteristic features of modern spiritualism. Nevertheless, his presentation is highly original and personal. The main emphasis falls on the range and validity of the principle of identity. The effort of idealism, he points out, was to make the empirical world rational by showing that it is governed by the same principles—identity and non-contradiction—that govern the world of concepts. This effort cannot succeed; nature remains a realm of appearance, never conformable to the *a priori* concepts. These, deriving from the principle of identity, become logical imperatives according to which the world of experience is interpreted, with no pretense of asserting that these concepts are the actual organizing principles of nature. The value of the *a priori* principles lies precisely in their power of organizing experience on this imperative basis. They constitute the realm of spirit as distinct from that of nature; and nature is ordered only by reference to the realm of spirit.

Spir's doctrine culminates in the identification of the unconditioned, imperative order of the *a priori* with God. God is discovered at the heart of human existence, just as the *a priori* principles are discovered when man examines the basis of his reflective life; indeed, it is only in relationship to God that the unconditioned order of the *a priori* takes on unity. This unity is not reached, in its character as divine, by an act of criticism as are the logical *a priori* principles. It is revealed by a sentiment of unity with God. The relationship of man to God is *a priori* but not critical; it is immediate and not of a secondary order, as are the *a priori* principles discovered by the critical operation. Man achieves coherence in life when he conducts the whole of his empirical existence on the basis of this primary unity in sentiment with God.

The range of Spir's influence was not large, but it was historically important. His most significant conquest was the Italian spiritualist thought of Piero Martinetti.

B. *Modern Spiritualism in Italy*

In the Italy of the nineteenth century, positivism, reaching its fullest and most intransigent expression in Roberto Ardigò, established a firm hegemony over intellectual and cultural life for a long period. For this reason, the reaction against positivism, when finally it was aroused, was all the more violent and determined. This reaction took three principal forms, all related in differing ways to the renewal of spiritualism in philosophy. The first was the return, in neo-scholastic thought, to the classical spiritualism of the Catholic tradition. The second was the return to the idealist tradition, deriving principally from Hegel, but also determined to establish continuity with pre-Hegelian and indigenous sources of spiritualist thought, such as Vico and Campanella. The third sought to establish spiritualism on neither of these historical bases, but to find an autonomous basis in the direct examination of human nature and the human condition. The return to the Catholic tradition of spiritualism in the neo-scholastic and neo-Thomist movements is studied in the next volume (V, Part I, Chapter VI); so too is the return to spiritualist philosophy by way of the idealist tradition, both in its immanentistic form (Croce and Gentile: Part II, Chapter II) and in its transcendental form (Christian spiritualism: Part II, Chapter V). In this place our attention will be limited to the third form of neo-spiritualism, that which seeks to estabish it autonomously in the direct examination of human nature. The most significant representatives of this form are Martinetti, Varisco, and Carabellese.

Piero Martinetti (1871–1943) is considered the founder of *metaphysical* spiritualism in Italy. Though his thought is strongly religious in tone, he eventually subordinates religion, as well as all other aspects of man's spiritual life, to an intellectualistic metaphysics. His thought is expounded chiefly in two works: *Introduzione alla metafisica* [Introduction to metaphysics], 1904, and *La libertà* [Liberty], 1928.

Martinetti's philosophical purpose is to reestablish metaphysics as a valid science on grounds and by a method whose validity would have to be recognized by the dominant positivism. His scientific metaphysics would meet all the requirements of scientific methodology. Adhering to data which science must recognize, it is no mere synthesis of the sciences but interprets their findings to determine their *meaning* as distinct from their mere *facticity*. His objective: an inductive metaphysics which, on *a posteriori* grounds, might achieve successive unifications of empirical data until the absolute is reached.

This projected unification would take place on three successive levels or grades. The first is the level of the "I," or self, as unity of sensuous consciousness. The "I" is the central point about which perception is synthesized. Here no distinction is achieved between subject and object save that between unity and multiplicity. The self, at this level, possesses a rudimentary transcendental character in the form of the invincible persuasion that my sense perceptions are identical with those of all possible subjects. But this persuasion is a mere datum. The rudimentary intimation of the transcendental provides Martinetti with the means of passing to the second level of synthesis, the *logical*. His *a priori* forms are not *a priori* in the Kantian sense, however, but are "connatural" with their empirical content. The passage from sensible to logical forms of unity is natural, i.e., not itself logical. Logic is the "science of the natural conformations of human thought" (*Introduzione*, 1929 ed., p. 433). Logical relations are therefore empirical relations. The third level, that of absolute unity, cannot be achieved in thought, though it is implied in the dynamic of thought. We can achieve no speculative concept of this unity, but only a symbolic intuition which may be expressed by substituting ideogramic complexes for objects of representation. Nevertheless, our knowledge cannot be called merely phenomenal; the absolute unity is always present, for it enters structurally into all of the levels of synthesis. This omnipresence of the absolute Martinetti calls "mystical": "Our knowledge is a mystic unity with the eternal *Logos*" (*Introduzione*, 1929 ed., p. 473). Finally, Martinetti transposes this process of synthesis from the cognitive to the practical order. The transcendental principle here is freedom. Morality exhibits a primary synthesis in the form of necessity freely achieved. It is continued and extended by art and religion.

The conflict with positivism which is the historical background of Italian spiritualism is attested by Bernadino Varisco (1850–1933), for he himself passed through an early positivistic phase, which found expression in his work *Scienza e opinioni* [Science and opinions], 1901. The first dim outlines of his ultimate position, however, are already discernible in this work; for he insists upon religious faith and its vision of life as fact as much as any indubitable fact of the physical or psychic orders. His first intention is that religion should be brought under the all-leveling force of science. The key to his subsequent development is precisely his perception that this reduction is not feasible and that, instead, the primacy of the spiritual order, of which religion is the supreme testimony, would eventually have to be asserted.

In his subsequent works—*La conoscenza* [Knowledge], 1905; *I massimi problemi* [The master problems], 1910; *Conosci te stesso* (*Know Thyself*), 1912; the *Sommario di filosofia* [Summary of philosophy], 1928; and finally, the posthumous *Dall'uomo a Dio* [From man to God], 1939—he records the progress of this reassertion of the primacy of the spiritual order. The first of these works, *La conoscenza*, is considered especially important for an understanding of the transition from positivism to spiritualism in Varisco's thought.

The first phase of Varisco's spiritualism reflects the preponderant influence of Leibnitz; it is a monadism. Reality is constituted by a multiplicity of particular subjects, each the center of the phenomenal world. Within each of these subjects can be discerned two zones: that of clear and distinct consciousness and that far more extensive zone of the subconscious. There is no realm of the thing-in-itself. Each subject varies or differs from all the others by a spontaneity which is its own. The monads are the centers of two orders of unity: the inner unity of each monad and the unity among the monads, which constitutes the order of the universe.

To account for these orders of unity, Varisco has to venture beyond the confines of his adherence to Leibnitz. He has recourse to certain basic insights of Rosmini, especially to the Rosminian idea of Being. The idea of Being, as Rosmini conceived it and as Varisco adopts it, unifies the particular spiritual and thinking subjects because it is, on the one hand, the concept common to every thinking principle, and, on the other hand, the concept under which every object of thought is apprehended. This idea of Being cannot be resolved into the act of thought, because it always reveals itself to analysis as the object of thought, informing and yet transcending thought. Being thought is a state of Being in its pure idea. Being as thought by particular spiritual subjects is, however, the very act of self-thought of Being as universal subject; for all that is thought, including the act of thinking, is within the range of the idea of Being. Therefore, Varisco concludes, the being and unity of particular subjects, and hence of the phenomenal universe can be reduced to their being thoughts of the universal subject. "God's knowledge is the cause of things." The universal subject is the self-consciousness of Being, of which every phenomenon and every secondary unity of phenomena are only a determination.

This analysis confronts Varisco with a dilemma which he finds difficult to resolve. What is the nature of the supreme being? How is the choice between theism and pantheism to be determined? His own statement of this speculative situation cannot be improved. Are the determinations of which the phenomenal world is constituted, he asks in *Know Thyself*, essential or nonessential to Being? The first case would be clearly pantheistic because any assignment of other determinations to Being would be gratuitous. In the second case, other determinations *must* be assigned to Being, and these would constitute Being as *person;* theism would be the result. Eventually, he decides the issue in favor of theism, and his philosophy acquires a definitely religious tone. Once the issue has been decided in this way, however, a second problem demands consideration: how to maintain the autonomy of the individual consciousness with respect to that of God. To meet this problem he has recourse to an ingenious, though hardly persuasive, argument. He postulates self-limitation in the omniscience of God; and this self-limitation of God's knowledge is reflected in his limited knowledge of the movement of the world. Hence, human activity is free to be free, so to say, to act on its own and to collaborate in God's action through the creation of values. This line of reasoning leads Varisco to an unqualified acceptance of the basic concepts of the religious, and specifically Christian, life.

Pantaleo Carabellese (1877–1948), in the opinion of not a few critics, is the most acute of the earlier spiritualists of the modern period. He developed the position which he called "critical ontologism" with great learning and equally impressive dialectical skill. Because of their rich historical context, the principal documents of his position present the dual aspect of historical exegesis and theoretical construction. Chief among these works are: *Il problema della filosofia da Kant a Fichte* [The problem of philosophy from Kant to Fichte], 1929; *Il problema teologico come filosofia* [The theological problem as philosophy], 1931; *L'idealismo italiano* [Italian idealism], 1938; *Le obbiezioni al cartesianesimo* [The objections to Cartesianism], 1946; and *Da Cartesio a Rosmini* [From Descartes to Rosmini], 1946. He was an influential teacher, and valuable insights into his thought are to be garnered from his published lectures.

The central problem of his thought is clear: What is the meaning of "critical ontologism"? He speaks of "ontologism" because *Being* is the foundation, object, and end of all philosophy. Further, the Being which thought seeks to discover or unveil is not a being which is opposed to, "other than," consciousness in the thinker and investigator; on the contrary, thought seeks the Being which is the substance of that consciousness. The philosopher's task is to render explicit the conditions or elements which constitute subjectivity and thus to bring to consciousness the Being which establishes consciousness. Philosophy is thought seeking the Being which is its own principle.

The critical basis of his ontologism is clearly defined by Carabellese. The way to ontologism lies along the thorny path of the refutation of both "realism" and "idealism." All three of the positions engaged in this dialectic have one principle in common: the quest of being. All, too, are constrained to cast this quest in the basic terms of the relation of consciousness to being. Both realism and idealism fail, for similar but opposing reasons. Seeking "objectivity," which implies freedom from the conditions of subjectivity and consciousness, realism seeks a being which is other to consciousness, other to subjectivity; a being which is "independent" of our thought. But what would be the character of such a being? Kantian criticism has made this clear. It must be being which is indistinguishable from non-being in the only terms which are significant for the characterization of being: its relation to consciousness. For such "independent" being would be without intrinsic relations to consciousness, and consciousness would be without intrinsic relation to it. An abyss is sunk between consciousness-appearance, to which all significant discourse is restricted, and being-in-itself which evades all characterization. Consciousness is therefore a form of non-being for realism, and philosophy is but the critical process of making this character evident.

The insight of idealism is sound in its beginning: Consciousness provides the only terms in which being can be enunciated. But once entered upon, the path of idealism leads to a self-defeating conclusion.

Seeking to clarify or render explicit the conditions of its own being, consciousness eventually resolves into itself, into the ultimate act of self-consciousness, all of the contents of consciousness, identifying them absolutely with itself and itself absolutely with them. By thinking itself, thought or consciousness realizes the absolute conditions of its own being; in the same process, moreover, it envisages itself as the ground of all its alleged contents, as the generator and creator of its world. It does not generate this world as something other in relation to itself but as something in which it is entirely immanent and which is entirely immanent in relation to it, so that transcendence is excluded both in the direction of the object and in the direction of the subject. This is the point at which Gentile, the most rigorous and logical of all idealists, arrived; and it is the point at which any idealist possessed of any rigor of method must inevitably arrive.

Consciousness, in realism, possessed no intrinsic relationship to being; consciousness, self-consciousness, in idealism equally possesses no direct relationship to being but becomes involved in the circular process of autoctisis. Such is the criticism which Carabellese directs against these opposing positions, and it is on a middle ground which nullifies the extremism and the latent nihilism of each that he seeks to construct his "critical ontologism."

Between the extremes of realism and idealism lies the solid ground of being revealed by philosophical reflection. It is the being *of consciousness*. Excluding on the one hand, a "being" which is without intrinsic relation to consciousness and, on the other, a subjectivity which generates self and world in one spontaneous process, the being of consciousness reveals itself as a complex structure in which subjectivity and objectivity appear as constitutive poles in a unified field. For Carabellese this being of consciousness has within itself both the order of existing subjects and its foundation, God. To identify either of these terms or poles with the other is to annihilate them and any meaning which can be ascribed to the term *being*. In his own words, "The nexus Being-Knowledge is not the distinction One-many. . . . The many are not the positivity of the One; nor is the One the positivity of minds" (*L'essere* [Being] 1947, p. 53). What is positive, therefore, is being itself, which is always the being of consciousness; what is positive is always concrete and is, therefore, that *founding relation* into which, in order to be established, the terms of the relation being-knowledge enter. Our knowing the *Truth*, which makes it possible to know any particular truth, is not a relation *to* Truth or *to* Being. It is never a relation to the object. It is always a relationship *in* Truth and a relation *within* Truth, and thanks to the presence of the object, with other minds. Being, therefore, is a field within which the structure of the plurality of subjects in a world mediated through the ultimate object is revealed. The determination of the order of objects and of the founding, mediating object (God) and of the order of subjects are problems within this field.

It is clear how, in the construction of this position, Carabellese has returned to a central position, or better perhaps, *possibility,* of western thought, ontologism. His predecessors are St. Augustine and the neo-Platonics, and more proximately Anselm and Malebranche; but he seeks to give this possibility a critical formulation which makes it the mediating force between the conflicting alternatives of realism and idealism—a mediation which nullifies both these extremes in order to direct philosophical reflection to the field of being as both ground and object of thought.

C. *Modern Spiritualism in France*

Spiritualism, it has been said, constitutes the classical tradition of philosophy in France. Most of the great names of modern French thought adhere to it, beginning with Montaigne, the master of the introspective method and most "interior" of philosophers, and including Descartes, Malebranche, and Pascal. True enough, during the period of the Enlightenment, under the mesmeric influence of Newton and English empiricism, a naturalistic orientation inserted itself directing attention to the "outer" world, the world of nature as the object of philosophical reflection based upon observation. But almost at the height of the influence of the Enlightenment, the older and deeper current began to reassert itself; at this point reference to the name of Maine de Biran is again inevitable. The naturalism of the Enlightenment takes on, therefore, the aspect of a parenthesis. Modern spiritualism in France, taking up this theme and attitude anew, is concerned not only to continue and enrich it, but to establish it with greater clarity against the menacing forces of positivism and materialism, which the advance of the natural sciences tended to fortify.

Because he published nothing during his lifetime, Jules Lequier (1814–1862) might have become the forgotten man of the spiritualist current in France. This eventuality was prevented by the intervention of an important figure of that current, Renouvier. Understanding the value of Lequier's achievement, Renouvier, in 1865, published a collection of Lequier's writings, for the most part fragmentary, under the title: *La recherche d'une première vérité* [Quest of a first truth]. A new edition of this work appeared in 1924. The interpretation which Renouvier placed upon Lequier's thought has seemed to some to conceal rather than reveal its true form. However this may be, the basic value of Lequier's thought has become so impressed upon subsequent consideration that any account of French spiritualism during this period which does not mention his name must be thought deficient.

That basic value lies in his affirmation of the central place of freedom in the life of spirit and in his efforts to place the character of spiritual freedom in clear relief. This effort is the more significant because it was undertaken at a moment when the victory of determinism seemed complete. Lequier rests his development of the notion of freedom and its place in the life of spirit on one point, above all: Freedom is the absolute condition for the quest of truth. Necessity, he points out, is the basic postulate of modern natural science; on it rests the order of nature and the possibility of prediction, which is the essence of scientific knowledge. This concept of necessity, however, will not withstand careful scrutiny. Not only does it confound good and evil, but necessity itself can be recognized and affirmed only by freedom or liberty. To distinguish truth from error, the subject must be free. Necessity may be the postulate of science, but freedom is the postulate of consciousness. Without liberty, no affirmation is possible.

While he thus gave a fundamental intonation to modern spiritualism, the defense of man's constitutive freedom, Lequier differs from many subsequent spiritualists in his conception of this freedom. The latter have frequently held that man's freedom is an immediate datum of introspective observation. Lequier holds, rather, that freedom is a postulate of the life of spirit—indeed, of its very idea. He thus introduces into the notion of freedom and into the life of spirit that element of risk which is also to be encountered in such thinkers as Kierkegaard, with whom he has on occasion been compared.

Though he is numbered more frequently among men of letters, Henri Frédéric Amiel (1821–1881) nevertheless deserves a place among philosophers. The pages of *Journal intime* [Intimate journal], published in part in 1883–84 and more amply in 1922, both in their substance and in their form contribute richly to the spiritualist current. The journal form is, with the essay of Montaigne, the form most consonant with the spiritualist attitude as a mode of life and thought. The treatise, by contrast, which seeks to objectify the life of spirit and subject it to rigorous explication, loses in the process much of the attitude of spiritualism. The substance of Amiel's journal may be considered under two aspects, both important to the idea of spiritualism: self-communion and reflection. These are the living actuality of that *interiority* which is absolutely essential to the notion of spirit. This interiority also is twofold in Amiel: the interiority of reflection, in which the whole world as he knew it is reflected in his own intimate consciousness; and, further, the interiority of self-establishment and creation, in which

Amiel discovers the key to the meaning of all that is reflected in his soul within that soul itself. He realizes in a very subtle and delicate manner Augustine's injunction: *In te ipsum redi,* not to find there only the self, but, as Augustine averred, the key to truth itself.

Amiel's pages are rich in comments on the reality of the spiritual life. For Amiel, the life of spirit is a delicate tension between passion and action. The soul which cannot suffer must remain alien to being and alien to itself. This is true with respect to the self in its intimate nature. We suffer ourselves, we undergo ourselves, and in this passion not only come to know but come *to be* ourselves. But this suffering, this passion, revealing itself as the inward process of the self-creation of spirit and its world, also reveals itself as the highest and most intensive form of action.

In his major work Charles Secrétan (1815–1895), one of the major figures of modern French spiritualism, takes up the note which Lequier had sounded, that of liberty. The title of this work is significant for the whole attitude of spiritualism: *La philosophie de la liberté* [The philosophy of liberty], 1849. All his other works, it is universally recognized, are but specifications of this basic work in regard to concrete problems of ethics, social thought, and religion. These include *La raison et le christianisme* [Reason and Christianity], 1863; *Le principe de la morale* [The principle of the moral life], 1883; *Les droits de l'humanité* [The rights of mankind], 1890, and others.

Secrétan had been a student of Schelling, a fact which considerably influenced the form of his spiritualism. The point of departure of his thought is the contraposition of the domain of external experience and that of consciousness. In consciousness, we encounter being and, by reflection, possess it philosophically. Being, as manifested in consciousness, is liberty or freedom. He intends, apparently, in contrast to Lequier, that this freedom is a first datum of consciousness—not merely a postulate—and, as well, a lived experience, the immediate form in which we possess being. Liberty is highly significant in a metaphysical sense; it reveals that while man is indeed spirit, this principle in man is not fully actuated or realized. This reflection opens two lines of speculation. The first concerns freedom in man and the discipline of the spiritual life, the life of liberty. The second leads him to the consideration of God as the actuality of that absolute liberty of which man's freedom is but a reflection.

Man's freedom, though most real, is but a limited freedom. Its limited character is evidenced by the fact that it moves within anteriorly prescribed bounds which are both physical and moral. Even while eliciting the activity of freedom, physical nature imposes the bounds within which it may deploy itself and beyond which it may not pass.

The moral law and moral duty limit man's freedom as effectively as does nature by any anterior imperative. From these considerations Secrétan draws the inescapable conclusion: man is contingent; he depends upon a higher principle for his being. The actualization of his life, within due limits, is the work of man's freedom, but that life and being itself, whose essence is freedom, is not from himself. He does not exercise the ultimate act of freedom, the creation of his own reality, the positing of his own being by a free act. This act alone would make man absolutely free and would endow him with absolute being, i.e., being that is absolutely within his own power and discretion.

Man's contingency turns Secrétan's attention to two further issues: the nature of the principle upon which man depends in the metaphysical order and the mode of that dependence. This is to say, he turns his attention to God and to a metaphysics of creation.

Man, Secrétan affirms, has no true idea of God, that being upon which his own being is dependent; that is, no idea in the Cartesian sense. He can, however, reach certain conclusions about God which are grounded in his apprehension of self rather than in any direct intuition of God. Thus man is led to affirm God, first, as absolute freedom, absolute liberty. This in turn justifies the assertion that God must be person, for the person is but the elaboration of the implications of liberty on the metaphysical plane. Person is that being which freely posits itself and possesses itself through consciousness. An absolute free principle, such as God must be, is personal in the absolute sense; his being is entirely an act of self-positing and self-possession. Man, too, within the limits of his freedom, can claim the title "person." But the term belongs radically only to God, for only in him is the self-positing act of freedom metaphysically ultimate.

Since man is dependent upon God in the order of his being, Secrétan is led to consider the nature of this dependence. God is absolute freedom; hence, the form of this dependence is clear: Man's being is the result of a free act of God. Man is a creature of God, i.e., the real consequence of God's free action. But the question arises, what is the reason for man's creation? Or, how is it that the effect of God's creative will should fall outside the divine being itself? Secrétan holds that God's creative will *must* have its effect outside the divine being itself. Two levels of the divine will may be distinguished in order to provide the context for this conclusion. God, as absolute freedom, *is* through his own will. But the act of will which is the principle of God's being is not creative. God is not his own creature nor his own creator. He *is*, as the character of absolute liberty demands. Within him there can be no order of cause and effect, will and its consequent. His will is related to an effect outside himself. It is not the ground of his being, but its superabundance. God creates solely in view of the being of the creature which he wills for its own sake. This is Secrétan's interpretation of the classical view that the motive principle of creation is love. It is not by an act of self-love that God creates, but through an act of love for the creature. Secrétan draws important conclusions from this thesis from the point of view of the creature as well. The act of love is reciprocal. The meaning of man's liberty ultimately is love of God, that is, the establishment of his being on an act of will, the object of which is God's being. Only through willing the divine being, does man will his own. The supreme act of his liberty is the establishment of his own being on the being of God.

These reflections provide the key to Secrétan's interpretation of history and to his view of the ethical character of the social bond among men. The meaning of man's historical life in time is the realization of history. History is the history of liberty. At the same time, however, the quest of liberty is the quest for union with God, which finds its historical and temporal expression in the perfect social community among men. Such a community is both established on the love of God, its only adequate motive, and is the expression of that in its most concrete form.

In the thought of Secrétan, we are at the very sources of the traditions of interiority and personalism in modern spiritualism. It provides many of the basic motifs which later spiritualistic reflection develops and enriches.

Felix Ravaisson-Mollien (1813–1900) was a man of great cultural attainments, with a rich preparation in the classics and a talent for archeology which made him one of the foremost men in that field during the nineteenth century. Early in his career he laid the foundations for his spiritualism in his *Essai sur la métaphysique d'Aristote* [Essay on the metaphysics of Aristotle), which received the prize of the Academy of Moral and Political Sciences in 1837. This work, still considered one of the best contributions to Aristotelian studies during the last century, combated the unilateral interpretations of Aristotle then current by insisting that Aristotle enclosed himself neither in the sphere of sense experience nor in that of pure logic. Rather, he achieved that "superior point of view of pure reason in which the real and the ideal, the individual and the universal are united in the activity of thought" (Vol. I, p. vi). This point of view, which Ravaisson discovers in Aristotle, is the classical position of philosophical spiritualism.

In the constructive phase of his philosophical thought, Ravaisson aligns himself more immediately with the work of Maine de Biran, whom he sees as the restorer of this original spiritualistic point of view. The chief document for this constructive effort is the essay *De l'habi-*

tude, 1839, which even in its title reflects the influence of Biran. In his *Rapport sur la philosophie en France au XIXe siècle* [Report on philosophy in France in the nineteenth century], 1867, Ravaisson spells out clearly his conception of Maine de Biran's influence and work: He had liberated philosophy from the empiricism to which Locke, Hume, and Condillac had subjected it. Maine de Biran had also emphasized the important fact that we are revealed to ourselves as beings which stand outside the course of nature and that every true existence is of this character, while that which appears in time and space is appearance only (p. 13 ff.). Therefore, in contrast to "external" experience, which the Enlightenment had placed in the foreground of attention, Ravaisson emphasized the "experience of consciousness," "interior" apperception, which makes of philosophy the supreme science because it is the science of the internal spirit and its living causality (cf. his essay on *Philosophie contemporaine* [Contemporary philosophy] published in 1840). This point of view immediately raised a question with which spiritualism had to deal before it could make any headway in its own development. How is the order of material nature, the spatial-temporal world, with its mechanistic laws, etc., to be accounted for?

This problem is the first concern of his essay *De l'habitude*. The area of habit is crucial to this problem of the *why* of nature as well as to that of the activity of spirit, because in habit the characteristics of nature are produced by the activity of spirit itself, in the living existent agent. Here, then, if anywhere, the questions both of the *why* of nature and the ascendancy of spirit may find an answer. This answer is that nature is a trope of spirit, a strategy by which spirit organizes its own activity in such an efficient manner that it can place it, under certain aspects, in brackets and not maintain it in the forefront of its active attention. Nature, in a word, is a technique of efficiency and utility in the life of spirit. Even those characteristics which nature exhibits can be understood and accounted for only when referred to the activity and decision of spirit. Habit is a spiritual activity free and self-conscious in its initiations; through the repetition of its acts, it gives rise to movements in which the role and function of reflection and will become progressively smaller; in the end these activities and movements become completely automatic and take on the characteristics associated with nature. But at no point does their direct dependence upon spirit disappear.

Obviously, then, to assume the principles of such natural movement as primary, as self explanatory, or as capable of explaining anything else, is absurd. When taken in themselves, the patterns and principles of natural activity are pure appearance. They must be referred to another principle, namely spirit and consciousness, for their explanation. Nature is, therefore, economic, in the sense which Croce was eventually to give to this term; but it is only a free and reflective principle like that of spirit which can establish an economic system within its own activities, as the area of habit testifies. Habit is the model for the comprehension of the whole of nature. Nature is intelligible and real when it is understood as emerging from the activity of spirit and constituting a moment of spirit. Here Ravaisson is outlining patterns of thought which will become basic to nineteenth-century spiritualism as it is developed at the hands of Lachelier, Boutroux, Hamelin, and finally, Bergson.

Jules Lachelier (1832–1918) wielded a powerful influence over French thought through his teaching in the Ecole Normale Supérieure of Paris. His writings are few, but they exhibit great care in structure and composition. His chief work is *Du fondement de l'induction* [The foundation of induction], 1871, with a number of subsequent editions, each enriched by new essays. Second to this stands his *Etudes sur le syllogisme* [Studies on the syllogism], 1907, which takes up the theme of his Latin doctoral thesis of 1871, *De natura syllogismi*. In the *Du fondement de l'induction* Lachelier is concerned to establish the reality of the finalistic order of nature in contrast to the appearance of mechanism which it exhibits. He makes a distinction (which will have a large place in Gentile's thought) between the abstract existence of the objects of science, reflecting the abstractness of science itself, and the concreteness of the objects of thought. Both science and its objects are necessary but abstract, while thought and its objects are concrete and contingent. But the former can be conceived, in their mode, only on the basis of the latter. Reality, he therefore concludes, is universal contingency, which is liberty. The true philosophy of nature must be a spiritualistic realism, according to which every being must be a force and every force a thought which tends always to a more complete consciousness of itself (cf. *Du fondement de l'induction*, p. 102).

In the essay "Psychologie et métaphysique" appended to the second edition (1902) of the *Du fondement*, Lachelier examines the structure of this spiritualism in itself. He distinguishes two forms of the interiority of man and relates them respectively to these sciences, psychology and metaphysics. Psychology has sensible consciousness as its domain; metaphysics, thought itself. The nature of the spiritual principle is thought, rather than will; thought, that is, as an activity which objectifies itself in existing reality in order to return to itself as pure consciousness. If thought did not posit its concrete existing object, it must reestablish that object in consciousness and thus become pure affirmation of itself. Lachelier invests this spiritualism with a heavy religious cast. The philosophy of nature as spiritualistic realism leads to the conclusion that reality is God. And the same is true of the philosophy of man, for all that is in man that is spiritual and immortal proves to be divine, proves to be God.

Emile Boutroux (1845–1921) is known principally for his *De la contingence des lois de la nature* [On the contingency of the laws of nature], which was originally the French thesis he presented for the doctorate in 1874. He developed its implications in later writings, such as *De l'idée de loi naturelle dans la science et la philosophie contemporaines* [On the idea of the law of nature in contemporary science and philosophy], 1895. Boutroux carried the spiritualistic revolt against positivism into the field of science itself. He establishes an order among the objects of scientific investigation: matter and material bodies, the organism, and, finally, man. The order rests on the increasing richness of qualities, of variety, of individuality in the ascending orders. As a consequence, no reduction from one order to a lower is possible. Each ascending grade exhibits a novel character with respect to the lower. Hence, the higher grade cannot be related to the lower by any causal necessity. Each higher level is *contingent* with respect to the antecedent; hence, the order of nature is freedom, rather than causal necessity. At the apex of this gradation stands man, whose being and life is spiritual, for he cannot be reduced to mere organism, any more than the latter can be reduced to the status of physical body, nor this to the abstract concept of matter. This freedom also governs the interior life of man, which, in its turn, cannot be brought within the pattern of necessary causality. The *motive* is not a necessary cause in human action; the will assigns preference to one motive over another, and the stronger motive is never such independently of the will but because of the preference which the will assigns it. In this way all of the basic motives of spiritualism are vindicated by Boutroux within the ambit of the world of science. His spiritualism gains strength from this relation to science, and he believes that the opposition between them is resolved.

Without basically altering these reflections, Boutroux elaborated on them in the work *De l'idée de loi naturelle dans la science et la philosophie contemporaines*. His position achieved a kind of classic status and exercised a wide influence inspiring more or less directly such men as Croce and Bergson. Of equal interest is the defence of religion offered by Boutroux in his later work *Science et religion dans la philosophie contemporaine*, 1908. The scope of science appears to him very limited. Beyond it there exists a world of values incomprehensible to it. Value justifies attitudes in man which cannot be comprehended by science. Chief among these attitudes is faith. Quite differently from science, faith generates ideal objects which arouse love in man. Science is incompetent to judge these ideals and the attitude man assumes toward them. "Religion has an object different from that of science; religion is not an explanation of phenomena. . . . Phenomena, in the eyes of religion, are valued for their moral meaning, for the sentiments they arouse, for the interior life which they express and excite and no scientific explanation can change this character in them" (*Science et religion,* p. 383).

Octave Hamelin (1856–1907) always presented his thought as a form of idealism. Nevertheless, the chief themes of spiritualism are presented in it in so perceptive a manner and with a systematic power so unusual among spiritualists that his own denomination of his thought has frequently been called into question. His chief work, in addition to solid historical studies on Aristotle, Descartes, and his own teacher, Renouvier, is his *Essai sur les éléments principaux de la représentation,* 1907, a work to which he devoted most of his creative speculative effort. The principle achievement of this work is the construction of a *dialectic of correlation* which enables Hamelin to reconstruct in principle all finite, human reality, from the most general and abstract category he can discover, that of relation, to the most concrete, consciousness. It should be noted that this is a dialectic of finite reality, not the dialectic of the infinite or the idea as was the case in classical idealism. Hamelin's position is clearly humanistic, and upon reaching the limits of finite being in human consciousness, he recognizes the existence of a transcendent God, who is the ground even of that finite reality, though in no sense immanent in it or subject to its dialectic.

This dialectic of correlation, which he explicitly contrasts to Hegel's dialectic, leads him by a triadic movement from the world of nature, whose mark is causality, to the world of spirit, whose mark is finality, to the world of the person, whose mark is freedom and consciousness. Consciousness is a creative activity which produces at once object, subject, and their synthesis (cf. *Essai,* p. 373). This finite dialectic, reaching its term in consciousness, which is "existence in itself," does not exhaust reality. In sensing its own finitude, it exhibits an awareness of the reach of being which lies beyond it but is not directly or with certainty apprehensible by its method. Toward this further reach of being and existence it can entertain but probable conclusions. On this basis Hamelin offers his theistic position. There is a universal Consciousness, which is God; both materialism and pantheistic idealism are held to be highly improbable. Theism offers the only conceptual form of representing God. But at this point Hamelin returns to a thesis which his teacher Renouvier had maintained. Since God is absolute goodness, the world could not have been his creation. It could only have come into being through an original fall.

D. *Spiritualism in England*

The chief and most characteristic traits of spiritualism also found defenders in England, though here the position did not reach the speculative brilliance or solidity that it achieved on the Continent. One of the most impressive of the English spiritualists is A. J. Balfour (1848–1930). Though primarily a man of affairs and of considerable political stature, Balfour wrote vigorously in defense of religion and the spirituality of man. His most noted work is *Foundations of Belief*, 1895. Another English thinker representing a vigorous spiritualism is Andrew S. Pringle-Pattison (1856–1931); his *Idea of God in the Light of Recent Philosophy,* 1917, is a balanced defence of the classical spiritualistic theses. Finally, James Ward (1843–1925), primarily a psychologist but twice Gifford lecturer, must be placed in this brief list. His two volumes based on his Gifford lectures: *Naturalism and Agnosticism,* 1899, and his *Realm of Ends,* 1911, are strong and lucid expositions and defenses of the classical spiritualistic theses on human consciousness, personality, and the transcendence of God. In this exposition, Ward conducts a polemic chiefly against those forms of agnosticism which rest on a naturalistic basis.

The philosophy of spiritualism, which has been briefly depicted here in the forms it took in the nineteenth and early twentieth centuries, laid the foundations for the spiritualism of the middle twentieth century, although the latter has other preoccupations. The adversaries have changed and the methods of analysis have been refined, but the great principles to be expounded and explained—consciousness, God, personality, and liberty—remain.

Readings

Material in English on the origins of modern continental spiritualism is sparse. The items listed will prove useful. For Fichte and Schelling reference should be made to Volume III, Part IV, Chapter II of the present work. Some foreign titles are indicated for the sake of completeness. For figures of the early phase of modern Italian spiritualism reference may be made to the articles *sub nomine* by the present author in *The Encyclopedia of Philosophy* (New York: Macmillan, Free Press, 1967).

Books

Booth, Meyrick. *Rudolf Eucken: His Philosophy and Influence.* London: T. Fisher Unwin, 1913.

Crawford, L. S. *The Philosophy of Emile Boutroux.* New York: Longmans, Green, 1924.

Fessard, Gaston. *La méthode de réflexion chez Maine de Biran.* Paris: Librairie Bloud & Gay, 1938.

Gibson, William R. B. *Rudolf Eucken's Philosophy of Life*. London: Adam & Charles Black, 1912.

Hamelin, Octave. *Le système de Renouvier*. Paris: J. Vrin, 1927.

Jones, Henry. *A Critical Account of the Philosophy of Lotze*. Glasgow: Maclehose, 1895.

Jones, William Tudor. *An Interpretation of Rudolf Eucken's Philosophy*. London: Williams & Norgate, 1912.

Sesmat, Augustin. *Dialectique: Hamelin et la philosophie chrétienne*. Paris: Bloud & Gay, 1955.

Simon, Jules. *Victor Cousin*. Translated by M. B. Anderson. Chicago: A. C. McClurg, 1888.

Thomas, E. E. *Lotze's Theory of Reality*. New York: Longmans, Green, 1921.

Essays and articles

Abril Castello, Vidal. "Biranismo, Blondelismo Neotomismo." *Crisis*, XIV (1967), 163–195.

Ballard, E. G. "Jules Lachelier's Idealism." *Review of Metaphysics*, VIII (1954), 685.

Caldwell, J. W. "The Epistemology of Edward von Hartmann," *Mind*, II (1893), 185–207.

_____. "Hartmann's Moral and Social Philosophy." *Philosophical Review*, VIII (1899), 465–483 and 589–603.

Greenwood, T. "The Logic of Jules Lachelier." *Proceedings of the Aristotelian Society*, XXXV (1934), 75–94.

Hall, G. Stanley. *Founders of Modern Psychology*. (Regarding E. von Hartmann, pp. 181–246.) New York: D. Appleton, 1912.

Lavelle, Louis. "Maine de Biran, l'homme et le philosophe." *Bulletin de l'association Guillaume Budé*, December 1949, pp. 597–610.

Parodi, D. *Du positivisme à l'idealisme*. (Regarding Hamelin, pp. 183–206). Paris: J. Vrin, 1930.

Santayana, G. "Lotze's Moral Idealism." *Mind*, XV (1890), 191–212.

Schiller, F. C. S. "Lotze's Monism." *The Philosophical Review*, V (1896), 225–245.

Siwek, P. "Pessimism in Philosophy." (Regarding E. von Hartmann.) *New Scholasticism*, XXII (1948), 249–297.

Smith, Colin. "Destutt de Tracy's Analysis of the Proposition." *Revue internationale de philosophie*, XXI (1967), 475–485.

CHAPTER VI

The Philosophy of Nietzsche

Introduction

Nietzsche is without question the best known and most celebrated thinker of this period; at the same time, he is the least understood as a philosopher. One of the most interesting events in the history of philosophy during the last decades, it may be said, has been the rediscovery (or more accurately perhaps, simply the discovery) of Nietzsche as a philosopher and his rescue from a maze of ambiguity, misinterpretation, and pseudo-mystique. The reader interested in how this rediscovery came about is well-advised to read Walter Kaufmann's *Nietzsche* (Princeton, N.J., 1950). Here we can only take advantage of these rectifications and try to present his thought as it possesses value for the continuing process of philosophical dialogue.

Mario Manlio Rossi has well summarized the difficulties involved in presenting even a simple exposition of Nietzsche's thought (cf. *Enciclopedia filosofica* [Venice-Rome, 1950], Vol. III, cols. 899–901). These difficulties stem both from the external structure of his writings and from the internal process of his philosophical reflection. For the most part, Nietzsche's ideas are expressed, not in systematic treatises and essays, but in isolated affirmations and aphorisms, which only in his most celebrated book, *Thus Spake Zarathustra*, achieve some exterior coherence through being presented as the sage enunciations of a prophet. His thought is asystematic, highly personal, and not entirely free from outright contradictions. This asystematic and personal character springs from the fact that Nietzsche's is an agonizing mind and spirit. Philosophical reflection is not, with him, a calm scientific inquiry but his own wrestling with the most profound enigmas of human existence. The insights he achieved were struck out of his inward labor of spirit like sparks from a forge. Little wonder then that only with effort on the part of the reader can something of the inward pattern of their form and movement be discerned. Nevertheless, Nietzsche well rewards efforts to overcome these difficulties.

Nietzsche establishes relations between his reflection and the dominant currents of his time—evolutionism, irrationalism, vitalism, even positivism; though he is filled with the afflatus of romanticism, he is opposed to idealism and spiritualism and made it his special task to initiate a "transvaluation of all values." But he cannot be considered as belonging to any of these movements; he uses them only as dialectical elements for the forging of his own thought. In this way Nietzsche both belongs to his time and rises beyond it, offering a fresh and revealing perspective in which contemporary speculation may exhibit new aspects. For this reason, the only way his thought can be studied is monographically.

The story of Nietzsche's life is sad and briefly told. Born in 1844, he was left fatherless at the age of five. His widowed mother supervised his upbringing and that of his sister, Elizabeth, who was to have considerable responsibility for the subsequent formation of the Nietzsche myth, that maze of distortions, suppressions, exaggerations, and direct misrepresentations which forced his thought into such odd postures and compromising relations. He studied classical philology with the celebrated Ritschl and received his first teaching post in classics at Basel, Switzerland, where he became the colleague of such celebrated scholars as Jakob Burckhardt. In 1872 he published *Die Geburt der Tragödie* (*The Birth of Tragedy*), in many respects his most expressive work. This was followed in 1873–76 by the *Unzeitgamasze Betrachtungen* (*Untimely Reflections*). In 1879 he was forced to resign his teaching position because of ill-health. He spent his remaining years in physical wandering and in the composition of his works, the documents of his ceaseless inner struggle toward a vision of truth. His last years were spent under a cloud of mental incapacity, a gentle madness, as it has been called, not without affinities with that of Hamlet. Chief among the works of these years are *Menschliches, Allzumenschliches* (*Human, All Too Human*), 1879, the document of a period of human isolation; *Die fröhliche Wissenschaft* (*The Gay Science*), 1882; *Also sprach Zarathustra* (*Thus Spake Zarathustra*), his great philosophical canticle, composed during 1883–84; *Jenseits von Gut und Böse* (*Beyond Good and Evil*), 1886; *Zur Geneologie der Moral* (*On the Genealogy of Morals*), 1887. Most of his other works were published only later. The work which was to give systematic expression to his thought, *Der Wille zur Macht* (*The Will to Power*), remained incomplete.

Given the intrinsically unsystematic character of Nietzsche's

thought, every exposition of it must assume the responsibility of imposing some order which will facilitate the presentation. The order followed here has tried to profit by other such efforts and aims only at
the same utilitarian purpose. We shall first briefly treat Nietzsche's
"method" (if so formal a term is permissible); then his acceptance of
"life" with all of its inward contradictions and abrasions of the spirit;
thirdly, the Nietzschean view of art; next, the moral life and the transvaluation of values; and finally, his "propaedeutic atheism," the fruit
of his life-long personal struggle with Christianity. About these central themes, it would seem, most of Nietzsche's basic insights can be
brought into focus; however, it must constantly be kept in mind that
no exposition can communicate the particular character of his thought,
the sense of inward struggle, the pathos and the aura of imminent
tragedy and great destiny which it manages to generate.

A. *Nietzsche's "Method"*

By "method," in this context, nothing formal or rigidly procedural
is intended. The only concern is to convey, if possible, some notion of
the elements which enter into Nietzsche's thought and which influence
the manner in which problems appear urgent to him and in which he
seeks to come to terms with them. (The idea of "solving" them would
be entirely out of accord with his genius.)

As with all of the other thinkers of his generation, Nietzsche's basic
orientation in philosophy as an undertaking and activity is toward
Hegel. Hegel is the touchstone of the age; thinkers tend to line up
with him or against him, especially on the concept of philosophy, its
method and what it may hope to achieve. To some the entire Hegelian
enterprise seemed the only possible way of philosophical salvation; the
method, dialectic, and the system, both in its architectonic structure
and in its particular doctrines, seemed undoubtable. For others it was
possible to accept the method, the dialectic, but impossible to accept
the system as Hegel had formulated it; among these were some, like
Marx, who could accept the dialectic only if they were permitted to
make serious alterations in it ("set it on its feet"). Finally there were
those to whom both the system and its method were unacceptable,
indeed anathema; who could not see that the end of philosophy was
the system, that the method of philosophy could be the dialectic, or
finally that philosophy could achieve that universal irenicism, that
reign of eternal peace, the reconciliation of all contradictions in the
serenity of the idea.

Nietzsche, like Kierkegaard, most clearly falls in this third group.
The irenicism of the Hegelian synthesis was farthest from his spirit,

for his spirit was the abode of eternal conflict and agony. This opposition to Hegel never reached in Nietzsche the status of a formalized criticism and attack; it was an unspoken, but very much acted out, opposition. Nietzsche never worked under the illusion that every contradiction is eventually capable of resolution into a "higher synthesis"; on the contrary, one of his most profound and abiding insights is that human thought must always move on troubled waters, ever be buffeted by contrary winds, and perhaps like the *Flying Dutchman* of Wagner, be eternally banished from any final port. The ultimate formulation of this insight was to flower into his theory of the eternal return, which is the supreme evidence of the unassuageable inner torment and conflict of the human spirit and of being itself.

Because of this patent antipathy to the spirit of the Hegelian system, some interpreters, especially the eminent philosopher Karl Jaspers, have thought to subsume Nietzsche's genius under the rubric of existentialism. (Cf. Jaspers, *Nietzsche: Einführung in das Verständnis seines Philosophierens* [Berlin, 1950]). They hold, first, that an "existentialistic" interpretation alone can bring out the sense and truth of his spirit and, second, that his method of thought is "existentialistic" when existentialism is conceived as a method. This is probably too extreme a view and is liable to lead to extravagances and confusions. Nevertheless, there is a certain element of truth in the attempt.

Although Nietzsche cannot be classified without qualification as an existentialist, he is one (and perhaps the first) of those philosophers who see philosophy as springing from the inner movement and turmoil of life, as the interior effort to reach a saving, and not merely declarative, truth. Even more, he sees that effort within the intense circle of his own life, and he believes that every man will and must, in his turn, live that experience just as intensely, just as personally. What philosophy will thus engender is not an abstract transcendent "truth" but a truth which is the inner form of a direct and personal encounter and struggle with being, with one's own being and its terrible possibilities. In this sense, Nietzsche is at once the prince of "existentialists" and beyond existentialism, in a realm where categorizing is meaningless and where only the entire dedication of the living person to the conquest of a personal truth is real. Disinterestedness, he says in *The Gay Science*, has no value either in heaven or on earth. It is one thing if a thinker takes a personal position before his problems so that he finds his destiny, his pain, and his greatest joy in them; another if he approaches them in an "impersonal" manner, with frigid curiosity.

One of the earliest and strongest influences upon Nietzsche was the thought of Schopenhauer. Nietzsche drew from Schopenhauer the insight that philosophy involved a direct evaluation of life—of life in its widest aspects, ranging from the amoeba to God, but also of life in its most intense personal aspect, as each individual subject has to live, and not merely contemplate, it. Even more, he imbibed Schopenhauer's own evaluation of life, which was to remain the presupposition of his own reflection. However, he rejected the conclusions that Schopenhauer drew from it and sought to forge a courage out of the despair implied by the Schopenhauerian view.

Life, as one experiences it directly, is struggle, sorrow, uncertainty, error, cruelty, injustice. All of these add up to saying that life is the very opposite of reason; it is the reality of unreason. No rational principle guides its coming to be, its floresence and decay, or its end, death. Chance dominates it at every turn. Man envisages values and ideals only to find that life offers them no support or justification. This was Schopenhauer's diagnosis, and Nietzsche acquiesced in it. But the question is: what attitude is one to take before it? Withdrawal, renunciation, abandonment of the enterprise of life, is Schopenhauer's reply; this is also, Nietzsche goes on to say, the reply of Christianity and of the general spiritual atmosphere which it had spread over European culture. But it is not the only attitude possible. Neither is it the attitude which life itself counsels when one has felt its full surge within one. Life counsels rather the acceptance of life in the very characteristics under which it presents itself as lived experience, the acceptance of life on its own terms and the prosecution of these terms to their fulfillment. The unreason of life has a logic of its own, greater and stronger than the logic of reason. To say "yea" to this reason of unreason against the admonishments of the reason of intellect is the acceptance of life, the fundamental act of the sane and wholesome living subject. This is the attitude which Nietzsche, counter to Schopenhauer and to the spirituality of Christianity, affirms and seeks to assume. All of his thought is an exhortation to this acceptance. This is the primary act of life, which he presents in divine form under the figure of Dionysius and which he preaches through the lips of the mystic-prophet of his greatest work: Zarathustra.

Under the image of Dionysus (which first appears in *The Birth of Tragedy*), Nietzsche celebrates, as he himself says, the religious affirmation of total life, life neither denied nor fragmented. Dionysus represents intoxication with the world as it is, without the intrusion of the distinctions, the diminutions, the choices which reason would force upon it. Dionysus, as he points out, is the god of wine, and wine is the symbol for the celebration of life in the totality of its power. Dionysus is the God of the dance, of the orgy, of song. He rejects any attitude of renunciation before life and finds in the very characters of life the values and virtues that man seeks.

The full meaning of the Dionysian acceptance of life in its direct and primitive terms and the exaltation of these to the rank of absolute values is to be found in the innermost consequence of this act, which is, in a profound sense, the key to Nietzsche's most personal vision. The acceptance of life reveals the inner dialectic of life, the only movement of dialectic which Nietzsche recognizes. By the dialectic of life, all of the characteristics of life, as it first appeared, are transmuted. The acceptance of life carries with it an inward revelation which shows that the characteristics of life which had first seemed negative and deplorable are the true categories of value. In the light of this acceptance it is clear to Nietzsche that all that had hitherto passed in our culture as virtue is precisely the opposite of virtue. For virtue in its most primitive sense is precisely the affirmation of life as power. (The affinity of this conception of virtue with the concept of *virtù* as encountered in the Renaissance has been noted more than once; though no direct equivalence between the Renaissance use and Nietzsche's can be established.) What has passed in our culture for virtue is not some superficial table of values but the act which saps virtue at its root: the negation of life. The table of values in post-classical culture (and in some aspects of classical culture itself) is the schematization of the negation of life into the catalogue of the "virtues." There emerges as the fundamental dynamic principle of Nietzsche's philosophy this contrast and tension between the yea and the nay, the affirmation of life and its negation. In the one and the other lie the fundamental possibilities of man, and all that he is, all that he can be stems from the one act or the other. This is man's fundamental choice, before which all other choices pale and lose significance, for if man once has uttered the "yea," not with his lips only, but from the very depths of his personal being and existence, the whole of life opens before him in its inward "reason of unreason," the deeper wisdom which the merely reflective reason of intellect can never grasp. If he utters the radical "nay," life is withered at its roots; the perspective which then opens before man is the shrinking of his life from within and the spurious growth of the non-values or non-virtues which he mistakes for true values and for life itself.

This utterance of the "yea" is for Nietzsche a completely personal and individual act. It cannot be rendered collective, for no collective affirmation of life can substitute for the personal affirmation. It cannot be participated; it must be individual, direct, and originative. Only upon the basis of this radical and personal affirmation does participation, brotherhood with other men, become possible. Neither can this act be rendered public. By this Nietzsche means that it can never be made to rest, can never be grounded (in the sense which Hegelianism had made current) on a secondary act, a reflective act which derives its character and validity from its universality or transcendentality. Here again, he perceives a radical inversion. It is only on the basis of the originative and personal "yea" to life that any universal and transcendental structures of meaning and value can be erected. These find their validation in that original affirmation of life, and not vice versa.

The supreme test case is death. The life-affirmation is the pure rejection of death. The originative "nay" embraces death in the place of life and therefore is the intimate suicidal act of man. Before the affirmation of life, the idea of death loses all its meaning. The only meaning which death can have is that life is not; that, in its essence so to say, it is not merely an appearance but an illusion or a delusion. Correlatively the innermost meaning of the "nay" is the denial of life and the affirmation of death in its place. The value system of the "nay" is death itself erected into a schema of non-life under the appearance of life. Man's true immortality, his conquest of death, lies in the fundamental and founding "yea."

This notion of the acceptance of life offers the key to all of Nietzsche's subsequent reflections: his views on art and the moral life; his struggle with theism and specifically with Christianity, its value system and its effect on western culture; and, finally, his difficult, inchoate, but haunting doctrine of the "eternal return."

B. Art and the Affirmation of Life

The affirmation of life finds its fullest expression and realization in art. Art and life are correlatives, if not synonyms. Art generates beauty, which is nothing else but the radiance, the plenitude which attends this affirmation. By contrast, all forms of ugliness reduce themselves in the last analysis to forms of the negation of life and draw from the aesthetic man a resounding "nay." As Nietzsche says in *The Will to Power:* "Every time the idea of degeneration, of impoverishment of life, of impotence, of decomposition, of dissolution is born, the aesthetic man reacts with a nay" (*Friedrich Nietzsche: Complete Works*, ed. Oscar Levy [New York, 1964], XIV, 357). By contrast, he states (taking up the theme of the intellective process as the negation or arresting of life) that objectivity, abstractness, impoverishment of the senses, ascetic tendencies are non-artistic, non-aesthetic attitudes which involve the negation of life and issue in ugliness. Art is the supreme soteric force in human life; through its expressive affirmation of life, it changes the weakness of human nature into strength, its impotence into power, its problems into certitude.

Nietzsche displays great wisdom concerning both the form and dynamics of the artistic life and the close relation between art and tragedy, the tragic sentiment of life. Though art is rooted in the Dionysian affirmation of life, art is not the surrender to instinct; it is not the free and untrammeled headlong rush of vitality. On the contrary, art is the domination and direction of these forces. In this sense, it is the first and the truest expression of the will to power. The will to power is not the simple will to dominate, the will to power over another, but the will to dominate oneself, the life which is in one. To dominate means to impose order, form, meaning. Hence, from the artist Nietzsche demands a kind of inward asceticism, a self-control and self-direction which he compares to chastity. The artist in his view takes on a priestlike character. He is the priest of life, dedicated to its service but mastering it. Similarly, from the work of art, Nietzsche demands, not a formless upwelling of the animal powers of life, but a perfection of form which holds life in thrall. In the work of art which has achieved some degree of perfection we possess the moment of perfect equilibrium which only art can achieve: the surging power of life held in the thrall of a commanding vision and will and brought to perfection by this domination and control.

This is the meaning of Nietzsche's treatment of the tension between Dionysus and Apollo. For him there is no direct contrast in these images. Rather, they share one basic principle: Both represent the fulfillment of the life-affirmation in art. The fullness of this affirmation is in Apollo—in the perfection of order, the containment and fulfillment of life within form-shaping limits. But this perfection of form rests not upon a negation of the Dionysian forces beneath and within, but upon their affirmation. Art is born in the Dionysian moment of the inebriate affirmation of life against all negation. This exuberant life-intoxication is the matrix of all art. But within this exuberance, the shaping power of the Apollonian vision is generated. In the Dionysian moment, life affirms itself but does not possess itself. The will to power is present but without effect. Through the inward agency of the Apollonian vision, life takes possession of itself, takes on the form in which it is most fully realized and expressed. The two moments are strict correlatives. The Dionysian affirmation without the Apollonian generation of form is life with movement but with no significance. However, the only matrix for the activity of the Apollonian spirit is the Dionysian affirmation. This supports it; this is the medium in which it dwells and acts.

What is the meaning which is achieved through this delicate, mutually-supporting inner tension between Dionysus and Apollo? It is the tragic sense of life. Nietzsche gazed on supreme Greek art and read there the message which had been his truth since his first reading of Schopenhauer: that the tragic sense of life is the highest affirmation of life. There is present here not only paradox, but profundity, an insight which passes beyond any simple exposition. There is paradox, for, in gazing upon those serene monuments, or in reading the lyric passages of Oedipus, are we not drawn to think that the Greek spirit came to a final peace in which the tragic sense had been banished, to be replaced by an all-embracing, all-understanding, and all-accepting tranquillity? But Nietzsche sees beneath this specious calm. He reads the highest affirmation of the tragic sense of life within the very serenity which Greek art wears. What then is the secret of that art? What is the tragic sense that it reflects? It is the unbanishable tragedy which lies in the recognition that all human order, all human reason, all human beauty rests upon the radical absurdity of human existence. The entire role of art is to render that absurd existence tolerable. Once the spell of art is broken, the absurdity again swiftly overwhelms us. For this reason man is an artist in his soul, invoking that spell to make his absurd existence bearable and living in the knowledge that by the spell of art he holds that absurdity in thrall. This experience is the supreme but tragic moment of his will to power.

C. *The Moral Life and the Transvaluation of Values*

From what has been said about the relation of art and the tragic sense of life, it may be seen how profoundly *moralistic* was Nietzsche's view of art. The inner reality of the artistic transaction is the profound moral act of human life, its taking possession of itself and its expression of itself in truth and vision. For Nietzsche, consequently, the moral life, in its highest reaches, is inseparable and indeed indistinguishable from the life of art. Nothing could be farther from his vision than the notion, so prevalent in his own time, of "art for art's sake." For him this attitude is only another evidence of the great "nay" to life; moreover, it is an exceedingly corruptive form of this "nay," since it invades the precinct of the only saving act available to man: art.

The moral life, therefore, must be conceived as the extension of the artistic life. Morality is art extended to embrace the full concrèteness of every single life. The principle at work in both art and morality is the same: truth. The moral life can rest only upon the direct vision of the truth of human life and the real values which embody its truth and meaning. The moral life is the life of the virtues, and the inner essence of each of the virtues is a moment of truth engendered by art. The truth of the moral life lies in the virtues which it espouses.

On the basis of this insight Nietzsche moved to his vast and inclusive criticism of western spiritual life since the advent of Christianity and its triumph over the classic vision which he had read in the features of Apollo. He considered the Christian conception of spiritual life a lie.

For this reason, Christianity became his mortal and life-long enemy. For this reason also, he took upon himself as a personal mission, the "transmutation of all values." As he wrote in the rather terrifying book *Ecce Homo:* "My truth is terrible for hitherto lies have been called truth. The transmutation of all values; this is my formula for mankind's greatest step toward coming to its senses, a step which in me became flesh and genius. My destiny ordained that I should be the first decent human being, that I should feel myself opposed to the falsehood of millenia" (*Complete Works,* XVII, 131–132). What this transmutation of values proves to be is the extended and sometimes vehement criticism of Christian morality.

This criticism rests upon an opposition of cardinal principles. The true principle of art, of morality, and of life itself, as he had pointed out, was the affirmation of life taken as struggle, brutality. The principle of Christianity is the opposite of this: the denial of life. It is the direct opposition of the "nay" of death to the "yea" of life. Despite its insistence upon the resurrection and the future life, the Christian moral system is a death-morality because its cardinal principle is the denial of life in its immediacy. The "yea" to a future life, in Nietzsche's view, cannot counterbalance the present negation of life.

Seeking further, Nietzsche believes that he comes upon the very source of this "nay" of Christianity. The source is resentment—one might say bitter envy; it is the resentment of those to whom, for one reason or another, the true reaction to life, the utterance of the radical and life-giving "yea," is interdicted. The reasons for their inability to affirm life are many and varied. It may be some personal failing, as celibacy may have its root in impotence. But in this form Nietzsche pays it little heed, for it is with the corruption of the whole of western culture, and not with the corruption of an individual, that he is concerned. He seeks its root in a social impotence, a social, political, and cultural inferiority. The Christian morality, he affirms, is the morality of the inferior slave classes directed against the aristocratic and superior classes. At this point an ambiguity seems to invest Nietzsche's thinking; he seems to pass uncritically from historical to psychological-typological terms. Apparently he meant his criticism to embrace both dimensions of meaning. As a historical phenomenon Christianity represents the revolt of historical classes against their masters; but in psychological-typological terms, the same transaction takes place in individuals and in lesser groups. Still, his major emphasis seems to be on the collective-historical phenomenon. Christianity represents, in historico-cultural terms, the power of the "nay" to overwhelm the "yea" of life.

All of the values which Christianity offers as primary and salutory are, for Nietzsche, masks of this basic resentment. Humility, self-sacrifice, disinterestedness, abnegation, charity toward one's neighbor are the names, not of true virtues, but of non-virtues and non-values masking as values. The ascetical ideal, which Nietzsche insists is the very essence of the Christian moral vision, is a device for continuing and maintaining life in that state of degeneration and decadence into which the fundamental nay to life had plunged it.

By a strange and unexpected trope Nietzsche includes in this denunciation the attitude of science before objective truth. Science, he says, is linked to the ascetic ideal of Christianity by its adulation of *objective* truth, that is, the truth of an *other* and not the truth as it exists and is manifested in oneself. It would seem to be but an intellectual form of that same resentment to which he had traced Christian morality and asceticism. Science appears to him as a negation of life, a retreat into abstraction and intellectual dialectic, and abasement before a world which is other, alien, and dominant. Thus, counter to the main drift of nineteenth-century thought, science becomes for him one of those values of western culture which must be transvaluated into a truth founded in the immediacy of the subject.

Nietzsche reserves his final criticism for the Christian ideal of the *good man*. The good life of the good man is founded on a lie. Closing his eyes, he refuses to see life as it is. Life as it is neither favors his sentiments of benevolence nor easily tolerates his foolish and sometimes disastrous intervention in the name of "good will." Unable to face this truth, he rejects the full struggle of life, which, through art, is the only source of value, and he retreats into a world of ideal values. His will is directed, therefore, to the annihilation of life.

But the denunciation of false values is not enough for Nietzsche. The transvaluation of values involves establishing an order of values founded on truth which would displace and replace the non-values which have drawn his ire. First among these superior values must be placed commitment to earth, to this world with its ambiguities and contradictions. I teach men, he has Zarathustra say, not to hide their heads in the sands of heavenly things; I teach them to carry their heads high here on earth among the things of earth. I teach them to follow *knowingly* the path which men before them have followed *blindly*, to approve this way and not to fly from it as do the sick and the decrepit. Man's life is wholly terrestrial, wholly of this world. The true values of his life are those which can be realized here, those which are defined by the true state of his earthly life. Man must accept himself, as he truly and actually is; this is his truth and his basic value. He must accept himself and his mundane life with the same Dionysian force with which he has affirmed life itself: as creature of time and body, history and death.

This will yield the same result as the basic affirmation of life itself: the earth and the body of man will be transformed and transfigured. The earth, this world, will cease to be a desert to which man has been exiled from some celestial home; it will become his joyous habitation. His body will cease to be his prison or his tomb, and will become his very *self*. Above all, life will cease to be a problem for him and will become, instead, a conquest and a triumphal march.

The final answer to the transvaluation of values, however, is to be found in the figure of the "superman." The temptation, from what has gone before, might be to regard Nietzsche's point of view as a simple, though greatly exaggerated, humanism. If this were so, the notion of superman would be unintelligible. However, Nietzsche does not equate man with life, nor the acceptance of life with the acceptance of man. Life is the much broader concept. Man is but a stage in life's course toward its higher and more complete fulfillment. For this reason, life is accepted *in* man, but man is accepted only as the vehicle of life. He must be transcended if life is to realize itself. Nietzsche has Zarathustra say: "Man must be overcome, transcended. . . . The superman is the meaning of the earth. What makes man great is that he is a bridge and not a terminal point. What makes man an object of love is that he is a passage and a sunset" (*Complete Works*, XI, 7). But even the will to life is not enough. Indeed, Nietzsche denies Schopenhauer's assertion that there is a will to life as such. The living subject wills more than life; it wills *power*. The superman is not merely the expression of the will to life; he is the realization of the will to power. Only in the perspective of the will to power can the image of the superman take form; in this perspective, the new order of values, destined to replace the outworn, deceptively generated values of Christianity, becomes clear.

The first and primary value embodied in the ideal of the superman is freedom of spirit. He must break with all the customary ties of life, renounce what all others desire, Nietzsche says in *Human, All Too Human*. Again, in *The Gay Science*, he says that the superman must give up all faith, all desire of certitude and security, and must orientate himself toward the free play of life's possibilities. The freedom of superman consists in a vast range of possibilities; he is not held to a choice among them but seeks to realize them all. The superman seeks above all to differentiate himself from other men, to wrap himself in his exceptional character, to take refuge in an inaccessible, inner solitude. His inner solitude will never be a wasteland because within him there are depths upon depths of possibilities closed to other men. Other men seek to compensate their own inner poverty by attaching themselves to those whom they see as possibilities. But the superman has no need of such external bonds. Nietzsche closes his picture of the superman by announcing that he will be the philosopher of the future. By comparison all the philosophers of the past have been but crafts- men; superman takes on the stature of lawgiver and founder. His utterances concern what ought to be. He is the master of becoming, not the mere contemplator of what is. Above all, superman is the ful- fillment of truth. He can look reality in the face, in all its hostility, cruelty, struggle, and hardship, and affirm it as the basis of his own transcendence of it.

D. *Nietzsche's Atheism*

"God is dead." As the author of these terrible and terrifying words, Nietzsche has unquestioningly been held the prince of atheists. But even a superficially more intimate acquaintance with his words and an approximation of the moving spirit of his thought calls this judgment into doubt. As more than one student of Nietzsche has pointed out, an atheist could hardly have written the words which Nietzsche penned in his poem *To the Unknown God:* "I wish to know thee, Oh Unknown —You who bear me into the depths of my soul—You who sweep over my life like the whirlwind, You, The Incomprehensible . . . You my Blood-neighbor, You I wish to know, You I wish to serve. . . ." That terrible phrase of Nietzsche must be understood, not as a flagrant denial of God, but as an indication both of the turmoil of his own per- sonal thought and of a general crisis in our culture on the problem of God of which his thought is the vehicle. When seen in this light, Nietz- sche emerges, certainly not as a theist in any conventional sense of the term, but (as has been said of Spinoza) as a man "drunk with God"; with a God who is not possessed in an ecstacy of mystical vision or speculative thought but who is desperately sought in the labyrinth of doubts, possibilities, and negations.

Nietzsche's "atheism" may be approached on a number of levels. The first is his encounter with Christ, specifically with Christ as claim- ing to be God. It is immediately evident that his attitude toward Christ is ambivalent. On the one hand he is repelled by the moralizing Christ, the imputed author of the moral system which he had attacked in his anti-Christian denunciations. Although he could not see this Christ as standing above the moral code advanced in his name, Nietzsche did not reject him outright. Drawn by the powerful figure of Christ, he seeks to disengage him from that involucrum of moralism. Even less could he accept the Christ of the theologians who, in order to establish his divinity, had enveloped him in the speculations of the Hellenic theosophies; indeed, he said, it was the theologians who killed God. In an effort to validate his own insight into the positive character of Christ, he sought to approximate him to the central point at which divinity might seem to appear, namely, that affirmation of life which Nietzsche associated with the name of Dionysius, and to that other transcendent affirmation of life, the superman. Nietzsche sought to place Christ on the line between Dionysus and the superman in the order of the pure affirmation of self-transcending life. In this circuitous way there is a recognition of Christ in his never unilineal or unidirectional thought.

But the problem of God is not limited to that of Christ. Nietzsche seemed also to see the problem in other terms, which, from a strictly speculative point of view, are even more radical. His was a philosophy of life as ever-becoming, self-transcendent. What could be the relationship between such a philosophy and the classical conception of God as the absolute, the beginning and the end, the pure and unchanging act? The answer would seem to be that God is a temptation to be resisted. The vision of the ever self-transcending and ever-returning cycle of being and life is a vision to stagger the human mind. The human mind is tempted to take refuge from it in the rocklike solidity of the God who *is* and with relationship to whom anything else is. But this temptation must be resisted because it is a denial of the life-philosophy. What could be the essence of God within the terms of such a pure philosophy of life-affirmation?

In reply to this question, the closest approach possible to Nietzsche's projected view of God is to be found. In the context of the philosophy of life, God can appear only as the directing force of that vital movement, as the supreme *ratio* of the will to power. In this form, he loses the attributes which the traditional theology, based on pure act and pure idea, had assigned him and takes on new ones deriving from this new role. To the degree to which Nietzsche recognized this role as involving a privileged mode of subsistence, he may be said to have envisioned God. This certainly does not make him a theist in the traditional meaning of the term. But to impose the traditional meaning of the term upon his thought as the only admissible criterion would be peremptory. His vision, however dim, makes it impossible to think of him as being completely negative regarding the concept of God. As in almost everything else, it leaves Nietzsche in the position of one who seeks, rather than one who possesses; a thinker in whom the urgency of quest is the whole meaning of philosophy and the supreme object of that quest, as his own poem affirms, is the unknown God he seeks to know and to serve.

E. The Eternal Return

Many interpreters of Nietzsche's thought have sought to place the concept of the "eternal return" at the very center and to interpret all else in its light. In these brief pages the temptation to follow this example has been resisted, however enticing it may be. The warning sign is that on this basis the most contradictory characterizations of Nietzsche's thought have been advanced with complete confidence.

We must begin rather with the fact that the notion of the "eternal return" is one to which Nietzsche has recourse at various points in his reflections with the obvious purpose of bringing them into some all-embracing frame of reference. But the frame of reference itself is left undefined. What did Nietzsche mean by this enigmatic doctrine? The version which sees the doctrine of the eternal return as the cosmic projection of the Dionysian spirit of life-affirmation would seem to be the most plausible. The world, the cosmos, accepts itself with the same unrestricted "yea" that Nietzsche urged upon man. In this "yea" it dissolves all harsh distinctions, all rigid orders, by turning upon itself in a rhythm of self-creation and self-destruction in which the all returns to the naught and the naught becomes the womb of all.

But the full force of this projection of the Dionysian "yea" upon the world is ambiguous. It is not clear whether Nietzsche intends that man should surrender himself to this eternal cyclical movement of the world or whether he sees that movement as the passive theater of the unidirectional movement of the development of life in the order of the superman. At any rate, it is very clear that on these two central points, the notion of the eternal return and that of the superman, Nietzsche's thought seems to stand in immedicable opposition to itself. As many commentators have insisted, however, to impose system upon his thought is an unwarranted imposition, quite contrary to his creative genius. For this reason, the vision of the eternal return remains yet another dimension of Nietzsche's vast kaleidoscope of insights. It cannot be wholly integrated with the rest nor can it be employed as an integrating or systematizing principle to bring all his other insights into clear focus.

Readings

Books

Chaix-Ruy, Jules. *The Superman From Nietzsche to Teilhard de Chardin.* Translated by Marina Smyth-Kok. Notre Dame, Ind.: University of Notre Dame Press, 1968.

Copleston, Frederick. *St. Thomas and Nietzsche.* Oxford: Blackfriars, 1955.

Danto, Arthur O. *Nietzsche as Philosopher.* New York: Macmillan, 1965.

Harper, Ralph. *The Seventh Solitude.* Baltimore: Johns Hopkins Press, 1965.

Hollindale, R. *Nietzsche, The Man and His Philosophy.* London: Routledge & Kegan Paul, 1965.

Jaspers, Karl. *Nietzsche: An Introduction to the Understanding of His Philosophical Activity.* Translated by C. Wallraff and F. J. Schmitz. Tucson: University of Arizona Press, 1965.

Jette, Celine R. *Philosophy of Nietzsche and Thomistic Principles.* New York: Pageant Press, 1967.

Kaufmann, Walter. *Nietzsche, Philosopher, Psychologist, Antichrist.* 2nd ed. Princeton, N. J.: Princeton University Press, 1968.

Lea, Frank A. *Tragic Philosopher: A Study of Friedrich Nietzsche.* New York: Philosophical Library, 1957.

Lubac, Henri de. *The Drama of Atheist Humanism.* Translated by E. Riley. London: Sheed & Ward, 1949.

Morgan, George A., Jr. *What Nietzsche Means.* Cambridge, Mass.: Harvard University Press, 1941; reissued New York; Harper & Row, Harper Torchbooks, 1961.

Essays and articles

Collins, James. "A Kantian Critique of the God-is-Dead Theme." *The Monist,* LI (1967).

Copleston, Frederick. "Foreground and Background in Nietzsche." *Review of Metaphysics,* XXI (1968).

Heidegger, Martin. "Who Is Nietzsche's Zarathustra?" *Review of Metaphysics,* XX (1967).

NAME INDEX

SUBJECT INDEX

Absolute, the
  and contingent existent, 170–172
  in Royce, 258–259
act
  primordial, in Spencer, 218
aesthete, the
  as type, in Kierkegaard, 179–180
aesthetics
  in Schopenhauer, 129
agnosticism
  in evolution, 213
aid, mutual
  as optimal principle of evolution, 207
alienation
  Hegelian concept of, criticized, 151
  and philosophy, in Marx, 142–143, 151–154
  in Schopenhauer, 112
altruism
  in Comtean positivism, 104
America
  destiny of, in Emerson, 52
anarchism
  in Proudhon, 73
anthropology, philosophical
  in Marx, 146–151
apologetics, Christian
  task of, 168–169
art
  in Schopenhauer, 116–118

asceticism
  in Schopenhauer, 113
ateliers sociaux
  in Louis Blanc, 70
atheism
  in Feuerbach, 134
authority
  in de Maistre, 37
autoctisis, 269–270

being
  in Gioberti, 32
  in Rosmini-Serbati, 28–29
Being, the Great
  in Comte, 102–104
benevolence
  in ethics of Spencer, 222
biography
  and philosophy in Kierkegaard, 163–165
body
  in Schopenhauer, 115–120
  union with soul, in Rosmini-Serbati, 28–29

Catholicism
  liberal, 58
  and romanticism, 27–43
causality
  and evolution, 204
  four forms of, in Schopenhauer, 115
  in Mill's logic, 195–196

315